THE GOOD FRENCHMAN

THE GOOD
FRENCHMAN

The True Story of the Life and Times of

MAURICE CHEVALIER

EDWARD BEHR

VILLARD BOOKS
NEW YORK
1993

Villard Books is a registered trademark of Random House, Inc.
Originally published in Great Britain by Hutchinson,
a division of Random House UK, Ltd., 1993.

Library of Congress Cataloging-in-Publication Data
Behr, Edward, 1926–
    The good Frenchman: the true story of the life and times of Maurice Chevalier/Edward Behr.
        p.   cm.
    ISBN 0-679-41518-1
    I. Chevalier, Maurice, 1888–1972. 2. Singers—France—Biography. I. Title.
ML420.C473B45 1993
782.42164′092—dc20
[B]92-33481

Manufactured in the United States of America on acid-free paper
9 8 7 6 5 4 3 2
First American Edition
Book design by Jo Anne Metsch

For Cameron Mackintosh

"There are two nightmares for every biographer, he says. One is that everybody gives you the same story, and the other is that everybody gives you a different story."

—Philip Roth,
Deception

Acknowledgments

In the preparation of this book, I was helped by many: First of all, I would like to acknowledge the debt I owe Madeleine and François Vals, Maurice Chevalier's business managers and "confidents" from 1953 on. My thanks to: Yvonne Vallée, Nita Raya, and Janie Michels, for their patience and unfailing courtesy; to Odette Meslier, for allowing me to visit Chevalier's home in Marnes-la-Coquette; to Lucette and René Chevalier; to Henri Betti, Chevalier's former accompanist, not only for subjecting himself to long debriefing sessions but for loaning me a copy of his own, unpublished autobiography. I would like to thank the following, in France, without whose help and cooperation I could not have written this book: J-C Averty, Leslie Caron, Georges Cravenne, Pierre Daninos, Pierre Galante, André Halimi, Colette Laly, Madame Harold Lesser, Herbert Lottman, Robert Manuel, Olivier Merlin, François Périer, Lucien Rioux, Jean Sablon, Thérèse de Saint-Phalle, Jo

Siritsky, and the staff of the Bibliothèque Nationale, and Arletty (who died while the book was still in progress).

The following were of invaluable assistance in America: the late Sam Marx, whose last fax to me arrived almost simultaneously with news of his untimely death, and the late Robert Wagner; Robert Spencer; Gustav Vintas; Billy Wilder; Ned Comstock of the University of Southern California; Sol Shapiro; Charles Silver, of the film department of MOMA; the Library of the Performing Arts, Lincoln Center, and Maynard Parker, *Newsweek*'s chief editor, for allowing me to use the extensive *Newsweek* archives; Margot Mayne and Richard Mayne, for their valuable comments, Richard Mangan, director of the Raymond Mander and Joe Mitchenson Theatre Collection, the staff of the Newspaper Library, Colindale, and of the British Museum Reading Room, as well as Hélèna Goujeon.

Finally, my many thanks to Ed Victor, Peter Gethers, and MWT, for riding herd on this project and for their unfailing support and sustenance.

Introduction

$\mathcal{I}$ learned of Maurice Chevalier's death in unusual circumstances. Covering one of the numerous wars between India and Pakistan for *Newsweek*, I had just spent a week with an Indian Army brigade commander, an old friend from my own wartime Indian Army days, at what we both laughingly called the "front," somewhere between Amritsar and Lahore. Changing camps, at *Newsweek*'s bid, to cover the aftermath of the war from the other side, meant flying first to Teheran, where I spent a miserably cold and lonely Christmas, then on to Karachi, where I arrived on January 1, 1972.

By now the war was over. It had been a spectacular defeat, and these were grim days for Pakistan, shorn of its eastern portion (soon to become Bangladesh), humiliated, uncertain of the future. But the collapse of its government, the news that tens of thousands of Pakistani troops had been taken prisoner, and speculation about the country's very survival did not prevent the *Pakistan Times* from running a banner-headlined story about Maurice Chevalier's death on its front page.

Such interest in a part of Asia so far removed from the world of the French music hall was both touching and unexpected. It set me thinking. What *was* it about Maurice Chevalier that made him so special all over the world? It was to be my fate, as a roving reporter, to be in equally remote parts of the world when other famous show-business figures died. There was nothing, as far as I could recall, about Steve McQueen in the Indian papers, and precious little about Rex Harrison in Saigon, when *they* passed away. Even Yves Montand's death—mourned in France almost on the scale of de Gaulle or Jean-Paul Sartre—attracted only moderate attention in the United States.

Chevalier had been one of my boyhood heroes, though I had never actually watched him perform on the stage. In my childhood, in Paris just before the Second World War, I had seen him in several movies, listened to his records and interviews. Much later, writing a script for a British film company, I instinctively turned to Chevalier when I wanted to demonstrate the suitability of one of my American characters for service in the Office of Strategic Services (the OSS, the CIA's forerunner) in (then-French) wartime North Africa: the Chevalier leitmotiv worked well. I realized that one had only to summon up a cane, a boater, and one or two tunes to conjure up a quintessentially French archetype.

My interest in Chevalier grew as, all around me, his legend waned—to such an extent that I was somewhat disheartened when, at JFK Airport, my answer to the young immigration official's question about the purpose of my visit ("I'm researching a book about Maurice Chevalier") elicited a puzzled "Morris *who?*"

It was strange. Some twenty years after his death, he had become a nonperson in some parts of the world, at least as far as the younger generation was concerned, yet one only had to evoke the boater, the Gallic accent, and the songs for the penny to drop. And for good reason: In his day, he was not only the best-known Frenchman in the world, but probably the world's best-known living showman, an Elvis Presley and

Michael Jackson rolled into one. In the early thirties, he was among the "top ten" highest-paid Hollywood actors in the world. He was even more popular in France. When a Paris cinema showed one of his films in its American, instead of its French, version, his angry fans burned the theater down to the ground. The pauper from Ménilmontant became hugely rich (his music-hall fees were the highest in the world) at a time when income tax was a negligible 3 percent.

Present-day megastars owe their fame largely to television or to rock music; Chevalier was famous in the pre-TV era. I was curious about that. *How did it happen?* Chevalier's widow, Yvonne Vallée, whom he divorced in 1932, was still bemused by her countrymen's short memories when I talked to her. "These days nobody realizes what a star he was," she said. "He was like a king. The huge crowds at railway stations, the knots of people outside restaurants, wherever he went, nobody remembers that." There was a time, in the early thirties, when Chevalier was far, far better known in America than Herbert Hoover, who happened to be president at the time.

One of the extraordinary things about Chevalier was that he came to fame the hardest way, then lost almost everything, then clawed his way back to stardom not once but again and again. It happened in World War I, after his return to France in 1935, at the close of World War II (with the collaborationist smear threatening to put an end to his career for good), and again in the early fifties when, absurdly, he was branded as procommunist in McCarthyite America.

He not only endured, he triumphed. In his late seventies, in America at least, he regained much of his aura. It was not just his longevity that audiences celebrated, but his uncanny professionalism. His stage presence was unequaled, his buoyantly optimistic act a cure for all the ills overcoming America in the sixties—the growing drug problem, the Vietnam War, and, finally, the emergence of Japan as an economic superpower. The single most surprising aspect of his popularity, toward the end of his life, was that he was still, in the 1960s, performing the same kind of act that had brought him fame as early as 1913. What was his particular secret?

There was another side to Chevalier that the public never saw. For most of his life, he was a deeply unhappy, insecure man. This was surprising, for he had everything in the world that he had craved as an underprivileged youngster—riches beyond measure, the adulation of millions, feminine conquests galore. Only those closest to him knew the cost of that famous Chevalier grin, of the endless rehearsals required to project a stage cheerfulness that eluded him in real life. He constantly feared an irrevocable downturn in his fame and fortune; his petty miserliness was part of his conviction that it might not last, that he might himself become one of the pauper ex-actors whose retirement home he endowed. In the end, the dark side prevailed. Writing about the last eighteen months of his life, I was often close to tears.

It was not easy to get behind this facade, for he did everything possible to conceal the *real* Chevalier—not only from his fans, but from posterity as well. His eight-volume memoirs reveal only those aspects of his life and personality he wished to present to the public. He was extraordinarily successful in this respect. It may come as a shock to realize how different Chevalier was from the image he sought to project. In the course of my research, I was to discover how skillfully he went about it. He was, in real life, a consummately private man, able to conceal his real feelings with a veneer of charm that fooled almost everyone but his most intimate entourage.

Chevalier's life span encompassed the Belle Epoque, the two World Wars, and the May 1968 social upheaval, and the story of his life closely mirrors that of France from the start of the twentieth century almost to the present day. The World War I slaughter, the great slump of the thirties, the short-lived Front Populaire, the German Occupation and Pétainist France, the postwar growth of French communism and the student uprising of '68, all played more of a part in his life and work than he himself realized. He was not just a product of his time: He gave it form and expression.

So this book is not just about Chevalier; it is also about the events that shaped, and explain, his life and art. Born nearly a half-century after

Chevalier, and brought up in both French and English cultures, I experienced some of these events at close hand myself, and was as deeply marked by some of them. Perhaps that is why I feel closer to Chevalier than to any of the subjects of my previous biographies: He remains, for all his attempts at inscrutability, *mon vieux complice, mon frère.*

THE GOOD FRENCHMAN

CHAPTER 1

"I really wasn't cut out to be an artist."

—Maurice Chevalier

*P*aris: dazzling, seductive, eternal but ever-youthful Paris. Onstage and in films, Maurice Chevalier celebrated the glory of his birthplace with far more genuine emotion than he ever bestowed on love or beautiful women.

At the height of Chevalier's fame, his lavish revues at the Casino de Paris ritualized this worship of place: They had titles like *"Toujours Paris," "Encore Paris," "Pour Toi, Paris," "Paris Qui Jazz," "Paris en L'Air," "PA-RI-KI-RI."* In the public's mind, throughout the world, the town's glamour was inseparable from his own. He became, especially in American eyes, the Parisian par excellence. The late president Georges Pompidou told him once that he would have made a better envoy to the United States than any professional diplomat.

Never mind that Chevalier's private life differed considerably from his carefully structured public image, or that the last twenty years of Chevalier's life were spent not in Paris, but in the decidedly rural, millionaire suburb of Marnes-la-Coquette. He was, as *Variety* writer Abe Green put it, "a one-man Paris Chamber of Commerce," an ambassador-at-large of Parisian charm.

However, except for a privileged minority, the Paris he grew up in was neither dazzling nor seductive. By the time of Chevalier's birth—September 12, 1888, with the exception of the spacious VIe, VIIe, VIIIe, IXe, and XVIe arrondissements, where wealthy Parisians lived either in "*hôtels particuliers*" or in new, imposing stone-building apartment blocks (soon to have newfangled elevators), the French capital was an unsanitary, overcrowded, rat-infested place. Most Parisians lived in appalling squalor in its many inner-city slums.

Very few dwellings had running water or heating of any kind; wages were wretchedly low; tuberculosis was endemic, the single-largest killer disease; class distinctions were rigid and highly visible: Male workers and artisans wore high-buttoned Mao-type "blouses," corduroy trousers, and caps, which set them aside from the more formally attired, dark-suited, hatted, starch-collared clerks and shop attendants. Working women were immediately recognizable by the coarse cloth of their simple clothes, bonnets, and sensible shoes, all in marked contrast to the extravagantly hatted, feathered, and furred women of the gentry and "haute bourgeoisie." Cars were unknown: Carriages were horse-drawn, the streets gaslit and smelling of horse manure.

Like Victorian England, it was an "upstairs-downstairs" society; there was even a Paris music hall, La Pépinière, (on the rue de la Pépinière) specializing in sketches and satirical songs about master-servant relationships, and patronized almost exclusively by coachmen, cooks, butlers, and housemaids. The "good life" of the Parisian middle and upper class would have been impossible without them. Wages were low, social security, as we now know it, almost nonexistent, and though rudimentary crèches, paupers' homes, free hospitals, and medical treatment were available for the most underprivileged, those running such institutions were either stern-faced nuns or brutally impersonal bureaucrats, straight out of Dickens.

Emile Zola (1840–1902), at the height of his creative powers at the time of Maurice Chevalier's birth, repeatedly used Paris (the Paris of the proletarian Faubourg Saint-Antoine, not the Champs-Élysées) as a backdrop for his melodramatic accounts of the agony of French working-class life. Inspired by the daily spectacle around him of degraded, hopeless, prematurely aged working-class men and women driven to drink, disease, and early deaths by overwork, tawdry surroundings, and the many other inexorable pressures facing them, Zola painted an apocalyptic picture of contemporary society. In his day, most affluent Parisians preferred to dismiss him as a caricatural do-gooder and romantic champion of the underdog, obsessed by the seamy side of life. But before him Victor Hugo had drawn on the same raw material, and Paris had not changed all that much since the publication of *Les Misérables*, twenty-six years before Maurice Chevalier was born in Ménilmontant, in the heart of the traditional "East End" of Paris.

With its twin district, Belleville, it was Paris's equivalent of the Bronx in New York, the place the poorest workers and most recent immigrants drifted to, either to be near relatives or fellow workers, or simply because the old slum buildings were carved up into tens of thousands of dirt-cheap matchbox apartments. In his memoirs, Chevalier drew a subtle distinction between the Belleville of his youth, with its cheap nightclubs, louche cabarets, brutal pimps, and criminal reputation, and industrious, peaceful, respectable, almost bucolic Ménilmontant.

Number 29, rue du Retrait, the slum house on a long, narrow street at the very top of the rue de Ménilmontant, Chevalier's birthplace, has long since been pulled down, and is today a featureless office building. The Chevalier family moved out while he was still a babe in arms, and he had no recollection of it. He vividly remembered the place they moved to, however: a dark, windowless two-room apartment on 15, rue Julien Lacroix, a street nearer the center of Paris, but also just off the rue de Ménilmontant, where he would spend the next fourteen years of his life.

Chevalier would instantly recognize this building today. Now a fearfully run-down and nameless slum hotel for North African workers living five or six to a room, it is probably in worse shape than it ever was in his own childhood. None of the current tenants were aware that

Maurice Chevalier had once lived there. Most of them had never heard of the country's most famous entertainer, and when they heard the name assumed it referred to the absentee landlord, whom they dreaded—and had never encountered.

In Maurice Chevalier's day, the rue de Ménilmontant catered to the needs of a subproletariat, mainly from the poorest parts of France like Brittany and the Auvergne, with a profusion of cheap food stores, tailors, and estaminets. Today its new poor are no longer French but Greeks, Turks, Indians, Bangladeshis, Egyptians, and above all North Africans. There are still a few French working-class bars and cafés on the rue de Ménilmontant, but these are heavily outnumbered by Tunisian, Greek, and African-owned restaurants and shops selling cut-rate goods. A kosher butcher struggles to make a living still, a reminder that this district of Paris was once an enclave of poor Jewish immigrants, too, but the overall impression is of a Middle Eastern souk, with hole-in-the-wall mint-tea bars and cheap couscous restaurants, and a tiny French resident minority struggling to retain its identity against heavy odds.

Almost opposite Maurice Chevalier's childhood home is an imposing landmark: the huge white stone church of Notre-Dame de la Croix, where his devout mother prayed daily. Nearby is a surviving "traditional" eating place, the hundred-year-old Le Ménilmuche, flaunting the same slogan (on its handwritten menu in purple ink) as it did a hundred years ago: "Don't forget that a glass of wine is one coin less in the doctor's pocket." Maurice's mother could read only haltingly, so she may have been unaware of the irony of it, for it was a coin less in her own pocket too. Her husband was an alcoholic, and the whole Chevalier family could have stepped straight out of a Zola novel.

Charles Victor Chevalier was a housepainter, a conscientious worker when not on a drinking binge. After hours, he would stop off in estaminet after estaminet on the way home, often too stupefied with drink to do anything but sleep it off, sprawled across the bed—until it was time to go to work the next morning.

Joséphine Chevalier, born Van der Bosche, was Flemish. She had left Belgium to seek work as a seamstress in Paris as a teenager, and after marrying Charles never returned. Photographs taken of her in her old age show a wizened, resigned, kindly, distinctly gnomelike face on a tiny body. She spoke French with a marked Flemish accent. When Maurice was born, she was thirty-six years old, but looked far older. He was her ninth child. All but two others, both boys, had died in childbirth. Maurice grew up in the tiny apartment alongside Charles (who was thirteen years older and bullied him mercilessly) and Paul, five years older, whom Maurice, brighter, quicker, and tougher, was able to dominate intellectually, and bully physically.

"My mother's work never stopped," Chevalier recalled. All day she was cooking, cleaning up, washing dishes, repairing her husband's clothes, or earning pitifully small sums by piecework sewing. One of his earliest memories was the spectacle of his mother sewing by candlelight late at night, tears streaming down her face. Poor eyesight soon compelled her to give up her work as seamstress and lacemaker, and she became a cleaning woman. Trapped between a drunken husband and three turbulent sons, constantly worried about money for bare essentials, probably embarrassed by her foreignness, she lavished all her love on "Patapouf," as she called Maurice, and he responded in kind.

His devotion to "La Louque," as he and his brother Paul called her (neither could remember why they did so, except that the nickname had a Flemish sound to it) was exceptional. Later, he would turn his love for La Louque into a cult: He talked about her all the time, his numerous girlfriends later recalled, adding that "she was the only woman he ever loved." Even Jeanette MacDonald, his Hollywood costar, complained that "his mother was his sole topic of conversation." He would compose a song in memory of her during the Second World War (*"Toi, Toi, Toi"*), and his veneration was such that his exasperated young accompanist, Henri Betti, in later days, would find it necessary to remind him, "You're not the only one who loves his mother, you know!"

After her death, in 1929, he commissioned a bronze bust of her, which he kept in the garden of his house at La Bocca, near Cannes, itself named La Louque in memory of her. This bust was later moved to his huge estate, also called La Louque, in Marnes-la-Coquette. He had her remains transferred to the Marnes-la-Coquette cemetery when he moved there, and both Maurice and his mother are buried in the same massive charcoal-colored marble grave. In his final will, handwritten a few months before his death, Chevalier specified that no other member of his family was ever to be buried there.

In his old age, Chevalier claimed he talked to La Louque every day, and that her spiritual presence permanently influenced his life. On a flight back to Paris over the Atlantic in 1948, during an appalling storm, he wrote, "My distress becomes unbearable. I call on La Louque to save my life, silently at first, then whispering her name." In the terrible last few months of his life, frail, suicidal, with paranoid visions of betrayal all around him, he spent most of the time in his bedroom, but he prayed daily, on his nurse's arm, before his mother's effigy in the huge garden.

As a small boy, Maurice was chubby, almost overweight, with a disproportionately large head and huge hands on spindly wrists. At the age of six, in a local primary school run by priests, he reacted to some boys teasing him and shouting "*Grosse Tête*" (Swollen Head) by knocking one of them down. This turned out to be a boy who had not taken part in the ragging, but Chevalier's ready fists made him something of a hero at school from that day on. "I had two vices," he recalled, "sugar-coated almonds and cigarettes," which he used to smoke in the school toilet "till I almost passed out." He ran neighbors' errands to earn his pocket money, also acting as go-between, carrying messages written by pining lovers in the district unwilling, for obvious reasons, to entrust their love letters to the post.

Extreme family poverty compelled him to count every sou. All his life, he would be able to recall with computerlike precision how much he had earned, at any stage of his career, just as he would recall that, when he was six, the local butcher gave him slices of sausage as a tip, the baker's wife stale croissants, and the dairy-store owner nothing at all.

At the age of seven, Maurice became a choirboy at the église de Sainte-Croix, and had a vivid, painful memory of the church gate being slammed accidentally on his hand as he watched a wedding party emerge onto the church steps. In great pain, with a finger "hanging by a thread," he was taken to a hospital in a horse-drawn carriage, and he recalled that this cost his mother one franc fifty, "half a day's wages for her."

Though he idealized his mother, he had vivid memories of the grimmer side of his early life: His eldest brother, Charles, something of a sadist, or perhaps jealous of Maurice's privileged status as a "Mama's boy," regularly beat him up; Maurice himself took it out on Paul, who was a passive, impressionable boy, no match for young Maurice's own lively temperament and tantrums. Sunday family picnics—involving a long and tiring walk to the Bois de Vincennes—usually ended in family recriminations, bickerings, and tears. Though Chevalier draws a veil over his parents' relationship, it is clear that Joséphine was fed up with her husband's drinking, and that the nagging and bickering between them occasionally escalated into violent rows.

Then one day the father simply vanished, never to return. The circumstances of the disappearance suggest that he went seeking feminine company elsewhere, but Chevalier gave several contradictory versions of this traumatic event. He wrote in later years that his father walked out the door in a drunken fury and never returned. In another account, he told reporters that his father went on a prolonged binge after work and never came home. But to Percy Cudlipp, a British journalist who wrote Chevalier's first biography, in 1930,[1] he gave a third version: "A terrible blow overcame my family when I was eleven years old, for then my father died," he told him. He was in fact not eleven but seven when his father left. He may well have seen this as a symbolic death, but in 1930, Chevalier was not as proud of his working-class origins as he would later become, and this innocent deception may also have reflected his social aspirations at the time: He told Cudlipp, for instance, that his brother Charles "worked in a bank" when he was in fact a housepainter, like his father.

Soon after his father's disappearance, Charles announced that he was getting married, and because he would soon have a family to support, would no longer be contributing to the family budget. Young Maurice hated his eldest brother, and was not sorry to see him go. In Volume I of his autobiography, *Ma Route et Mes Chansons*, he pointedly noted that in his later life, he settled considerable sums on Charles, enabling him to become a rentier—a remittance man—but that he never saw him again in his life.

Charles's departure drastically reduced the family income: La Louque now depended on Paul to supplement her meager earnings as a cleaning lady, and as a metal engraver's apprentice he earned a mere pittance— three francs a day. La Louque took on more work than she could cope with, and, before long, collapsed (with "bleeding eyes") and was taken to a hospital. Paul was able to manage on his own, but Maurice was sent for a time to a state institution, a boarding school for underprivileged children, where, he admitted, he had rather a good time: The food was plentiful, the sheets were clean, and he met friends his own age.

His mother recovered, and Paul became a full-fledged metal engraver (at seven francs a day). Rid of the drunken father and hated eldest brother, Maurice basked in La Louque's love, and the three of them were able to move from their dark, wretched third-floor apartment to a brighter, cleaner two-room apartment on the first floor of the building.

Show business, in all its forms, had enthralled Maurice ever since, when he was five years old, his mother first took him to the Workers' Palace, a local entertainment locale, part working men's club, part music hall. To him, even this somewhat tawdry hall, with its bright spotlights and plush red seats, seemed an almost unbelievably glamorous place. Before leaving home, his eldest brother, Charles, had tried to become a professional singer, at a local cabaret called the Bat-à-Clan, but had given up, conscious that he had neither talent nor looks nor voice for that particular line of work.

At the age of ten, however, Maurice's ambition focused exclusively on the circus: He was determined to become an acrobat. He convinced his brother Paul that they should put on a double act, as "the Chevalier brothers." This was the time when English double acts were all the rage in Paris, and English titles were fashionable, even for French performers. At first, Maurice and Paul thought the word "brothers" was an English surname like any other—they had no inkling of the real meaning of the word. Paul devised a poster, cunningly substituting their own name for an existing "brothers" act. Somewhat prematurely, the two boys even had some printed. Years later Maurice confessed to Mistinguett, the world-famous vaudeville star, that he "posted one up over his bed and used to stand in front of it for hours, striking an attitude, bowing to an imaginary public, dizzy with the unheard applause."[2] Apart from the glamour involved, the aim, of course, was to supplement the family income, but it's also clear the yearning for applause—and approval—was there almost from birth.

Paul and Maurice practiced out of doors, on a vacant lot. Then they rented a tiny gardening plot, of the kind used by working-class Parisians to raise vegetables—for twenty francs a year. It was an hour's walk away from Ménilmontant. The brothers dug up the soft earth to cushion their falls. Theirs was a romantic, exhausting, but fatally doomed endeavor: Both underestimated the skills needed to succeed; at the local elementary school they had attended, there had been no gymnastics course, and the two boys simply tried, with no teacher and little success, to duplicate what they had seen in the circus. When this failed, they began their self-taught acrobatics all over again in a local gymnasium on the rue de Ménilmontant (costing five sous, or twenty-five centimes, per person for entry for an unlimited time in any one day), and promptly discovered they had neither the build, stamina, nor strength, to perform even the simplest acts without nasty, painful falls. Worse still, their act did not improve with practice.

Thin, gangling, bandy-legged Paul, especially, was a figure of fun in gym clothes, unable to lift even the lightest weights other hard-faced athletes tossed about with ease. Maurice, at ten, was still on the pudgy side, neither strong nor supple enough to make a go of it. He also—perhaps as a result of an unbalanced diet, heavy on carbohydrates, for La Louque fed her boys potatoes because they were cheap, perhaps because of an as-yet-undiagnosed appendicitis condition that was to plague him throughout his youth—suffered from occasional catatonic bouts, when he would simply sit, in a daze, staring blankly into space, oblivious of his surroundings.

After a few months, Paul bowed out: Working as a metal engraver was tiring enough, and he knew by now he was not cut out to become an acrobat, ever. Maurice persisted briefly, hiring himself out as an unpaid apprentice to an acrobatic team at a local circus, but soon suffered a painful fall, acquiring facial cuts and a sprained ankle. To La Louque's relief, he, too, abandoned the project.

Now eleven, and with his elementary school certificate in hand,

Maurice seemed doomed to follow in his brothers' footsteps, a work-shop apprentice hopeful of, in time, graduating to the status of skilled artisan, becoming part of the huge work force without which the French "industrial revolution" would never have occurred. This was all his limited schooling and deprived background fitted him for. Maurice was eventually apprenticed to his brother's engraving workshop. That lasted only a short time, for he had neither the enthusiasm nor the powers of concentration required. There was no lack of jobs, but none were attractive. He got a job as a carpenter's apprentice, was fired, was taken on by an electrician but let go soon after. Turning to the retail trade, he sold sheet music in a small shop but mooned over the songs he was supposed to sell, humming them to himself instead of attending to customers, and was again dismissed. The manager of a small toy factory hired him to paint dolls' faces, but his output was low, and he showed no talent for this either. Finally, he got a job making tin tacks. It required no skills, and precious little concentration. All Maurice needed to do was to punch out the tacks in a hand-held machine—piecework that paid a few francs per thousand. Even this proved above his capacities: He caught his finger in the machine. The accident left him idle and ban-daged for several months.

Throughout, La Louque was patient and supportive: She knew that Maurice had strange catatonic lapses, and these spells, she believed, explained the successive disasters at work, though there was nothing wrong with the boy that she could discover—he was strong, even if he *was* on the small side, and had a healthy appetite. In those days, in poor working-class families, doctors were summoned only at the last possible extremity. But there was another possible reason for his failure to thrive in a trade: Maurice Chevalier had become obsessed with the notion that he had a stage vocation, not as an acrobat but as a comic song-and-dance entertainer.

In retrospect, such a discovery seemed preordained: His attempt to make it in the circus world had been an abject failure but had given him a sense of rhythm, of physical mastery over his own body; in the music shop, he had learned by heart some of the songs on sale, performing them secretly in the toilet and at home, in front of a mirror. He liked what he saw: a small, impish, agile boy, slavishly imitating existing performers but with considerable poise, energy, and pitch. He could not read music and had none of the instinctive singer's ear for tunes. But he thought he could do an act à la Dranem, or Mayol, or any other of the noted comic performers of his day, as competently as any of the rank amateurs whose acts he monitored in local cabarets in Belleville and farther afield, on the Boulevard de Strasbourg and Faubourg Saint-Martin.

His bandaged hand gave him unlimited freedom to roam the streets, and though he was a "good son," carefully avoiding street gangs or bad company, he often stayed out late, haunting as many cabarets and "café-concs" as he could. Clearly, he felt that should he ever become part of this world, this would ease the financial pressures at home.

From the moment he began his secret, private rehearsals, his vocation was determined for all time: For Chevalier, in some respects surprisingly mature at eleven, was determined not to follow in the footsteps of either of his brothers if he could possibly help it. He was, whether aware of this or not, instinctively trying to break out of the environment into which he had been born.

In later years, he would display a marked weakness for the rich, aristocratic, socially powerful personalities whose backgrounds were so different from his own, preferring their company to any other, turning his luxurious estate at Marnes-la-Coquette into a kind of Maurice Chevalier museum full of memorabilia, including innumerable pictures of himself rubbing shoulders with European—and Hollywood—royalty. This longing for acceptance, for official recognition, was a trait that came to the fore surprisingly early in his life: From the age of eleven on, young Maurice, instinctively rejecting the drab workshop world and the dull, predictable company of fellow apprentices of his own age, deliberately sought out those members of the music-hall and café-conc world who might prove useful to him. All were naturally more sophisticated and far older. He was able to trade on his youthful appeal, as the irresistible, innocent working-class boy from Ménilmontant.

In so doing, he displayed all the charm, ambition, perseverance, and ruthlessness for which he would later become famous. The cutthroat

world of show business, as he quickly discovered, excluded real sentiment, and he learned fast. Even in the early days, the moment he no
longer needed people he dropped them abruptly, and this characteristic
became more noticeable after he had become a megastar. All newcomers
would be dazzled by Maurice Chevalier's charm, but many later learned,
at their expense, that it was a coldly calculated commodity that he turned
on and off at will.

This was apparent in his interminable nine-volume memoirs. He
freely mentioned the names of those unimportant, ephemeral minor
characters who, long ago, at the very start of his career, helped him on
his way. But there were also surprising omissions, deliberate distortions,
and some outright lies. His craving for approval was such that he never
wished to be perceived as anything but perfect. His breathless "Oh my,
just look at me, the poor little boy from Ménilmontant, how on earth
did I ever become such a great man?" sense of wonder, with exclamation
marks on almost every page, makes for increasingly tedious reading,
though part of the blame may be laid at the door of René Laporte, his
neighbor, friend, and literary adviser—though at the time of publication
of the first volume, *Ma Route et Mes Chansons*, (*My Road and My Songs*) the
French publishing firm headed by René Julliard was adamant that
Chevalier had written it all himself. René Laporte died in a tragic traffic
accident in 1954, and never, in his lifetime, admitted advising Chevalier,
though he acknowledged he had been Mistinguett's "ghost."

Ma Route et Mes Chansons began with the phrase "At heart, I wasn't really
cut out to be an artist." Chevalier described himself as "totally different
from those of the majority in my profession whose career (or lack of it)
I was to witness, sincerely astounded to have deserved to frequent the
artistic world in any capacity. Is it the proof of humility to reveal oneself
exactly as one is?" The fact is that Chevalier, in his memoirs, rarely did
anything of the kind, often covering his tracks to discourage anyone
seeking the "real" Maurice Chevalier.

He also claimed that he had never anticipated such a glorious career,
had done nothing to deserve it, and that his "greatest ambition was
simply to earn my keep (*ma soupe et mon pain*) without owing anybody
anything." But the "real" Chevalier was not only inordinately ambitious

and something of a snob, but also—especially toward the end of his life—convinced that his had been an exceptional, almost divinely inspired, destiny from the start.

His reluctance to admit the truth about himself was a shame, for the real Maurice Chevalier was far more interesting than the highly pasteurized version of himself he marketed so successfully and for so long. But to appreciate why he was so intent on making his mark in vaudeville, and why the world of the *café-conc* was so important to him, it is essential to understand what the music-hall world represented, a century ago, to people like young Maurice Chevalier when, at the age of twelve, he embarked on his meteoric career.

CHAPTER 2

"Paris . . . You've taught me all that a kid could be."

—Song sung by Maurice Chevalier, specifically written for him by Charles
Aznavow, at his final farewell Paris performance

*I*t is difficult, at this remove, to see the world through the eyes of twelve-year-old Maurice Chevalier, for such a world no longer exists.

Not only has the social order that seemed immutable in his day vanished without a trace; it is also almost impossible, in this day and age, to imagine ourselves without television, movies, cassettes, or even radio.

A hundred years ago, all entertainment was live, and music halls, *café-concerts,* and hole-in-the-wall cabarets were so cheap that even the poorest people patronized them regularly. Since opera, ballet, and "straight" theater were the preserve of a small, educated, and affluent minority, the only popular distraction for the working-class majority—sport and cockfighting excepted—was "variety" or, as it was known in America, "vaudeville." It fulfilled a twin role, with both the French *café-conc* and the British music hall providing entertainment, food, and drink—and, in some cases at least, betting facilities as well—all under the same roof. In America, "vaudeville was the national relaxation, the theater of people"[1]—the word stemming from Olivier Basselin's songs and ballads from the Val de Vire (or Vau de Vire) area in medieval France.

Top music-hall performers at the turn of the century achieved something of the status of present-day rock stars, and some of them—the Great Macdermott, Marie Lloyd, Little Tich, Dan Leno, Vesta Tilley, Harry Lauder, and George Formby in Britain, Félix Mayol, Dranem, Fragson, Mistinguett, and, of course, Maurice Chevalier in France— remain household names to this day. So do veteran American stars like Fanny Brice, W. C. Fields, Buster Keaton, Eddie Cantor, George Jessel, and Fred and Adele Astaire, most of whom went on to star careers in films and television. Even Judy Garland began her career in vaudeville, though she did not like to be reminded of this.

Some of the variety and vaudeville personalities of the early Edwardian era can be seen in flickering, lovingly preserved silent-film clips, but the few surviving recordings of their voices are of such poor quality that it is difficult to appreciate what they were really like. Also, with very few exceptions, fashions change so fast—and the shelf life of music-hall art is so woefully short—that we are sometimes left wondering what our grandparents saw in them.

The music-hall "industry" developed on parallel lines in Britain, France, and the United States, but British and French music halls had such a reputation, and were such lucrative poles of attraction, that Americans crossed the Atlantic to make their fortunes and reputations in Europe. The European cachet was such that in the early twentieth century Continental luggage labels were prized and prominently displayed as proof of an American vaudeville performer's worth (those who had failed to make the coveted trip to Europe bought fake European labels to stick on their luggage in the hope of fooling theater bookers and theater managers). Later, Americans came to be in great demand in British theaters during the First World War, when almost all Britain's native-born male performers were in uniform.

In all three countries, tough, imaginative entrepreneurs made their fortunes building new theaters, promoting shows, and booking artists. Léon Volterra, later one of Maurice Chevalier's producers, was a millionaire showman who started life handing out leaflets on the streets, but he could barely read and write. (Jacques-Charles, the dapper upper-class impresario, who also dominated French music-hall life in the twenties and thirties, had to guide Volterra's hand to get him to trace the words *"lu et approuvé"*—"read and approved"—on artists' contracts). Henri Varna, another hugely successful entertainment tycoon, came from a similar background. In England, some music-hall moguls like Sir Alfred Butt, owner of the Palace Theater in London and, later, the Mogador in Paris, came from the "respectable" world of the City or of commerce (Butt himself had started out as a Harrods employee), and George Robey was a graduate of Jesus College, Cambridge, but most music-hall producers, like most music-hall artists, sprang from the working class.

In America, as might be expected, the fierce, cutthroat capitalism of the late nineteenth and early twentieth centuries spawned an exceptionally ruthless, predatory kind of show-business entrepreneur: In their concern for artists, New York's Lee Shubert and Marcus Loew were exceptions. Typical of the hard world of vaudeville were Martin Beck, who dominated West Coast theaters, F. F. Proctor, who transformed the raunchy "men only" American vaudeville routines into family entertainment, and especially the tandem of Benjamin Franklin Keith (1846–1914) and Edward Franklin Albee (1857–1930) who—in close association with Proctor—were to vaudeville what the first Rockefeller was to railroads. In their determination to dominate the industry and maximize profits, imposing drastic working conditions and eradicating all competition, Albee and Keith used strong-arm tactics reminiscent of those of Al Capone. So feared was the Keith-Albee partnership that it took exceptionally brave men to challenge him. When crusading *Variety* editor Sime Silverman began campaigning against his dictatorial, penny-pinching, strike-breaking tactics, Albee announced that any performer mentioned in *Variety* or even found reading it would be blacklisted. At its peak, the Keith-Albee partnership dominated vaudeville circuits, with over four hundred theaters under the Keith and Proctor Amusement Company management, and while they imposed higher standards, banning outright obscene patter and devising shows for "family" entertainment, they were hard, ruthless taskmasters. When Keith died, and when, shortly afterward, Albee retired, they were "lightly mourned."

Music halls became fashionable when snobs started patronizing them, even mingling socially with a few outstanding performers: Success on the music-hall stage became one way of breaking through the otherwise almost impenetrable nineteenth- and early twentieth-century class barrier. But the bulk of the audience remained working class—rough, noisy, seldom completely sober, often illiterate, but nevertheless curiously discriminating. British "variety" dominated the rest of the world: Maurice Chevalier, who visited Britain several times as a very young man, first in 1905, at seventeen, then in 1908, and again in 1913, this time with Mistinguett, at the very peak of British music-hall popularity and excellence, spent all his time going from one show to the next. He was struck by the huge range and skill of British music-hall artists, and later unashamedly adapted some of their themes and mannerisms, incorporating them into his own acts.

Max Beerbohm wrote that people "flocked to the halls to be cheered up by seeing a life uglier and more sordid than their own," and it is true that a great deal of the success of the halls was due to the way bathos, class differences, and social injustice were exploited. The content had to appeal to the uneducated, who at the turn of the century were to a large extent uninformed about the world around them. There was room for the occasional literary or political reference only if, through popular writers like Dickens or Kipling or calamities like wars, earthquakes, or the San Francisco fire, such references had entered the national consciousness and were understood by all.

Hardly surprisingly, a large number of music-hall themes dealt with sex, sometimes explicitly but more often through salacious, crass "wink wink nudge nudge" allusions and double entendres. American vaudeville was probably the crudest in its earthy exploitation of sex and natural bodily functions. One of the earliest vaudeville stars, Johnny Forbes, became famous for his ballad about a young woman who was so refined that

"She wouldn't touch a flowerpot, oh no dot rot 'em
For the nasty things had holes in their bottoms."

Such was the level of American vaudeville that so delighted country and working-class audiences in still largely rural America.

There was also considerable room for emotion, often forcefully conveyed, especially of a patriotic nature. The American Civil War spawned a whole school of songs, of which the most famous undoubtedly was Constance Loseby's

"On a bright May moon in 'sixty-three
And ready for the action,
On the battlefield of liberty
Fell Stonewall Jackson."

But nothing, in Britain at least, could compare with The Great Macdermott's

"We don't want to fight,
But by jingo if we do,
We've got the ships, we've got the guns,
We've got the money too.
We fought the Bear before,
And while we're Britons true,
The Russians shall not have Constantinople."

These lyrics led to a new word—"jingoism"—entering the English language at the time of the Crimean War.

Songs about the army often dealt with the Kiplingesque theme of the public's ingratitude for the erstwhile defenders of the Empire, as in Charles Godfrey's sketch "On Guard":

"Be off, you tramp, you're not wanted here.
—'But at Balaclava—I was wanted *there!*' "

A particular favorite in France after the 1870 Franco-Prussian War, blending jingoism and the "she-was-poor-but-she-was-honest" theme, was a song sang by Rose Bordas, a noted French patriotic singer, about a French wet nurse refusing to sell her milk to an anguished German father:

> "On your way, kraut,
> My bosom's not for your ilk
> Not for your babe
> Will I sell my French milk."*

and it comes as something of a surprise to discover that the tune of the "Internationale" ("*C'est la lutte finale . . .*") began life not as a paean to internationalist socialism, but as a "patriotic" song, with words penned by Georges Pottier a decade after the same Franco-Prussian War. Later on, Vesta Tilley's "Jolly Good Luck to the Girl Who Loves a Soldier" was to become so popular during the First World War that recruiting soared when she first sang it in London.

Not all the themes were grim. Some combined sex with topicality. James Hillier became a star through a song about changing sexual mores brought about by the railways:

> "A tickle in the tunnel is a lark, my boys,
> 'Tis nice to take your Marie Jane
> A-riding in a railway train
> And have a jolly tickle in the tunnel-O."

A typical number, so popular that Chevalier almost certainly saw it on one of his first London visits, was the voyeurish "There'll be no show this evening" often sung by Herbert Campbell, a comedian of Falstaffian girth, with a strip-tease act in "shadowgraph" taking place behind him:

*"*Va, passe ton chemin, ma mamelle est Française*
Je ne vends pas mon lait au fils d'un Allemand."

"No show this evening, no show tonight,
I'd go home if I were you,
You've seen all you're like to do,
Mother's blown the candle out,
There'll be no show tonight."

There were no qualms about advertising, whether subliminal or direct. George Leybourne, a performer whom Chevalier greatly admired and who looked astonishingly like him, became famous for his "Champagne Charlie," containing the unambiguous plug:

"Whenever I'm going on the spree
Moët and Chandon is the wine for me."

Other songs contained similar brand-name references to whisky, snuff, and tobacco, with suitable compensation—in kind—to the performers. Leybourne, of whom a noted music-hall critic wrote that "he could have been the best light comedian on the English stage if he had been educated"[2]—proof of the social gulf that existed between "popular" music-hall comedians and straight actors—used show-biz tactics to draw attention to his act that even contemporary pop stars and Hollywood press agents of the thirties could not have bettered. During one music-hall run, he had himself conveyed to the Canterbury Theatre every night in a brougham drawn by four white horses, prompting another, lesser-known music-hall comic to have himself taken to *his* theater in an open carriage drawn by four white (painted) donkeys.

Social criticism on music-hall stages was implicit rather than explicit, with a strong emphasis on stoically maintained standards of respectability. England's Victor Liston sang:

"I'm too proud to beg, too honest to steal,
I know what it is to be wanting a meal,
My tatters and rags I try to conceal,
I'm one of the shabby genteel."

Chevalier may have recalled this song when, many years later, he first started to sing "*Ma Pomme,*" his own famous piece about a carefree, happy tramp, which had none of the British pathos or self-pity, but closely paralleled the earlier American vaudeville tradition of jovial "tramp comics," who "swarmed through vaudeville almost as a national symbol" in the first two decades of the twentieth century.[3] One of the more famous "tramp comics" was W. C. Fields, who started out as a "tramp juggler," his act a huge hit in Parisian music halls in 1911. The notion of the "happy tramp," as Chevalier instinctively realized, had universal appeal, both because of its inherent pathos and the sentiment that "but for the grace of God"[4] this could well have been the fate of most audiences watching the show.

In Britain, France, and especially America, a consistent theme was race: Chevalier himself, in his first appearances as a twelve-year-old, would crudely ape the comical provincial accents of Auvergnat or Breton country hicks; regional differences, especially Scottish and Irish, were a constant delight to English audiences, and the famous music-hall comic Harry Lauder probably did more to put his beloved Scotland on the map than the poet Robert Burns himself. But it was in the American melting pot that American vaudeville found its most enduring themes. "Racial comedy was an integral part of vaudeville,"[5] wrote Douglas Gilbert.

The possibilities were vast. There was the German immigrant theme, as in the amazingly popular vaudeville musical *The Prince of Pilsen,* performed by John W. Ransome. All over America, his trademark line, "Vaz you effer in Zinzinnati?" became a recognized catchphrase. Ransome also did imitations of the few nationally known Americans whose mannerisms were familiar to all—President William H. Taft and various Tammany Hall bosses. Another comedian, Ed Bush (who happened to be Irish), became the best-known of the large school of "Jewish vaudeville" comedians. Acts like his were not regarded as anti-Semitic in the least, relying heavily on accent and fractured Yiddish-English, as in Bush's song about a Jewish tailor:

> "Solomon, Solomon Moses,
> Hast du gesehen der clotheses

Hast du gesehen der kleiner kinder
Under der sox in der vinder?"

But the most common theme, of course, spreading all over the world, was that dealing with the American Negro. "The shuffling, improvident negro was the stock comic figure" of early twentieth-century vaudeville.[6] Though there were, of course, black vaudeville comedians, white performers in blackface outnumbered them vastly. For every ravishing star of "Blacklands," like Florence Moore, there were at least a hundred white performers in "Negro minstrel shows." It would take almost a century for Americans to wake up to the fact that minstrel shows—and "blackface" in particular—were seen in a very different light by the black community, as a bitter mockery of race and origin.

There were so many genres that a successful music-hall show was one that contained a cocktail of most of them. In France, for example, "patriotic" singers apart, some of the labels were almost untranslatable. The women performers were either *"diseuses"* (speakers and storytellers rather than warblers, in the style of Rex Harrison in *My Fair Lady*), *"gommeuses"* (also known as *"épileptiques"*—hysterics), *"pierreuses"* (or *"gigo-lettes"*—sexual tempters), or *"demimondaines"* (fake genteel); the men were *"gambilleurs"* (knockabout comedians), *"sentimentaux," "scieurs"* (those simulating excessive naïveté bordering on idiocy), *"gommeux"* (the romantic seducer type), *"comiques troupiers"* (army jokers), *"vieux beaux,"* or *"fantaisistes de charme."* Chevalier, in his early days, ran the gamut of all these types, though a British music-hall critic who recalled seeing him in his teens put him in the "sentimental coster [i.e., cockney] comedian" category.[7]

The going was quite extraordinarily tough. Chevalier himself would later write about the brutal, unpredictable behavior of upper-circle audiences, whenever they reacted unfavorably to a new performer. As Willson Disher, once a music-hall performer himself, wrote:

> With little warning one suddenly found oneself pushed onto a platform
> in front of a merciless mob. If not stunned by a bottle while striving to
> recover from stage fright, one might get as far as the first verse. Catcalls,

boos, old boots, dead cats and even rivets might come one's way. By far the wisest thing would be to break into a clog dance to change from a stationary into a moving target. Hundreds retired heartbroken from the struggle.[8]

The toughest audiences in Britain were in the north, in France in the south, especially Marseilles. Mistinguett recalled the reaction of a startled, demoralized teenage singer in Enghien faced with cries of "Higher! Higher, you bitch!" because her voice didn't reach the balcony. "She gathered up her skirts till she showed everything she had, shouting 'is that high enough for you bastards?' before flouncing off the stage in tears. She was among those who never made it,"[9] Mistinguett added.

The performers were equally tough: Paulus, the famous French comic singer, became even more popular with his fans after roughing up a member of the audience in the middle of a performance. The provocation had been considerable: The "victim" had shown up, night after night, in a front-row seat, and ostentatiously begun reading a newspaper whenever Paulus came on stage. Trombetta, another popular *gambilleur*, shot and killed his theater manager after a row about free tickets.

In America, things were perhaps even tougher: In many vaudeville theaters, entertainment was continuous, so that performers were on duty from 10:00 A.M. until late at night, when the last performance ended. At intervals, "barkers" attempted to hustle spectators out with cries of "This way out" after each show, but they often refused to leave—in which case the last performer had to return and repeat his act, once, twice, or more, until audiences finally tired of it and got the message.

In France songwriting was a specialized art long before the turn of the century, and the Faubourg Saint-Martin was where aspiring performers flocked, purchasing songs and sheet music they would try out later. Copyright laws were chaotic, and established performers often bought for a pittance the rights to songs that later became hugely popular. In many British music halls, performers supplemented their meager salaries by selling the sheet music of their songs to the audience during the intervals.

British music hall was the almost accidental creation of two men:

Samuel Haycroft Lane, who first presented a "variety of artists" at the Britannia Theatre, Hoxton, and Charles Morton, a publican born in 1819, in Hackney, who first hired professionals—including acrobats, magicians, mimics, and contortionists—to perform inside his Saint George's Tavern. This proved so successful that when he opened the Canterbury Theatre in Lambeth, he charged entry fees: threepence (later sixpence) for men, and a shilling for women (when they were eventually allowed in) because they drank less. Other theaters opened by competitors, like the Holborn Empire and the Tivoli, proved equally successful. By the time of his death, Morton, an eccentric who never used a typewriter, a telephone, or any form of transport that was not horse-drawn, was a rich man, managing the Palace Theatre and half a dozen others. For all his Victorian habits and formidable appearance, with vast muttonchop whiskers and stern expression, Morton was no puritan: It was he who tried to combine music halls and betting shops under one roof (this became illegal in 1853), first imported the cancan to Britain (to one of his theaters, the Alhambra, where it was banned), and first introduced nude *tableaux vivants.*

Both French and British music hall required a presenter, but "the chairman" was a unique British phenomenon. Whereas in France the role was usually held by a relatively unimportant soubrette-type figure, holding a notice board with the title of a song and the performer's name on it, in Britain the M.C. was a toastmasterlike figure of considerable girth and consequence who introduced the successive acts from a thronelike chair where he remained throughout the evening, at the head of a table with his back to the stage, monitoring the show through a mirror. In the early days of music hall, privileged guests were invited to sit at the chairman's table—and were honored to be allowed to ply him with drink and cigars. The chairman played a key role in other respects: He could boost careers and call for encores by hammering the table like an auctioneer, "knocking down" to invite applause and voicing his own enthusiasm, or, on the contrary, introducing artists in derogatory terms, encouraging and even provoking boos and catcalls. Because of this, he wielded formidable power, and woe betide the artiste who failed to tip him adequately. An essential difference among French and British music halls appears to have been the systematic gouging of the British performers not only by the chairman, but by the orchestra members, sceneshifters, and electricians as well. A fifth of their earnings probably went in tips of various kinds to keep on the management's right side.

By 1920, there were hundreds of *café-concs* in Paris, many of them in the Boulevard de Strasbourg/Faubourg Saint-Martin areas within easy walking distance of Ménilmontant, over sixty music halls in the London area alone, and hundreds more in provincial France and in the rest of Britain. In America there were some two thousand registered theaters, most of them specializing in vaudeville, and thousands more beer halls and "honky-tonks." In these establishments, at any rate prior to Prohibition and the proliferation of puritanical "moral watchdog committees," stage performances were not the only entertainment provided: In America "vaudeville"—and the different attractions that went with it— rapidly differentiated from both the French and English music-hall tradition.

In the American honky-tonks and "store shows," the real profits came not from tickets but from liquor sales: Chorus girls and "wine waitresses" were expected to mingle with the customers and push liquor consumption. This was the beginning of the long-established, American-instituted "hostess" tradition, later prevalent all over the world.

Prostitution, at least until the "new morality" wave and Prohibition laws took effect, was an integral part of vaudeville honky-tonks. The process was made easy by the existence of curtained booths from whose vantage point town notables could watch the show without being seen—and without being observed dallying with showgirls and prostitutes. At the Silver Palace in Texas, at the turn of the century, chorus girls—who, like American showgirls in all honky-tonks, earned a percentage on every drink sold to customers—emptied the beer from their glasses or bottles into a trough that flowed back to the bar, where the liquid was rebottled and resold.[10] Almost invariably, "vaudeville champagne" was sold. At four dollars a bottle, it consisted of pear cider, which normally cost sixty-four cents a bottle. Theater owners rightly presumed that the multiplicity of attractions—onstage, in the audience, and in the booths—would distract the customers' attention from the quality of the drink.

The honky-tonk side of American vaudeville, with its emphasis on chorus-girl hostesses, was not the only major difference between American music-hall entertainment and the French or British kind: "Wonderlands" and "dime museums"—forerunners of the quintessentially American theme-park phenomenon—also injected a circus note, for American vaudeville was not an offshoot of the theater, but encompassed freak and circus acts. P. T. Barnum, the circus entrepreneur, was a major figure in the world of vaudeville; B. F. Keith had also begun his career as an unsuccessful circus owner-manager; and the legendary impresario "Willie" Hammerstein was a showman with an intuitive understanding of the value of hype and sensationalism.

For Hammerstein, vaudeville talent invariably came second to headline-making notoriety. So he booked murderers (preferably murderesses) and anyone else he could find who combined scandal with a stage presence. After two young women, Lilian Graham and Ethel Conrad, had shot and seriously wounded a young man on the "social register," he had them perform as "the shooting stars," although they sang excruciatingly, prompting one vaudeville colleague to say, "They'll have to *kill* someone to get another week." It was Hammerstein who realized the vaudeville possibilities of showgirl Evelyn Nesbit, whose husband, Harry Thaw, killed Stanford White, the famous architect, in 1906, at the Madison Square Garden Roof Theater during the "premiere" of "Mamzelle Champagne"—it was one of the most publicized murder cases of the century.* As soon as she became "news," Hammerstein decided Nesbit was worthy of star billing.

Hammerstein's flair was unique, particularly when it came to turning lack of talent into a plus. He built a particularly mediocre singing

---

*Thaw, who pleaded temporary insanity, allegedly murdered White for sexually abusing Nesbit in 1901. Then only seventeen years old, she had just achieved a modicum of fame as a chorus girl in *Floradora*, for her outstanding beauty rather than her somewhat average talent.

ensemble act, the Cherry sisters, into an audience-participation hit by the simple device of ostentatiously rigging up a net in front of the stage, just before they appeared, to catch the eggs and vegetables that audiences invariably rained upon them. But perhaps his most exemplary brashness—and lack of scruple—came with his "discovery" of Abdul Kadar, court artist of the Turkish sultan, and his three wives. Hammerstein, who brought the polygamous "Abdul Kadar" to New York, duly summoned the press to witness his being turned away from its leading hotels after requesting a room for himself and his three wives. (Hammerstein, of course, had anticipated this and had provided him with a rented Manhattan apartment for the duration of his stay). The act, as such, was innocuous—and had been routine in vaudeville for years: Surrounded by his Oriental "houris" in diaphanous veils, "Abdul Kadar," in flowing Oriental robes and turban, simply drew fairly skillful cartoons of random members of the audience who volunteered to come up onstage and sit for him. His real name was Adolphe Schneider, he was Swiss, and his "wives" were his German-Swiss wife, daughter, and daughter-in-law.

For all these reasons, American vaudeville lacked the respectability conferred on it by British royalty. In Britain the music-hall profession was so well established that Edward VII himself attended the inaugural show of the newly built London Coliseum in 1906: To preserve the royal dignity, a specially designed "mobile box" was built to get him from his carriage into the theater (it got stuck halfway). British music-hall professionals were by then so well organized that when theater owners decided to increase the numbers of matinees, in 1907, without increasing artists' salaries, the entertainment world was brought to an abrupt halt by a general strike of music-hall performers, and they also successfully lobbied—through a music-hall Artists Railway Rates Association—for 25 percent reductions when traveling from one town to the next on business. Some London music halls, like the Prince of Wales, specialized in continuous entertainment—the "nonstop revue" formula first devised by America's B. F. Keith at the Gaiety Theater, Boston, in 1894, and on the same lavish scale (the Boston Gaiety, built by Albee, had cost $600,000).

Continuous performances required huge outlays and considerable logistical skill. Backstage, there were three separate stage canteens, one for technicians and musicians, one for women, and one for the management and stars, functioning nonstop, except, of course, for Sundays.

For all music-hall performers, whether in Britain or France, conditions were hard: For the juniors, on their way up, successful bookings meant a succession of sordid lodging houses. In Britain, where "circuits" were highly organized, performers had virtually no time to call their own: They performed six days a week, usually with twice-nightly shows and several matinees, and on the seventh day—Sunday—moved on to the next town. The French system was more anarchic, for there was nothing that could compare with the Stoll Theater empire; the "agence Dalos" that booked performers nationwide had a dubious reputation, and most bookings were made through personal contact. They also lasted longer. The *café-conc* formula was flexible: Shows could last as long as four hours, with audiences drifting in and out, rather as in Japanese Kabuki theater. British music-hall was more organized: Schedules were more rigidly adhered to, each performer's time monitored by a system of flashing lights, unseen by the audience, indicating how many minutes were left.

The first "Royal Command Performance," the benefit gala in aid of indigent music-hall performers and a hugely popular media event, was attended by King George V and Queen Mary in 1912: Almost all the stars Chevalier admired most—Harry Tate, Vesta Tilley, Little Tich, George Robey, and Harry Lauder, took part, along with Anna Pavlova, the world-famous ballerina, in the inevitable Tchaikovsky ballet excerpt "The Swan." A notable absence was that of Marie Lloyd. Sarah Bernhardt considered her "the best actress in the whole of Britain," but her witty, double-entendre numbers and suggestive body language scared Palace officials—and thus she was banned. They feared, probably correctly, that she might break into one of her favorite songs, such as "She's Never Had Her Ticket Punched Before." Such squeamishness was hypocritical, for Edward VII, an authority on both the French and English music hall, was a connoisseur who enjoyed nothing so much as bawdy, near-the-knuckle humor, and to say that he was no puritan is the mildest of British euphemisms: As Prince of Wales, he had epitomized the roué and libidinous stage-door Johnny, though to minimize the risks involved to his reputation, he preferred to indulge in his passion for vaudeville—and vaudeville artistes—in Paris rather than London.

The official "royal" recognition extended to music hall as an art form was not extended to its artists and entrepreneurs in France. Not that French politicians, aristocrats, and businessmen shunned the music hall, but their interests were mostly of a different nature, focusing backstage, on the scantily clad dancers of the opposite sex. For adolescents like Chevalier, music hall could become a stepping-stone to a straight acting career, as Raimu, Fernandel, Jean Gabin, and Paul Meurisse were to prove. For women, it could also be a step up of a different nature: Yvonne Printemps, the leading actress of the thirties, and one of Sacha Guitry's many wives, started out as a chorus girl, as did Arletty, the unforgettable heroine of Marcel Carné's *Les Enfants du Paradis*. But "La Belle Otéro," Adrienne d'Alençon, and Cléo de Merode, who all began as circus and music-hall performers, became more famous as prominent "demimondaines" with royal or ducal lovers than as performers in their own right. Small neighborhood "*café-concs*" were proving grounds for music-hall talent. Chevalier owed his own remarkable climb from seedy neighborhood *café-concs* to the Folies-Bergère in less than four years to his outstanding energy and talent, but also to the fabulous music-hall boom that occurred at the turn of the century.

Though there was, in France, no single figure of Morton's stature, the rise of the music hall followed the same lines, and in both countries "straight" theater owners reacted protectively to this new, rapidly grow-ing, popular art form. In France, during Napoleon III's "Second Em-pire," alarmed at the success of the mushrooming "*café-concs*," theater owners tried to put them out of business. Docile, suitably corrupt members of Parliament introduced new legislation, strictly regulating what could be seen on French music-hall and *café-conc* stages: Performers could sing but were forbidden to dress up, act sketches, or use theatrical decor of any kind. In the same way, in Britain legislation limited music-hall entertainment to monologues, songs, and ballets: Sketches, playlets, and double acts were forbidden. This was the price music halls were made to pay for the privilege of being able to serve food and drink.

Pioneers like Morton were constantly infringing the rules, gladly paying their fines when caught. These laws failed to inhibit huge new theater investments, either in France or Britain: The Folies-Bergère opened in 1869, the Gaité-Rochechouart in 1870. In France both the large, plush music halls and the seedier *café-concs* coexisted until the First World War, when the introduction of the spectacular revue, and the growing popularity of the cinema, killed off the smaller, poorer establishments: They went under, one by one, becoming theaters, cinemas, restaurants—or office blocks. In Britain music halls thrived for far longer—right up to the Second World War and the advent of television.

Whether in Britain or France, the popular music halls, located centrally and in working-class districts, attracted not only "mashers" but large numbers of prostitutes, though their modus operandi differed from those in American honky-tonks. Some practices were appalling. In France it was common practice to stage a lottery at the end of the evening: The winner (shades of *Miss Saigon*) had the right to spend the night with the female singer of his choice. At the Folies-Bergère in Paris, prostitution on the premises was legalized, if not officially encouraged, with management itself becoming a party to a vice it officially condemned, extracting a fee from all those wishing to ply their trade on the premises. Well into the 1930s, the Folies-Bergère *"promenoir"* was an established meeting place. Prostitutes paid the theater twenty francs for a monthly "pass" allowing them unlimited entry; as soon as the doors opened, Jacques-Charles, the well-known French impresario, noted, "There would be a furious rush, the girls eyeing themselves in the huge foyer mirrors as they took up their battle stations. We called this the nightly 'practice gallop.' "[11] Since the Folies-Bergère, when Maurice Chevalier first started performing there, was more of a vast nightclub than theater, with tables, chairs, and busy waiters, the girls made a beeline for unaccompanied males or all-male tables, quickly moving on if they were rejected, or if they were offered drinks but nothing more. Trading was brisk, noisy, and distracting to the performers, who, faced with the hubbub and the competing spectacle of openly soliciting prostitutes in suggestive garb, had to impose themselves by sheer noise and force of personality.

Some of the Folies-Bergère prostitutes were almost as well known as the artistes themselves. One buxom black woman, in particular, with her raucous laugh and sense of repartee, was invariably the center of attention, drinking champagne at her putative client's expense, telling jokes, exchanging banter—a Folies-Bergère geisha. The women on the prowl in the *promenoir* became bolder and more desperate as the evening went on, offering themselves at lower and lower prices as the evening's entertainment progressed, even grabbing potential clients on the way out after the show. The Folies-Bergère management worked hand in glove with the Paris police, Jacques-Charles noted without any trace of embarrassment. "The card registration system was useful to us because we gained access to all their records, we knew whether they had been in trouble with the law and who their pimps were."[12]

In Britain and France alike, sex was a favorite music-hall subject, bawdy songs outnumbered all the others, and Maurice Chevalier, as a twelve-year-old, was singing songs whose allusions he may not even have fully understood. There were subtle differences between the two countries: British music-hall songs were on the whole wittier and less crude than the French music-hall repertoire, at least in the early 1900s, when Chevalier began his career. One recurring theme, much more prevalent in Britain than in France, was that of the henpecked husband victimized by a nagging wife and predatory mother-in-law. Another revolved around the sexual predator—whether lodger, window cleaner, or plumber—cuckolding the innocent and usually totally deluded husband. In such songs, almost invariably, the victim told the story not only humorously but against himself, pretending—or preferring—to remain unaware of his wife's infidelity. Not so in France, where the narrator was usually the seducer, boasting of his sexual conquests, rather than the victim.

The difference went further than mere genre. It underlined a very definite British music-hall leitmotiv: the conviction that British males were sexually inadequate while British women had an unlimited appetite for sex. In England sexual references alone were not enough: The best bawdy songs told a complete story, as in "I'm the Plumber" or "Our Lodger's Such a Nice Man," sung with delicious double-entendre innuendo by Vesta Victoria, or in George Formby's "When I'm Cleaning Windows." An additional reason for the more subtle double entendre was almost certainly the "watch committee," the local authority that, from the twenties onward, monitored music-hall shows with a keen eye for obscenity. Marie Lloyd, and later Max Miller and Tommy Trinder, were past masters in the art of getting around the censors. Had the same moral standards prevailed in France as in Britain, many of Chevalier's later French songs would have remained unperformed. His song "Prosper," glorifying the profession of pimp and brutal sexual dominator, beating up his girls or sending them off to army bordellos if their earnings dropped, could not have been performed in Britain, at any rate in English. In France censorship was of a different nature: Apart from brief liberal spells throughout the nineteenth century, all *café-conc* and music-hall lyrics had to be approved by a special French government department. During the MacMahon presidency, some twenty-five hundred Paris cafés were closed "for political reasons."

For all the sexuality, there was room, too, for sentiment: "Two Lovely Black Eyes" became an overnight hit, and "My Old Dutch," that moving song about an old couple's long-standing mutual dependence and affection, made the fortune of the other (British) Chevalier, Albert. Though there were no accurate ratings, a successful tune could turn an unknown into a star overnight.

Despite the absence of television and mass-produced records, some British music-hall performers became stars in France as well. "Little Tich," the dwarf with the body of a seven-year-old and the timing, mimicry, and clowning skills of John Cleese, took Paris by storm. He wore huge bouffant trousers to make him look even smaller, huge, elongated shoes, with a tiny gray bowler perched on top of his head, and a clown's red nose. Jacques-Charles recalled his irresistible skit as a female Spanish ballet dancer in a tutu covered in spangles, "gripping a rose between his teeth, showing off his muscular little legs." Marie Lloyd, Jacques-Charles wrote, "combined the narrative talents of an Yvette Guilbert, the lewdness of Odette Dulac and the dynamism of Mistinguett." British blackface was common, its practitioners calling themselves "Ethiopian serenaders." Chevalier, nearly twenty years younger than "Little Tich," Mary Lloyd, and Harry Lauder, later drew considerably on their acts. After witnessing Little Tich's number in Paris, where he became an overnight sensation, Chevalier adapted some of his mannerisms and props, including the clown's nose and bowler.

Though formal copyright laws existed, to protect the livelihood of composers and lyricists (in France, Offenbach helped establish the SACEM, the Société des Auteurs et Compositeurs de Musique) exclusivity was another matter: Performers stole one another's acts, imitated one another's mannerisms, and there would be a whole school of Mayol (and later, Piaf and Chevalier) clones. When Chevalier started out in *café-concs,* there were distinct categories of singers who performed as licensed imitators of other, better-known artistes. Chevalier himself would try his hand at imitation in his early years. But he would later realize he was at his best in his own, distinctive, style.

At the peak of his music-hall popularity, hundreds of professional entertainers around the world (including Britain's Jack Warner) would "do a Chevalier," and twenty years after his death, Sacha Distel was doing his Maurice Chevalier imitation on French TV to enormous critical and popular acclaim.

CHAPTER 3

"Les femmes qu'on embrasse, ça léche ou ça pique." ("The women you kiss
either lick you or stab you.")

—Maurice Chevalier
Ma Route et Mes Chansons

$\mathcal{M}$aurice Chevalier's first, calamitous stage appearance
took place on the small stage of the Café des Trois Lions in
Ménilmontant, where amateurs performed for free at weekends
before an exclusively local working-class audience. The low entrance fee—twenty-five centimes, which included a free drink—
made it accessible to almost everyone. By the time he plucked up
the courage to ask for an evening slot, Chevalier's repertoire consisted of two songs: a well-known country-bumpkin act called *"V'la
les Croquants"* ("Here Come the Country Bums")* and a knockabout comic act called *"Youp Youp Larifla."* There were no prelimi-

---

*"To Paris Ah've coom
The capital to see
The sight makes me go 'boum,'
With joy ah'm all at sea."

nary auditions. Almost anyone claiming to be able to sing was welcome. The decor could not have differed much from Zola's description of Le Chat Noir a few years before, so reminiscent, as Richard Dorment* pointed out, of Toulouse-Lautrec's portrayals of low music-hall life in nearby Montmartre. As Zola wrote:

> Gas jets without globes flamed, scalding the open air, furiously heating the thick, stagnant vapour, made by breath and the smoke through pipes. One could see through that blur flushed, sweaty faces, while the acrid odour of all those crammed-in people increased the drunkenness, the cries of which the audience whipped up each new season.[1]

Just before going onstage, the following Saturday night, the pianist asked him, "What key do you want to sing in? Taken by surprise but unwilling to display his ignorance, Maurice replied, "Anything will do." The result was predictable: Young Maurice sang at the top of his voice in one key, the pianist played in another, and the hideous cacophony had the entire café audience in stitches. La Louque and Paul loyally applauded, but even they noticed something was amiss.

Maurice had been so intent on getting the words out that he was unaware, at first, of the fiasco. With considerable gall, he assumed that the laughter was friendly. It was left to another amateur performer, a young clock repairer called Boucot who did imitations of Mayol, to explain what a musical key was, and why there had been raucous laughter.

The experience was humiliating, but it could have been worse. "I knew," Chevalier wrote later, "that I could at least face an audience." This was not entirely true, for he had been unable to look them in the eye, and had his eyes glued on the ceiling for as long as he was onstage.

Then and there, he began showing the compulsive tenacity and passion for detail for which he would become famous. Leechlike, he attached himself to Boucot, following him everywhere—to music shops, to the Café des Trois Lions, watching him perform, gaining the rudiments of a musical education.

*Richard Dorment, "Lautrec's Bitter Theater," *New York Review of Books*, December 19, 1991.

One day, in a famous sheet-music shop owned by the legendary Henri Christiné, (who would later write songs for Chevalier) Boucot pointed out Félix Mayol, then at the top of his form. Exquisitely turned out, with a bowler hat and silver-topped cane, Mayol expressed considerable interest in *"le petit Chevalier"* when Boucot told him he was a budding amateur singer. Completely unaware of Mayol's sexuality, Maurice had no inkling that Mayol was trying to pick him up. All he knew was that Mayol had a "strange, soft look" that scared him.

Having learned about keys, and after considerable practice over several weeks, Maurice felt able to face the Café des Trois Lions crowd once more, and this time was able to sing in tune with the music. The audience was sympathetic: He was by far the youngest performer ever seen there. But no amateurs ever became permanent fixtures at the club, and after a couple of weekend performances Maurice, Boucot, and the others were told their time was up. The habitués wanted new blood.

There was a disastrous interlude at another sordid *café-conc* before a raucously drunken audience of ten. Young Chevalier despaired of ever going onstage again. But the *café-conc* phenomenon was at the peak of its boom: A new establishment, pompously calling itself the Élysée Ménilmontant, opened on his very doorstep, and Maurice Chevalier's professional career began there in earnest, though he was still being paid in kind—a *café-crème* for every song. He was billed as *"le petit Chevalier— comique miniature,"* "little Chevalier, the miniature comic."

He now had a new mentor, Jean Gilbert, who also did Mayol and Fragson imitations. Gilbert introduced him to the owner of another *café-conc,* the Casino des Tourelles. Audiences there were invariably informed whenever newcomers did tryouts. When the time came for Chevalier to appear onstage, a notice board with the word "audition" on it was placed on the stage. Usually, this was enough to destabilize all but the most self-assured performers, for the public was merciless toward beginners. Again, Maurice's extreme youth, and charm, saved the day. Gilbert was overjoyed with his protégé's progress. "They like you, you make them laugh . . . but if you really want to come back, you're in for a lot of hard work."

Maurice's repertoire still consisted only of those two songs, but he promised to learn more and was hired for two weeks at twelve francs a week for two appearances a night, four nights a week—two francs more than he had ever earned. He ran all the way home to break the news to La Louque, adding, "No more tin tacks for me." His adoring mother timidly suggested he might have to change his mind, but celebrated with him.

They went on a shopping spree. He bought himself a cheap but flashy overcoat, with a velvet collar, and a high-crowned man's felt hat called a *girondin*. Both were Gilbert hallmarks, for Chevalier badly wanted to look like his mentor. It was only when he started wearing them, and was jeered at in the street, that he realized he looked grotesque—a small child dressed as a man.

La Louque's fears were confirmed: After his two weeks were up, Maurice was not asked to stay on. He found another slot at another small *café-conc*, the Concert du Commerce, for a paltry five francs a week. By this time, he had lost his shyness, and spent all day canvassing for jobs, finally landing a one-week-but-renewable contract at twenty-one francs a week at the Ville Japonaise on the Boulevard de Strasbourg, the Pigalle of its day. The Boulevard de Strasbourg was the *café-conc* area par excellence, and the money seemed like a fortune to him.

He found himself instantly catapulted into another world. La Ville Japonaise was a cut above the other *café-concs* he had known. It was also far less respectable than the working-class *"beuglants"* and "amateurs' night" cafés in Ménilmontant. Neither a brothel nor a *"maison de rendez-vous,"* it was a convenient place for "free-lance amateurs" to meet potential clients, and for married men to seek out chance acquaintances for an extramarital fling. At the tables, there were always plenty of very young women pawing fleshy, bearded "bourgeois" twice their age.

Here the young and hitherto incredibly sheltered Chevalier, now thirteen years old, first became aware of sex. The casual promiscuity of shared, unisex dressing rooms, the predatory games being played in the audience, the knowing, and incredibly obscene, comments of the *café-conc* waiters in the wings, all provided him with an instant education.

Until then he had indulged in a childhood flirtation with a girl of his own age called Georgette (they held hands on the church steps in

Ménilmontant on moonlit nights), and he had worshiped, but only from afar, a sexy cabaret singer called Mademoiselle Daudibert.

His first experience was predictable. A young woman in the audience took him out to dinner, flirted with him outrageously, introduced him to the French kiss, and would have taken him to bed if he had not taken fright. He was then unwise enough to tell the woman's elderly lover what had happened. According to Chevalier's memoirs, they both turned on him, calling him a "little shit." It is possible he embroidered on the story, but it may well have been his first evidence of duplicity in women, and of the virtue of secrecy.

A highly charged, diminutive sex bomb called Spinelly, only two or three years older than Maurice, behaved with equally outrageous immodesty in the dressing room (where she provocatively displayed herself in the nude to Chevalier) and onstage. Her act consisted of songs like *"Un P'tit Coup de Piston"*

"A little poke of the piston-rod
Does you a world of good."*

while unabashedly miming sex onstage. As Chevalier quickly discovered at the Ville Japonaise, the raunchier the song, the greater the applause. As a result, he now concentrated on Dranem imitations.

Dranem (1869–1935) was a self-taught, working-class entertainer who had started off as a street hawker. His real name was Armand Menard, his stage name spelled backward. He had practically invented the French "double-entendre" lyric genre, and was almost as widely imitated as Félix Mayol. Whereas Mayol ostentatiously flaunted his mincing effeminacy, Dranem onstage used the staple comic's "I don't know what you're laughing at" gimmick. By any standard, his songs were unbelievably crude, even granted Alan Jay Lerner's caveat that "a lyric,

*"*Un p'tit coup d'piston*
ça n'a l'air de rien
mais ça fait beaucoup de bien
pour trouver une position."

without its musical clothes, should never be allowed to parade naked across the printed page." Dranem himself was a likable spendthrift, generous to a fault, as improvident as his erstwhile partner Mistinguett was miserly, in real life riotously funny but totally unable to complete a sentence without an obscenity or a crude sexual allusion.

To the tough audience that haunted *café-concs* like la Ville Japonaise, the spectacle of a thirteen-year-old boy doing a Dranem act was irresistible, and young Maurice immediately exploited this for all it was worth. "The more laughter I generated, the more obscene I became," he wrote later. By the time he left la Ville Japonaise to go on to the even raunchier Casino de Montmartre, he had a whole repertoire of Dranem and Claudius songs to draw on, including songs like "I Stuck It in the Starch (to Keep It Stiff)"—and another where, strutting round the stage with his hands in his pockets, simulating an erection, he sang:

> "My iron determination
> Is the main thing that I know
> The male part of a nation
> Had better let it show."

By now Chevalier had an agent, who booked him into *café concs* not only in Paris but in the provinces. In Tours, a casual acquaintance invited him to lunch. Unused to aperitifs, wine, and liqueurs, he ended up drunk and incapable, unable to go through with his act. The following morning, he was fired. Maurice never dared tell his mother the truth. He himself, as a result of this experience, believed that alcoholism was in his blood, and henceforth, with only minor lapses, rationed himself to a glass or two of wine a day, or a Dubonnet, his favorite drink. Onstage, he was "*le petit* Chevalier," the foul-mouthed, cheeky little prankster delighting in shocking, sexual badinage. Offstage, after Tours, he turned into an abstemious, almost neurotic worrier, carefully hoarding his money, at a time when most *café-conc* performers flaunted their heavy drinking habits.

He no longer worried about his sexuality, though: In his memoirs, he would later boast that when he finally went to bed with a girl ("a robust, chesty girl singer") at the age of fourteen and a half, he made love to her seven consecutive times. From then on, until his first real love affair five years later with the singer Fréhel, sex would be a casual, almost mechanical, activity.

He was now skinnier and more worldly-wise. In the backstage world of the *café-concs*, there was no shortage of attractive, willing, equally casual girls. Though his act required him to wear a clown's outfit—red nose, funny hat, floppy shoes—and despite the large mole on his left cheek, he knew they found him exceptionally handsome. His mother may have guessed that her "Patapouf" was becoming "a little man," as he himself put it, but he never told her about this side of his life, and she never asked embarrassing questions when he failed to come home at night. In addition to his growing legion of female admirers, Félix Mayol made a pitch for the handsome Maurice, offering him a thousand francs—and a bicycle—if he would spend the night with him. Chevalier was able to fend him off tactfully, without turning this powerful music-hall star into an enemy.

In his memoirs, for all his early sexual initiation and the company he now kept, he gave the impression that his dearest wish was for his childhood to last forever. His increasingly frequent sexual conquests were unimportant to him. His greatest thrill was to bring home to La Louque the tangible tokens of love and success: the earnings he handed over to her with the touching devotion of a retriever returning a stick to its master. His fees grew steadily, for in the small world of the down-market *café-concs*, he was acquiring a reputation as a box-office draw. When Paul left to get married, La Louque and Maurice, now fifteen, moved several times, ending up in a slightly larger, more expensive apartment on the Faubourg Saint-Martin, in the heart of the entertainment district.

What young Maurice Chevalier understandably failed to realize at this juncture was the huge class difference that existed between the cheaper, popular *café-conc* audiences and those attending the classier, more prestigious music-hall theaters, where stars like Dranem, Fragson, and "Little Tich" were performing. He believed his near-the-knuckle repertoire, full of sexual innuendos, was a sure formula for success. They had certainly delighted audiences in the past. But, as in English music-hall and American vaudeville, tastes were changing. Parisian audiences, in the more fashionable theaters at least, were becoming more demanding. What they now wanted was more wit and less smut.

Maurice learned this the hard way. Booked for one week at the Petit Casino at nine francs a day, by a theater manager who had seen him perform the previous year—but with a possible extension if he proved a success—he was dismayed to find that the brand of humor that had delighted audiences on the Boulevard de Strasbourg was not at all to the taste of the new crowd. The Petit Casino, for all its small size, was *the* testing ground for music-hall performers: It was said, in the trade, that if you made it there, you could make it anywhere in Paris. The Petit Casino audiences were partly made up of affluent Parisians slumming, thrilled to be mixing with the fauna from the French underworld. It was not an easily satisfied working-class Ménilmontant crowd.

During his "iron determination" act, there were catcalls, whistling, and shouts of "Disgusting" and "Send him back to school." Chevalier had never experienced rejection: He left the stage and burst into tears. What had gone wrong? How could audiences be so different? He toned down his act in subsequent performances, but such an adjustment was now meaningless, and he was not kept on after the first trial week.

He went back to canvassing the small *café-concs* with only limited success. La Louque had been unable to save any money, and they were once more eating potatoes and drinking a weird concoction of boiled cherry pits and stalks, which for some reason his mother believed was good for him. He had a large hole in his only decent pair of shoes, so he stuffed them with paper. That summer of 1903 he was reduced to singing, on Sunday afternoons, at a *guinguette* (roadhouse) on the Seine, passing around the hat to eke out a pitifully small fee. He even seriously toyed with the notion of finding a "normal" job, answering a newspaper advertisement for secretaries "with good handwriting to address envelopes."

Then, as so often in show business, a minor miracle occurred: A *café-conc* manager, unaware of Chevalier's Petit Casino disaster, had just been hired as the manager of a small but fashionable music hall, the

Parisiana, far more prestigious than the Petit Casino, and the real stepping-stone to top establishments like La Scala and the Alhambra. He offered Maurice nine francs a day to perform there for the whole autumn season. Chevalier was by no means the star of this new revue, for he had only one solo song, but he was also in the singing-and-dancing chorus. It was his first experience of organized, structured rehearsals, of theater and company discipline. By this time, he had a better idea of what a Parisiana audience would fall for, and he had a largely new repertoire, with less sexual innuendo and more stage comedy.

The opening night was attended by the music-hall "tout Paris." Mistinguett was there, and so were the famous courtesans like Cléo de Merode (with her publicly acknowledged lover, Leopold, king of the Belgians), Liane de Pougy, La Belle Otéro, and the critic Catulle Mendès. Chevalier got a small but creditable mention. This season was followed by a long booking at the Eden-Concert d'Asnières, a suburban *café-conc* with a good reputation, where he was a big hit. His agent was now able to book him in top music-hall theaters in the provinces and in Belgium, at twenty francs a day and more.

He began to work continuously, and his post-office savings account grew and grew. After his Petit Casino flop, he and La Louque had decided that half of what he earned should be put away for a rainy day. He now knew—and this conviction would remain with him for life— that no entertainer was ever fully secure. New talent, faces, and styles always threatened to ease out the old. By the time he was sixteen, he was determined this would never happen to him. In brief spells between bookings, he started going to music halls to watch major stars, including "Little Tich," shamelessly incorporating some of their stage business into his own act. No one noticed the appropriation. He was particularly fascinated by an English entertainer called Norman French, a huge hit at the Alhambra, whose top-hatted elegance was so very different from the grubby vulgarity of most French stage comics. He also crossed the Channel and spent a week in London, staying in a cheap hotel room near Victoria Station, to take in all the shows in town, to see what he could learn from them. The fact that he spoke hardly any English was no drawback.

He decided to take singing, dancing, and boxing lessons, and invested in a completely new wardrobe, in what he thought was the latest "English" style. And he began taking a greater interest in the fashionable audience on the other side of the footlights, even indulging in a brief affair with a society lady far older than he. This left him painfully conscious of his social inadequacies. He realized he had never read a book, except those imposed by his elementary-school curriculum. He knew virtually nothing about politics or the world around him. Even his "English" wardrobe was a travesty of the real thing, he discovered.

The most prestigious—and roughest—music-hall theater outside Paris was the Alcazar in Marseilles. A booking here, in 1905, at the end of a provincial tour of smaller towns in the *Midi*, turned him, almost overnight, into a minor star. Maurice, now seventeen, chose a series of his older repertoire songs, rightly assuming nothing could be too raunchy for a Marseilles audience. Appearing two thirds of the way through, after the intermission, he came on after a couple of turns that had stimulated the well-known Alcazar audience's wrath. Having vented their contempt on others, the audience was prepared to sit back and be amused. Racked with stage fright, Chevalier could scarcely believe his good fortune when he heard encouraging laughter coming from the audience. Afterward, the applause, and the encores, were unmistakable signs that he had made it into the big time, that he was perhaps in the same league as Dranem and Mayol. The delighted manager immediately signed him up for the following year.

News of his Alcazar triumph spread rapidly. From then on he was continually in demand, both in the provinces (where his fee was now a hundred francs a night) and in the classier music-hall theaters like the Casino Saint-Martin and the Casino Montparnasse. He was still not quite in the very first rank. La Scala, the classiest of the Parisian music halls, did not yet want him—he was still considered a little too vulgar. But he was becoming well known and was delighted to find, in Bordeaux, during a booking there, that his name on the billboards was in larger type than anyone else's except Mayol's.

His reputation kept growing, throughout 1908 and 1909. In the music-hall business, he was acquiring a reputation for driving a hard bargain, for negotiating with managers far more efficiently than any agent. He was not, at this time, universally liked. These were the years that the well-known writer Colette (1873–1954) was trying to combine a literary career with that of a music-hall artiste, doing a lascivious "seven veils" Oriental dance. In her only lightly disguised autobiographical account of life in a second-rate traveling music-hall repertory company, *La Vagabonde*, written throughout 1907 and 1908 but only published in 1910, all the main characters she wrote about were taken from real life. Maurice Chevalier makes a cameo appearance, under the name of "Cavaillon." As Colette, then thirty-five, wrote:

> Everyone envies Cavaillon, who is young and already famous. The buzz is that even Dranem feels threatened by him, and that theater managers agree to pay him the most outrageous fees. He is tall, has a swaying, snakelike stride, appears to be boneless, with huge fists attached to tiny wrists. He is almost a pretty boy, with blond hair cut in a fringe, but his anxious violet eyes, constantly on the move, reflect a violent neurasthenia close to madness.
>
> His catch-phrase is "I'm burning myself out." He lives only for his nightly stage appearance, for this is the only time he is able to forget his worries, look his age and conquer his public. He neither drinks nor parties, invests all his money and is bored.[2]

Since all the other portraits in *La Vagabonde* were about real people and, according to experts, astonishingly accurate, the glimpse she afforded of the young Chevalier had the ring of truth to it. She later claimed, in a newspaper column in *Le Petit Parisien* written in 1941 about her music-hall traveling days, that Chevalier, as she knew him then, was obnoxious and brutal to the "little people" in provincial theaters, always ready to create a scene, to react to imaginary slights—the opposite of the charming, grinning young man who so delighted his audiences.

She wrote that he always came to the theater too early, and could be "observed, motionless, with his head in his hands in his dressing room." He may of course simply have been repeating his act to himself: He had a lifelong fear of forgetting his lines, and, though he tried to conceal this from even his closest acquaintances, his stage fright never left him. But on the road, his seems to have been a singularly unenviable existence. Colette wrote that he

> spends his sinister evenings in this fashion, prostrate, silent. He makes me shudder. I want to chase away the memory of this man hiding his face. I fear I may one day become like him, stranded, wretched, lost among strangers, conscious of his solitude.[3]

There was another cameo portrait in Colette's book. This was "la petite Jadin." In *La Vagabonde,* Jadin epitomized the flighty, promiscuous, hopelessly irresponsible but immensely talented performer, always late, often skipping rehearsals or even performances when one of her many rich lovers offered her a more attractive alternative.

Jadin was the barely disguised, highly accurate portrait of Fréhel, the up-and-coming music-hall star sensation, three years younger than Maurice but already beginning to lose her fabulous looks, with whom he was to embark on an ill-matched affair. Its consequences would be incalculable, influencing Chevalier's attitude toward women for the rest of his life.

CHAPTER 4

"Contre l'amour y a rien à faire"
("There's nothing you can do about love")

—Song by Maurice Chevalier

Fréhel's life story is one of the most tragic sagas in show-business history. The adorable toast of the Belle Epoque ended up a penniless, bloated, alcoholic junkie, exhibiting herself like a two-headed sheep in "freak" booths in the Foire du Trône, a sordid Paris street fair. In comparison, the disintegration of Professor Emmanuel Unrath (played by Emil Jannings) at the hands of Lola (Marlene Dietrich) in Joseph von Sternberg's film *The Blue Angel,* seems like a mildly unfortunate hiccup in an otherwise distinguished career.

By the time she was forty, Fréhel had become so coarse and overweight, with hideous gaps in her blackened teeth, that it was difficult to imagine her earlier radiance. Her septum was so damaged by cocaine that she could do a frightening parlor trick, inserting a silk scarf up one nostril and exhaling it down the other.

Though she also had more than her share of sheer bad luck, she was willfully self-destructive and could blame only herself for her vertiginous downfall. Plumbing the depths of alcoholism and squalor in later life, she rejected all attempts, including Chevalier's, to help her.

The history of show business is full of textbook histories of gifted performers who fell by the wayside, but Fréhel's case is unique, for in her extreme youth she showed a potential for stardom almost as great as that of Mistinguett, Edith Piaf, and Marlene Dietrich combined. When, at eighteen, at the height of her precocious fame, she laid eyes on Maurice Chevalier and deliberately picked him out to be her "official" lover, he could no more resist her than he could have turned down an offer of top billing at the Scala, Paris's most famous music hall.

Fréhel's show-business career had begun even earlier than Chevalier's—singing while perched on café tables at the age of five. There were other similarities in their backgrounds. Her father, too, had left her mother when she was little, and she, too, went to work by the time she was eleven. But there was no loving La Louque in Fréhel's life: Her mother, a domestic servant, took on a succession of lovers, neglected her daughter, and was interested only in the money she was able to bring in. Her favorite trick was to burst in on a theater where Fréhel was performing and threaten to call the police because her daughter was underage and parental consent had not been obtained. She was invariably bought off, but the word got around that Fréhel's mother was trouble, and several theaters refused to hire "la Môme Pervenche"—Miss Periwinkle—as Fréhel called herself at the very start of her career.[1]

Her real name was Marguérite Boulc'h. She was just as single-minded as Chevalier in her career plans, at least as long as she was on her way up. Working as a pharmacist's assistant, selling face masks "guaranteed" to get rid of wrinkles, she called on La Belle Otéro, the leading star and demimondaine. While she failed to make a sale ("Come back in twenty years, *ma petite*," she was told), she did make a friend. La Belle Otéro took her on as teenage servant, part companion, part clown, and they became inseparable companions.

Fréhel learned a great deal about men by observing La Belle Otéro's way with them: This buxom, Spanish-born ex–circus performer and former Flamenco dancer was said to be greedier, more ruthless, and more expert at getting her lovers to part with their money than any of her Belle Epoque contemporaries.

Thanks to coaching by La Belle Otéro, and the encouragement of another well-known singer called Damia, Fréhel developed her natural stage and singing talents fast, favoring a stark, realistic street-singer genre that anticipated the later heartbreaking, lyrical outpourings of Edith Piaf.

As with all her relationships, Fréhel's friendship with Damia was a complicated one, for Damia was Fréhel's husband's mistress, and they enjoyed, for a time, a harmonious ménage à trois. Fréhel had met her husband when she was fourteen, while singing at the Olympia. A somewhat colorless Frenchman-about-town, Robert Hollard took her out to dinner after the show, sent her candy, and soon afterward became her first lover.

All she knew about sex, she later told a magazine writer, was that handheld vaginal sprays called "irrigators" had to be used immediately after intercourse. Hers could not have been very effective, for she quickly became pregnant, Hollard agreed to marry her, and, two months after the wedding, at age fifteen, she gave birth. The child was taken to Brittany, where her grandmother lived. But Fréhel's budding career was more important to her than her daughter's welfare, and the infant soon died at the hands of an incompetent country nurse, a victim of everyone's neglect.

Hollard became a kind of Pygmalion, teaching his young wife correct intonations, choosing her repertoire. She rapidly made her mark, and not just as a singer: Though her songs could make the most hardened Parisians cry, she had the irreverent wit and gift for repartee of a Bette Midler. In some respects, her stage appearances must at times have been a bit like Barry Humphries's "Dame Edna Everage" one-man shows— no one ever had the last word when Fréhel got going.

She could be shocking, abusive, or even falling-down drunk, but she was never either predictable or dull. In one mood, she became, onstage, a remote, tender, haunting female *gavroche* with an astonishing range and an unerring choice of lyrics. In another, she traded foul-mouthed insults with her audience, in the course of highly scatological, improvised monologues about their vileness, often sweeping offstage to riotous applause without having sung a note. People did not come to hear Fréhel sing. They came to see her flaunt her wit and impertinence and be herself. By the time she was nineteen, she was known to have had a string of famous paramours. Her disrespect for the rich and aristocratic was not just a pose and spilled over into real life—but those she insulted and treated like dirt often came back for more, sometimes ending up as her lovers.

In his memoirs, Chevalier was not just discreet, but outrageously self-serving about his affair with Fréhel, not even mentioning her by name. "A pretty woman's face comes into my life," he wrote. "The long, sensual folly of it all leaves me bruised, nauseated, diminished.... Those outings in Montmartre, those riotous, macabre and exhausting parties, those quarrels, partings, the self-respect of the gutter, all this I experienced, up to the hilt, as a price of the sensual pleasures I enjoyed in her arms." Their affair was disposed of in a couple of paragraphs. He left out a great deal. There was, of course, far more to it all than he was prepared to acknowledge, perhaps even to himself. He once told an American reporter that the reason he so admired Shirley MacLaine was that she looked like Fréhel in her prime.

When Fréhel first set eyes on Chevalier, she was infinitely better known than he was. She was still beautiful, with a mop of red hair and large greenish eyes, but, at nineteen, was already starting to lose her figure. Her face was puffy, and her once-dazzling white skin had an unhealthy tinge. Chevalier was immensely flattered to be picked out by her, but there was also an element of calculation in his willingness to be selected. For all her idiosyncracies, at best such a liaison would help his career and, at worst, could do it no harm. He could not possibly guess that his year with her would be catastrophic on all counts.

Fréhel's frenzied life-style should have given him food for thought. Chevalier lived an ordered life, which revolved around his nightly stage performances, his mother, casual sex, and occasional drinks with music-hall cronies, most of them older men on their way down, at the Café Pagès, on the Faubourg Saint-Martin.

Fréhel's life was unbelievably disordered: She was incapable of living a normal existence, squandering away her gifts in drinking clubs, bars, nightclubs, and at private parties with an assortment of hangers-on who included Argentinean millionaires, aristocrats, playboys, socialites, but also gangsters, pimps, con men and drug peddlers. She sustained her suicidal pace with lethal doses of cocaine, then freely available, seldom ending her nightly revelries till dawn, often waking up in strange surroundings with strange company in strange beds.

She was excessively extravagant, promiscuous, incapable of any stable relationship, hopelessly incompetent in her financial affairs, and a poor judge of people. Hangers-on took advantage of her, rich men took her up, gave her expensive toys, and then, tiring of her, cut off her funds and turned her loose. By the standards of today, she was, in many respects, indistinguishable from a high-class call girl, but she was not necessarily venal. She had no misgivings about going to bed for money, but took pride in the excessively high price she extracted, as proof of her desirability. Despite their shared working-class background, Chevalier and Fréhel were hopelessly mismatched.

At first Chevalier was intrigued by her life-style, accompanying her after their shows to bar after bar, where she was invariably the center of attention, escorting her to the stately homes of Argentinean socialites where parties, impromptu performances by Fréhel, and cocaine orgies continued well into the night. Even in the early days of their relationship, she cuckolded him spectacularly, but her hold over him was surprisingly strong. However badly she behaved toward him, she proclaimed to all and sundry that he remained her real love. Some of the members of the Fréhel gang concluded that Chevalier was a consenting party, perhaps even her pimp—a ridiculous supposition to anyone who knew him.

His biggest humiliation was the lack of consideration shown by members of the rich set she introduced him to. In their eyes, he was totally insignificant: Fréhel's latest craze, or *béguin,* and everyone knew how long *that* lasted. He lacked the social graces they were used to, and had none of the scandalous aura of her gangster, cat-burglar, shady businessman, and prizefighter entourage.

After a while, Chevalier could no longer stand it, and refused to go out with her after their shows, waiting up for her instead. There would be furious quarrels when she returned at dawn, befuddled with drink and the aftereffects of cocaine, but the fights were usually followed by passionate lovemaking and an ephemeral peace. There were times with her he would treasure all his life: Nearly half a century later, in November 1948, while singing in London, he made a special pilgrimage to Little Newport Street, near the London Hippodrome, where he and Fréhel spent an "idyllic" week in 1908, taking in the shows.

His love affair was not proceeding along the lines he had expected: Far from improving his chances, it threatened to jeopardize his career, for the quality of his work was suffering: He was not getting enough sleep. Nor was he rehearsing new acts. More ominously, the abuse of ether, cocaine, and alcohol (for with Fréhel, it was almost impossible not to indulge in whatever she wanted to sample) was having serious consequences on his health.

He continued to move upward, for all that, with prominent billing at the Eldorado, and then, unexpectedly, he was offered work at the Folies-Bergère, including a contract for three consecutive seasons, at eighteen hundred francs a month in his first year, two thousand francs in the second, and twenty-five hundred francs in the third. His debut there in 1910, in a stage solo, was not an unqualified success, for here again the public was very different from anything he had experienced previously. But he stuck it out, even performing a dance number with Gaby Deslys, the Folies-Bergère star and best-paid performer in Paris of her generation.

From time to time, Fréhel and Chevalier appeared together in the same music-hall shows, but always accidentally. They had already begun to drift apart. He must have known she was destroying herself, must also have been aware there was nothing he could do about it. In any case, she, not he, was the more important star—and she had not yet started to unravel. Somehow, despite her totally disordered life, she was able to choose songs, rehearse them, memorize them, and deliver them with incomparable feeling and skill. Hers was an untrained voice, but, like Piaf's, it had a unique resonance.

Fréhel's feelings toward Chevalier were complex. He was certainly one of the handsomest men on the Paris stage at the time. As she later told a reporter, "He was tall but onstage he looked huge, he wore this formfitting outfit that showed off his trim waist, he moved across the stage with slinky, boneless grace . . . and he did this incredible balancing act with his hat." There were plenty of good-looking men around who were wittier and richer than he, but just as he was flattered to have been singled out by her, so she was proud of being seen with someone who, though less famous than she, nevertheless was the growing talk of the music-hall world. She also seems to have thought that his strength was not merely physical, but also moral—that he could protect her from the consequences of her compulsively flawed, self-destructive ways. She also believed that because they were both of working-class origin, they were natural allies—that it would be Fréhel and Chevalier against the "haves." Her antiestablishment populism was no pose.

She was, of course, dreadfully wrong: Chevalier, for all his background, had an innate respect for law and order. His outlook, at this time, was petit-bourgeois, materialistic. He later told a reporter that when he was twelve, his ambition had been to own a gold watch, a fur coat, a car, and a house in the country, in that order, and that he was proud to have fulfilled these objectives. All were unexceptionable goals, but they were completely at variance with Fréhel's crazy, deluded whirl, her illusion that tomorrow would take care of itself.

La Louque was a silent witness to all this. To prove that, come what may, and despite her nightly fugues, he remained her only "real" lover, once, while Chevalier was away, performing in Marseilles at the Alcazar, Fréhel surprised everyone by showing up unexpectedly at his apartment on the Faubourg Saint-Martin and moving into his room. Gossip had it that she did so only because one of her latest lovers, the marquis de la Torre, who had allowed her the run of his *hôtel particulier* on the ultrafashionable rue la Pérouse, had finally chucked her out.

On his return, Chevalier "made a strange face," Fréhel later told a magazine writer, and they did not remain under the same roof for long. La Louque may have had something to do with it. The disapproving neighbors also complained that Fréhel's nocturnal habits kept them awake. She rented a pied-à-terre where Chevalier would occasionally spend the night, waiting for her to return.

The crucial break came in 1911. One day Fréhel was injured when her taxi collided with a truck on the rue Lépic. At first, in a daze, propped up against a café bar, she refused to see a doctor. When he was told the news, Chevalier dropped everything, rushed over, and insisted on taking her to the hospital, where she was discovered to have a mild concussion.

She discharged herself after five days and took a taxi straight from the hospital to the Folies-Bergère, to surprise Chevalier and thank him for his concern. Chevalier had, by this time, begun his second-year stint at the Folies-Bergère, and had been chosen to be Mistinguett's dancing partner—a singular, unexpected promotion. Fréhel never got farther than the stage-door reception area, walking out of the famous theater in a total daze. From casual remarks she overheard as she walked in, she realized that Chevalier was having an affair with Mistinguett, his partner onstage and the leading music-hall star of the day. He had taken advantage of the accident to make a clean break, and relegate Fréhel firmly to the past.

It must have been a horrible discovery, for despite her wild ways, Fréhel believed that Chevalier represented something valuable and permanent in her life. But she now had a wonderful opportunity to indulge in a series of spectacular offstage performances. Her mourning for her lover was highly publicized. He had betrayed her, she tearfully told her cronies at the various drinking clubs and late-night insiders-only clubs, displaying the knife and pistol she intended to use on both Chevalier and Mistinguett. She even made a halfhearted attempt to lie in wait for him in a café on the rue de Ménilmontant, but when a bystander who knew them both agreed that Chevalier was nothing but a cheap, rotten swine, a pimp and a gigolo, and deserved everything that was coming to him, she whipped out the knife to stab the man who dared slander her beloved Maurice, and had to be forcibly restrained.

French tabloids indirectly referred to their rift, never mentioning names, in their underhanded, allusive, and somewhat simpering style, though all readers knew who the identities of the "famous music-hall couple" were. A cynic would construe it all as a remarkable publicity stunt, except that, in a curious way, Fréhel's despair was genuine. She decided to "tell all" to a popular magazine, *La Rampe.* "My heart is bleeding," she told its reporter, but blamed Mistinguett for spiriting him away more than Chevalier, consoling herself with the certainty he would come back to her. How could he possibly stay with someone thirteen years older than she?

She continued living it up with a succession of playboys, thugs, shady entrepreneurs, and millionaire sugar daddies, establishing a semipermanent relationship with a locally famous boxer who had also recently had an unhappy love affair. At the same time, she continued showing up regularly at the fee-paying "Fréhel supper clubs" and "Fréhel tango club" that were supposed to provide her with some of the money needed to sustain her extravagant life-style. In this as in other ventures, unscrupulous entrepreneurs pocketed most of the money.

From this time on, Fréhel's and Chevalier's paths would cross only occasionally, and by tacit consent they treated each other like strangers. These casual backstage encounters did not last long, for in early 1914, perhaps to make a clean break with everything, Fréhel embarked on a series of performances in Bucharest, St. Petersburg, and Vienna. Stranded in Russia at the outbreak of the First World War, she returned to Romania: On her earlier visit, she had fallen passionately in love with a dashing Romanian cavalry officer.

Her Russian tour had left her with a sizable treasure chest, for she had been the toast of St. Petersburg and Moscow, and had been able to spend little, however hard she tried: The Russian princes, grand dukes, and other wealthy admirers had lavished incredible hospitality on her. It was in character with Fréhel's doomed life that the only time she ever saved any money (in this particular case, over two million rubles), the 1917 October Revolution made it worthless overnight.

This was only one of the calamities that beset her: Her Romanian lover died a hero's death, fighting against the Germans on the Romanian border, and she herself remained stranded in the Carpathian Mountains, where she had gone to be near him. Broke, distraught, her looks fading fast, she patriotically entertained the French expeditionary force that had been brought in to shore up the hard-pressed Romanian Army, becoming their somewhat shop-soiled mascot. The French officers now shunned her, and she ended up living with a French Army cook.

The French authorities decided to repatriate her to France, and put her on a Marseilles-bound troopship. It stopped on the way, in Constantinople. She went ashore and liked the place: Some of her White Russian friends were moving there, it was full of shady adventurers, there was an interesting nightlife, and cocaine was dirt-cheap—reasons galore for not returning home. She jumped ship, acquired a string of Italian lovers, and stayed for four years. Only on the brink of death from drug and alcohol abuse did she allow herself to be repatriated once more. Her ex-husband met her at the Gare de Lyon in 1922 and scarcely recognized her. In Paris, after eight years' absence and the devastation resulting from the war, hardly anyone remembered Fréhel.

Somehow, she kicked the cocaine habit, and made a minor comeback at the Olympia, in November 1923. In 1932, after kicking the habit again, she got a limited engagement at the Comoedia, and Gustave Fréjaville, a veteran critic, who had seen her in her prime, wrote that "the unforgettable one" (*l'inoubliable inoubliée*) was "as astonishing as ever." She was only forty-one, but looked at least sixty. In the thirties, she appeared in cameo performances in a dozen French films, invariably playing herself: the drink-sodden ex-cabaret artiste with a heart of gold and lots of memories. She was the unforgettable "Casbah" singer in *Pépé le Moko,* the film that turned Jean Gabin into a star in the part of the French gangster on the run.* She sang a song about the old times in a Paris she—and Pépé le Moko—knew they would never see again.

In 1935, she married again. Her husband, a Belgian metal worker who became her self-styled impresario, swindled her out of her few remaining possessions—all but a famous diamond she claimed Queen Marie of Romania had given her, which she managed to pawn, for a minuscule lifelong annuity. The couple soon separated, acrimoniously.

During the Second World War, Fréhel was recruited by a German organization to sing in French prisoner-of-war camps. She made several

*Charles Boyer took over his part in a Hollywood remake.

trips to Germany, proving a considerable embarrassment to both organizers and fellow performers. After the war, she lived in a succession of
tiny rooms in cheap hotels in Pigalle, often seen in the company of
equally destitute underworld characters she had known in her early life.
No longer able to afford cocaine, she acquired a phenomenal capacity
for cheap wine, often keeling over in front of cheap cafés after closing
time, a filthy, bedraggled old bag lady in bedroom slippers, sleeping in
the gutter till sunrise.

In the last two years of her life, she became a familiar figure in Pigalle
and on the rue Mouffetard, the haunt of homeless tramps and panhandlers, a local attraction in cafés and bars where she would sing her old
songs, or at least what snatches of them that she still remembered, in
return for a glass of *gros rouge.* A year before her death, a gala was staged
for her, but it was an unmitigated disaster: She turned up drunk and
unable to sing. She remained a landmark in Pigalle, propping up the bars
there, a befuddled, wine-sodden "Ancient Mariner" figure full of improbable tales that she told again and again, occasionally breaking into
raucous song. One of the stories she liked telling best was how Mistinguett "stole" Chevalier from her.

In 1950, a few months before her death, Maurice Chevalier, through
an intermediary, tried to give her 200,000 francs (about $450), to tide
her over. She sent the check on to the French Society for the Prevention
of Cruelty to Animals. In February 1951, almost totally destitute, she
died of natural causes. Staff and inmates of the sordid Pigalle Hotel
where she died helped raise the money for her funeral.

CHAPTER 5

"It has often been said that I created Chevalier."

—Mistinguett

For all his meteoric rise, Chevalier was not in the same league as Mistinguett when he was hired as her leading man at the Folies-Bergère. He was in fact very much her junior partner. From his autobiography, it is clear he believed that Paul-Louis Flers, one of its managing directors and an outstanding music-hall talent-spotter, had been the sole deciding factor in his selection. Flers, who had initially drawn up Chevalier's contract and kept a watchful eye on him since, had indeed put him forward as a possible candidate. Years later, in *her* autobiography, considerably franker and more revealing than Chevalier's but nevertheless somewhat sanitized, Mistinguett made it quite clear that *she* had picked Chevalier, as, indeed, she picked the rest of the cast. She had complete control of her shows: The director, choreographer, stage designer, and lighting director were her minions. She even made sure that the girls in the chorus would not be *too* pretty—so they would not provide unfair competition. Her decisions were final. Nobody contradicted "La Miss."

When Chevalier and Mistinguett became stage partners, and, almost immediately, lovers, in 1911, Chevalier was in his twenty-third year. Mistinguett was thirty-six. The thirteen-year age gap was already apparent in those formal, "Harcourt"-type staged pictures of them together. Mistinguett, with her distinctly chubby arms and mature looks, is in startling contrast to the absurdly young-looking Chevalier, in the smart suit and pinstriped shirt she undoubtedly picked out for him but almost certainly didn't pay for. Even in the stiff, affected poses that were de rigueur in those days, hers was a remarkable presence. Dark, with huge eyes, a wide mouth, and very prominent teeth, she had something of Isabelle Adjani's fey, haunting little-girl look, deceptively innocent but clearly full of depthless guile and sexual promise. Her voice, an early critic wrote, could be both velvety and harsh. It certainly needed to be powerful: Both Chevalier and Mistinguett made their music-hall debuts without the aid of microphones, which were introduced onstage only in 1931, and though Chevalier would quickly fall into the habit of using them, Mistinguett, to the very end of her life, hated doing so.

Just as it is quite impossible to do justice to Chevalier as a performer through the criteria of voice or delivery alone, so Mistinguett's magic defied analysis. Jean Cocteau, her devoted admirer, wrote of her that she was "typically and essentially French, a Parisienne of the Parisiennes. Perhaps one must be a Parisian oneself to understand to the full that little gamine's face that looks as though it were always having its ears boxed, and to recognize that haunting voice."

As was the case with Fréhel, Mistinguett and Chevalier had a great deal in common. Both had Belgian blood in their veins, and both were stagestruck practically from birth. Mistinguett's background and family environment was almost as grim as Chevalier's: Her real name was Jeanne Florentine Bourgeois, and her parents, Antoine and Jeannette, were small-time artisans, incorrigible drunks (at least according to their neighbors), idle and feckless, with thieving tendencies, living on the wrong side of the tracks, 5, rue du Chemin de Fer in Enghien, today a Paris outer suburb but then a small, rural town well outside Paris, known chiefly for its imposing lake and casino. The witnesses who signed her birth certificate were one of the "lake watchmen" (a retired gendarme) and one of her father's fellow carpenters. Her father's signature was in a spiky, painfully illiterate scrawl.[1]

Antoine worked, intermittently, as a carpenter, also restoring used beds and mattresses, which Mistinguett, as a small child, had to collect and deliver on a pushcart. Jeannette made women's hats part time, and also, for a time, managed a café, later becoming a considerable embarrassment to the local Enghien authorities. As her drinking problem worsened in her later years, she was frequently picked up in the streets for disorderly conduct, for when drunk, she was liable to take off all her clothes.

For all her alcoholism, Mistinguett's mother had genteel pretensions for her daughter, sent her to a Catholic school, insisting she take violin lessons and become a little lady. Mistinguett was a rebel, constantly in trouble, without any of the filial devotion Chevalier had for his mother; for all her lively intelligence, she hated school and soon gave it up. From what she hints at in her memoirs, she probably hated her parents as well. Instead of a lady, she became a flower girl, selling carnations outside Enghien Casino to elderly gamblers in evening dress, getting up in the middle of the night to take the train to Les Halles flower market to buy them wholesale. Her gamine charm and persuasiveness were such that she almost invariably sold out her wares. Her first direct experience of the theater came when one of the gamblers bought up all her flowers and ordered them delivered to an actress in a local theater. What struck her most, she recalled over forty years later, was the backstage squalor, taken for granted by all those working there.

This did not, however, discourage her from wanting to go on the stage: She parlayed her violin lessons into singing lessons, and by the time she was fifteen, she was well known in Enghien, a show-off singing in cafés and *café-concs*, desperately eager to become a star and already something of a local celebrity among her own Enghien generation, with a retinue of student groupies who followed her about. She would later claim that Léon Blum, eventually the socialist prime minister of France and leader of the Front Populaire (whose cousins had a house in

Enghien) was one of them. She also claimed that, because of her boyish good looks, in her extreme youth she attracted the attention of Oscar Wilde.

To escape her oppressive family environment, as a teenager she ran away and joined a circus and, like Chevalier, briefly trained to be an acrobat. Later, she became a skilled acrobatic dancer. Her strength and stamina were legendary. She was among the first to introduce the *valse chaloupée*, or *dance des apaches,* as an art form on the French music-hall stage. It was her performance in this brutal pas de deux with its overt sadomasochistic overtones—for it explicitly described, in body language, the rapport between the prostitute and her pimp, his brutality endured not just passively but with erotic abandon, with the victim deliberately coming back for more—that had initially brought her to the attention of the future King Edward VII.

The *valse chaloupée* required considerable strength, as well as agility, for she was hurled to the floor, dragged by the hair, twisted into knots, thrown up in the air, on the receiving end of simulated blows to the face and body. There was no love lost in real life between her and her best-known partner, Max Dearly. He hated her so much that he was often unnecessarily brutal during performances, and they were not on speaking terms.

Unlike Fréhel, Mistinguett took her work seriously. She was physically tough and worked out every day. She was also a good "straight" actress, able to learn her lines fast, perfectly suited for minor roles in Feydeau farces. She could have had a respectable theater career, but her ego was such that she had to be the sole focus of any audience's attention. To French audiences, at least, she was ageless. "At seventy she could still be a convincing sixteen-year-old flower girl, and could walk down the staircase of the Casino de Paris trailing seven meters of plumes and wearing spangles weighing seven kilos," wrote Jacques Damase, France's leading music-hall historian.[2] In one of her last stage appearances, at the age of seventy-four, she amazed critics by bebopping on stage for twelve consecutive minutes with no apparent sign of exhaustion while starring in a revue at the ABC Theater in Paris, her "million-dollar legs" shapely to the very end. (She had actually insured them for

500,000 francs: The million-dollar figure, she admitted, was simply "good publicity.")

At fifteen, she claimed, she was so ignorant of sex that she believed a kiss on the lips was enough to induce pregnancy, but such chaste naïveté didn't last long. While still in her teens, she had a son by an aristocratic Latin American lover barely older than she was. At birth, the child was removed by the father's family, the Dos Santos, who compensated her generously for this loss, and later, when she became rich and famous, allowed her access to her son. At the outset of her stage career, her fee was a mere five francs for an evening performance, three francs for a matinee. When she first began appearing in small theaters and *café-concs*, she called herself "La Môme Flora," but quickly changed the name to "Mistinguett" because, as a teenager, she remembered a popular operetta coming to Enghien whose leading character had been called "Miss Helyett," and felt this was an unusual, memorable name.

The "Miss" appellation was a stroke of genius, aging her (at a time when maturity could only help her career) and giving her, subliminally, an aura of virginal, vaguely British authority. To her colleagues, and, very soon, to her many subordinates and hangers-on, she was "La Miss." To her intimate friends and lovers, she was simply "Mist." Chevalier may have had a more precocious sex life, but when they became a couple, she was by far the more experienced, sophisticated sexual partner, infinitely more versed in the art of seduction. Chevalier's sexual adventures—with the exception of his doomed affair with Fréhel—had been mostly one-night stands with chorus girls or suburban *grisettes*. Compared to Mistinguett, he was still the innocent working-class lad from Belleville-Ménilmontant. The company he had kept with Fréhel had included socialites and aristocrats, but on the whole the crowd she ran with had been, to say the least, flashy and second-rate, and Chevalier had very quickly distanced himself from it. By 1911, Mistinguett was a veteran demimondaine, as well as a star performer, who mixed only with the best people. After her unfortunate pregnancy, she had acquired a string of lovers, most of them old, all of them rich—and at least two of them of royal blood.

Very early on, she displayed an almost frightening self-confidence and cynicism where male relationships were concerned. Amoral, uninhibited, and totally manipulative, an irresistible mixture of childish playfulness and greed, she was quick to take advantage of her potent sexuality, reveling in her power over the awkward, tongue-tied, but tumescent sugar daddies and "mashers" who were attracted to her like bees to pollen. When she found out that the doorman at the Eldorado was demanding money from the stage-door Johnnys clamoring to meet her after the show, she institutionalized the procedure—twenty-five francs for the old or ugly, twenty francs for the young and good-looking—splitting the proceeds with him.

While at the Eldorado, in the early days, still an unknown but up-and-coming tomboyish singer specializing, like Chevalier in his earliest days, in her portrayal of popular street characters, she also worked out a deal with a hatter across the street. Whenever a naive-looking, nervous new admirer came to see her in her dressing room, she would pick up his hat and say, "That's a terrible, shabby old hat, I hate it," crushing the crown and throwing it out the window in mock disgust. Leaving the theater, the visitor would almost always cross the street and buy a new hat, and "I got the usual commission."

She was also fond of telling, again and again, how, one day, while in her first year as an Eldorado performer, she was inside the Casino de Paris, begging for free tickets, when she observed the Eldorado's leading man, Dranem, in earnest conversation with the Casino's manager. Dranem told her, afterward, that he had applied for a job there, since performers at the Eldorado were traditionally underpaid. They worked out a scheme together. "That evening I spread the news, confidentially whispering to anyone who would listen: Dranem had got himself a fabulous deal at the Casino de Paris." The Eldorado manager got to hear of it, doubled Dranem's salary to keep him—and also substantially raised Mistinguett's.

She picked her lovers with a ruthless determination to rival those established music-hall stars she admired from afar. There were three outstanding role models: La Belle Otéro, Fréhel's mentor, who had started life as an equestrian circus performer before becoming a star—and the mistress of some of the most aristocratic scions of the French nobility; Émilienne d'Alençon, also a former circus performer of working-class origin, despite her spuriously aristocratic name, who had become the *maîtresse en titre* to the duc d'Orléans; but most of all, Mistinguett envied Cléo de Merode, in her day the music-hall performer whose pale, milky skin and virginal, refined good looks so entranced King Leopold of Belgium that he had a highly publicized affair with her for years, becoming known, in music-hall circles and in the French and Belgian tabloid press, simply as "Cleopold."

By the time she brought Chevalier into her show, Mistinguett had become their equal, if not their superior. In her late teens and early twenties, she had been the mistress of a wholesale butcher, Monsieur Androt ("I used to steal the odd twenty francs out of a jug on the mantelpiece where he kept his small change"), but soon took on more socially acceptable lovers. She was courted by an Indian prince of "unbelievable wealth" whom she nicknamed "Lord Sun" because of his "radiant looks," who traveled with a court retinue and displayed "an iron-bound chest he carried everywhere with him filled with precious stones and jewelry worth hundreds of millions of francs." All this would be hers, he promised, if she would become his wife. She finally turned him down, in a letter revealing something of the passion both she and Chevalier shared:

> Can you imagine what it is to have in front of me a theatreful of people, all unknown to me, from all over the world, and yet able to strike a chord of sympathy out of them? To be able to swing them over, by a gesture or a phrase or the catchline of a verse, from laughter to a moment of emotion? No, I'd be too bored down there, in your Oriental palaces, covered in hundreds of millions of francs' worth of diamonds. And how would I ever get the chance of hearing—as I hear every day over here—some little shopgirl humming a few bars of my song in the street?[3]

Then there was royalty. She coyly admitted, in her memoirs published in 1954, two years before her death, that she regularly met the future King Edward VII in a discreet Paris apartment belonging to a friend of hers, and that a scandal was narrowly averted when he mistakenly left his walking stick, and perhaps other items of a more intimate nature, behind. There was, in fact, the distinct possibility that it was the king himself, acceding to the throne in 1901 at the age of sixty (when Mistinguett was twenty-six), bored or scared by his affair with Mistinguett, who passed her on to his Indian friend, for she had been introduced to him, she wrote later, "by a 'Very Great English Personage,' " the usual way Edward VII's friends referred to him when they wished to be exceptionally discreet.

Edward VII was not the only "royal" in her life: Her affair with King Alfonso XIII of Spain was common knowledge all over Europe.* As she was to write, shortly before her death, "He played an important part in my life." Her first meeting with King Alfonso gives some insight into her character: The Spanish king and queen were expected at the Eldorado Theater, and Mistinguett anxiously eyed the box reserved for them as the theater filled up. It remained empty. After the show, the king's majordomo showed up, profusely apologetic. The king had deferred to the queen's wishes, he explained, and they had seen another show that night. But Their Majesties hoped Mistinguett would join them for supper. The majordomo had a carriage waiting. "Fine, then you can drive me straight home," Mistinguett told him. "But what on earth will I tell His Majesty?" the distraught court official wailed. "What will the king say?" "I imagine he'll use the same word I used when I realized he had stood me up," said Mistinguett, "but I imagine he'll say it in Spanish." Subsequently, King Alfonso and Mistinguett were to have many, many intimate suppers together, without the queen, meeting not only in Paris but in hideaways in Deauville. He was to prove a powerful ally when, a few years later, disaster struck both Mistinguett and Chevalier.

There were other royal admirers: The Swedish king, when in Paris, invariably saw her shows, smiling broadly at her from his box, but never attempted to meet her backstage. And shortly before the outbreak of the

*King Alfonso XIII (1886–1941) was king from birth until 1931, when he abdicated, a huge Spanish majority having pronounced itself in favor of a republic. In 1923, he had helped the first "caudillo," General Primo de Rivera, become dictator, and went into exile in 1931, never to return to Spain.

First World War, she refused pressing assignations from the German Crown Prince. "He doesn't need Mistinguett to increase his popularity in France, and Mistinguett doesn't need the Crown Prince to help her with her publicity in Germany," she told a go-between.

Mistinguett came of age during the Belle Epoque. For all the wave of strikes in the 1890s, the quiet, underestimated growth of militant, Marxist socialism (Karl Marx himself died in 1883, five years before Chevalier was born) and the occasional bomb outrages perpetrated by the anarchists, this was a period of relative calm in France, coming between the traumatic "Commune" uprising of 1871 and the even more traumatic First World War. It was to be the last time Europe's over-privileged elite, and its nouveaux riches, were able to enjoy their wealth openly, with no fear of crippling taxation or social unrest. After the social upheavals of 1848 and 1871, it was also a time of unabashed hedonism for the wealthy and highborn: the last time Europe's royals, aristocrats, leading politicians, and industrialists would be able to indulge in their private weaknesses and sexual whims to the full, supremely indifferent to gossip or scandalous press reports. An amendment to France's *Code Pénal*, introduced by French parliamentarians who had good reason to curb the power of journalists to write about their scandalous affairs, forbade the media to refer to the private lives of citizens, and in any case much of the French press was highly venal, its publishers always ready to refrain from running potentially libelous articles in exchange for hard cash. Social and moral values and attitudes differed enormously anyway: In both France and Britain, the extremes of society—the very poor and the very rich—had no time for the stifling Victorian middle-class morality that was still, after Queen Victoria's death, a feature of the times.

During the heyday of the Belle Epoque, royals and top aristocrats, whether British, French, German, or Russian, could get away with almost any behavior, making the present-day antics of Europe's surviving royal families, whether from Windsor or Monaco, look like the innocent cavorting of Boy Scouts at a jamboree. As Prince of Wales, Edward VII had an encyclopedic, and, indeed, biblical knowledge of the leading women stars of the French music hall, from La Goulue to Jeanne Garnier and Hortense Schneider, three of Mistinguett's role models of the past.

His private life was highly scandalous, but he seemed impervious to attacks against him, frequently visiting Parisian brothels, where special rooms were decked out for him. In one of these "royal rooms," a hollow swing seat, suspended from the ceiling over the bed and activated by a pulley system, enabled his sexual partner to bring him to the requisite climax without being crushed by the grossly overweight monarch, all without excessive royal exertion.

As Prince of Wales, he had indulged in grand theatrical gestures, and Mistinguett bitterly regretted that, unlike Sarah Bernhardt, she had never been able to enlist his services onstage. In Victorien Sardou's play *Fedora*, admittedly long before Mistinguett's time, the future Edward VII would slip into the coffin supposed to contain the body of the murdered prince, which was then wheeled onstage for Sarah Bernhardt to weep and wail over—the unseen royal presence a huge private joke to all those in the know.

Mistinguett's avarice was legendary, to the extent that she herself, in her heyday, would refer to it in her own songs:

> "They say I don't pay my tradesmen—and it's true!
> They say I hang on to my shekels—and it's true!
> But if Monsieur Sarraut*
> Were to take a leaf out of my book
> *His* books might show a credit
> And if they put Mistinguett
> In charge of the budg-et
> We'd not be in this pre-di-ca-ment!"

There had been no compulsive need for her to sell flowers outside the Enghien Casino—unlike Chevalier, she was not, as a child, supporting her family, and knew that any money handed over to her parents would probably be spent on drink—but she required it to indulge in her own glamorous tastes.

*France's finance minister at the time

Freud, whose *Interpretation of Dreams* appeared in 1899, would have been fascinated by her attitude toward money and would doubtless have found deep-seated reasons for them. She never paid for anything if she could help it; haggled in stores, demanding rebates; stole cutlery from the expensive restaurants and hotels where she expected to eat or stay free of charge, or, failing that, demanded huge discounts she claimed were her due because of the attendant publicity. In later years, she would plug almost anything from hair oil to laxatives if the price was right. She earned a fortune advertising a brand of sherry (*"Le sherry de mon chéri c'est mon sherry."*) She drove loaned Délage and Peugeot cars at high speed and with outrageous lack of consideration for pedestrians and all forms of traffic, correctly surmising that her notoriety, and the irresistible smile she flashed at charmed Paris policemen, who always recognized her, would inhibit them from bringing her to court.

In an unintentionally hilarious encounter with "La Miss," Michel Georges-Michel[4] a journalist (and later a nightclub owner in partnership with her) described how, after days of waiting, he was finally admitted into her sanctuary. Mistinguett, oblivious of his presence, kept up a running stream of instructions, to minions and on the phone. To a Délage representative, she ordered, "You must change the machine, the Peugeot people have offered me a more powerful model. If you don't, I'll switch." Responding to a clamoring posse of would-be product endorsers who wanted her to praise the qualities of a face cream, she shouted, "Tell them five thousand francs, like all the rest." Georges-Michel also observed her haggling with a record producer for a bigger share in royalties. Told she already got a far higher percentage than anyone else, she replied, with a typical "Mist" non sequitur: "What about when [the records] are played on the streets? I don't get a sou when they play and sing my songs out there." She was referring to the large army of Parisian panhandlers and beggars who habitually cranked out her songs on portable gramophones at street corners.

A somewhat pompous British music-hall critic, Herbert Griffiths, invited to Paris to meet her and see her show, years later, was asked to pay sixty francs for his tickets.[5] When he refused, arguing that critics invariably got them free, they were promptly sold under his nose—for she was playing to a full house. To get into the theater, he had to settle, at the last minute, for vastly inferior seats costing fifty francs. When they met, Mistinguett was unrepentant: "In any case," she told him, "seats are much cheaper in Paris than in England."

What shocked people were her brashness and her complete indifference to public opinion. In those days, individual stars lacked the retinue of agents, business managers, and endorsement specialists to deal with such matters on their behalf, and in any case Mistinguett's distrust of others, where money was concerned, was such that she would never have entrusted anyone else with her affairs. As a very young woman, she had been swindled by an unscrupulous manager who took her on assignment to Russia and failed to pay her what had been initially agreed. Mistinguett then vowed she would never fall into the clutches of agents again, and bitterly resented the fortune of all successful theatrical entrepreneurs, who, she claimed, "have made hundreds of millions of francs out of us." Fréhel, too, when Chevalier first met her, had been besieged by publicists begging for endorsements at almost any price, but because of her wild life-style and total financial incompetence, she probably allowed a considerable fortune to pass her by. Chevalier, who started putting aside half his earnings from the age of fourteen "for a rainy day"—and would do so for the remainder of his life—was impressed by Mistinguett's shrewdness, and respect for money, which mirrored his own.

Her very language was unconsciously mercenary, and her description of the show-business music-hall world well in advance of her time:

> What one sells to the buyer is a mirage. Nothing actual or concrete has changed hands. We sell them a trip! A trip to nowhere, with canvas landscapes, moonbeams made out of gelatin. . . . Those people out there have bought a ticket to a country that doesn't exist, to never-never-land, "the land of ultimate unreality."

At the height of her fame, in the thirties, traveling on the Chief, the famous Chicago–Los Angeles express train, she noted that it was one and a half hours late after the four-day journey, which meant that the company, which guaranteed on-time schedules, reimbursed her for half her fare, and "I found this highly gratifying."

By this time, she kept a huge Chrysler in Antibes, where she had bought a house. Jean Sablon, the music-hall singer who had an outstanding career both in France and in the United States from 1936 onward knew "Mist" well and liked her, for all her foibles. He recalled with wry amusement that it was always advisable to carry plenty of cash when in her company. "I can't count the number of times," he said "she would offer me a lift—we were practically neighbors on the Riviera—then stop the car and say: 'Oh, my goodness, there's no gasoline and I've forgotten my purse!' "[6]

Commenting on her reputation, she wrote:

> I encouraged the legend because it was useful to me. It discouraged spongers. It focused the public's attention on one aspect of my personality, not perhaps a very laudable one but one that was nevertheless remarkable enough. The public likes to label its stars. I was stingy, therefore they did not saddle me with other vices. Certainly I like money. I like money very much.

Chevalier was to acquire a similar reputation. Fréhel's contempt for money had shocked him, and one of the reasons he had put an end to their relationship may well have been the additional burden of expense it incurred. There can be no doubt that it was Mistinguett, in this as in other matters, who molded him.

Such was the character of the celebrity who, after a spell at the Theatre of Varieties, in London in 1909 (where a critic noted that she "showed her legs with more generosity than is consistent with the normal standards of decorum") became the star attraction at the Folies-Bergère.

For Chevalier, entering Mistinguett's world must have come as a huge shock: Her life-style was very different from Fréhel's. Though Fréhel was no stranger to luxury, she was the quintessential bohemian, her own small apartments hopelessly untidy and her dressing rooms none too sanitary. Her real life was elsewhere. During the brief time she shared Chevalier's Faubourg Saint-Martin apartment, she turned it into shambles, though La Louque constantly cleaned up after her.

Now, Chevalier experienced real luxury for the first time. He was also conscious that he was a mere consort. Despite his own growing stardom, he was not in the same league as Mistinguett. Griffiths would later note with amazement that crowds outside the ABC Theater, where she was currently appearing when he was in Paris, were prepared to wait for hours merely to catch a glimpse of her—she attracted them "like royalty."

Like Fréhel, Mistinguett was never alone. Both attracted coteries of admirers and hangers-on. But while Fréhel's crowd included thugs, boxers, members of the underworld, and flashy high rollers with mysterious means of support, Mistinguett's inner circle was very different, with a leavening of artists, fashion designers, composers, and songwriters. Many of her admirers were gay, and this, too, was a new experience for Chevalier, who routinely ridiculed homosexuals in his songs, and who regarded the outrageous Mayol as their archetype.

In her Folies-Bergère dressing room, there were feathers and aigrettes everywhere, a gramophone constantly blaring jazz tunes. The place was cluttered with dolls, woolly dogs, artificial flowers. Her dress designer and stylist, the talented, girlish Gesmar, still in his teens in 1911 but with penmanship gifts that rivaled Aubrey Beardsley, was constantly at her side. In a reversal of conventional roles, she called him "*Maman,*" and their shared dependency and affection, entirely platonic, was touching, giving many outsiders the impression he was her son. But Mistinguett's capriciousness made her difficult to work with, and despite their constant, extravagantly public displays of mutual adoration, the relationship would end tragically: Gesmar, a few years later, killed himself when he felt that Mistinguett had tired of him. And *his* successor, the stage decorator Louis Gaudon, whom everybody called "Zig," who worked closely with "La Miss" on most of her shows since Gesmar's death, would share Gesmar's fate, committing suicide in May 1936 for the same reasons.

Mistinguett lived on a grand scale. Her apartment, on the rue des

Capucines, was reached by a staircase that was littered with trunks labeled MISS. There was a room containing nothing but the plumed and aigrette headdresses of previous shows, displayed like precious exhibits. Her drawing room looked like a museum of Victorian bric-a-brac: there were pianos, more gramophones, more dolls and woolly dogs, scattered sheet music, old "Toile de Jouy" tapestry on the walls, and a daybed, a narrow divan surmounted by a canopylike cradle, done up in lace and chinchilla. In her bedroom, her bed was "Chinese antique," decorated with lacquer paintings of fabulous beasts and fantastic flowers.[7] Many years later, Chevalier would have his own "Chinese bedroom" in his Boulevard de Courcelles apartment, but he kept it as a guest room.

Her country houses, first in Villerville in Normandy and later in Bougival and Antibes, were equally spectacular. Her Bougival house was full of Chinese lacquer cabinets and Dresden figurines. Her bedroom there was paneled in pink satin with mirrors everywhere. The dressing table, desk, lamps, radiators, and even the bed were made of mirrored glass. Her bathroom was pale blue, with the bath deliberately placed immediately below the window looking out onto the main drive so that she could spot any arrivals.

She was inordinately fond of pets and kept several dogs, a parrot, and a pet monkey called Jacko, traveling with her menagerie like an early Brigitte Bardot. In old age, she would buy a large tract of land near Le Lavandou, "Le Clos Mistinguett," specifically to house superannuated, and increasingly choleric, monkeys and marmosets. Characteristically, she liked her dogs to fulfill a useful purpose, too, and her successive Brie and Afghan hounds were made to work for a living, frequently appearing onstage with her. Live chicks wandered around the floor of her dressing room, often trodden on. Her whole life-style, with its breathless, hysterical, frenzied quest for pleasure, almost nightly after-theater tours of fashionable nightclubs and "boîtes," with a camp entourage of twittering hangers-on invariably by her side, was a strange foreshadowing of Madonna's, and, as with Madonna, behind it all was a hard-as-nails, tyrannical businesswoman who knew perfectly well what she was up to, with views far in advance of her time. As she was to write, many years later:

All this high life was a sort of testing ground for my reputation—an extension of the sphere where I learned my living. My pearl necklace and crocodile-upholstered Rolls were the talk of Paris. The newspapers were full of pictures of the gymnasium where I worked out in my red silk star-embroidered tights. Publicity. Publicity, too, my innumerable lovers. Not all of them, perhaps, let's be honest, one or two were for pleasure. Outside of Chevalier, I have never loved anyone. My lovers, offstage, meant very little to me. I have always thought that a couple is essential for the success of a music-hall show. A stage couple gives the public something to think about. . . . One must know how to satisfy the public. The ideal partner is one who makes the public say: They go well together, and not necessarily the one you like most. The public has chosen you as an instrument of its pleasure and object of its applause: Let it also choose your partner.

She was unusually modern, too, in the way she prepared for her shows. She paraded the entire staff of a large Paris couture firm before her, when about to play the part of a waif, and selecting "the lowest of the low," a poor little girl almost in rags, whose job was picking up the pins in the atelier, pointed and said, "I want everything *she's* got on." The rags she stripped from the "pin girl" became her extraordinarily effective stage costume.

Mistinguett almost certainly had Chevalier in mind as a possible lover from the start. When he first started rehearsals, she noted, he was "just a great timid chap with a friendly smile, his shoulders too broad for his narrow coat, which was an awkward fit." Surreptitiously looking him over before he was actually hired, she went to a small Montmartre music hall to see his act. "I watched him—and it was a revelation. Using very little in the way of gesture, smiling his ordinary smile of everyday life, he put his songs across as though he were humming them for his own pleasure."[8] "In spite of his immaturity," she noted, "my immediate judgment of him was that he had got the vital quality of the '*fluide*,' or current."

There was to be an uncanny similarity in the way Mistinguett coached Chevalier, from 1911 on, and the way Edith Piaf would deal with Yves

Montand, also her lover, over thirty years later, in 1944. In their professional lives, at least, both women were dominant, brutally hard taskmasters. Having spotted raw talent, they worked hard to transform their lovers into stars, and in each case success led to bitterness: Neither Piaf nor Mistinguett realized, at the time, the pitfalls of playing Pygmalion.

For all their later protracted feuds, in his first few months with Mistinguett, Chevalier was a docile, attentive, and, at least at first, immensely grateful pupil. And Mistinguett, for all her hard-as-nails practicality and ruthlessness, never quite got over her love affair with Chevalier, in later life regretting they never had a child together.

Shortly before her death, she pointed to her entry in the French *Who's Who*: It read, in part: "1911—discovers and launches Maurice Chevalier." All her long life, she remained proud of the fact, adding, with uncharacteristic modesty:

> It has often been said that I "created" Chevalier. This is untrue. I simply passed on a few of the tricks of technique that I had learned in the course of my experience, to him who was destined to become so dominating a figure in the stage life of our epoch. I merely held out a hand to him across the threshold of the domain I already possessed: Welcome to the world of lavish and spectacular entertainment that the jangled nerves of our epoch demand. . . . Enchant them with that smile of yours, and that gleam of genuine Parisian gaiety of which we both, you and I, know the full worth—for we've both known what poverty is, and what the struggle to earn bread is, from childhood up! Come across into this strange revue world with me— and *they*, the public, will follow. . . . I may have launched him, but if I had not given him his first real chance, he would have found some other jumping-off ground."[9]

CHAPTER 6

"Oh my man, I love him so!
He'll never know!
All my life is just despair,
But I don't care!"

— *"Mon Homme,"*
sung by Mistinguett

$\mathcal{M}$istinguett had been Maurice Chevalier's "unattainable ideal" ever since his childhood. In his teens, "she was everything that turned me on," he wrote in his memoirs. A fellow performer, who knew "La Miss," had once, after Maurice's persistent entreaties, taken him to see her in her dressing room at the Eldorado. "How old are you, *mon petit?*" she asked him distractedly. Fifteen and a half, he told her. Patting him on the cheek, she said, "So you're Maurice Chevalier? Carry on, young man. I, Mistinguett, swear you'll go far, because you have such a sharp little face [*une belle petite gueule*]." It had been his most memorable boyhood thrill. Their paths had crossed subsequently, but, as Chevalier somewhat disingenuously noted, "she didn't seem to remember me."

It is amusing to compare Chevalier's and Mistinguett's versions of their love affair. Just as, in his memoirs, Chevalier made as little as he possibly could of his relationship with Fréhel—for who wanted to be associated with failure?—so he gave the impression, with Mistinguett, that after their initial, unexpected romantic encounter, theirs was a long-drawn-out, romantic courtship, and that he spent days and nights mooning over her beauty and relative inaccessibility.

Mistinguett, for all her genuine, lifelong fondness for Chevalier, was much more down-to-earth. While Chevalier idealized her in his memoirs, she was far more lucid about him, recalling examples of his selfishness, his all-encompassing egotism, and his habit of "using" people. In *her* memoirs, she also noted that "his comfortable sentimentality, his honest poverty, his conscientious striving—all this reassured me."

Both acknowledged that everything began the moment they began rehearsing an act thought up by Paul-Louis Flers, "*la valse renversante,* "the knockover waltz." In this number, Chevalier and Mistinguett started out by having a lovers' quarrel, followed by a mimed reconciliation ending with a passionate waltz around the stage in what was supposed to be her bedroom, seemingly so wrapped up in each other that they were unaware that, as they danced, they knocked over dressing tables, lamps, and chairs, finally tripping up on the scattered, overturned furniture and ending up, still trying to dance, rolled up in the carpet—which was in fact a length of coconut matting. It all required split-second timing and careful planning. The idea may not have been oversubtle, as Chevalier himself acknowledged, "but I can assure you it was excellent music-hall material." The whole thing was designed as a tongue-in-cheek skit on the "*valse chaloupée*" for which Mistinguett was famous, with the furniture taking a beating instead of the leading man's partner.

From the moment they started rehearsing, the right note of easy intimacy was struck between them. "We spoke the same language," Chevalier wrote later, "our common origins led to an immediate, comradely bond." As professional dancers, with a good sense of rhythm, they found it easy to work together—their bodies were perfectly synchronized. He also discovered he was able to make her laugh, "and she told me that in the circles she moved in, this rarely happened. She must also have been aware," he wrote, of the effluvia emanating from my body as I held her tightly in my arms. Which is why you will readily understand why, during the course of one particular rehearsal, rolled up in the carpet, isolated from the rest of the world, we found ourselves admitting, quite naturally and without words, in the most unequivocal way possible, that there was no reason to seek love elsewhere."[1]

After that particular rehearsal, Chevalier hinted, Mistinguett whisked him away in a carriage, and they made passionate love. In subsequent rehearsals, they spent more and more time rolled up in the coconut matting, until the director had to call them to order, like an umpire ordering two boxers to break their clinch. The whole staff of the Folies-Bergère was immediately aware of Mistinguett's new man in her life.

As Mistinguett herself wrote, with fewer embellishments, "it was that damn carpet that started it all."

For that strip of coconut carpet seems just as beautiful as any setting of the legend of Tristan and Yseult. . . . Rolled up in the carpet, we no longer met as Chevalier and Mistinguett, but much more as the flower-seller and the young Paris apprentice, speechless, lost in wonder at our discovery, just like their counterparts, the *midinette* and the little counter-jumper, under the flare of the street lamp, at their place of tryst in the dark of a rainy street. . . . I did not realize at first the importance Chevalier was beginning to have in my existence. I had other commitments after that first show together at the Folies-Bergère. I fulfilled them, but they began to weigh on me. We spent more and more time in each other's company, lunching together, meeting after the show, going home together."[2]

Chevalier recalled at length, in his memoirs, his astonishment that such a star would have anything to do with him, her overwhelming impact, and, again and again, his sense of inadequacy in her company whenever they were offstage. This inferiority complex vis-à-vis those he considered his social superiors would never completely disappear, even after he had become world-famous. "I was extremely naive and timid whenever I was outside the theater," he wrote. "This awkwardness arose out of the gap in my education. I felt out of place in elegant restaurants or in fashionable places. I was mixing with a world that was superior to me. I got the impression people were looking at me with contempt. I couldn't wait to be back in more modest company." Mistinguett, he added, was aware of these tendencies and "wanted to get rid of them." She insisted he order an expensive, tailor-made tuxedo for when they attended fashionable parties together. He wore it the first time for a performance of *La Vie Parisienne*, the musical comedy Mistinguett was starring in while at the same time attending rehearsals with Chevalier. The tuxedo, Chevalier wrote, felt like a suit of armor but he was reassured, from his seat in the front row, "by the way she eyed me from the stage with gentle tenderness. . . . I was in a mood of perpetual enchantment."

Unlike Mistinguett, he was singularly discreet in his memoirs about the physical details of their affair, all the time stressing that "she was not free," since it was well known that she was having an affair, at the time, with a celebrated stage actor, also performing in *La Vie Parisienne*. This was Louis Verneuil, whom Chevalier did not name. He painted a sad, somewhat humiliating portrait of himself as enduring a "back street" existence after their first sexual encounter, hoping at best for a snatched kiss, waiting for hours for her in a café on the Boulevard de Strasbourg where they met, discreetly, in a back room. To some extent, Mistinguett may simply, at this stage, have added Chevalier to her list, and may have enjoyed the trappings of a covert love affair with such a handsome, naive young man, wearing a hat with a thick black veil for her afternoon encounters with him, meeting him "incognito" (but the waiters at the café knew perfectly well who she was) reveling in his eager, innocent ardor. After the curtain went down on their highly successful "premiere," Chevalier went back to his mother, while Mistinguett had her own separate celebration with her cronies—and with her still official lover, Louis Verneuil. Chevalier, in his memoirs, sadly reminded himself that "she hasn't promised you anything." Mistinguett, in her memoirs, recalled that she turned down his marriage proposals. Chevalier did not mention this at all in his memoirs, except to say that she "was not the marrying type."

Since Mistinguett and Chevalier reminisced in print about their initial encounter almost half a century after it occurred, long after they had become national monuments, both yielded to a certain amount of self-indulgent nostalgia. Inevitably, they chose to idealize the relationship somewhat, remembering only its glamorous side.

This was understandable: It had been a uniquely exciting time for them both, and, by the time they wrote about it, they were looking back on a singularly alluring, incredibly secure world that had vanished without a trace. In the immediate, pre–World War I years, there had been unlimited confidence in the future: These were the times cautious French investors put their savings into what appeared to be the safest, as well as the most profitable, investment possible: Russian railway bonds and securities, guaranteed by the Czar himself, which would shortly become as valueless as Fréhel's hoard of rubles after the 1917 Russian Revolution. In 1911, the notion that sheltered Europe would ever jeopardize its prosperity by war was, to most people of Mistinguett and Chevalier's generation, almost unthinkable.

In any case, Mistinguett and Chevalier were so wrapped up in their own music-hall careers that neither had much time for the world around them, then or later, though Mistinguett's horizons were vaster than his. She had traveled to Russia. He had only been as far as London. She was familiar with key figures on the world stage—King Edward VII, King Alfonso XIII, but also playboy fortune-hunters like Boni de Castellane. Part of their conversation must have ranged over the state of the world as these eminent personalities viewed it. But neither the crowned heads of Europe, nor the leading politicians of the day, nor her other hugely rich, pleasure-loving fans had any inkling that they were partying on the edge of an abyss. The fortunes of the titled foreigners who flocked to Paris, like the extravagant, reckless spending of Russian grand dukes, were taken for granted, and their resources were thought to be limitless. No one could possibly imagine that some of these former grand dukes, only a few years later, would be lining up for fares in their taxis outside the very same Paris nightclubs where they had dissipated fortunes on girls and champagne.

For Chevalier and Mistinguett, part of the privileged elite of the booming music-hall world, there was an additional reason for recalling those days with nostalgia: 1911 was the year the really big music-hall theaters began staging hugely costly, elaborate "revues," with large casts, numerous extravagant "tableaux," and countless complicated costume and scenery changes. The Folies-Bergère itself was then one of the best-known, most fashionable theaters in the world—not yet, as it later became, the venue for an eminently predictable, all-inclusive night out for tourist groups bused in by Japanese and German tour operators before closing for "extensive renovations" in 1992. Men like Flers and Jacques-Charles wielded immense power and were as well known as today's leading Hollywood film directors. The new kind of revue, in turn, glamorized still further those leading members of the music-hall "star system" like Mistinguett and Chevalier, on whom the success of these unprecedentedly expensive shows depended. They were earning huge sums and getting the kind of press exposure film stars get today. No wonder, then, that for both Chevalier and Mistinguett, the "damned carpet" evoked a host of memories of all kinds.

"We would act, dance and stay together for the best part of ten years," Mistinguett wrote.*

> In those days he was a great, shy, unsophisticated lad, completely wrapped up in his own dreams. For hours at a time, in the evenings, he would sit, without saying a word, imagining himself at the top. Then he would catch my eye and come tumbling down again, smiling wryly at his giddy fancies. My presence reassured him, gave him confidence. I was the living proof, the tangible guarantee, of his future. In spite of myself I became all tenderness, and so captivated by that charm of his that I was excited and anxious at the same time to find I was holding in my arms not Maurice, but a confused bundle of possibilities. I would shake myself

*"La Miss" is not strictly accurate: She and Chevalier were together from 1911 to 1913, then from October 1916 until shortly before the end of the war (Nov. 11, 1918). By 1919, they were living separate lives.

mentally and him, too, determined to bring him back to reality; I wanted him in the present.[3]

Mistinguett's authoritarian streak, and the conviction that her show-business decisions were invariably correct, made her toy with the notion of changing Chevalier's stage name to Carpentier—and it's likely that, had she insisted, she would have got her way. As it was, she transformed him, for, as she wrote:

> he was extraordinarily badly dressed. Maurice later said I was always making fun of him and of his repertoire. [Before appearing at the Folies] he wore on stage a pair of blue and white sailors' trousers that barely came down to his ankles, a short browny-colored jacket and a tiny bowler hat. He did the most amazing things with it—as though by accident. He could make it slide down over his eyes when he got to the naughty parts of his song, and he'd knock it back over his ears when he came to his jokes. . . . He made it all extraordinarily amusing, and at the same time extraordinarily evocative of the Paris street type.[4]

In the wings, listening to him onstage, in a solo number, of the memorable "first night" of their first show together, she recalled:

> The scene comes back to me. I can see myself again, standing hidden in the prompt corner, watching and listening. My heart's beating madly. . . . And Chevalier begins to sing. He sings easily, charmingly, with his usual absolute naturalness and geniality—and suddenly all sense that the occasion is a "first night," and all sense of the responsibilities on my own shoulders leaves me. . . . How can I explain myself? Chevalier had *got* me—*me*, a fellow professional, just as he had *got* every member of the audience that I could see through my little hole in the curtain. The whole vast circle of the house was merely a reflection of his smile. The audience was gripped and held, just as I was myself gripped and held. It was the same boy from the tiny Montmartre music hall who was singing out there, but with something else added to him—a newfound maturity. He had become an artist, and he was holding his audience in the hollow of his hand—he was controlling the reactions of two thousand people.

. . . What his smile was saying to the audience in front was: "Tell me—d'you like it all right? Of course, I don't say it's great literature or classical music; but we're here, aren't we, just for a little pleasant amusement together, and we're doing harm to nobody. Right?"

She said to herself, "He's got them! He's made it. Now I can start teaching him his job, and first and foremost how to walk properly."

She did so quite literally. As Jacques-Charles, the noted stage director and impresario, wrote nearly half a century later:[5]

> I would pick them up at her apartment on the Boulevard des Capucines on the way to the theater. We made him walk in front of us to correct his posture, for he swung his body around like all the suburban bully-boys of his day. "La Miss" would say: "Keep your back straight [*tiens toi droit*], no, not too much, pull your bottom in, look where you put your feet, don't swing your shoulders like that [*ne roule pas des épaules comme ça*]."

Only some forty years later would Chevalier dare criticize Mistinguett in his memoirs, commenting adversely on some of her mannerisms, such as her overeager insistence on audience participation and her habit of calling on acquaintances in the audience to sing a particular verse of her songs solo. But in his memoirs, he never mentioned her dictatorial ways during rehearsals, or her habit of systematically rejecting all new material composers and librettists submitted to her. It was Jacques-Charles, in *his* memoirs, who described Mistinguett as she really was during rehearsals,[6] foul-mouthed, shrieking, yelling, losing her temper with all around her, Chevalier included. He also witnessed Chevalier's and Mistinguett's intimate, almost childish moments together: In the heyday of their relationship, in 1913, he noted that their favorite game was to turn out the lights when they were alone in a room together. Each would make an excruciating face in the dark. When the lights came on, whoever made the other laugh won.

Chevalier's admiration for Mistinguett was genuine, and his "eagerness to learn," she wrote, "amounts almost to a vice with him. He thinks one can learn everything." He knew that his sudden promotion was causing resentment among his peers, and that Mistinguett's other lovers were jealous (for her relationship with Chevalier, as she herself had been the first to admit, was at first only one of several "commitments.") Verneuil, after finding one of his love letters to her, challenged Chevalier to a fistfight and was ignominiously beaten in an alleyway behind the Folies. Verneuil may not have known that Chevalier had been taking boxing lessons for the last two years, and took considerable pride in his friendship with the young but already up-and-coming future champion Georges Carpentier. (Later, one of his favorite stories was how, in 1911, he had fought Carpentier in a friendly match in a Paris gym and attracted the attention of a boxing promoter who urged him to turn pro). "He came a cropper of his own doing that night," Chevalier wrote somewhat pompously of Verneuil's humiliating rout that evening, "poor dislocated puppet of *La Vie Parisienne*.[7] Even at this idyllic point in their relationship, he was not blind to Mistinguett's cold-blooded self-centeredness, recalling that she had watched them exchange blows with no apparent show of emotion, and that afterward, "she behaved as though nothing had happened."

At some point in the months that followed, her emotional involvement with Chevalier increased. She finally dismissed Louis Verneuil from her apartment, though they continued to meet and remained friends; she met La Louque and began spending some time in the apartment, now on the Boulevard de Strasbourg, that Chevalier officially still shared with his mother. La Louque approved of Mistinguett as much as she had disapproved of Fréhel. Mist also paid a surprise visit to Marseilles, where Chevalier was performing, simply to surprise and comfort him—he had written her that he was feeling lonely and miserable.

In 1913, Chevalier and La Miss went to London together, staying at the Savoy in the same suite as man and wife, to take in the London shows, for Chevalier still had a thirst to learn. They took in shows from early afternoon till late at night, going from the Coliseum to the Holborn Empire to the Palace Theater and then on to the Café de Paris for its midnight cabaret. Chevalier particularly admired Gerald Kirby's elegance, and—though he could not understand their jokes—the stage presence of George Robey, George Grossmith, and Wilkie Bard. During their stay in London, Mistinguett also took Chevalier in hand sartorially—insisting he order a complete change of wardrobe. Jack Buchanan was then a young, up-and-coming vaudeville star, the epitome, in her eyes, of British sartorial elegance. "That's the kind of person I want you to look like," she told him.[8]

Shortly before their London trip, which set the seal on their "permanent relationship," they renewed their onstage partnership for a single gala performance, leading to what was probably the first-ever mention of Chevalier in the American press. Describing Mistinguett as "thin, gawky, hugely advertised and frightfully popular," a *New York American* dispatch from its Paris correspondent, dated June 2, 1913, read:

> Mistinguett directed the orchestra at one of the dances, and then did an American contortion dance with a harmless man-person called Chevalier. He threw Mist around, listened to her peculiar English as she had to warble it, and was a handy thing to have around the house.

The *New York American* reporter marveled at the high prices: boxes cost eighty dollars, orchestra seats five dollars.

Because he was now showing considerable promise as an amateur boxer, organizers of a charity gala for destitute actors asked Chevalier not to sing, but to box onstage. His opponent was a leading black French professional with an English name, Young Joe Gains. Gains had agreed to "lie down" in the third round and pull all punches, but reneged on the agreement in the first two rounds, hurting Chevalier considerably before fulfilling his part of the bargain. Chevalier surmised that Gains had been "got at" by Fréhel, whom he referred to, in his memoirs, simply as "an ex-girl-friend."

He was fast attaining superstar status. Topping the bill at La Cigale after his London trip (one of the lesser comics in the show was Raimu, later one of France's best-known film stars) he was getting four thousand francs a month, "the same kind of money," he noted proudly, "that Dranem was making." With his stage partner Régine Flory, he devised a French version of the Ethel Levey–Gerald Kirby "Hullo Ragtime" number he had admired so much in London, insisting they both appear dressed from head to toe in white. Chevalier wore a white bowler for the occasion. Mistinguett alternated between music hall and a new medium—the cinema. As early as 1906, she had been one of the very first Éponines in Albert Capelloni's silent-movie adaptation of *Les Misérables.* Now she was becoming a silent-film star as well. Chevalier had also been in several French "shorts," but in minor roles. In this pre–World War I era, the cinema was of little importance to music-hall stars, and when, in Britain and America, music-hall producers interrupted their schedule of live entertainers to show a short film, the audience invariably protested—or left the theater.

Chevalier's glittering prospects were such that he seemed destined to overtake top music-hall male stars like Dranem, Mayol, and Dearly within months. He himself knew better. He had deferred his call-up four times, from 1908 on, "for professional reasons," and could do so no longer. French military conscription lasted two years, and there were precious few exemptions, certainly none for music-hall artists. On December 1, 1913, leaving a tearful Mistinguett and an anxious La Louque behind, he reported to the 35th Regimental Center in Belfort, where he was to train as an infantryman.

He was four years older than most of the other recruits, who were mainly peasants, infinitely more sophisticated and, of course, far richer. Fitter than most of them, too, Chevalier took the grueling training in his stride, and had sufficient spare time to hire a room with a piano in town, where he practiced new songs with a fellow conscript, a talented young musician called Maurice Yvain. Mistinguett sent them sheet music, and anything else Chevalier required. They found themselves in great demand, not just for army concert parties, but at dinner parties given by senior French officers' wives. A standard attraction, they were regularly invited to dinner alongside local dignitaries and French officers, then set down in front of a piano to do their act. Chevalier's company commander once insisted that he do his act in front of just the commander and his wife; the combination of a rigid class system and respect for military hierarchy was such that Chevalier dared not refuse. He was also able to take a very brief leave of absence to be a guest star at the annual concert party given by the leading shoemaking factory bosses, *"les chaus-sures André,"* in nearby Nancy. Chevalier got five hundred francs, Maurice Yvain, acting as his accompanist, three hundred francs, for an evening's appearance.

Chevalier was soon transferred to the 31st Infantry Regiment at Melun, near Paris. He claimed this was a routine move, authorized because he was the sole support of his aged mother. In his memoirs, Jacques-Charles claimed that, responding to Mistinguett's constant requests and to put an end to her tantrums, *he* was the one who used his powerful connections to get him transferred to Melun. Mistinguett shortly afterward underwent a major operation, and rented a country house at Bois-le-roi, near Melun, for her convalescence. There, Chevalier recalled, he spent every afternoon with her, from 5:00 to 9:00 P.M. "How I looked forward to those visits," Mistinguett wrote. "He was never out of my thoughts. Those brief hours were the loveliest I have ever known. We had no cares and we sat in the sun and laughed and talked and lazed as if our happiness could last forever."

The idyll was brief: A few days later, on August 14, 1914, war finally broke out, and four days later Chevalier's regiment was on its way to the north, to fight the Germans. Mistinguett and La Louque were outside the barracks to see him off. Mistinguett wrote:

> I was stifled at the sight of the helpless, useless grief around us and I felt helpless too. I have always found myself tongue-tied in the face of disaster—I should be angry if I could only find the words. . . . We were allowed one last embrace. The sergeants shrieked their orders. The little soldiers fell into line and we watched the column, with its bobbing kit bags and fluttering handkerchiefs, go marching out of sight along the high road.[9]

Chevalier wrote that "I was leaving behind everything in the world I loved. I caught sight of *Maman* and Mist looking at me with strange expressions. I managed to give them a smile. Let's get into the train, quickly." Chevalier placed the scene of his mute farewell not outside the barracks, but at the station itself.

The war affected everyone: Jacques-Charles recalled it was almost impossible to get the curtain up that night. "Everyone was in tears and the chorus girls' mascara streaked their faces." But when the staff of Paris theaters realized many of them would have to close because there were simply not enough replacements available to fill the jobs of those being called up, a wave of hysteria swept through casts' and technicians' ranks as well that night, everyone demanding to be paid at once before they actually went dark. What began as a day of patriotic fervor ended up, Jacques-Charles recalled, in an undignified scramble for money.

Only a few days after the outbreak of war, Chevalier was in action. On August 21, 1914, his regiment marched fifty kilometers from a small railhead station to a village called Cons-la-Grand'ville, near the Belgian border. Chevalier was among those ordered to attack a nearby village called Cutry. Scouts reported the Germans had cleared out of the village, and Chevalier and his squad spent the night there, dug in and relieved to be alive.

The following morning the Germans launched a frontal counter-attack. Chevalier described the noise of incoming artillery shells, the overall confusion, and how he fired his rifle again and again, from a wall parapet, at an advancing mass of gray-green uniforms. After taking heavy casualties, his unit was ordered to withdraw. As he crawled away from the parapet, there was a huge explosion, he felt a burning sensation in his back and knew he had been hit. Somehow he managed to keep moving, and was among the walking wounded led back to Cons-la-Grand'ville. The local château had been turned into a military hospital. He was stripped of his uniform and bandaged, and fell into a deep sleep. A shell fragment had penetrated his left lung. Had he not been wearing his haversack, which to some extent amortized the blow, he would almost certainly have died.

When he woke up, the hospital was in German hands. Those, like Chevalier, who were only lightly wounded were marched a few days later to a station, and after two days on a slow train, he found himself in Alten Grabow prison camp, a huge stalag a hundred kilometers south of Berlin.

Chevalier adapted to his life as a P.O.W. with surprising ease. Partly, this was because, once his wound had healed, he was able to resume doing what he liked best—appearing onstage under the appreciative gaze of his peers. Among fellow prisoners were stage designers like Joe Bridge, ballet dancers from the Opéra, professional actors like Maurice Chevillard and Louis Tunc, all of them acquaintances from his prewar days. Chevalier was, in the military pecking order, the lowest of the low, a buck private (*soldat de deuxième classe*), but he soon became one of the key figures of the stalag because of his notoriety as a music-hall star and the enthusiasm with which he devoted himself to staging shows for his fellow P.O.W.'s in the improvised theater they called *La Boîte à Grabow*.

Chevalier seems not to have suffered overmuch from his enforced celibacy, noting with disapproval the growth of homosexuality among prisoners: "What had at first seemed scandalous became almost the norm. Couples paired off, at first timidly, then cynically."

From later arrivals, Chevalier learned that rumors had spread in Paris that he had lost an arm, been badly tortured by his captors, even that he had gone blind. For the first three months of the war, until the flow of Red Cross letters and messages began, Mistinguett was in a state of near collapse, but from 1915 on, Chevalier noted, the flow of weekly letters and parcels from her and La Louque never stopped. "Mist behaved admirably during my captivity," he noted.

> She took good care of *Maman* and visited her often. When I compared my fate to that of the poor guys around me who learned that after a few weeks' captivity, their girlfriends had irrevocably cast them off, I felt grateful for this woman, this Queen of Paris where a gay, insensitive life had started up again like dry wood catching fire, who had decided to remain loyal to the man of her choice.[10]

Mistinguett was indeed faithful to him, in her fashion. While Chevalier's whereabouts were still unknown, she determined to use her influence to set the Swiss Red Cross in motion, and, if at all possible, to get him exchanged. By now the French authorities were seeing spies everywhere, and, lacking the necessary travel permits, she was taken off the train to Geneva at Sens for questioning, before being allowed to resume her journey. A director of the Red Cross promised to help, and was as good as his word, soon locating Chevalier at Alten Grabow. On the advice of a senior French government official, Mistinguett also enlisted the help of her illustrious former lover, King Alfonso XIII of Spain. He wrote back he would do what he could. Meanwhile the Germans continued their advance across northern France, and Mistinguett rented a house for La Louque south of Paris before embarking on a disastrous tour of Italy, where, she claimed, she was cheated by her Italian impresario, who also impounded her expensive costumes.

Returning to Switzerland, she was again arrested as a suspected spy before being allowed out of France. French counterespionage agents had been warned that a German woman spy in a gray car was trying to leave the country. Mistinguett's car was gray.

> I was stopped on the main road, and once again I found myself locked up in a room. This time I was stripped and anointed all over with a sort of citrus paste. The two harpies in charge of this operation were, however, unable to discover on my body any traces of invisible ink and so I was released.

With tantalizing vagueness, Mistinguett wrote that "this time, my main preoccupation was to be the liberation of Maurice, and this was to lead me into tricky situations." She hinted, in her memoirs, that the French Deuxième Bureau, the Military Intelligence Department, had promised to do its best to get Chevalier repatriated if she would "cooperate" with them. From sparse hints dropped, it seems that this involved approaching the Germans and promising to work for them if they would agree to let Chevalier go—all the time, in classic "double agent" fashion, informing the Deuxième Bureau of the details of the German espionage organization in Switzerland she was able to infiltrate.

Mistinguett consistently refused to elaborate, in her lifetime, about this episode, to such an extent that many of her friends believed she had made it all up. But there must have been an element of truth in it, for just before the end of the war, in September 1918, she was summoned as a prosecution witness by a French military court to determine the fate of members of a German espionage network whose activities she had

THE GOOD FRENCHMAN · 91

helped uncover. Because they dealt with security matters, records of the proceedings have never been released.

Chevalier, meanwhile, was keeping busy in Alten Grabow. Thanks to his new prominence, as one of the chief stalag entertainers, he was given the job of medical orderly. This was originally intended as a sinecure, providing him with better food and quarters, more privacy, and the companionship of the senior medical officers, many of whom had seen him onstage before the war. Joe Bridge, a sergeant and former music-hall employee, was also given a job in the stalag infirmary. Both Bridge and Chevalier found themselves working around the clock during a typhoid epidemic inside the camp in 1915. Chevalier became highly sought-after for the skill with which he painlessly administered injections.

He was also learning English. Ronald Kennedy, a fellow prisoner, Durham Light Infantry sergeant, and former Yorkshire schoolmaster, agreed they should exchange lessons—Chevalier teaching Kennedy French, Kennedy providing Chevalier with English lessons. It didn't work out quite as Kennedy had intended, for he proved a far better teacher of English than Chevalier of French. After a few sessions, Kennedy was so delighted at his pupil's excellent progress that he gave up any hopes of being taught conversational French and concentrated on Chevalier's artistic as well as linguistic talents, teaching him English music-hall hits and traditional English songs. Chevalier began performing them at the regular concert parties. They were a huge success.

In his memoirs, he claimed that the thought never occurred to him that he might in any way exploit this achievement commercially. "I felt, very sincerely, that I lacked the talent to dare try my luck in countries where there were already such admirable music-hall stars." As with some of his other self-deprecatory assertions, this one should not be taken at its face value, for Chevalier's skills as a mimic were considerable, he was already familiar with some of the songs he now sang from having heard them performed in London, and was perfectly aware of their impact on his British audience.

In the third year of the war, the Swiss Red Cross was organizing exchanges of German and French P.O.W. medical personnel—and both Bridge and Chevalier applied for repatriation as medical orderlies. Both knew their chances were slim: Officially, despite their camp affectations, they were infantrymen, not medical corpsmen. A selection board consisting of senior French and German medical officers met to examine each case on its merits. Bridge passed the test. Chevalier knew he would fail if asked even the most elementary questions. But he was not required to. The German senior officer in charge muttered a few words in the ear of the camp interpreter, who told him he was on the list.

Whether the Spanish king's unofficial request to the German authorities or the Deuxième Bureau's intrigues were responsible for his inclusion will never be known. Possibly, his very notoriety as an entertainer was responsible for the German decision. The fact is that, the following day, a small group of French P.O.W.'s left Alten Grabow by truck, first for a transit camp in Mercebourg, then, by train, for Zurich, where they changed trains for Lyons, and were given a heroes' welcome.

There were a few hours to kill before the train's departure for Paris. Chevalier and Bridge immediately made for the local music hall, the Casino Kursaal. "Real women! a real music-hall orchestra!" Chevalier wrote later. "We go backstage, as out of place as two peasants visiting a town for the first time in their lives." Hours later, at the Gare de Lyon in Paris, he waited impatiently for the official welcoming speeches at the Gare de Lyon to end. They seemed to go on forever. Mistinguett was there. At last, they were free of the interminable ceremonial. "We are a little embarrassed," Chevalier wrote in *Ma Route et Mes Chansons*:

> In her car, we drive like mad to the apartment. We climb the stairs like kids. There is La Louque! There am I. Mist too. One on each arm. These two women are all my life. What else is there to say? *Maman* is already pottering around the kitchen, making coffee.

For the first time in his account of his years with Mistinguett, Chevalier waxed explicit about his sex life:

> I am alone with Mist in my room. She is in my arms. This moment I had avidly looked forward to for twenty-six months, like a sick man, like

a madman, finds me in such a state, trembling, emotional, that an inconceivable, dramatic failure prevents me from . . .

The chapter ends there, on that cryptic yet unquestionable note. His fiasco, understandable under the circumstances, would nevertheless be an ominous foretaste of their disintegrating relationship.

CHAPTER 7

"I was convinced he would do well in moving pictures."

—Elsie Janis

Chevalier's release from captivity occurred at a time when the toll of war was reaching unprecedentedly murderous heights. The battle of Verdun, in May–June 1916, with over sixty thousand French casualties, had taken place while he was still a prisoner of war, and he must have heard firsthand accounts of the carnage from captured French survivors sent to Alten Grabow. A year after his return, several French Army units mutinied, refusing to go "over the top" to almost certain death in futile frontal kamikazelike assaults. The shocking ruthlessness with which discipline was restored was a lasting, if largely hushed-up, blot on a country priding itself on "Liberty, Equality and Fraternity": One man out of ten in the offending units was indiscriminately selected and executed by firing squad in front of the others. So sensitive did this particular issue remain for decades that Stanley Kubrick's fictionalized account of the event, *Paths of Glory*, was banned in France for over ten years when it was first released in 1957.

Chevalier was proud of the military cross (Croix de Guerre) he received for his war wound and twenty-six months imprisonment, and was photographed in uniform wearing it after his release. Though he prided himself on being the quintessential "good Frenchman," he was atypical in one respect: He hated jingoism in any form. The only two military men Chevalier ever admired were Philippe Pétain and Charles de Gaulle. De Gaulle, at this time, was still a junior captain, himself a prisoner of war and completely unknown. But General (later Marshal) Pétain was acquiring a huge following among men of Chevalier's generation. He was brought in after the mutinies, did his best to restore the morale of the troops under his command, and put an end to suicidal frontal attacks. By 1917, Chevalier had become a lifelong Pétain fan.

For all his new command of English, his stalag concert-party successes, and Mistinguett's touching concern for him, Chevalier's morale was at rock bottom in Paris during the winter of 1916–17: He remained on sick leave for several months, until a review board finally decided to invalid him out of the army. His was the classic ex-prisoner's syndrome, a combination of agoraphobia, resentment, and a sense of exclusion. For an ambitious stage performer, the condition was far more serious than for most other categories of former prisoners of war. Chevalier felt, with reason, that he had remained in a time warp while events, and fashions, had passed him by. Though the war was raging less than two hundred miles away, Paris was full of people frenetically enjoying life while they could: Theaters and music halls were in the midst of a wartime boom, playing to full houses. Mistinguett wrote of "the sea of blue and khaki" that made up her audience, night after night.

Chevalier's main fear was that he would never again be a star, and this was part and parcel of a financial angst he would never shake off. The specter of poverty and deprivation, which would never leave him even after he had become a multimillionaire, came to the fore. As he put it, plaintively, to Mistinguett, shortly after his return, "Mist, there's no way I'll ever get six thousand francs a month again."[1] He tried out some of his old songs in a series of small music-hall theaters in Paris and in the provinces: He lacked confidence, and though not a complete failure, this initial return to the stage was only a moderate success. In theater-booking circles, he got the impression he was treated as a newcomer, all his past promise forgotten. Audience responses were disappointing.

There was further reason for Chevalier's gloom. Though he only obliquely hinted at this in his memoirs, he was also conscious that Mistinguett now had a circle of new friends and admirers in high places, some of them totally unaware of his relationship with her, or, indeed, of his very existence. Since his year with Fréhel, Chevalier had been averse to noisy parties and "smart," fast crowds. Mistinguett reveled in them, and for all her almost maternal attitude toward him after his release, her temperament was such that she simply could not sacrifice her life-style, or her career, for any length of time for sentimental reasons alone. As time went on, she became increasingly averse to quiet evenings at home in his silent, morose company.

Slowly, Chevalier began to adjust to this new situation. He was entirely lucid about his altered prospects, for times *had* changed, memories were fickle, and in many respects Chevalier's act *was* part of a remote past, even though it was less than four years since he had last been seen on the stage. The first two and a half years of the war had profoundly altered the tastes of the French public, now living furiously in the present.

Jacques-Charles, back at the Folies-Bergère helm after being in-validated out of the French Army with a war wound, was himself quite ruthless as far as Chevalier was concerned, now regarding him as a far reduced, almost insignificant box-office draw. When Mistinguett pleaded with him to take on Chevalier again as her partner, he offered him a mere hundred-francs-a-night fee—an insultingly small amount for someone who, only four years previously, had been getting five times as much. Mistinguett, with unprecedented generosity in light of her attitude toward money, insisted that a hundred francs be taken out of her own nightly fee and given to Chevalier, without his being told of the arrangement.

The new contract at the Folies-Bergère provided Chevalier with the necessary incentive he had hitherto lacked to change his repertoire. He showed what would henceforth be one of his main strengths as a performer—the intuitive ability to select songs that were in accordance with the times. When he began partnering Mistinguett again, Chevalier jettisoned many of his prewar acts, bringing others up-to-date. He modified an earlier, prewar boxing skit, now challenging members of the audience to fight him onstage for a large fee. Invariably, a previously briefed (and suitably paid) professional boxer called Lenaers clambered up onstage, put on gloves, and, in an outrageously phony fight, hit the floor in a simulated knockout. One night, Lenaers failed to show up, and Georges Carpentier, already a well-known boxer who would later fight Jack Dempsey for the world heavyweight boxing championship, took his place, without Chevalier being aware in advance of the switch. A few years younger than Chevalier, Carpentier had been his initial coach and sparring partner when Chevalier started taking boxing lessons. They were close friends, but Chevalier was by no means sure he could rely on his ex-teacher to take a humiliating fall onstage. He kept muttering, in a loud stage whisper, overheard by the first few rows in the audience, "No funny stuff, okay?" Suitably briefed, and intensely loyal, Carpentier allowed himself to be knocked down.

Paradoxically, it was Chevalier's stint in the stalag that was responsible for his professional rebirth. After America's entry into the war, on April 2, 1917, members of the American Expeditionary Force started showing up at the Folies-Bergère, first in a trickle, then in large numbers—to such an extent that some Parisian music halls, from 1917 on, were given over to all-English-language shows, targeting British, Canadian, Australian, and American troops on leave (on July 4, 1918, at the Casino de Paris, there would even be a special, one-night-only Grand American Gala to commemorate American Independence Day). Chevalier altered his routine, incorporating some of the songs he had performed at Alten Grabow. His fluency in English, and his familiarity with English hits (largely thanks to Sergeant Kennedy) turned him, once more, into a huge success, and his heavily accented version of "How Shall We Keep Them Down on the Farm, Now That They've Seen Paree?" invariably brought the house down.

Success rekindled self-confidence—as well as bringing higher fees.

He and Mistinguett were now, as in 1913, a couple in real life as well as a team onstage, and Mistinguett, at least at first, was delighted to witness his physical and moral convalescence. Folies-Bergère theater programs were now printed in English as well as French for the benefit of British and American servicemen, and Maurice Chevalier's war record, Croix de Guerre, and honorable discharge were specifically mentioned in the program notes. This, too, was good for his morale.

He showed considerable panache when the German long-range "Big Bertha" cannon and enemy bombers started attacking Paris by night in the winter of 1917. On several occasions, this happened while he was onstage, but thanks to his presence of mind and stage patter mocking the raiders and the noise ("I assure you it's not part of the show"), nobody left the theater. Mistinguett also recalled how, returning home after the show, she, Gesmar, and Chevalier were set upon by a gang trying to steal her handbag and jewelry: "Gesmar's girlish screams and Chevalier's useful fists quickly sent them packing."[2] But Chevalier never lost his loathing for the champagne parties he and Mistinguett were constantly urged to attend, in the company of increasing numbers of British and American officers and the inevitable "hard-faced men who had done well out of the war."

In May 1918, with the tide of war turning irrevocably against the Germans, Mistinguett and Chevalier deserted the Folies-Bergère and were lured away to head the bill at the new Casino de Paris, Léon Volterra's refurbished theater, which had opened in December 1917 with a new revue called "Paris Qui Danse," originally starring Gaby Deslys and Harry Pilcer, whom they replaced.

Chevalier's relationship with Mistinguett was changing. His dependency on her decreased as he regained confidence. As his morale returned, so, too, did his own sex drive—and with it the confirmation that he still had considerable sex appeal. He was also becoming more aware of the age difference between them: Mistinguett was now forty-three; he was only thirty, and at the top of his physical form. He resumed his philandering as soon as he no longer needed Mistinguett as a moral prop.

She found this out by accident. Chevalier, while still "officially" living with his mother, had rented a small apartment of his own, in the heart of the theater district. Mistinguett went there one afternoon, on the spur of the moment, because she wanted to have a look at the place, intending to redecorate it, at her expense, as a surprise gift. The place was empty, but the feminine underclothes, perfume, and knickknacks strewn all over the apartment were not hers. Chevalier, she realized, was having an affair with someone else. Never challenging him to his face, she simply made him aware that her own apartment, on the Boulevard de Capucines, was no longer available to him, except by prearranged consent. In her memoirs, she wrote that she told Chevalier never to visit her if he spotted a bright red handkerchief tied to the ironwork of her balcony. They still, on occasion, spent the night together in her place, but Chevalier was no longer, from that moment on, the only man in her life. Needless to say, Chevalier failed to mention the incident, or his philandering, in his own memoirs, referring to their gradual drift apart in general terms, alleging as its sole cause Mistinguett's fondness for late-night parties and fashionable nightclubs—and his disinclination to be ruled by her.

Despite Mist's unwelcome discovery, they continued their joint appearance at the Casino de Paris. "Until the armistice," wrote Jacques-Charles, "they remained a model couple." Then, probably aggravated by Mistinguett's sexual jealousy, the falling-out took on a novel dimension. Léon Volterra had hired Jacques-Charles to put on a new revue at the Casino de Paris called "*PA-RI-KI-RI*" (Laughing Paris), and Chevalier, now completely cured of his earlier self-doubts, wanted his name, on posters and all program billings, in the same bold type as Mistinguett's. He was no longer prepared to be her junior leading man. She refused, and he walked out. This delayed the opening night unexpectedly: *Le Figaro* had announced the new show would begin on October 3, 1918, but because of Chevalier's row with Mist, and his refusal to continue rehearsing with her, the premiere was delayed for two weeks (opening night was on October 19) and then proceeded only after considerable behind-the-scenes work by Volterra to bring them together again. But not for long: By 1919, he had decided that he would not perform with Mistinguett again.

The incident left lasting scars. Both parties, in their respective memoirs almost half a century later, were still intent on justifying their behavior. "For all the very sincere feelings Mist had for me," Chevalier wrote, somewhat cattily, apparently forgetting her crucial role in grooming him for stardom from 1911 on,

she had always, in her own mind, confined me to the role of junior partner who would display her in the best possible light. I was cast as the dancer, the carrier, the straight man, never as the potential challenger.[3]

Referring to the incident over thirty years later, Chevalier gave Elsa Maxwell a somewhat one-sided version. "I was going up, and she was not any more going up," he told her. "So she became jealous of me—just because I was younger. She could not bear to grow old. We had to part. . . ."[4] In fact, Mistinguett's career would remain in full swing well into the thirties, and even beyond.

Mistinguett saw it all very differently. As she wrote:

I couldn't grant him this [billing request]. Our joint success had gone to his head a bit and he thought I was trying to sabotage his performance. He stopped calling for me after the show [they were still performing together] as he had every night previously.[5]

Had she not made the fateful discovery in his apartment, the matter might have been resolved more amicably. But his womanizing may have affected her more than she herself was prepared to admit, for, as Jacques-Charles recalled, "she began making life difficult for everyone and especially for Chevalier. She was by temperament highly despotic, and wanted to reign without discussion." After a spell in the new revue, Chevalier abruptly resigned, and Mistinguett, noted Jacques-Charles, "became a queen without subjects."

Chevalier presented the facts to his best advantage in his memoirs, claiming that it was simply a chance encounter with Elsie Janis, the famous American music-hall star currently visiting Paris, that led to her sudden proposal that he join her in a new show called "Hullo America," about to go into rehearsal in London at the Palace Theater in 1919.

In fact, Jacques-Charles recalled in *his* memoirs:

> Chevalier asked me to get Sir Alfred Butt [the owner-director of the Palace Theater] to hire him in London. He said he wanted to get away from Mist and "see more clearly in my head, and also in my heart."

Chevalier swore Jacques-Charles to secrecy—he didn't want Mistinguett to know. Sir Alfred Butt proposed a three-month contract at one hundred pounds a week, all expenses paid, and Chevalier accepted. Both Mistinguett and Léon Volterra were taken aback when he announced his imminent departure. "You'll lose out over there," said Volterra, "but it may turn out to be a welcome lesson."

His first overseas assignment was not an unqualified success. Chevalier was well aware that British music-hall standards were the highest in the world. His latent inferiority complex came to the fore: He believed people were staring at him in the street because of the outlandish French cut of his clothes; at his request, he had been booked into the Savoy Hotel, in a "sad-looking, small single room," and the headwaiter at the Savoy Grill where he lunched on the first day in London "lost all interest in me as soon as he discovered I was alone, without Mistinguett." Calling in at the Palace Theater, he professed to be overwhelmed by the skills of the other members of the cast, their superb dancing techniques and, above all, by Elsie Janis's multiple talents as singer, *diseuse*, mime, mimic, and dancer, which overshadowed his own. He was also, for the first time, coping with an entire show in English, a very different proposition from the occasional English song he had belted out at the Folies-Bergère and the Casino de Paris. He knew, too, that his London audience would inevitably judge his performance by the standards of other English comics, many of whom, like the much-loved Brazil Allen, whose act resembled Chevalier's, had been killed in the war.

For some reason, the new show began with a Monday matinee—and matinee audiences are notoriously unresponsive. Chevalier's first number, a Cole Porter song called "On the Level You're a Little Devil," fell flat. So did a brief tap-dance number. After the show, Chevalier was so despondent he told Sir Alfred Butt he was prepared to pull out altogether. "Don't be so temperamental," he was told. "The evening show will be splendid." Gradually, the audience warmed to him. The three-month spell in London was not, as Volterra had predicted, an unmitigated disaster, but neither was it the outstanding personal triumph he had hoped for. "I was ill at ease all the time," Chevalier recalled later.

Elsie Janis, the star of "Hullo America," had something to do with Chevalier's malaise. This totally career-oriented American vaudeville sensation, whose good looks revealed her strong-jawed determination, was a type of woman Chevalier had never come across before. A star practically from the age of five, when she started imitating President McKinley in theaters (for $125 a week), she was a formidable all-around talent—an indefatigable writer, fluent in French, iron-willed, and with limitless tomboyish energy. Because she had entertained the American Expeditionary Force at considerable risk and discomfort near the front line during the Great War, she had become something of a heroine to the American public. As well known in America as Mistinguett was in France, she was temperamentally very different. Her autobiography, *So Far, So Good*, published immediately after her mother's death, in 1932, though absurdly discreet as far as her own emotional life was concerned, was revealing despite itself. In the book, Elsie Janis accounted for almost every show, and every major traveling assignment, from the age of ten on, but it was impossible to gauge her feelings, at any time, toward men, her quintessential "stage mother" who practically never left her side, or the numerous high-society figures she mingled with, flirted with, and observed with amused condescension—for she regarded herself as their equal in every way.

She had had one official fiancé, but, as her book made clear, she never slept with him. Elsie Janis's mother was a ubiquitous chaperon when they were together, never leaving them on their own together, even when they rented a houseboat near Windsor during a brief holiday spell between shows. He was a Bertie Wooster–type English music-hall artiste called Basil Hallam, famous for his song "I'm Gilbert the Filbert," which turned him overnight into a vaudeville sensation. Elsie Janis had been responsible for this metamorphosis: Before they met, he had been a relatively unknown actor in a series of unmemorable drawing-room comedies.*

Elsie Janis's cold-bloodedness came to the fore in her description of their relations after the outbreak of the war: Hallam, she wrote, was no hero, but pressures of all kinds had compelled him to enlist. "He didn't want to fight, poor boy," Janis recalled, "he was peace personified, and when he did so, he said to me: I don't mind being killed, but I don't want to be maimed. Darling, I couldn't face life if I couldn't be on the stage." She added, somewhat dryly, that "he was saved the trouble of doing so."

Hallam became an officer in the Balloon Corps. In his last letter to her, he wrote, "I'm not 'deaded' yet, darling, and as soon as the present 'show' quiets down a bit, I will come over. Stay in England."

But she was never to see him again. As she wrote, somewhat cold-bloodedly:[6]

> He got his endless "leave" on 22nd of August, 1915. The observation balloon in which he and another had gone up in a stiff wind broke loose from its cable. Basil said: "let's jump for it. Let's sit on the edge of the basket and count three." The young man who was with him landed safely and wrote me a most beautiful letter giving me the details. "I never thought," he said, "it would be Gilbert the Filbert who would give me the courage to face death." Every bone in his body was broken but his face was intact and he was almost smiling.

There was no further reference to him after that—no expression of grief, nostalgia, or regret—and she rapidly seems to have put him out of her mind.

It was after Hallam's death that Elsie Janis embarked on a career as "the sweetheart of the American Expeditionary Force," treated like a VIP wherever she went. She and her mother had been in Paris in 1917,

---

*"I'm Gilbert the Filbert, the nut with a K,
the pride of Piccadilly, the blasé roué.
Oh Hades, the ladies, who leave their wooden huts
for Gilbert the Filbert, the kernel of the Knuts."

at the Casino de Paris, watching Chevalier and Mistinguett, when an air-raid warning sounded. *"Mesdames, Messieurs, les Gothas* sont arrivés, la réprésentation continue,"* the MC announced, but Elsie and her mother left the theater—not to seek shelter but, characteristically, to observe the raid from closer quarters in the streets. (They were disappointed: It turned out to be a false alarm.) Elsie Janis's description of Paris complements Chevalier's: She mentions the lack of street lighting, "no taxis, no hot water except at weekends, maimed and bemedalled waiters at the Crillon, and no food after 8.30 pm."[7]

Chevalier was no stranger to Janis: After seeing him perform in 1913, she had told him, "Don't forget that when you do play in London, you play with me."

Chevalier had been intrigued by Elsie Janis's directness, and her apparent flirtatiousness, when they met once more in Paris in 1917. Only when he got to London did he realize that this was a pose, and that the promise of sex had been either a ruse or a figment of Chevalier's imagination. She had no intention of going to bed with him—as he had undoubtedly assumed she would. Her professional life was far too important for her to risk jeopardizing it in any way with a junior leading man. Besides, what would her mother have said? Elsie Janis's sex life would not in fact begin until after her mother's death, when she married and immediately quit the stage forever.

For all her reluctance to communicate her real feelings, Elsie Janis did hint at problems with Chevalier in London:

> Maurice in interviews gave me credit for helping him a great deal. The only thing I did of real value was to insist that he was my (onstage) lover more than a "comic," and to coax him not to take the first boat back to France when he heard the sentimental duet he had to sing with me. He thought it was more in his line to fall for the audience than have all the women in it fall for him. There were times during the rehearsals when he really was so like a naughty boy, with that alluring lower lip of his pulled into a pathetic pucker, that I was tempted to let him go, but

---

*Nickname by which the German bombers were known

considering that as far back as 1913 I had seen a certain *quelquechose* which now makes him the ladies' Waterloo, I stuck out my chin, which already had a good start, and would say: let's go to the hotel and talk things over. Mother, who was crazy about him, always had a large loaf of real French bread (the kind they carry through the streets under the arm), a hunk of cheese, and some *vin ordinaire* ready in case Maurice flourished his inferiority complex, and after a talk in his own language instead of the one which at the time he did not know well enough to get mad in, we would dance a bit, laugh a lot and say good night! The next day the Chevalier smile would be shining, and so he finally made his debut![8]

With the rest of the cast, too, Chevalier remained an outsider. His fellow performers had their own lives and, offstage, did not mingle. He found no candidate worthy of replacing Elsie Janis in his "narrow little bed" at the Savoy.

His loneliness was not due to a lack of recognition. As Elsie Janis noted, "just as the gallery girls nearly fell from their heights above, the duchesses reached for their lorgnettes or fans when he came on and sang, 'On the level, you're a leetle devil, but I'll soon make an 'ongell' of you.' " Everyone in London wanted him at parties. I coaxed him to several but gave it up as hopeless. 'Elsie,' he said, 'I am a bourgeois! I like simple things!' And so, he spent a lot of time with Mother and me!"

Chevalier was homesick: He did not yet understand the English, and their habit of concealing their dislike of foreigners under a veneer of polite cordiality and superficial bonhomie. Above all, he missed the close circle of French male music-hall performers he met with regularly in Paris cafés around the Boulevard de Strasbourg, where they would exchange the latest gossip about the French music-hall scene, who was in, who was out, who was sleeping with whom. There was no one in London to turn to when he became depressed—no La Louque, no Mistinguett—although, as Elsie Janis mentioned in her memoirs (Chevalier did not), La Miss did make the trip to London specially to see Chevalier perform, and was not impressed either by the show or by his act. She particularly disliked Chevalier's new hairstyle, slicked back instead of the low brow "bang" she had insisted on. How could it have been otherwise? Mistinguett was convinced that he and Elsie Janis were having an affair.

In ensuing years, he would come to terms with occasional loneliness, when on tour in foreign countries, but this was his first experience of it—and he did not yet have the allure and snob appeal of a worldwide star.

The experience was not entirely negative, however: Ever sensitive to current fashions, he jettisoned his wardrobe, ordering new, tailor-made suits, coats, shirts, and shoes. The 1913 Jack Buchanan image no longer corresponded to the impression he wished to project. "Mistinguett had turned Chevalier into a *Monsieur*," Jacques-Charles noted. "Elsie Janis turned him into a gentleman." It was not only Elsie Janis, but also London itself, that led to the change.

Elsie Janis was probably the first American to appreciate Chevalier's potential as a film star. He always maintained that his first contact with Hollywood came, in 1926, with Irving Thalberg's visit to Paris. But his first film test came seven years previously. As Elsie Janis wrote:

> I was convinced that he would do well in moving pictures, so with the assistance of Al Kaufman, who represented Famous Players–Lasky in London, and who agreed with me about Maurice as a film possibility, we made a "test." Al furnished the camera. He, Mother, Maurice and myself went out to a secluded spot in the grounds of the Zoo! I played straight for Maurice, asking him questions to bring out various expressions, putting him through a series of acrobatics (we were after Doug Fairbanks' line). Maurice stood on his hands, turned cartwheels, and to us was altogether marvelous. We thought we had the contract in hand and were bowing. The film was sent to America to the "Judges" in power at Famous Players–Lasky. Not only did they think nothing of it, but they did not waste the postage to tell us so.[9]

The same "Hullo America" show opened, shortly afterward, but without Elsie Janis, at the Palace Theater in Paris, recently built by Sir Alfred Butt. It flopped, to such an extent that he was compelled to sell the theater to recoup his losses (it was renamed the Théatre Mogador).

Chevalier then took on limited assignments in French provincial towns, putting his English experience to good use: He now saw himself as a dandy and jettisoned all the props he had used in previous numbers that made him look like a vulgar clown. His favorite stage getup was now a tuxedo and top hat. It was only after returning to Paris, once more in Volterra's good graces at the Casino de Paris (Mistinguett was no longer performing there) that he discarded the top hat for the straw boater (or skimmer), perhaps the most important single career decision in his life.

In later interviews in the thirties, he told reporters he could not recall what made him opt for the boater—he had been trying on different kinds of hats and had picked one out almost by accident. In his memoirs, begun later still and published in 1946, Chevalier wrote that he had seen a London "gay blade" wearing a tuxedo and a boater in the West End one night, and that the unusual combination had looked good on him. He was not entirely candid about his "boater" discovery: A well-known American vaudeville comedian, Harry Richman, whom Maurice Chevalier had almost certainly seen onstage during his London visits in the twenties, was in fact the first entertainer to use the famous "straw hat" prop, and it is virtually certain that Chevalier, always on the lookout for new ideas and gimmicks for his own act, appropriated the "trimmer" device. In later years, without any bitterness, Richman himself wryly noted that he had inadvertently provided Chevalier with his trademark.[10]

He had no idea, at the time, that it would become world-famous, that the Chevalier "look" would lead to a small boom for an English factory making them (A. E. Olney and Co., of Luton, which supplied them free to Chevalier), and that he would end up traveling with trunkfuls of them, distributing them to fans, friends, and, occasionally, in lieu of tips, to bemused hotel concierges. His first straw-hat appearance was in a Casino de Paris revue called *"Dans un fauteuil"* ("In an Armchair") in 1921, with an Australian music-hall artiste called Jennie Golder with whom he had a lighthearted affair. Prior to that, however, there had been one final attempt to patch things up with Mistinguett.

In 1920, Mistinguett had taken a trip to the United States, in the company of Jacques-Charles, not to perform, but simply to take a look at the American music-hall scene and discuss future shows with the likes of the Shuberts and other American producers. On her return, Chevalier met her at Le Havre, and they spent two weeks together in her house in Villerville. Prior to her trip, Mistinguett and Chevalier had not been on speaking terms, and their tryst, Jacques-Charles noted, "was in the nature of a last attempt at a honeymoon." But Mistinguett had been so uneasy at the prospect of two weeks alone with Chevalier that she had asked Jacques-Charles, and Alfred Willemetz, the famous librettist, to come along too.

There was another reason why Mistinguett was reluctant to be alone with Chevalier: While in New York, she had renewed her acquaintance with Earl Leslie, the ruggedly handsome American vaudeville star. She had done a dance number with him at the Folies-Bergère in Paris the year before (to Chevalier's considerable annoyance) and found him very attractive indeed. In New York, as was her habit when she was sexually attracted to anyone, she took the initiative and seduced him. Leslie was married, with a family, but Mist, as usual, had been irresistible when roused. Chevalier must have become aware of her new liaison, for she was soon to bring Leslie over to Paris.

It must have been an awkward reunion, but it was not unproductive, for it was here that she first rehearsed "*Mon Homme*," the song that was to make her world-famous. The music was by Maurice Yvain—the same Yvain who had been Chevalier's fellow conscript (and pianist) in Belfort in 1913—and the lyrics by Albert Willemetz and Jacques-Charles himself. At first, as was her habit, Mistinguett complained that the music and words were awful. For once, Chevalier was bold enough to face up to her, perhaps because, no longer her lover, he was less in awe of her, and freer to speak his mind: "You're crazy," he said. "If you don't take it, I'll put it in my own repertoire." Later, Chevalier did just that, singing a parody of her song entitled "*C'est Ma Bonne*" ("She's My Maid"). "*Mon Homme*" became Mistinguett's single most famous hit, before its English version was taken up by Fanny Brice. Other than that, the two weeks were not a success: Chevalier and Mistinguett came to the conclusion that their emotional and professional life together was over, though they parted good friends.

In later life, Mistinguett said she never despaired of winning him back

some day, though she did combine nostalgia and bittersweet recriminations in her memoirs. "Chevalier's presence," she wrote,

> never brought me anything special, but his absence dominated the rest
> of my life. Was it my fault that he left me? Or was it because I couldn't
> stop thinking about the boy on the boulevard, trying to impress everyone
> in his first tuxedo? His head was so swollen with newly found impor-
> tance, yet he was incapable of scratching his own bottom. It is true that
> he wanted to marry me . . . yet how could someone like me settle down
> with a man like that? Mind you, I don't think badly of him, even though
> he treated me badly. In our oasis of happiness, the garden was artificial,
> the water always unfit to drink. I never found a single reason to justify
> loving him. He used me, and as soon as he got what he wanted, he
> dumped me.[11]

She readily conceded that all the later men in her life—Earl Leslie,
Harry Pilcer, also a partner in the twenties and thirties, and Lino
Carenzio—had all been Chevalier look-alikes. "I never really lost sight
of him," she wrote with some pathos. "When he was no longer there,
I insisted on an imitation of him. . . . The great mistake in my life has
been to make do with facsimile Maurice Chevaliers. I should have
reconquered the only man who ever made me vibrate"—though only a
few pages later she was at pains to point out that Chevalier "was a lousy
lover."

Jacques-Charles, the insatiable gossip who continued to work closely
with Mistinguett for many years, had grave misgivings about her change
of partners. He had witnessed the beginning of their affair and knew that
Leslie had a serious drinking problem. He later wrote that Mistinguett
took on Earl Leslie as her new American partner, and as her lover, only
to make Maurice jealous, "to prove she could have a younger and more
handsome lover than Chevalier." But by this time Chevalier couldn't
have cared less, for he was on top of the world—a hugely successful star
once more and the lover of one of the most gloriously sexy music-hall
stars in Paris, his new stage partner, Jane Myro.

Without in any way belittling Chevalier's phoenixlike reemergence as a star, the nature of the war, from 1917 on, its immediate aftermath, and the social changes it triggered undoubtedly had something to do with it. Losses had been horrifying: Nearly 1.5 million French dead, 4 million wounded, 740,000 of them permanently disabled, 350,000 French houses destroyed, along with 5,000 kilometers of railroads, 62,000 kilometers of roads, and 3 million acres left unfit for cultivation. France suffered physically far more than any other country, for most of the time the war had raged on French territory. Germany, the loser, emerged, physically, practically unscathed.

While the huge numbers of French women in black widows' weeds were to be a constant feature of France for years to come, the nightmare's end led to an unprecedented sense of euphoria. "It is quite impossible to describe the mood of France immediately after the First World War," said Arletty, then a young chorus girl.[12] "Theaters were packed. People wanted to forget the war, they spent without counting, went out night after night, living from one day to the next with the sole notion of catching up for the wasted four years that had gone by."

The gathering of the victorious powers for the Versailles conference, leading to the Treaty of Versailles, which restored official peace among the nations, turned Paris into the diplomatic center of the world, with thousands of delegates on lavish expense accounts eager to take in the delights of Paris after their haggling around the conference table—and committees continued to meet in Paris long after the Treaty was signed, on June 28, 1919. Tens of thousands of affluent civilian tourists from all over the world were also able to enjoy the delights of Paris for the first time in four years. Theaters, music halls, and nightclubs were packed, and Chevalier, like Mistinguett and, later, Josephine Baker, rode the crest of a boom that only slackened off in the thirties, for the full impact of America's stock-market crash (October 1929) was not felt in France for some years. Later, France would pay the price, not just of war but of a misguided economic policy that relied on the promise of German reparations to bring about French recovery, and would lead, instead, to a devalued currency, inflation, protectionism, and growing unemployment. But in the twenties, French pride in victory turned Paris into a euphoric capital, the future seemed radiant, with France, in Denis Brogan's words, "the most glorious of victors."[13]

It was not just the new postwar boom in entertainment that gave Chevalier his much-needed fillip. As Lucien Rioux, the veteran French music-hall historian, pointed out,[14] the war had helped to blur France's once-rigid class distinctions. The uniform had been a great social leveler, and "WWI heroes and the 'nouveaux riches,' the hard-faced men who had done well out of the war [many of them of working-class origin] could identify with new entertainment personalities like Maurice Chevalier, and new sporting personalities like Georges Carpentier." Chevalier was the prototype of a new kind of star, the *titi en smoking*, the working-class lad in a tuxedo, who now enjoyed a new, glamorous status. He was the first of a new breed of stars—men like Albert Préjean and Jean Gabin, who shared Chevalier's background, but did not, as would have been the case before 1914, do anything to conceal their working-class origins, reveling, on the contrary, in the fact that they came from the long-neglected, underprivileged majority. This was the time Chevalier began using his *"gosse de Ménilmontant"* image so successfully, though it would be another decade before his social pretensions eased. In 1930, he would still pretend that his father had "died" and that his eldest brother "worked in a bank," but shortly after that date he fully assumed his working-class heritage. The shift in social values was akin to that which would occur in Britain, during the sixties, with the emergence of the Beatles and the newly fashionable working-class photographers, designers, directors, and writers, all lionized by a fascinated, fawning former ruling class.

Chevalier was now, perhaps for the first time in his life, to realize that his music hall triumph was no flash-in-the-pan accident, but something that would lead him to ever-greater heights. He now treated theater managers like Volterra and Jacques-Charles with a new self-confidence, high-handedly even, dictating terms for his new contracts. His thrift remained, but he now indulged himself in those trappings of success— gold watch, fur coat, car—that he had longed for as a boy. Soon he would be wealthy enough to buy a large piece of land outside Cannes, on which to build La Louque, his luxurious country home, complete with tennis court and swimming pool. But the "black dog" inside Chevalier was only dozing. What he experienced had little to do with the war, or the dire poverty of his childhood: He would soon discover that depression was liable to strike at any time, regardless of his star status, his bank balance, or the ease with which he attracted beautiful women.

CHAPTER 8

"These little worries won't endure.
Everything will be just great."

—from *Dédé*,
sung by Maurice Chevalier

The early twenties continued to be boom years for the French music-hall theater, and such was the hunger for popular, light-hearted entertainment after the First World War that even highly derivative, mediocre productions achieved undeserved success. But two musical comedies in Paris stood out as *the* plays to see: *Phi-Phi* (a lighthearted romp with a Greek mythological theme, *Phi-Phi* being the diminutive of the sculptor Phideas) and *Dédé*. Sold out from the start, they made a fortune for their librettist, Albert Willemetz, already the most successful French songwriter of his generation, his composer-partner Maurice Yvain, and above all for Gustave Quinson, owner-director of the Théâtre des Bouffes Parisiens, where they were staged. *Dédé* succeeded *Phi-Phi* on November 10, 1921, three years almost to the day after the World War I armistice. It ran for nearly three years, turning two of its young actresses, Lina Sakhy and Alice Cocea, into top-ranking stars. In *Dédé*, Maurice Chevalier played the part of a rakish, spend-thrift man-about-town who ends up, inevitably, both in the money and getting the girl of his choice.

By today's standards, at least, *Dédé* comes across as an unbelievably old-fashioned piece of part-spoken, part-sung theater, with a creaking, contrived plot and a host of cardboard characters. It owes something to Georges Feydeau, but Feydeau farces have more pace, more humor, and considerably more depth. *Dédé* reads like a bad Feydeau farce, and surviving recorded excerpts are of such poor quality that the tunes can hardly be discerned. It must have had *something*, for it was revived again and again, and veteran theatergoers still remember it as *the* thrill of the Paris theater of the twenties. Veteran *Le Monde* entertainment critic Olivier Merlin recalled playing truant as a schoolboy to stand in line for a cheap upper-circle seat, seeing the show again and again. For Jean Sablon, the famous singer, "Chevalier was my boyhood hero: seeing *Dédé* as a kid was one of the reasons that compelled me, later, to go on the stage. He had unimaginable presence," he said. "All he had to do was appear, and a thrill ran through the audience. In my entire experience, only Mistinguett had this magnetic, almost hypnotic appeal."[1]

Audiences responded to the story of the eccentric absentee shoe-store owner who hires totally inexperienced, amateur salespersons of dubious virtue to sell shoes to largely hypothetical customers (only one of them actually buys any, and only because he is in love with one of the shop assistants) because of *Dédé*'s stunning set, expert choreography, and compelling dance numbers. And it did have Chevalier, positively oozing cheerfulness, optimism, and charm, in tailor-made numbers by Willemetz and Yvain. In all French newspapers, he was singled out as the play's real star. All Parisians were soon humming the play's theme song:

> *"Dans la vie faut pas s'en faire,*
> *Moi je ne m'en fais pas.*
> *Ces petites misères*

Seront passagères
Tout ça s'arrangera,"

and Chevalier's answer to his irate wealthy uncle:

"Faut travailler, prendre un métier,
C'est le conseil que je vous donne.
Je lui dis: comment? Vous voudriez
Que j'vole le pain d'un ouvrier?"†

Dédé's frothy lightheartedness came just at the right time, for in 1921 the French, like their victorious World War I allies, needed relief from the growing problems caused by unemployment, political unrest, and inflation. A dramatic split among the left had led to the birth of the French Communist party in 1920, and inextricable international conflicts loomed in the wake of the Treaty of Versailles. The immediate postwar mood of victorious euphoria among the allies had not lasted long. The most divisive issue among French, British, and American leaders was over the military occupation of the Rhineland, and French insistence on German reparations. France regarded hefty, almost crippling German "reparations" as an inherent right, and the United States ended up funding defeated Germany to enable it to repay part of its debt to the French—but France was refusing to reimburse the United States for the debts it had incurred during the 1914–18 war.

For Chevalier, *Dédé* was a major challenge. His part, though not the lead, was a major one—he was onstage, singing, dancing, or speaking dialogue, for the best part of three hours. As only his most intimate

---

*"Life's too short to dissipate,
And I never make that mistake.
These little worries won't endure,
Everything will be just great."
†"He's constantly nagging me: do some work,
Be a swot, not a heel.
"What rot," I say, "you'd have me steal
The bread from a working-class berk?"

friends and colleagues knew, he lived in fear of forgetting lines of even the simplest songs, and found memorizing them a major ordeal at the best of times. Once he had agreed to appear in *Dédé*, he worried constantly. "My famous inferiority complex made me dread the long monologues," he wrote. By this time, the rhythm of the music hall and the revue had no secrets for him, but he had never actually been in a play before. Now he had to stand onstage, listening, motionless, to someone else. He discovered that he had an irrepressible tendency to overact, projecting himself in *Dédé* "as I would in a music-hall number," and its director, Edmond Roze, had his work cut out to restrain him. Chevalier knew that his peers would do their best to find fault with his performance, for his decision to move from music hall to operetta had not been popular: Volterra, furious at this latest betrayal of "straight" music hall, once again warned him he had made the wrong career decision. "Whatever possessed you? Weren't we treating you right?" he asked Chevalier, reminding him he was among the few artistes now commanding 1,000 to 1,500 francs a day. In the final days before the premiere, the play had to be cut drastically—and this, too, was a new, painful experience for Chevalier: Having memorized his lengthy part, he now had to learn it all over again.

The rave reviews, singling him out for special mention, should have put his mind at rest. But Chevalier was the worrying kind. His workaholic compulsion never allowed him to relax. Now that *Dédé* was a surefire success, he gave himself no respite; he decided it was time to become a film star as well.

As early as 1908, he had had walk-on parts in silent one-reel (roughly ten-minute) comedy movies; he appeared in three of them in 1911, was filmed with Mistinguett doing *"la valse renversante"* in 1913 (it was actually released in 1914, after he had been conscripted), and again appeared in a short with Mistinguett in 1917. Now he embarked on a movie actor's career in the mornings and afternoons, (when there were no matinees) breaking off only to show up in time at the Bouffes Parisiens. These films, still silent, of course, were much more ambitious, and required more work than the earlier ones. In 1921, concurrently with *Dédé*, he was the star of *Le Mauvais Garçon* ("The Bad Boy"), originally a play by Jacques Deval, in an adaptation by Henri Diamant-Berger, who also directed this forty-five-minute "five-reeler" (his costar was Marguerite Moreno). Also with Diamant-Berger, he made *Le Match Criqui-Ledoux,* a short (one-reel) comedy about boxing; in 1923, while still appearing on the stage most nights, he was in *Gonzague,* a three-reeler, playing a man-about-town who poses as a piano tuner in order to visit the home of the girl he has fallen in love with. This was followed, the same year, by *L'Affaire de la Rue de Lourcine,* a black comedy also directed by Diamant-Berger. Finally, Diamant-Berger persuaded him to be in two more films in 1924: *Par Habitude,* a comedy, and *Jim Bougne, Boxeur,* with Chevalier as a love-stricken boulevardier who pretends to be a prize-fighter to be near his girl (the plot patterns were as predictable as ever, for successful formulas were exploited to the hilt, even more so than today).

Chevalier was at the peak of his physical and sexual powers, with a limitless number of showgirls eager to be at his beck and call (but no great love affair emerged from his innumerable casting-couch conquests). He was driving himself exceptionally hard, also drinking and smoking heavily, and almost certainly using cocaine (and perhaps ether as well) as a booster, for he had become, quite unexpectedly, the darling of the cosmopolitan jet set congregating in Paris at the time, and the strain of mingling with socialites was far worse, for Chevalier, than performing onstage.

The poetess-socialite Anna de Noailles was bowled over by his charm and sex appeal, and had no trouble seducing him. Their physical affair lasted only a few weeks. Chevalier quickly tired of her demanding, proprietary ways—but was shrewd enough to keep on good terms with her, and she remained a lifelong fan, introducing him to le tout Paris, as did Lucien and Sacha Guitry, the famous father-and-son acting and writing team. Nineteen twenty-one was also the year of Chevalier's first exposure to "royal" visitors from Broadway—George Gershwin and Irving Berlin—and from Hollywood, in the shape of Douglas Fairbanks, Sr., and his then-wife Mary Pickford. Chevalier, who never, ever, quite got used to mixing with celebrities, though he gradually developed a technique for appearing at ease in their company, was entranced with

Fairbanks. He admired the latter's nonchalant elegance, his athleticism, his easy, relaxed social style, his mastery of small talk. Despite his own solidly established reputation, Chevalier behaved toward Pickford and Fairbanks like a wide-eyed adolescent fan, openly asking them for their autographed pictures, which he was to treasure all his life (even traveling with them and hanging them in his dressing room, wherever he might be).

The Fairbankses were so taken with *Dédé* that they almost persuaded Chevalier to star in a Broadway version. Charles Dillingham, the owner of the Globe Theater in New York, drew up a contract for him. But Chevalier had tremendous misgivings about appearing onstage in a foreign language after what he regarded as an inconclusive experience with Elsie Janis. He decided to take another trip to New York while *Dédé* went dark for eight summer weeks in 1922.

It was a strange trip, for no sooner did Mistinguett hear of his plans than she decided to come to New York as well. By this time, Earl Leslie was her constant companion, and the three of them decided to travel together and be the best of pals.

Things did not quite work out that way. Mistinguett could not resist playing off Chevalier against Leslie. Also, to conform to current American hotel morality, all three had to stay in separate rooms, much to Mistinguett's fury—and Leslie's surreptitious visits to her room caused a scandal. Chevalier, from the moment of arrival in New York, decided to go it alone. He wanted, as usual, to take in as many shows as possible, and proceeded to do so, also arranging for daily tap-dancing lessons with the best Broadway professionals. Always the committed professional, he visited Harlem frequently, haunting the many jazz clubs there, and was bowled over by a vibrant, long-legged black dancer named Josephine Baker, clowning it up in "Shuffle Along."

Keeping Mistinguett amused was a full-time job, as Leslie soon discovered: the threesome split up, somewhat acrimoniously. Jacques-Charles, always eager to comment on his erstwhile charges, felt that Mistinguett had deliberately suggested the strange ménage à trois only to make Chevalier jealous: Furious when she realized her plan was not working, she deliberately made life impossible for both her companions, throwing tantrums that drove Leslie to morose, solitary drinking bouts, while Chevalier looked on with quiet "I told you so" amusement. On the return sea journey, Chevalier did not dine at the same table as Mistinguett and Leslie, and when they disembarked at Southampton did not even say good-bye. Returning to Le Havre, he must have congratulated himself that his liaison was over, for Mistinguett behaved abominably during the crossing, her stateroom echoing with her shrill abuse of the long-suffering Leslie.

Chevalier returned to *Dédé*, to a series of undemanding relationships—and to socializing with le tout Paris. Thanks to Anna de Noailles, he now met the Prince of Wales (later briefly Edward VIII before becoming the Duke of Windsor), King Alfonso of Spain, Mistinguett's former lover, and Leopold III of Belgium. He resumed his punishing theater, film, and occasional nightclub routines. He was in a professional, social, and sexual whirl, and something was bound to give.

While in his second year at the Bouffes Parisiens in *Dédé*, he attended a luncheon party with old friends, including Raimu—and drank too much. He decided to take a nap, woke up just in time to go to the theater, with a hideous hangover, and, once onstage, had a complete blackout: He could no longer remember his lines. The other members of the cast helped him through his performance, but Chevalier's fright remained long after he had recovered. He asked the theater manager to rehire the *souffleur*, the prompter, who is a traditional feature of the French theater and whose services had been dispensed with after the first year. When the management refused, Chevalier arranged to pay him out of his own pocket.

Retribution finally came in the shape of yet another hit musical comedy, *Là-haut (On High)* by the same Willemetz-Yvain team. By this time, it was unthinkable to stage such a show without Chevalier. *Là-haut*, like its predecessors, was a somewhat derivative Feydeau-type farce (set in heaven), but this time Chevalier made the mistake of allowing himself to be cast, for the first time of his life, in a relatively "straight" role. The comic lead was played by Dranem, the veteran, outwardly modest, lackadaisical music-hall star Chevalier admired and had learned so much from. But there is no such thing as a music-hall star with a small ego, and Chevalier had been lulled into a false sense of security. During rehearsals, the wily Dranem did not, in the jargon of the theater, give his all. Fully aware of Chevalier's inexperience as a "straight" actor, he had decided to hold back on a number of gags and subtle stage business that he introduced, to no one's surprise but Chevalier's, on opening night.

The result was that this time, it was Dranem, and not Chevalier, who got the rave reviews. Chevalier was not entirely ignored, but some critics were frank enough to write that he had allowed himself to be miscast. As Chevalier wrote, "The first night led to a bullish rise in Dranem stock, and a bearish dip in Chevalier stock." Chevalier was devastated: He felt Dranem had betrayed him and moodily toyed with the possibility of leaving the show, but decided against it, because he knew this would be interpreted as acknowledging his limitations as an actor. Besides, he was liable to punitive damages if he abandoned his role before the first hundred performances were up. So, night after night, as he had to stand by onstage and acknowledge Dranem's comic gifts and the rapturous audience reactions to his ex-mentor's performance, his morale plummeted. He drifted into a deep depression, made worse by the physical strain of filming most mornings, and partying after the theater.

Something had to give. He sank, without at first realizing it, into deep depression. Aghast, he went to several doctors, who recommended various—and mostly contradictory—courses of action. In his autobiography, Chevalier blamed both his indifferent performance and his depression on improperly diagnosed appendicitis. He took leave from the theater to have his appendix removed, but—returning to the theater—found that his "black dog" depression had not left him.

He now displayed all the clinical symptoms of someone in the throes of deep depression: insomnia, extreme tiredness, irritability. Appearing onstage had become excruciatingly painful, and he was obsessed by the fear that each new performance would lead to a repetition of his earlier mental block. After brooding for months over his Globe Theater contract, he bought his way out; he knew that in his present state of mind, he would be unable to master his part in English. He bought a revolver and toyed with the idea of blowing his brains out. In his memoirs, he even claimed that he bought his mother a place in the country and got her to leave Paris so she would not be in town when he shot himself. (He mentioned that, though he was thirty-three, they still "lived together," which was only half-true, for he had long since used his small studio in town close to the theater as a *garçonnière*, a convenient meeting place for sex, so much more discreet than hotels). Finally, unable to cope, he gave notice to the Bouffes Parisiens Theater owner and had himself admitted as a patient in a clinic in the country specializing in psychiatric cases.

Whenever Chevalier was in a depressive state, he turned to women who mothered him. Jettisoning a number of casual girlfriends who expected him to squire them to nightclubs and fashionable parties, he selected a young, dark-haired actress, Yvonne Vallée, who had a small singing and dancing part (her first) in *Là-haut*, and they soon became lovers. He was attracted to her, he noted, not only because of her petite, trim figure, expressive dark eyes, and good looks, but because she was neither demanding nor extravagant, and, while waiting to go onstage, would sit quietly, knitting in the wings. This domestic trait may have been the deciding factor. Yvonne Vallée accompanied him to Doctor Dubois's clinic at Saujon, near Bordeaux (which happened to be her hometown), never leaving his sight. They held hands constantly, he clung to her like a sick child, and she made sure he was well installed before returning to her small part at the Bouffes Parisiens.

He did not, at first, improve, and his letters to Yvonne became so pathetic that she gave notice to the theater and returned to Saujon to be with him. There's no doubt that it was her reassuring presence that helped him overcome his breakdown. Later, she recalled that part of Chevalier's depression focused on money matters: Such was his irrational fear of poverty that he believed, if his "black dog" mood lasted, as he was convinced it would, both he and his aged mother would end up in the poorhouse.

After a couple of months on a strict diet, taking plenty of exercise (it was then that Chevalier started his daily five-mile walks, a routine he maintained until he was in his late seventies), his morale started to improve. But, as in the immediate aftermath of his release from prisoner-of-war camp, his self-confidence had gone. He was convinced he would never again be able to face an audience. With Yvonne Vallée constantly at his side, encouraging him, he gradually made it back into the big time, after a series of provincial appearances, first in the Saujon town hall—a concert organized by his doctor for the assembled patients as part of his therapy—then in Melun, and finally in Marseilles. The knowledge that some French tabloids had hinted at an incurable drug addiction added to his determination to succeed.

By the autumn of 1924, after a six-month hiatus, he was back at the Casino de Paris, once more Léon Volterra's favorite star, and in 1925 the new revue, "*Paris en Fleurs*," was an unprecedented triumph. This was when the French cartoonist Kiffer drew his memorable cartoon of Chevalier as a dancing lily—the drawing used on "*Paris en Fleurs*" posters—which became, in time, Chevalier's official emblem.

His philandering days seemed over: Yvonne Vallée never let him out of her sight. At her insistence, she was given a small part in the revue, joining him in a somewhat stilted duet with a "Gallagher and Sheehan" routine. They moved to a villa in Vaucresson, appropriately named "When We Are Two" ("*Quand On Est Deux*"), and Chevalier bought some land four miles west of Cannes, on a hill called La Bocca in what was then a remote, bucolic spot. He commissioned an architect to design him a luxurious Hollywood-style ranch, complete with tennis courts and a large swimming pool. The good life was not simply at hand: It was being experienced.

He should have been once more on the top of the world, but something was wrong. Recalling this period of his life (1925) he wrote, somewhat condescendingly (using the present tense) that

> Yvonne is a little companion whose behavior I could only praise, but my natural instinct is to be attracted by extraordinary women. She is too . . . I know not what. She's not quite . . . I cannot put it into words, but I sigh. So? So I work like a black and I live like a monk. . . .

It was clear that Yvonne Vallée's very qualities, her protectiveness and feminine devotion, that had been pluses for as long as he had needed her support while sick, had become difficult to bear now that he was well again. Chevalier's attitude toward women was complex: He took it for granted that those he was sexually attracted to were instantly available, and had almost always been proven right (Elsie Janis was a notable exception). But for all his miserliness and craving for a mother figure who could console him and listen to his interminable woes without losing patience, his physical tastes did not run to simple, home-loving bodies: The two most important women in his life so far had been Fréhel and Mistinguett, both of them unusually temperamental stars with flamboyant life-styles, women almost impossible to live with for long, tolerating as they did only self-effacing consorts who accepted their theatrical mood swings and pandered to their considerable egos.

This was not Chevalier's style at all. He enjoyed the company of young, beautiful women who made no emotional demands on him. In the show-business world, there were plenty only too eager to appear in public at his side. But he also sought out, as he put it, "exceptional" women, who were sufficiently well known or talented in their own right not to have to depend on him, and at whose side *he* attracted attention. Yvonne Vallée, he knew, though a good dancer with a pleasing, light voice, would never be a star in her own right.

The same domestic qualities that compelled her to knit in the wings of the Bouffes Parisiens now began to irritate him. Though he wanted to possess, he did not like being possessed. Yvonne's protective concern for him started becoming burdensome the moment he recovered from his depression. Besides, being able to pick and choose from an almost limitless number of highly attractive young women, he was unable to sustain a physical interest in the same woman for very long—and in his eyes, Yvonne's physical attraction was waning. Probably for the first time in his life, he felt he was in a woman's debt, for Yvonne had played a crucial role in helping him overcome his recent breakdown. This, however, made him no happier.

On his return to the theater, in 1924–25, he launched "Valentine" (lyrics by Willemetz, music by Henri Christiné, whom Chevalier had known since his childhood days), which instantly became the hit of the year and was to remain the public's favorite Chevalier song of all time. Its comic erotic undertones made it, at the time, mildly shocking, but

Chevalier's charming, unerring delivery turned it into something more than a hymn to carnal love: The song was a haunting reminder that a woman's physical charms, though invariably remembered with nostalgia, did not last forever.*

He also participated, in 1924–25, in an extraordinary moment in Parisian nightlife. The Boeuf sur le Toit nightclub had become the late-night "in" rendezvous for almost everyone of creative talent living in or passing through Paris, a convenient meeting place not just for show-business stars like Chevalier and Mistinguett, or writers like Jean Cocteau (though he was largely responsible for its success), but for most of France's intellectual and artistic elite. Diaghilev was there frequently (invariably with Boris Kochno, his extraordinarily handsome private secretary, favorite ballet-music composer, and constant companion); so were Missia Sert, Picasso, Chanel, the Dadaist poet Tristan Tzara, the leading Surrealist, André Breton, Darius Milhaud, and practically all the "beautiful people," French or foreign, who happened to be in the public eye (the Prince of Wales was also a frequent visitor.) Chevalier, who hated conventional party-going, found the relaxed, informal café atmosphere of Le Boeuf sur le Toit to his liking. It became a regular port of call after the theater. Yvonne Vallée did not enjoy these visits: She feared Chevalier's roving eye, and the intellectual small talk did not interest her overmuch. For all her youth and good looks, at the Boeuf sur le Toit she was out of her depth. But for Chevalier, rubbing shoulders with artists and intellectuals was a novel and pleasing experience. He began, in a small, almost timorous way, collecting modern art (his first acquisition was an Utrillo *nature morte*, one of his many flower-vase paintings).

---

*"She had tiny little tootsies,
Valentine, my Valentine.
She had tiny little titties
Which I tickled with my mitties . . .
She had a tiny little chin
And besides her little feet
Her little tits,
Her little chin,
She was as curly as a lamb."

Meeting writers like Gide, Pierre MacOrlan, and Blaise Cendrars over a drink made him, for the first time, want to read their books.

For all his meticulous professionalism onstage, Chevalier was not unerringly successful in his choice of engagements. In 1925, having spent what he regarded as an astronomical sum on his new house at La Bocca, he was eager to go where the money was. An American impresario called Lew Leslie approached him with an offer he was unable to refuse, and Chevalier misguidedly accepted star billing (along with Yvonne Vallée) in a show called *White Birds*, at His Majesty's Theatre in London. The pound was exceptionally strong, and Leslie guaranteed him five hundred pounds a week.

White Birds was intended as a successor to *Blackbirds*, a highly successful American import, with an almost entirely black cast headed by the enchanting Florence Moore. Somewhat naively, Lew Leslie believed that British audiences would take anything, provided it was highly publicized, and bore the imprint of *Blackbirds*. He was a shamelessly self-confident self-promoting egotist in the tradition of nineteenth-century American vaudeville. What worked in America was bound to work in London, he felt, as the success of *Blackbirds* proved. A far better showman and promoter than director, he insisted on directing *White Birds* himself, indulging in American-style promotional overkill that grated on the British music-hall community—and on the media: On their arrival at Victoria Station, Chevalier and Yvonne Vallée were greeted by twenty-four costumed chorus girls and a posse of British reporters.

Though Chevalier would later write that almost nobody remembered him from "Hullo America" and British newsmen "didn't know how to spell my name," he did attract considerable attention. David C. Fairweather, a critic on the staff of the influential *Theatre World* weekly, clearly an expert on Paris nightlife, gave an admirative description of Chevalier in his Casino de Paris routine:

> The stalls and boxes are full of people in evening dress. The promenoir is crowded with a restless, cosmopolitan throng. On the stage scene follows scene in a glittering sequence of wonderful colors, greeted by

metallic applause from the claque in the circle and lethargy from the rest of the audience. Then suddenly a jaunty figure in an immaculate "smoking" saunters onto the stage to be greeted by genuine applause. With the first tune the audience sits up and takes notice. His burlesque equilibriste act is as funny as anything I have ever seen of its kind. In "Valentine" he asks the audience, now do you want it in Yiddish, American, 'military' or effeminate style? His American miming is extraordinary, taking an imaginary stick of gum out of his mouth and sticking it to his shoe, ending with "Ahm gonna show you how to kiss that goil."

His "light-brown hair in no way suggests the Latin race, he is as popular with men as he is with women," and his brand of humor was immediately comprehensible, whereas "English people can listen to Dranem or Saint-Granier for a solid hour without a smile on their faces."

Chevalier was photographed mock-sparring with Mickey Walker, the visiting American middleweight boxing champion, and in the company of fellow comedians George Robey and Leslie Henson—but none of these well-known personalities appeared in the show, and the advance publicity proved of little value when the much-ballyhooed premiere took place in May 1927. *Theatre World* had already noted that "much of the essential 'Maurice' will have to be sacrificed on the altar of our insular conventions," but few were prepared for its total fiasco.

For *White Birds*—though it was to struggle on bravely for two months—was a financial, critical, and popular disaster, and deservedly so. Leslie had spent far more time on promotion than on the show itself, which was under-rehearsed. Lyrics and music were derivative and undistinguished, the humor heavy and out of fashion. Chevalier had had second thoughts about it from the start, but as a foreigner, confined himself to his own particular act. His anxiety deepened when the opening was postponed twice so that some of the numbers could be rewritten and some of its more glaring flaws corrected. There was no dominant English vaudeville star to put an imprint on the show. Chevalier apart, the most talented member of the cast was probably Anton Dolin, later the world-famous ballet dancer and choreographer, then making his debut, but male soloist dancers did not make or break a variety show, however brilliantly they performed. London audiences were not impressed by the worn, stilted prologue ("Mighty Like a Rose," sung by Doreen Reed) or the off-color sketch ("The Business Trip") written by Lew Leslie himself. To make matters worse, on the first night everything that could go wrong onstage went wrong: Cues were missed, provoking a chorus of boos and catcalls from the upper circle. Worse still, the pace of the show flagged to such an extent that it dragged on for nearly an hour more than its allotted time—with most of the audience noisily leaving before the end. Maurice Chevalier, in his memoirs, claimed that he saved the show, but in fact, as the program shows, he appeared in only two scenes—once with Yvonne Vallée in a new English number called "Cuddle Up and Dance with Me," which was indeed one of the show's few successful numbers, vigorously applauded. To Percy Cudlipp, a few years later, he admitted that the show had had "no wit," no pace, and that the whole thing had been "a tragedy."

It was the kind of failure Chevalier had always dreaded, and he was thankful that this time neither Mistinguett nor any French critics came to see it. Chevalier was not superstitious, and Yvonne Vallée was as supportive as ever, but he felt profoundly humiliated that she had had to witness, and take part in, such a fiasco.

Back in Paris, soon afterward, Chevalier married Yvonne Vallée at Vaucresson. He did so, he wrote later, largely to please his aging mother. In her eyes, Yvonne Vallée was the ideal bride for Maurice—domestically capable, *sérieuse*, willing to subordinate her own life to his. The civil ceremony turned into an unplanned media event.

Over fifty years later, Yvonne Vallée lucidly appraised the Chevalier she had known at the time of their marriage as "a child rather than a husband. He had to be reassured constantly. He was never sure of success. Invariably, any unusual achievement brought on a black mood. He would querulously ask, 'Whatever can I possibly do now? It has to be downhill all the way.' But this constant worrying generated energy. When he was working, there was an impenetrable barrier between himself and the rest of the world."[2]

Chevalier was glad to start work at the Casino de Paris again. This was the time the movie business was expanding all over the world by leaps and bounds, and—though he was unaware of this—Chevalier's name had come up in Berlin, as a possible candidate for European film stardom. Billy Wilder, then a junior staffer on the payroll of UFA, the largest film studio in Europe, recalled that "we were looking for known performers we could turn into stars. We saw lots of pictures of Chevalier but the fools there decided to turn him down, because of the prominent mole on his left cheek."[3]

Though he was completely unaware of it at the time, Chevalier's music-hall fame had also brought him to the attention of a far more powerful film studio—MGM. By this time, Paris had become by far the most popular tourist attraction for affluent Americans. Sooner or later, anyone of note turned up there. But the visit to Paris of young Irving Thalberg, the "wunderkind" head of production of MGM, was not just a well-deserved holiday: The Fairbankses had spoken highly of Chevalier to Irving Thalberg and his wife, Norma Shearer, after their return to Hollywood. Thalberg and Shearer came to Paris in late 1927 and took in his show. Afterward, they went around to his dressing room, bringing fond greetings from the Fairbankses.

Thalberg had no reservations about Chevalier's mole, and promptly suggested he undergo a screen test. In his memoirs, Chevalier's version of events differed slightly from Thalberg's: Chevalier claimed that, amazed by Thalberg's youth and outward diffidence, he did not realize until almost too late that he was dealing with one of Hollywood's most powerful figures, and haughtily rejected the screen test as unworthy of his well-known talents. Belatedly discovering who Thalberg was, he ran after him to make amends, and accept.

By now, Chevalier had a full-time business manager, the Egyptian-born Max Ruppa, who had once worked for the Folies-Bergère on the management side. Ruppa advised Chevalier to drive a hard bargain and settle for nothing less than $25,000 for his first picture, to be revised upward for any subsequent work.* He also got Chevalier to insist that if he and Yvonne Vallée came to Hollywood, Ruppa (and Chevalier's

*Equal to at least $137,000 in current value, but probably worth far, far more.

full-time French cook) should also accompany them, at MGM's expense.

Thalberg was dumbfounded and countered by offering Chevalier fifteen thousand dollars. He was "not competent," he added, to decide on any additional expenditure. This, Chevalier claimed, was less than he was already getting as a music-hall star in Paris. Both men stood firm, and Chevalier ended up making his screen test but remaining in Paris.

But not for long. Arriving in Paris a few months later, Paramount's Jesse Lasky met Chevalier backstage and immediately made him an offer. Jesse Lasky, one of the founders of modern Hollywood, was outgoing where Thalberg was reserved, and almost recklessly extravagant with his (and Paramount's) funds where Thalberg was careful with MGM's money. Though no top stars trusted anyone where money was concerned (before Mary Pickford joined United Artists, her mother, legend had it, habitually checked the nightly takings of as many movie houses as she could on any given night to check up on her daughter's real worth), Paramount had the reputation of being not only the richest, but also the most generous and understanding, of all the Hollywood studios. Lasky, on the lookout for "bankable" stars as never before in 1927, had recently offered Gloria Swanson a $1 million contract—and been rebuffed. Immediately, he made an almost equally outrageously extravagant offer to Pola Negri, who accepted.

Lasky's own background also made him immediately receptive to Chevalier, for there were indeed extraordinary affinities between them: Both had been born with the show-biz bug. Jesse Lasky's family background was both more secure and more affluent than Chevalier's (his father owned a shoe store) but Lasky, before becoming a millionaire producer, had experienced the seamy side of vaudeville too. He had started off in show business as a cornet player, part of a seamy "ensemble" advertising "Doctor Crabtree's cure-all Indian herb medicine" at country fairs. He and his sister, Blanche (who married, and later divorced, Sam Goldwyn) became vaudeville comedians and quick-change artists. After losing the family savings gold-prospecting in Alaska, he had recouped some of the money playing the cornet in a honky-tonk orchestra there. The miners on a spree, if they liked the show, would throw minute quantities of gold into the orchestra pit. Like Chevalier, Lasky knew what it was like to face difficult, rough audiences in third-rate theaters. He knew the seamy side of show business: For a time, to earn a living, he had been agent-manager of "Herman the Magician." Sadly, it's unlikely that either compared notes on their difficult beginnings, or even that Chevalier was aware of the common vaudeville bond between them.

For by the time Lasky and Chevalier met, both men had adopted a more serious, businesslike "persona." Lasky looked the part of the high-powered executive, in his tailored dark suits and pince-nez. The onetime cornet player and quick-change artist had become one of the most famous, publicized figures in Hollywood, who had "discovered" Mary Pickford, Mae West, and dozens of other stars (and would later discover Archie Leach, also known as Cary Grant). Just about his only shortcoming, as a record producer in his early days (characteristically, he loved to tell the story against himself) had been his rejection of Irving Berlin's "Alexander's Ragtime Band."

In his autobiography, Lasky recalled his first meeting with Chevalier:

Chevalier sang a number of songs specially for the large proportion of American tourists in the audience and they were so captivated by his bubbling good humor and broken English that I couldn't help thinking that this ruddy-complexioned blue-eyed singer with a straw hat and an infectious smile would have the same appeal for Americans in Paris, Texas, as he obviously did in Paris, France. I impulsively went backstage and asked him if he'd like to go to Hollywood and become a picture star. His first reaction with a spreading grin was: "would I meet Doug and Mary?" I made an appointment to talk seriously about it the next day in the offices I used in the Paramount Theater in Paris, the architectural hybrid built under Al Kaufman's supervision and which he now managed.[4]

But Kaufman, remembering Chevalier's earlier London test (with Elsie Janis) was not enthusiastic.

When I told Kaufman I needed someone from the legal department to prepare a contract for a great discovery I had made and that it was Chevalier, he couldn't conceal a fleeting quizzical expression as though he were talking about someone who wasn't quite bright. "He's been around for years," Al said. "All the American producers have looked him over. Irving Thalberg and Louis Mayer saw him two months ago." His inference was that if Chevalier was such a prize, why hadn't someone signed him up before?

Lasky wavered. "I might have called off the appointment if there had been time to do so. I didn't know what I would do—until he came in, and his personality lit up the office."

On the Laskys' day of departure, Chevalier showed up unexpectedly with a large bouquet of roses for Bessie (Lasky's wife), "kissed her hand, and wished us *bon voyage*, beaming his radiant smile. Doting French fans looked on enviously as their idol enslaved another feminine heart."

The offer of an entirely new career came at a highly appropriate time: Chevalier's private life was in a shambles again. He bitterly regretted his marriage, now only a few months old. "I am faithful to her," he wrote, of his feelings toward Yvonne at the time,

> but am unable to give her the confidence that is needed if there is to be harmony between a couple. . . . Though I am the most envied of artists, I lead a miserable life. I don't know what to do. Get a divorce? That is not possible. Continue along these lines? How wretched! Added to all that, I believe that what prevents me from taking any kind of decision is my unhealthy fear of being alone. I feel as though I am drowning.

To add to the couple's crisis, Yvonne Vallée had recently suffered a miscarriage and had been dangerously ill for several weeks afterward. Chevalier, who later was to claim that a son would have brought him more joy than anything else in the world, never mentioned the loss in his memoirs.

Hollywood, he felt, would at least provide a change of background. The studio publicists who transformed every married Hollywood star into a paragon of domestic felicity did their job so well that few Americans, even at Paramount, realized that when the Chevaliers set foot in America, their marriage was already in jeopardy.

CHAPTER 9

Hollywood, here we come!

When Lasky signed up Chevalier for his first Hollywood film, this was not the act of a tycoon indulging in a sudden, whimsical impulse. Though still shunned by snobs in America, movies were not only finding huge mass markets all over the world, but transforming the behavior and thought processes of their audiences in unprecedented ways. "The Cabots and the Lodges won't be caught dead at the pictures or let their children go," Joe Kennedy, an early investor in movies, told Gloria Swanson in 1927, "and that's why their servants know more about what's going on in the world than they do."[1]

And Hollywood, the generic term for the group of hugely powerful, profitable, interlocking yet rival studios of various sizes, was facing the biggest opportunity in its history: the advent of sound. In 1929, the "silent pictures" era was coming to an end.

Lasky, like Thalberg, was looking for new faces that would also be acceptable new voices. Both found the going difficult.

Al Jolson's *Jazz Singer*, made in 1927 and released a year later, triggered the change. In most histories of the cinema, it commonly figures as the first "real" Hollywood talkie. It was not. Warner's *Lights of New York*, directed by Bryan Foy and made around the same time, came out first, and that supreme authority on the cinema, Leslie Halliwell, described it as "the first all-talking film, a backstage gangster drama notable for little except its continuous nasal chatter" (still separated by subtitles).* What made the otherwise undistinguished *Jazz Singer* a huge hit was the fact that Jolson not only talked—*he sang*. For the first few years of sound, Hollywood pictures would sing, too, the golden rule of movies, then as now, being that a successful genre could be milked almost ad infinitum.

Talking pictures took a vast toll of careers, reputations, and fortunes. Rodolpho d'Antonguolla, otherwise known as Rudolph Valentino, perhaps fortunately for his posthumous reputation, had died of appendicitis in 1926, at the early age of thirty-one. Otherwise he might have lingered on, like so many other silent-movie stars, reduced to the status of a has-been. Some of the greatest stars of the twenties, like Buster Keaton, never fully recovered, only posthumously achieving cult status after decades of shameful neglect. Sound was to have almost the same impact on stars like John Gilbert, Clara Bow, Colleen Moore, Agnes Ayres, Bill Haines, Charles Ray, Richard Dix, Bebe Daniels, and countless others that the Great Crash of 1929 would have soon afterward on millions of American investors. Even Chaplin found it hard to adjust to the new medium. Of all the silent movie stars, Greta Garbo, with her husky, inimitable contralto voice, William Powell, and Louis Calhern would be among the most successful survivors. Though Gilbert and Clara Bow went on making pictures, they were never to be in the "top ten" again.

Some studios recoiled from the huge cost involved, and some of the most creative filmmakers deplored the advent of sound, just as their later peers were to deplore the advent of television, and for the same reasons, forecasting that the art of the cinema would be hopelessly compromised.

Halliwell's Film Guide, (New York: Charles Scribner's Sons) 6th edition, 1989.

Warner Studios, small fry at the time in Hollywood, had produced *The Jazz Singer* without realizing its far-reaching impact on the industry as a whole. Several studios had dabbled with sound. Now all were faced with a do-or-die situation, and massive investments in electrical hardware for the new soundstages.

The example of *The Jazz Singer* was not lost on them. The public wanted their stars to sing, and, as Adolph Zukor, president of Paramount, endlessly preached, the public was never wrong. The reaction of both Paramount and MGM was not simply to follow Warner, but to celebrate the advent of sound in new, spectacular ways, giving audiences not just dialogue and sound effects, but—far more important to the success of the new "talkies"—rich musical spectacles with elaborate orchestrations. This in turn led Hollywood to make a new kind of film and turn to a new kind of director, to European imports like Ernst Lubitsch and Rouben Mamoulian, themselves proven theater specialists with a passion for musical theater and European "comic opera" (as the earliest nineteenth-century musicals were once called).

Today, with the exception of *The Merry Widow*, directed by Lubitsch, and *Love Me Tonight*, directed by Mamoulian, which retain their own timeless magic, most of Hollywood's early musical-comedy films seem hopelessly old-fashioned, patterned on the same formula, with almost identical plots creakily obeying formal rules, and lacking the verbal brilliance subsequently provided on stage and screen by wordsmiths like Alan Jay Lerner. Though the work of the two backroom boy geniuses of the musical-film genre, composer Richard Rodgers and lyricist Lorenz Hart, remains an unfailing delight, some of the music and lyrics by other writers and composers working on these early, and by and large overpraised, musical-comedy films, were caricaturally pedestrian. We tend to remember the more enchanting bits, but to sit through *all* the musical-film classics of the early thirties starring Chevalier is a wearing, rather than an aesthetic, experience. It is impossible not to wince at some of the lyrics, of which

> "With every bit of liver
> My heart begins to quiver"

is perhaps the most embarrassing, but by no means a unique example.*

Maurice Chevalier rode the crest of the musical-film wave from the moment he arrived in America. His timing was perfect. He was made for the Hollywood musical. He had extensive acting, dancing, and film experience, as well as a remarkable stage presence. Not only was he unusually good-looking, but he spoke English *and he could sing.* For all his narrow range, his voice was deep, resonant, and despite a marked French accent, easily understandable. Alan Jay Lerner would later say that his was the most perfect diction of any actor he had ever encountered.[2]

Paramount's reaction to Lasky's "find," however, was, at least at first, totally negative. Lasky received a cable from Adolph Zukor "begging me to lose him, reminding me that the public had shown definite antagonism to even the suspicion of an accent, that we were already stuck with Ruth Chatterton [an English actress whose Hollywood debut had proved disappointing] and insisting that a full-blown French accent would be ten times as bad." Coming from Zukor, whose Hungarian accent was the delight of Hollywood (Gloria Swanson, herself a Paramount alumna, did a fabulous imitation of him), the comment must have amused Lasky, who was not the type to give up easily. "I was nettled but determined to brazen it through and get myself off the hook," he wrote. He decided to turn Chevalier's arrival in America into a major news event. Paramount's publicity department was put to work: The first step was to corral Hollywood's biggest names into a greeting committee. A few days before leaving for America, Chevalier received the following cable, addressed to him care of Paramount, Paris:

We want you to know we are looking forward to welcoming you as a member of the motion picture colony of Hollywood upon your arrival here and feel that the results of your screenwork in America will bring

---

*"Breakfast Table Love," the duet between Claudette Colbert and Maurice Chevalier (lyrics by Clifford Grey, music by Oscar Straus) in *The Smiling Lieutenant.*

you the same esteem and popularity from the peoples of all the world that now exists in the hearts of your countrymen.

It was signed by Mary Pickford, Norma Talmadge, Clara Bow, Bebe Daniels, Charles Chaplin, Douglas Fairbanks, Sr., Emil Jannings, Adolphe Menjou, Wallace Beery, William Powell, Clive Brook, Walter Wanger, Albert Kaufman, Jesse Lasky and, of course, the man who had shown the most reluctance to allow the deal to be struck, Adolph Zukor himself. Needless to say, in his own, later, autobiography, predictably entitled *The Public Is Never Wrong*, Zukor never mentioned this initial reservation.[3]

There was an additional reason for Lasky's acquisition of Chevalier: "Paramount was one of the few studios that thought ahead in terms of global markets and released foreign language versions—hence the importance of bilingual performers like Claudette Colbert, Adolphe Menjou," and, of course, Chevalier himself.[4] The Paramount movie theater was the largest in Paris. Chevalier knew it well. Before it became a movie theater, it had been the Théâtre de Variétés, one of the most celebrated Paris music halls, and he had appeared there often. The lavish Paramount cinema in Paris was only one of several in Europe.

Zukor was not the only one to have doubts about Paramount's gamble in its new investment: Chevalier himself, as he recalled in his memoirs, was jittery, fearful of the consequences of a possible flop. There was an emotional send-off at the Gare d'Austerlitz, orchestrated by Paramount's Paris publicity staff. On the *Île-de-France*, in the company of Yvonne Vallée, Max Ruppa, and their pet, a ruby-encrusted tortoise called Frankie, Chevalier expressed his private fears constantly. They were not allayed by the young Mark Hellinger, also on board, who told Chevalier that he had seen his show and did not think it would work in America. Hellinger was not yet the powerful Broadway figure he would soon become, but his was already an influential voice: "I'm awfully sorry, dear Maurice," he said, "I like you personally very much, but what can I do?" Chevalier worked himself into such a state that by the time the French liner dropped anchor, within sight of the Statue of

Liberty, to allow reporters on board, he had a high temperature and was experiencing familiar stage fright.*

News assignments aboard the *Île-de-France* were much sought-after among New York journalists and photographers, and they swarmed around Chevalier in large numbers. He was, of course, a legitimate news story, but there was another explanation for their presence. The *Île-de-France* was French territory, not subject to Prohibition laws, and Paramount flacks had set up a huge buffet, with large quantities of liquor, including Chevalier's own favorite drinks—Dubonnet and pink champagne. The "photo opportunity" alone lasted over an hour, and afterward Chevalier had his first experience of American reporting brashness. His nervousness was not apparent. He answered all their questions with a mixture of innocence, charm, and sincerity that delighted Paramount. Asked whether he felt France would pay its war debts to the United States—a front-page topic, with France refusing to pay because Germany had defaulted on reparations the French claimed were their due— his reply provoked sympathetic laughter: "I had no idea we owed anything to anybody!" He delighted his audience with his praise of American performers, singling out Chaplin and the Marx brothers for special mention. That night, his fever abated after his successful confrontation with the press, barely installed in a suite at the Ritz-Carlton, he and Yvonne went to the premiere of the Marx brothers' *Cocoanuts* on Broadway. While in New York, they also went to see Al Jolson in *The Singing Fool,* and visited his erstwhile Paris colleague W. C. Fields, currently starring in a Broadway show, backstage. Always a close observer of the talents of others, Chevalier noted two performers he instinctively felt would have a great future: Bert Lahr and Ginger Rogers, then eighteen.

Part of Paramount's publicity buildup of Chevalier involved a docu-

*There was a compelling reason for Casino de Paris stars to travel aboard the *Île-de-France.* The Casino de Paris safety curtain lowered at intermission consisted of a huge billboard advertising the "French Line." In lieu of payment, Henri Varna was granted a number of free transatlantic trips, which he distributed to his favorite performers. Before World War II, Chevalier's frequent crossings were paid for either by Paramount, or indirectly by Varna, or else by the French Line in return for a Chevalier concert appearance during the voyage.

mentary, to be distributed by Paramount News, directed by the French-born Robert Florey, shot on arrival in New York. *Bonjour New York!* made over four days in Manhattan, showed Chevalier, with Yvonne Vallée, on Fifth Avenue, Broadway, in Chinatown, on top of the Empire State Building, eating hot dogs—and smiling ceaselessly. If Chevalier had any reservations about Paramount extracting its pound of flesh (for he did not get paid for this), he never showed it. Chevalier got on well with Florey, a likable French-speaking Paramount director, who later would co-direct *Monsieur Verdoux* with Chaplin. Chevalier's one reservation was that he felt that "Florey drank too much." Like all foreigners, he was baffled by the restrictions caused by Prohibition, and by the profusion of speakeasies all over Manhattan. Florey was impressed by Chevalier's poise, his fluency in English, his unfailing good humor. He was a little less enthusiastic about Yvonne Vallée, though even she was able to conceal her true mood. In Florey's film, the Chevaliers seemed very much in love.

Lasky's publicists also created a genuine "news event"—a three-hundred-guest banquet at the Ritz-Carlton Hotel attended by the French consul general in New York, and assorted Franco-American guests, what Lasky called "a real hands across the sea affair." Lasky wrote:

> I had a moment of panic when I introduced Chevalier to the discriminating audience and begged him to favor us with a few "impromptu" songs (I had planned it for the night after his arrival so he'd have plenty of time to rehearse the pianist). But I needn't have worried. Although virtually no one in the room had ever heard of him, he captured the audience with his first song and held them spellbound through encore after encore. Even Zukor and Kent [Sidney Kent, another Paramount executive] who hadn't been happy about my impulsive commitment, were impressed.[5]

Lasky need not have worried. Without warning him beforehand, Chevalier introduced each of his songs with a short English preamble, telling the guests what they were about. In his memoirs, he claimed the idea had come to him on the spur of the moment, but in fact he had practiced the introductions in his *Île-de-France* stateroom for hours daily. His delivery impressed everyone by its apparent impromptu casualness—so successful that he would almost invariably use this technique in his later shows in Britain and the United States. The French consul general was among those speechifying before Chevalier was called on to sing, and Chevalier noted that he spoke with such a caricatural, almost incomprehensible French accent that "if he can get away with it, I can." Chevalier also recalled that, before dinner, and despite Prohibition, a variety of "disguised" foul-tasting cocktails with a kick like a mule were circulated among the guests, some of whom were seriously under the weather by the time the banquet began.

The dinner also led to an unforeseen coup for Lasky that none of his publicity men had bargained for. The next day,

> Flo Ziegfeld, who had been at the banquet, phoned and implored me to let him have the sensational artist for his *Midnight Frolic* on the New Amsterdam roof. I told him that, as a special favor to him, I'd postpone Chevalier's first picture long enough to let him appear on the Roof for six weeks if he wanted him badly enough to pay $5000 a week.[6]

In fact, Chevalier's first Hollywood film had run into problems, and shooting would be delayed six weeks at least. Lasky was overjoyed:

> Chevalier's salary started from the time he arrived in this country, but instead of losing $1500 a week waiting for the script to be written, we made $3500 a week*—and we couldn't have got a better publicity build-up for the picture if *we* had paid Ziegfeld $5000 a week to put him on the Roof.[7]

The fee was indeed unprecedented for a non-American with no star image. In 1929, $5,000 was worth at least $27,500—in purchasing terms, far, far more—and income tax, in those halcyon days, even in top brackets, never exceeded 3 percent.[8]

---

*Chevalier got approximately a third of the fee—fifteen hundred dollars.

The tables at the New Amsterdam, the most fashionable New York nightclub, were specially furnished with small wooden hammers—and audiences expressed their appreciation of Chevalier deafeningly by hitting their tables with them. By the time he and Yvonne took the train to Los Angeles six weeks later, he was already famous.

Whenever a prominent newcomer arrived to star in a Paramount movie, the studio pulled out all stops, and its publicity machine went into high gear. When the Chevaliers arrived at Los Angeles railroad station on October 29, 1928, after a five-day journey aboard the Santa Fe Express, they received a spectacular reception. French flags bedecked a banner across the platform reading WELCOME TO MAURICE CHEVALIER FROM FRANCE, a posse of leggy showgirls was in attendance, as well as Lasky and all Paramount's top stars, including even Chaplin himself. (Such a welcome was invariably geared to the guest's nationality—and fame: Marlene Dietrich's welcoming committee, in 1930, would include a German band in regimental regalia playing Viennese waltzes and Silesian polkas, but a slightly smaller, less prestigious group of stars.)

With only a brief stopover at the Beverly Wilshire, Chevalier was taken to a Paramount party at the Roosevelt Hotel, a repetition of the Ritz-Carlton affair, with Chevalier introducing his songs in English. The Fairbankses, Chaplin, Zukor, Lasky, and most of the stars under contract to Paramount, or who had signed the welcoming cable, were there. The event, Chevalier noted wryly, was unusual, combining, as it did, extreme adulation for him with expressions of extreme hostility toward France, for one of the speakers was none other than William Randolph Hearst, who embarked on a violent, and interminable, anti-French diatribe on France's "vindictive" anti-German policy. Richard Dix, the Hollywood star, in an aside to Chevalier, told him not to take either the praise or Hearst too seriously: This was Hollywood.

Chevalier was billed as the "French Al Jolson," and columnists reported his every move, including the fact that he pronounced Hollywood "holy wood." Paramount stars would do their best to make the Chevaliers feel at home, hosting parties for him in the next few weeks. The very night after his arrival, Chevalier had dinner with Chaplin, at the house of his future director, Henri d'Abadie d'Arrast. Chevalier was tongue-tied, and the evening was only partially successful. Chaplin, who came alone (he had just broken up with Lita Grey) wanted to talk about current events in Europe, the growing postwar disillusion, the catastrophic economic situation in Germany, the crisis between France and America over reparations, and the growing impact of Marxism-Leninism in Europe. Chevalier wanted to talk about practical, show-business matters that would be of use to him in Hollywood. As secretive about his own working methods as Chevalier himself, Chaplin proved reluctant to talk about them, and Chevalier's ignorance and lack of interest in international affairs made him an uninteresting dinner companion. They would never meet *en tête-à-tête* again. "I am too ordinary and he is too extraordinary," was Chevalier's verdict afterward.

Throughout his Hollywood years, though he occasionally entertained his fellow stars and Paramount executives, delighting them with impromptu performances, Chevalier never became a "socialite." Later, he would say that he had been too "unsophisticated" for the Hollywood "in" crowd. He remained, in many ways, insular as only the French can be outside their native habitat. Even some of the ways of Douglas Fairbanks, Sr., whom he admired more than any other living performer, baffled him: At a Sunday swimming-pool party, soon after his arrival in America, Fairbanks pushed the fully dressed Chevalier into the pool. He meant it as a boisterous piece of fun. Chevalier was outraged. He was, his fellow stars soon discovered, a very formal, serious, somewhat withdrawn guest, never at ease in the company of large numbers of people. He had mistakenly come to the party wearing a tailor-made gray-flannel suit (most of the other guests were casually dressed) and may have felt that Fairbanks's prank was a not-so-subtle critique of his attire. But his ill-concealed anger centered on more practical matters: He feared both his expensive, tailor-made suit, and his gold watch, were ruined.

He found Emil Jannings, the famous German actor and Academy Award winner (and Dietrich's former costar, "Professor Emmanuel Rath" in *The Blue Angel*) a more useful source than Chaplin, and a relief to turn to after overexposure to the exuberant Fairbanks crowd. Jannings told him never to worry about the presence of the cameras, to "be sincere and never worry about your looks." The new talking pictures, he said, needed personalities, not beauties. He also warned him about the sheer strain of appearing in "talkies." Chevalier learned, to his surprise, that he would be filming mostly at night, and that it would not be a pleasant experience. As Patrick McGilligan wrote, in his biography of George Cukor:

> Camera noise—the slightest noise—was picked up by giant unwieldy microphones. The cameras were placed in heavy, shrouded booths, insulated for sound. For further insulation, the crew hung huge blankets from the roof of the stage to the floor of the set. There was no air conditioning, the soundstages would become suffocatingly hot, and after two or three takes, everyone had to step out and get some air.[9]

Yvonne Vallée was appalled to discover that her husband would be filming most of the night and sleeping most of the day.

While Max Ruppa looked for a suitable, secluded house, which he soon found, Chevalier started familiarizing himself with Hollywood. He bought a small Ford and soon found his bearings. Thirty-seven years almost to the day (October 15, 1965) after his arrival, in a handwritten answer to a questionnaire submitted by Hedda Hopper, the doyenne of Hollywood columnists, Chevalier compared the Hollywood of the sixties with his first (1928) impressions. "Beverly Hills seems to have exactly the same kind of quietness it used to have. Very often I walk around Beverly Hills and I am absolutely alone, I can talk, or sing and I am alone, and it was the same 25 years ago. The big change is between Beverly Hills and Los Angeles along Wilshire. Twenty-five years ago it was almost countryside."

His official biography, part of the press kit compiled by Paramount, chronicled his early rise from rags to riches, his partnership with Mistinguett, emphasizing his huge reputation in France. It also contained a singular version of his return from his German P.O.W. stalag. Not content with the facts, an imaginative studio publicist turned the circumstances of his release into a wholly fictitious, more newsworthy tale. As the *Los Angeles Times* (along with many other newspapers throughout the United States, all based on the same handout) wrote:

If Maurice Chevalier hadn't had imagination and an imaginative pal—
when he was a German prisoner-of-war—he might not have been on the
American screen today. Because it was due to his imagination and that
of Joe Bridge, the said pal, that he escaped.

They were to put on an act one night to entertain the camp. "Let's
fix it so we can duck, and yet make it look like part of the act," suggested
Bridge. Chevalier assented, and they laid their plans. And so, while the
applause still rung on the air, the two were over the fence where they had
cut the wires, and were on their way, and Chevalier at once resumed his
career in Paris where Jesse Lasky discovered him.

The mention of Joe Bridge, his stalag companion, in the story,
suggested that Chevalier had indeed been debriefed by the studio about
his World War I experiences. It is highly unlikely that Paramount would
have released its Chevalier "bio" without his knowledge or approval, or
at any rate that of Max Ruppa. Nor was the Paramount "escape" version
to die an early death: The story was to pop up in the American media
for the next few years—right up to 1933, often with imaginative
embellishments: Bridge and Chevalier, in a variety of disguises, were said
to have walked their way across most of Germany (the Alten Grabow
camp was seventy-five miles south of Berlin). In some, they made their
way through the Franco-German lines; in others they reached the Swiss
border. Exactly how was never spelled out. One of the most detailed
accounts appeared in the *Philadelphia Daily News* on August 15, 1930,
under the byline of J. H. Keen, its dramatic editor:

His escape from the German POW camp was something of a strategic
military move. When his health had mended, he devoted his time to
entertaining others and by staging shows. His success established him as
one of the more important prisoners. One night he planned a show, and
with a cunning eye, cast himself as a Red Cross worker, so that he might
be outfitted in this garb which was a sort of open sesame in any portion
of the "war area." At the conclusion of the show, he calmly walked from
place to place, still wearing the Red Cross trappings, and finally succeeded in gaining the French lines.

The story was important on several counts: It revealed Chevalier's tendency to indulge in, or at any rate condone, "hype," as well as his contempt for the press in general; it foreshadowed other, less innocent, manipulations indulged in fifteen years later, at the time of the liberation of Paris, when he so successfully fought charges of collaboration and made his wartime record look far better than it actually was.

More important, it underlined Hollywood's mastery over the media, the Hollywood press corps' excessive reliance on studio-fabricated hand-outs, and, above all, the extraordinary docility and slavish deference to the studios of most Hollywood reporters in the early thirties. Not a single investigative-minded reporter challenged Paramount's version, or even bothered to check it. Admittedly, there were no permanent French correspondents in Los Angeles at the time, but there were plenty of British and American foreign correspondents in Paris who could have reacted speedily, and gotten in touch with the French Defense Ministry, or with Joe Bridge himself. No Hollywood editor ever requested clarification of this unlikely feat of arms.

At the time, accounts of genuine, daring escapes from prisoner-of-war camps, written by the protagonists themselves, were becoming a best-selling literary "genre" in the English-speaking world, and the improbable aspect of the Paramount version of Chevalier's "escape" must have been palpable. With hindsight, their lack of reaction could be explained only by the power of the studios. By 1931, Chevalier had begun denying the "escape" version in interviews, but even after he had left Paramount and gone to MGM in 1934, the myth persisted. An MGM publicity handout, in the form of an "authorized" life story by Howard Strickling, described how "Chevalier and another Frenchman, also an actor, by the way, walking out of Alten Grabow disguised as field hospital attendants. Slowly and cautiously they reached the French lines."

It was all part of the climate of the times. The star system had created larger-than-life characters. With scant respect for the general public, the studios' imaginative publicity departments concocted innumerable background notes about their stars' impressive if imaginary athletic prowess, their high-minded hobbies and pursuits. Jeanette MacDonald's favorite occupation was listed as "collecting the works of Victor Hugo"; Kay Francis "longed to be a trapeze artist." The public had to be able to believe in the perfection of the Hollywood stars they worshiped, in their happily ordered domestic lives and their unquestioning adherence to the American way of life. When, as in the case of "Fatty" Arbuckle, or the murder of director Bill Taylor, the seamy side of Hollywood was exposed, the consequences were devastating.*

The "star system" required absolute moral purity among the chosen. This explained the tyranny Hollywood tycoons like Louis B. Mayer, Zukor, Zanuck, and others exerted over their protégés, not only by contract, (the much-feared Paramount "moral turpitude" clause, which could lead to instant dismissal) but as marriage brokers and moral watchdogs—though they themselves scarcely practiced what they preached. When Zukor discovered that Douglas Fairbanks, Sr., and Mary Pickford were "seeing each other" (both, at the time, were married to other people), he made elaborate plans to conceal any trace of extramarital infidelity. "Thou shall not be found out" was the cardinal rule.

By tacit consent, ambitious Hollywood reporters and columnists did their best to further the studios' platonic image of their favorite stars. Until the infamous, but in retrospect refreshing, *Confidential* magazine began shattering this gentlemen's agreement (in 1937), columnists like the much-feared Louella Parsons and Hedda Hopper wielded amazing power, acting as they did both as self-appointed moral watchdogs *and* purveyors of gossip. Hopper had been a bit player in silent films before finding journalism more rewarding, and producers would later give Louella Parsons occasional cameo parts in their films more to ensure good write-ups than out of a regard for her talent. Both proceeded by allusion and innuendo, and while they usually confined themselves to simpering over the "lovely parties" and exemplary private lives of the

---

*"Fatty" Arbuckle faced murder charges after an alleged orgy in 1921 during which a starlet died. Though he was acquitted, his career ended abruptly, and he became a pariah. The unsolved mystery of director Bill Taylor's murder in 1922 virtually ended the career of Mabel Normand.

terrified stars they battened on, they could also destroy careers in a single sentence. Interpreting the hidden meanings of their syrupy prose remains an exercise comparable to deciphering editorials in the daily Beijing *Ren Min Ri Bao* during the Chinese Cultural Revolution or *Pravda* at the height of Stalin's hegemony over Russia.

On *her* arrival in Hollywood, many years later, Ingrid Bergman would be amazed by the extent of the power of the Hedda Hopper–Louella Parsons tandem, who were professional rivals but close friends. Bergman, while completing a picture produced by Walter Wagner, refused to attend a party honoring Louella Parsons, which he had organized for promotional purposes. She did not like the columnist's prying, two-faced ways, she said. Wagner told Bergman, "You *have* to go. *Everybody* must go. She has a list of those who refuse to go and we'll be in trouble with the picture." "I knew they were against me because I never sent them presents," Bergman said. "They couldn't get into their houses on Christmas Eve for all the gifts they were sent!"[10] Bergman was one of the Hollywood stars whose later career was almost wrecked by the malicious attacks and innuendos penned by Hopper and Parsons after her love affair with Roberto Rossellini began. Chevalier never made the mistake of underrating either lady.

Vestiges of the old Hollywood order remain to this day: Access is everything, as editors and show-business reporters well know—and even now, can be made to depend on the reporter's observance of the rules imposed by high-handed stars and producers. At the time of Chevalier's Hollywood debut, the power of the studios was far more awesome: The newsmen and women on the Hollywood beat who prospered were those who worked within the system, emulating the techniques of the unspeakable Parsons and Hopper.

Chevalier instinctively understood the situation. Perhaps because he was already used to an even more docile, malleable French press, he knew exactly when to appear to be forthcoming, and whom to cultivate: From the moment he arrived in Hollywood, he was extraordinarily deferential to both Hopper and Parsons. He flattered them grossly, even, in the case of Louella Parsons, inviting her to stay with him in Cannes, taking her into his confidence again and again, occasionally using her as a sounding board, knowing she would not betray him because she valued his friendship and access too much.

As all power brokers know, the method works uncommonly well. John F. Kennedy, many years later, would become especially adept at this kind of "off the record" manipulation, which appeals as much to reporters' vanity as to their sense of Boy Scout morality. Chevalier had an additional advantage: his charm and sexual aura, for after his first picture he became a sex symbol, not just in Hollywood but all over America and Europe, wherever in fact moving pictures were shown. Soon he would be pursued by squealing fans and mature women alike, the Elvis Presley and Mick Jagger of his day.

Paramount's extensive distribution network ensured maximum exposure. By 1929, it controlled over one thousand cinemas throughout the United States, including parts of rural America where it had a virtual monopoly, and a million Americans bought tickets every week to go to Paramount-owned or licensed cinemas, so that when Chevalier became an overnight star, he became instantly known not just in the big cities, but all over rural America as well. And because Paramount had an aggressive international marketing strategy, his films were seen in Europe (in French in all French-speaking countries) very soon after they were made. This new Chevalier cult, this overnight rise to stardom, which Paramount itself had not expected, changed his persona, though it never put an end to his insecurity.

Innocents of Paris was no masterpiece. Like so many Hollywood films of the time, it used a few stock shots to establish the setting of the intrigue—Paris—but the studio decor was creakily unconvincing. The intended director, Henri d'Abadie d'Arrast, who had grave reservations about the script, bowed out and was quickly replaced by Richard Wallace, a young competent "line" producer. A hybrid, with some "silent version" titles, dialogue, and song, the film told a trite story about a small-time Parisian junk dealer (Chevalier) with a passion for vaudeville who saves a small boy from drowning, after his disturbed mother has thrown him in the Seine. The junk dealer/songster locates the boy's grandparents and falls in love with the boy's young aunt (played by Sylvia Beecher). To keep her love, he agrees to give up vaudeville, but his farewell performance is such a success that she relents, and they live happily ever after.

Chevalier, too, was uneasy about the script, and insisted on the inclusion of some of his better-known French songs (including "Valentine") as well as the new hit song that began "Every little breeze/Seems to whisper Louise," specially written for the film. In a "prologue" to the film, along with the credits, he introduced himself to his American audience, and explained why the film, though set in Paris, was spoken in English. This was added because Lasky recalled how well Chevalier's introductory remarks had worked at his initial Waldorf-Astoria performance. Chevalier recalled that he was so inexperienced that he had no idea that the six-year-old child actor, David Durand, was continually upstaging him on the set, until Richard Wallace pointed this out.

Variety's review was totally negative ("Neither Maurice Chevalier nor his songs will last very long over here"), but nearly all other newspapers praised his performance to the skies, while admitting that the film's other virtues were hard to find. The *Los Angeles Examiner* said it was "a disappointment, but Chevalier seems to have survived the ordeal of a picture that could have been better," *The New York Times* said that "without Chevalier this latest specimen of audible films would be a sad affair," and that "when he is off screen the suspense consists of waiting until he reappears, to sing or talk in his charming manner." *Sound Waves* said Chevalier possessed "a pantomimic ability topped only by Charles Chaplin, a personality topped by no one living, a keen sense of humor and a rare histrionic talent." But the *Philadelphia Enquirer* (June 4, 1929) expressed mild disappointment: "In spite of his Parisian music-hall reputation one is inclined to think that his singing is somewhat overrated."

The impact of *Innocents of Paris* induced Lasky to put him on a far more lucrative five-year contract (far exceeding the original $25,000 fee per film and guaranteeing him a percentage of the gross), and his new stardom turned him overnight, between films, into one of the most sought-after nightclub performers in America. With each film, his repertoire of English songs grew and grew. Paramount, and later MGM, would provide Chevalier, at no cost, with invaluable new material.

He was quick to take advantage of this, appearing onstage with the California Ramblers at the Million-Dollar Theater in Los Angeles shortly after the general release of *Innocents of Paris*, at eight thousand dollars for a week's work. He followed this up with an eight-week booking, again at Ziegfeld's New Amsterdam Roof, at five thousand dollars a week, with Paul Whiteman's orchestra and a crooner ensemble, the Rhythm Boys, that included the as-yet-unknown Bing Crosby. This time Paramount got none of it. The New York audience's response was even more enthusiastic than for his first appearance. Night after night, they "whistled in the grand old-fashioned manner, putting fingers between their teeth," wrote Walter Winchell. He could not know that the first time this happened, Chevalier was scared out of his wits: In France whistling was the audience's ultimate rejection of a performer. His New Amsterdam routine included his new song, "Louise," and not only "Valentine," but a series of "Valentine" imitations—as sung, in turn, by a nervous performer, a patriot, a German, and—this one brought the house down—an effeminate performer. Chevalier, a lifelong homophobe, usually included at least one such number in his nightclub repertoire.

Paramount, like other major studios, was a highly efficient assembly line, turning out films like model-T Fords. Even before *Innocents of Paris* confirmed Chevalier's personal promise, he was being groomed for another picture. This was *The Love Parade*, directed by Ernst Lubitsch, then one of Paramount's most important, influential directors. It was to bring Chevalier consecration as a major Hollywood star. It would also lead to typecasting he would finally rebel against, with catastrophic consequences for his subsequent career. Because of its continental affiliates, Paramount offered directors far more latitude than actors, who, time after time, were "locked into type and ground into a truism."[11] The studio displayed far more tolerance for the demands and eccentricities of its directors than toward its stars under contract. In 1929, fresh from France and desperately eager to please, Chevalier was unaware of Paramount's reputation.

Idiosyncratic talent apart, the studio's respect for directors was one of the reasons for the ultrarapid promotion of Ernst Lubitsch, a tough, aggressively "European" individualist and quintessential Berliner who remained nostalgically attached to his pre-Nazi German cultural past until his early death in 1947. (His loss would be felt around the world. At his funeral, Billy Wilder turned to William Wyler and said, "He's dead." And Wyler replied, "Worse than that: There won't be any Lubitsch movies anymore.") Lubitsch became one of Paramount's most influential directors, promoted, in 1934, to be its head of production.

When he arrived in Hollywood, in 1922, Lubitsch already had a solid reputation. Like Jesse Lasky, he had considerable stage experience. In pre–World War I Germany, his stocky physique and somewhat saturnine looks had not prevented him from becoming a well-known comic actor. From 1914 on, he had become first a theater then a silent-film director in Berlin, specializing in historical spectaculars (*Carmen, Anne Boleyn, Pharaoh's Wife*). But above all he loved the music of Oscar Straus, the plays of Lothar Schmidt, and the operettas of Franz Lehar, and really wanted to make films with an "Imperial Austro-Hungarian" flavor. He had made only one of these for Paramount, the silent *Student Prince* (about a prince who falls in love with a barmaid), in 1927.

It was a happy coincidence for Lubitsch that the new Hollywood craze for musical comedy began just as his own reputation as a recently imported film director was steadily growing. He was one of the few directors to attend Paramount's executive-committee meetings, where major decisions were made (Jesse Lasky rarely attended them) and was thus able to influence the studio's filmmaking policy directly.

Film historians have analyzed Lubitsch's films in humorless detail, with a thoroughness he himself would have mocked, for the "Lubitsch touch" owed a great deal to his own sardonic sense of humor and ability to parody his favorite themes. "The last of the genuine continentals," as Andrew Sarris called him, was indelibly influenced, in his youth, by the Austro-Hungarian "comic opera" froth and pageantry, consigned to memory, if not to oblivion, by the First World War. The new "talking pictures" era allowed him to exorcise his nostalgia in films (with Chevalier) that could not have been made before 1929—for before that date there was no sound—or after 1934, when the self-imposed, puritanical Motion Picture Association "morality code" made it impossible to deal with sexual themes on film as he would have liked. Lubitsch's few films with Chevalier before the stifling MPA code came into force show "how erotic Paramount's elegance in fact was, how deftly it uncovers the trouble in paradise."[12] One of the surprises of early Lubitsch musical films is their potent if oblique sexual content and their constant "double entendres"—contributing to no small extent to Chevalier's extraordinary reputation as a sex symbol, but attracting mature women, and men, as well as teenagers. Lubitsch later showed he was also capable of directing elegant *comédies de moeurs,* as well as satires with serious themes (which he managed to turn into delicious lighthearted comedies) like *If I Had a Million, Ninotchka,* and *To Be or Not to Be.* Like Billy Wilder, another, later refugee from Germany, he brought to Hollywood a literacy, irony, and Jewish humor, both verbal and visual, which most of his contemporaries (with the obvious exception of the Marx brothers) lacked, for all the prevalence of Jewish talent in Hollywood.

When first approached by Paramount, Chevalier balked, initially, at playing the youthful "Count Alfred," the Ruritanian sexual charmer summoned home to become his queen's consort in *The Love Parade,* and was convinced that Lubitsch himself would find another, more suitable actor once he had seen him in his elaborate court uniform. He pointed out he was over forty-one ("In that case, he should stop acting like a twenty-year-old prima donna" was Lubitsch's reaction) and that his image was a popular, plebeian one.

Lubitsch's professionalism, and thoroughness, caused Chevalier to change his mind. He was flattered to be invited to script and music conferences, and to find that his advice was taken seriously, except for one, crucial area—casting. As Jesse Lasky wrote later, Paramount

> had no actresses who sang. . . . I began to look around for the right girl, and I made a point of catching Shubert's show featuring a new singer one of my assistants had told me about. I liked Jeanette MacDonald so well I secured her as Chevalier's leading lady, and turned the pair over to Ernst Lubitsch. . . .[13]

The "assistant" was none other than Lubitsch himself, always on the lookout for new talent, who had seen her in Chicago, dancing in an otherwise eminently forgettable extravaganza produced by the Shuberts called *Boom Boom*. At the time he thought, If this girl can sing, it would be a miracle. She could, somewhat operatically. Then he discovered that MacDonald had done a screen test for Paramount, in 1928, for a film called *Nothing But the Truth*, and that nothing had come of it. Paramount executives now had second thoughts, and Lasky was won over.

Once Lasky had spoken, the choice of Jeanette MacDonald, then twenty-seven, (though she claimed, in her official Paramount biography, that she was twenty-three), was never in doubt. The Shuberts asked for $75,000 to "let her go," but settled for less, and Jeanette MacDonald showed up in Hollywood with her mother and her business manager, a former New York stockbroker called Bob Ritchie who was also her lover (or perhaps her husband—no Hollywood columnist ever solved that particular mystery). When they first met, neither Chevalier nor Jeanette MacDonald could imagine to what extent, over the next few years, their relationship would degenerate into visceral mutual dislike bordering on hatred. Even on their first film, it was clear their incompatibilities were major ones.

Jeanette MacDonald irritated Chevalier considerably. He was unimpressed by her conventional beauty: She was definitely not his type. He was attracted to slight, dark-haired women; in his eyes, she was too blond, too much of a prude, with terrible taste in clothes and, despite her dancing skills, little natural grace. He disliked her agent, Ritchie, and his hold over her. Lubitsch, whose taste ran toward ample women, felt she was too skinny and made her drink malted milks and eat huge meals. By the time shooting was over, she had gained fifteen pounds.

Jeanette MacDonald would later call Chevalier "the biggest bottom-pincher I have ever come across." This habit apart, Chevalier's conduct on the set was exemplary. Always the consummate professional, he practiced his numbers and repeated his lines endlessly, and was invariably prepared for his daily "takes." MacDonald was often late, quickly revealed a temperamental streak and a violent temper, was quick to take offense, and treated the "little people" at Paramount with patronizing

hauteur. As Lubitsch later said, "She was very, very pretty and knew it
. . . but she was underdeveloped within."[14] Very soon after coming to
Hollywood, she developed the persona of a *grande dame,* well aware of her
value. Even in her early films, she displayed something of the stage
pomposity of a Margaret Dumont.

The cigar-chomping Lubitsch used a mixture of Berliner humor and
avuncular charm to coax the appropriate performance out of her. At first,
on the set, he called her "Mac." She retaliated by calling him "Lu." He
then called her "Donald." She addressed him as "Itsch." He reverted to
"Miss MacDonald," but continued to kid her, on the set, in his comical,
accented English. "Ach, you domb gurl," he shouted again and again, in
mock anger, when she failed to understand his directions. "If I'm so
dumb, why did you hire me?" she asked. "Ach, I vos even domber, that
day, I guess." In private, Lubitsch, too, was irritated by her prudishness;
she neither drank nor smoked nor would tolerate bad language, and
always worried that her bedroom costumes were too *déshabillé.* Like
Chevalier, Lubitsch puzzled over her relationship with Bob Ritchie, her
lover, and *his* relationship with her ubiquitous stage mother, for they
were an inseparable threesome.

Chevalier was astounded by the ease with which Jeanette MacDonald
managed to avoid the curiosity of Hollywood gossip columnists. "At the
time we worked together," he later wrote,

> She was very much in love with Bob Ritchie. But he was not the man for
> her. Their marriage, or arrangement—although I'm sure they were mar-
> ried, otherwise it's difficult to understand why she allowed him to
> mistreat her so—never seemed to interest any of the columnists or cause
> any gossip. And yet Ritchie would often come on the set, insult her,
> throw a jealous tantrum and leave after he had reduced her to tears. A
> moment later, when it was time to film a scene, she was ready to work,
> all smiles. . . . I never thought she had much of a sense of humor. When
> we worked together she always objected to anyone telling a risqué story."

No wonder film crews would later call Jeanette MacDonald "the iron
butterfly."

A trained singer in the operatic tradition, Jeanette MacDonald had nothing but contempt for Chevalier's loud voice and excessively limited range. For all their temperamental differences, *The Love Parade* was probably the only film where both stars kept their feelings in check and remained unfailingly polite to each other.

With one exception—Pierre de Rohan in the *New York Telegraph*, who found only "tuneless songs, trite dialogue and awkward attempts to introduce sex jokes"—critics greeted *The Love Parade* with almost ecstatic acclaim. At this vantage point, the praise lavished on it after its release in November 1929 seems exaggerated, almost inexplicable. Even de Rohan referred to Chevalier as "the outstanding personality of the screen," doing his best with weak material, and he was actually nominated for an Oscar, which went instead to George Arliss. In retrospect, the film seems no more than a rough, imperfect sketch for the later, far wittier, more sophisticated Lubitsch-directed *The Smiling Lieutenant* and *The Merry Widow* (the last film Jeanette MacDonald and Chevalier would do together). *The Love Parade* has its share of double entendres, especially in the sexually allusive Chevalier songs "Nobody's Using It Now," and "Anything to Please the Queen." Its opening, with the rousing, durable hit song "Paris, Stay the Same," makes one hope for more in the same vein. Alas, it never comes. All the songs in the film are divorced from its action, never an intrinsic part of it. Like all but a handful of musical films, it suffered from an uneasy blend of sung music and spoken dialogue: For no compelling dramatic reason, at regular intervals throughout the movie, its characters simply burst into song. The British actor Lupino Lane, playing Chevalier's valet, had a delightful cameo role, as did Lillian Roth (the queen's personal maid). In commedia dell'arte tradition, their own love affair paralleled that of the two principal stars. There was also a tiny role for the star of silent comic films Ben Turpin, fallen on hard times. As usual in Lubitsch films of this kind, the court dignitaries (admirals, cabinet ministers) were played by overweight, coarse-looking character actors with heavy New York accents. Looking for artistic or social significance where there was none, Lubitsch scholars would later claim such "countercasting" was deliberate, part of his masterful sense of derision—the cynical European's way of voicing an oblique protest at a retrograde social order. George Cukor, who witnessed the making of these films at close hand, believed Lubitsch had no such subtleties in mind: Simply, "Lubitsch never really spoke English very well."[15]

During most of *The Love Parade*, Chevalier staves off the increasingly direct advances of the queen of Sylvania (Jeanette MacDonald in vaporous negligees most of the time), and part of the film's originality lies in Lubitsch's depiction of Chevalier the seducer as a mere sex object at the hands of an increasingly shrewish, jealous woman. Chevalier displayed quiet dignity under adversity, the victim, for most of the film, of a spoiled woman's tantrums, provoked, as is made clear in various ways, by sexual frustration. *The Love Parade*, in its small way, was a musical *Taming of the Shrew* as well as Aristophanes' *Lysistrata* with a twist: Chevalier withholds all sex from his queenly bride until he gets his due: a fair share in the running of their Ruritanian kingdom. The happy end is somewhat contrived: The queen eventually demurs, and the satin sheets of the huge royal canopied bed eventually become suitably rumpled.

Perhaps only Chevalier could appreciate the true irony of the situation, for some aspects of *The Love Parade* plot were not all that different from his real-life predicament. In Hollywood, he complained to a friend,[16] Yvonne was becoming unreasonably, almost pathologically jealous: She insisted on accompanying him to the studio, remaining in his dressing room all day; she brought Chevalier his home-cooked lunch; she loathed the parties they were forced to attend, and, once there, monitored his every move. She hated Hollywood: As so often was the case where imported French stars and their companions were concerned, French insularity and cultural snobbishness clashed with the simpler, homespun American values. One Hollywood writer cattily noted that Chevalier bringing his wife to a party was like "taking an old ham sandwich to a banquet." By this he did not imply that she was ugly or undesirable—she was neither—simply that her ill temper and unpredictable, but usually morose, moods were palpable when she mingled with the Fairbankses, the Joan Crawfords, and all the Hollywood dignitaries who tried to make the Chevaliers feel at home. Adolphe Menjou, who had become a close friend of the Chevaliers, perhaps sensing

Yvonne's loneliness, gave her a wire-haired terrier. She called it "Adolphe." It died soon afterward, and so did Yvonne's ruby-encrusted tortoise. When visiting, she hardly spoke, and systematically resisted all American attempts to involve her in local community affairs, acquiring a reputation for standoffishness. In all interviews, she was at pains to keep up the pretense of a blissful marriage.

Paramount worked Chevalier hard: Immediately after *The Love Parade*, he was required to figure in *Paramount on Parade*, a musical extravaganza—in essence, nothing but filmed vaudeville—made up of twenty unrelated song-and-dance sketches, all supervised by Chevalier's old acquaintance Elsie Janis, still a huge star herself but now semiretired, spending most of her time nursing her ailing mother. Janis herself figured in one of the numbers, and wrote several of the songs in the show. (By this time, her relations with Chevalier had cooled considerably. In neither star's memoirs is there any reference to the other in connection with *Paramount on Parade*.) Chevalier made three appearances, as an Apache, as a French gendarme (in "All I Want Is Just One Girl"), and in the finale, "Sweeping the Clouds Away," as a chimney sweep with a chorus of leggy girls, all directed by Lubitsch. One performer made a great impression on Chevalier: This was Kay Francis, in a toreador number culled from Bizet. Not yet a star (her most important film role so far, her second, had been in the Marx brothers' *Cocoanuts*, where she did little but try to escape Harpo's gropings) her eye-catching dark-haired beauty and her independent, "fast" life-style were causing a great deal of comment on the Paramount lot. When Chevalier first became aware of her, she was twenty-six according to her official Paramount biography but actually three years older (according to the late, far more reliable Leslie Halliwell's *Film Guide*).[17] Evelyn Brent, then another up-and-coming star with a showgirl background, also in *Paramount on Parade*, was bowled over by Chevalier's charm—and later hinted that he had not been indifferent to her either.

While he was hard at work, Chevalier's adored mother, La Louque, died suddenly, on May 18, 1929. All transatlantic travel was by sea, and he would not have been able to attend her funeral in time even if he had been able to take time off and interrupt shooting to do so. Indeed, so secretive was he in his private affairs that, Yvonne apart, very few of his colleagues were aware he had just suffered the worst loss of his life.

He himself was to play a strange trick on his readers, and indeed on most of his future biographers, for he later wrote that he heard the news of his mother's death on the first day's shooting of *The Smiling Lieutenant* (actually made a year and a half later) and, indeed, graphically described how, at the actual time of her death, he had strange premonitions, and suddenly, during that fateful night, felt unaccountably close to death himself. In another, shortened version of his memoirs *(Bravo Maurice)*, he wrote that his premonition occurred the day he was due to give a concert at the New York Metropolitan Opera—again no date was mentioned—and that he found assuming the persona of "the Smiling Lieutenant" an enormous strain. Just why he shifted the date of her death is unclear; La Louque was by far the most important person in his life, and he cannot have been unaware of the real date of her death. Perhaps, in retrospect, he was angry at himself for not returning home for her funeral, and deliberately switched the date to the moment when he was just starting a new film, to give himself—and posterity—a more convincing alibi for not returning to France. It is even possible that because he had kept the news of her death secret when it actually occurred, in 1929, he was able to use its pretext to barricade himself in his dressing room a year later, avoiding all unwelcome contact with his colleagues during a particularly black depression brought on by his own marital problems.

When, after the final wraps of *The Love Parade* and *Paramount on Parade* but before their release, the Chevaliers returned to France in August 1929, he immediately became conscious of his new fame: Though Paramount's Paris publicists had something to do with it, there was no mistaking his new star status, or the significance of the huge crowds waiting to greet him at the Gare d'Austerlitz. *Innocents of Paris* (billed in France as *La Chanson de Paris*) had been a huge hit. Fans besieged the Crillon Hotel (where they stayed briefly before visiting La Louque's grave and leaving for Chevalier's Riviera home) to such an extent that the Chevaliers had to change hotels, moving to the more discreet Château de Madrid. That autumn he capitalized on his fame with a hugely lucrative two-week appearance at the Théâtre de l'Empire in Paris at an unprecedentedly high nine thousand dollars a week.

Yvonne Vallée cut short their first Paris stay deliberately, insisting they leave for La Bocca as soon as possible. International stardom was changing Chevalier, she knew. Hollywood was not just the golden Mecca ensuring a huge income and a constantly expanding repertoire of songs. For all its surface puritanism and "moral turpitude" clauses, it was the place where seemingly limitless quantities of easily available beautiful young women were eager to do anything to break into pictures. As his new American friends had been quick to whisper in Chevalier's ear when no ladies were present, its real attraction lay in the fact that it was a quintessentially masculine sexual paradise, a well-stocked bull pen for privileged producers, directors, and stars.

He had not, so far, been able to take advantage of this. But Max Ruppa, whose influence derived solely from his access to Chevalier, had, and his forays among showgirls and aspiring starlets had quickly become the talk of the town.[18] No wonder Chevalier found Yvonne's constant, motherly attentions highly frustrating. For Hollywood, as he quickly discovered, also had more than its share of the "exceptional women" he was instinctively drawn to, and these, he had sensed—unlike their complicated French counterparts—were simply anticipating his first move. He could hardly wait.

His marriage was at an even more unsatisfactory stage than when he first left for Hollywood. During those few weeks in La Bocca, however, the Chevaliers declared a truce: It was the one place where they could recapture the past and relive their time together in Saujon when, totally demoralized and convinced his career was over, Chevalier had turned to Yvonne for comfort and mother-love, and been tenderly nursed back to health by his gentle, admiring companion.

He needed her still: not for sex, certainly, nor really for companionship. What he required, then and for the rest of his life, was someone who never tired of hearing him voice his fears, enumerate his past successes, outline his future career plans, and tell of the esteem in which he was held by important people. These were his favorite topics of conversation, and he returned to them obsessively, again and again. For this was his only way of exorcising his lifelong, irrational dread of poverty and failure.

His mother had once fulfilled this role. Now that she was gone, it was a price Yvonne willingly paid, that summer of 1929 in La Bocca, to have him to herself once more.

CHAPTER 10

"Marlene and I were just good friends."

—Maurice Chevalier

The success of *The Love Parade* turned Chevalier into a star phenomenon surpassed only by Gary Cooper, Clark Gable, and a handful of others. "He had become," said Jean Sablon, "even more of a star in America than Al Jolson himself."[1] When he returned to Hollywood in October 1929, with Yvonne (and seven French newsmen in tow, invited to Hollywood by Paramount) he knew just how valuable he had become to Paramount. The studio readily acceded to his request that it foot the bill for two round trips to Paris every year for the Chevaliers, their cook, and Max Ruppa.

Love Parade reviews were ecstatic, at least as far as Chevalier himself was concerned. According to the *American*, "it more nearly approaches perfection than anything of the sort yet filmed." Louella Parsons, with a slight barb at Jeanette MacDonald, wrote that "It is Monsieur Chevalier's personality that is chiefly responsible for its great success. Scenes when Chevalier is not on the screen are flat and uninteresting." The *New York World*'s Quint Martin, noting its "silk sheets and languorous nights," felt that its "moments of clever- ness . . . are for the most part the result of M. Chevalier's own unquenchable, irresistible spirit. He is rather distressingly in poverty in the matter of individual material in song, in dance or in story, but he is a fascinating devil, and even so will have his day." The critics' somewhat muted praise for Jeanette MacDonald was one of the reasons why, temporarily, Paramount let her go, bringing her back later to make *One Hour with You* with Chevalier. Her knowledge that Chevalier had done nothing to make Paramount change its mind—bad-mouthing her, she suspected, behind her back—did nothing to improve their relationship.

Though the 1929 stock-market crash had just shaken America to the core, its ripples would not affect Hollywood for some time: Paramount's 1930 profits rose to a record $21 million before they started to plum- met, and its eventual bankruptcy would be the result not only of a drop in moviegoers, but of a multitude of unfortunate financial speculations. At first, before the Depression took hold, both American and European audiences alike continued to flock to the movies. Tickets were afford- able; though they might come as high as two dollars for galas and premieres, they cost as little as ten cents in small towns in the heart of rural America. In the immediate post-Crash mood, with the Depression just beginning, the more escapist the film, the more successful it was— another reason for Chevalier's stardom.

Between Paramount assignments, Chevalier found he now com- manded astronomical fees for guest appearances: The San Francisco Motor Show's organizers were slightly taken aback, in December 1929, shortly after the Crash, when Chevalier asked for—and obtained— $25,000, pointing out that Paul Whiteman and his large band had been hired for that sum the previous year. "Maybe," Chevalier replied, "but you are getting Chevalier and his trimmer."[2] This, the *Los Angeles Examiner* pointed out, was a lot of money for a week's work involving a single daily forty-minute appearance. Chevalier, and *The Love Parade*, also bene- fited from a different kind of publicity that winter: In a technological breakthrough as important, in its day, as the first satellite transmission, its sound track was beamed by radio, via Sydney, to the Antarctic base of Admiral Byrd, the famous explorer.

In Chevalier's next two films, *The Big Pond (La Grande Mer)* and *Playboy of Paris (Le Petit Café)* he reverted to more familiar "popular" roles—as a worker in the first, a waiter in the second. Neither film was particularly distinguished. *The Big Pond* was chiefly memorable for the appearance, among the writing credits, of Preston Sturges, for Claudette Colbert's first major film role (as an American heiress Chevalier falls in love with), and for the song "You Brought a New Kind of Love to Me," ("If a nightingale/Could sing like you . . .") immortalized shortly afterward in the Marx brothers' *Night at the Opera*, also a Paramount film. *Playboy of Paris* was adapted from a play by the French writer Tristan Bernard, a friend of Chevalier's and part of the Boeuf sur le Toit circle. Both films were made in two versions—French and English—and some of the episodes were reshot in French at Paramount's Astoria studio in New York, with Yvonne Vallée playing the wealthy café owner's daughter (in the film, she is called Yvonne too) in her one and only Hollywood role.

Critics felt the Chevalier magic was as strong as ever, but were slightly less gushing: "It is disappointing to observe Mr. Chevalier with a millstone of a story," wrote Mordaunt Hall in *The New York Times*, of *The Big Pond*, while even Louella Parsons, in the Hearst papers, admitted that "I doubt, without Chevalier, if the story [of *Playboy of Paris*] could be classed as anything more than mediocre." *Outlook*, (October 30, 1930) openly deplored its new content: "Hats off, ladies and gentlemen, flags at half-mast and a roll of drums if you please! Maurice Chevalier, the light-hearted Frenchman, is no more. In his place we have a stereotyped silk-hatted comedian who plays drunk and behaves just as all other second-rate American comedians behave. . . . The machine has got hold of Chevalier and squeezed all the personality out of him. I suppose this is an example of efficiency and international art."

Chevalier was experiencing what most artists rapidly propelled to stardom have come to accept as one of the rules of the media game: Proprietary critics, after unearthing new talents and praising them to the skies, almost invariably enjoy savaging their discoveries once they have become famous. Though he would later claim that he remained su-premely indifferent to what the press wrote about him, he was in fact surprisingly thin-skinned, highly sensitive to criticism and quick to see slights where none were intended.

He could hardly complain: For all the inadequacies of both *The Big Pond* and *Playboy of Paris,* he had, in a remarkably short space of time, established himself as America's heartthrob for young and mature women alike. Louella Parsons, one of his biggest fans, returned to this theme again and again. Of *The Big Pond,* she wrote, "Judging from the hundreds of letters we receive dwelling upon his insouciance and his love-making qualities, perhaps it's just as well there is only one Chevalier. The competition would prove too much for American husbands."

He benefited from his film-star status in other ways: He was the star turn at the Fulton Theater in New York, a sellout for two weeks, his performance winning the rare approval of J. Brooks Atkinson himself, then already an influential *New York Times* critic: "He is French," wrote Atkinson.

> He is tall and engaging in appearance. His manners are excellent. His smile can turn a klieg light into a shadow. . . . He has the sort of dynamic intelligence that makes Beatrice Lillie's fooling so electric. It is an art, as they say, but it is infinitely more.

Brooks Atkinson was less approving where Duke Ellington and his orchestra were concerned. Ever the attentive talent-spotter, Chevalier had been to the Cotton Club in Harlem several times, spotted Duke Ellington, and persuaded the show's producer, Charles Dillingham (who had once tried, and failed, to bring Chevalier to Broadway in *Dédé*), to hire his jazz orchestra both to accompany him and to play, on its own, for the first half of the show. No jazz fan, Brooks Atkinson saw in Duke Ellington only "the djinn of din," whose orchestra could "devote an hour to elaborate devices for making noise." This was Ellington's first exposure to Broadway, and, despite the supercilious Brooks Atkinson, would be a landmark in his own career. He rightly credited Chevalier with the requisite flair and obstinacy—for Dillingham had not, at first, been too keen on an all-black orchestra at the Fulton. For the rest of his life, Duke Ellington would be a devoted Chevalier fan. Chevalier, too, felt he owed composer-players like Ellington, Sidney Bechet, and Fats Waller a great deal. One of the reasons, he felt, why Americans took to him was that he combined old-style European and new jazz rhythms in his songs.

Paramount's efficient European distribution and theater networks ensured that Chevalier's films were released almost simultaneously in the United States, London, and (in French) Paris. If anything, British and French audiences reacted to his charm and screen personality even more favorably: He would later write that he found his popularity embarrassing, and undeserved.

In Hollywood, Paramount had responded to criticism of Chevalier's last two films, returning to the Lubitsch-directed *Love Parade* formula that had earned it the biggest plaudits—and the most money. *The Smiling Lieutenant*, a sound version of an earlier, silent German film called *Ein Walzertraum*, released in early 1931, so closely parallels *The Love Parade* that if the two are seen in quick succession, Lubitsch's highly acclaimed second film with Chevalier looks astonishingly like a remake. Curiously, at the time it did not seem so to critics.

In this film set in the early 1900s, Chevalier is, of course, "the Smiling Lieutenant." He commands the Imperial Austro-Hungarian Palace Guard in Vienna, and falls in love with Franzi (Claudette Colbert), a talented violinist and leader of an all-women's orchestra in a Viennese *bierstube*. There is a state visit: The king of a tiny Ruritanian kingdom, and his daughter, Princess Anna (played by Miriam Hopkins), come to Vienna by train, on the lookout for any possible slights inflicted by their more powerful neighbor—and there are many. Their journey is held up to allow a cattle train right of way. While turning out the Guard, Chevalier catches sight of Claudette Colbert in the crowd, smiles broadly, and winks at her. Princess Anna thinks Chevalier is attempting to seduce her. For this act of lèse-majesté he is sent to the neighboring Ruritanian kingdom to be punished as the weak, pompous, overweight king and his insufferably prim daughter think fit. Chevalier charms them both, and is promptly dragooned into a loveless marriage with the princess. Because he still loves Franzi, Chevalier refuses to share Anna's bed. As he tells her father, "You can lead a horse to water but you cannot make him drink." Claudette Colbert, sweetly bowing to circumstance, teaches Anna the feminine tricks that will, in the last reel, turn Chevalier into an amorous bridegroom at last.

By this time, cameras were not quite as noisy, or as unwieldy, as in *The Love Parade,* and the action was consequently less stilted. Shot in New York, at Paramount's Astoria studio, the film was chiefly notable for one truly atrocious song ("Breakfast Table Love") and Lubitsch's malicious use of deftly humorous, sexually implicit lyrics. From Chevalier's opening number ("To arms, to arms, we're used to night alarms/We're not afraid to skirmish in the dark") and a song called "Every Man Deserves a Medal Every Night" to the concluding scene ("I've found a new commander to obey/I must report for duty right away") *The Smiling Lieutenant* lyrics resembled nothing so much as those "naughty" Edwardian music-hall numbers that so delighted British audiences when Chevalier was still a boy. There are Groucho Marx innuendos in some of the dialogue. To Chevalier's "Some day we must have a duet," Colbert replies, "Oh yes, I love chamber music!" After what has clearly been a night of passionate lovemaking, Chevalier tells her, archly, "Nobody plays the violin like you."

Chevalier was in his element, able to project his sexual charm in ways the later, draconian MPA code would probably have prevented. There was no mistaking the meaning of sound or gesture during his "Boulevard Grenadiers" song: "We give the girls a ra-ta-ta-ta-ta/When we are out campaigning/ And they give us a ra-ta-ta-ta-ta" (the last "ra-ta-ta" unmistakably burlesquing the sound of a shrill, high-pitched lovemaking climax) "so we are not complaining." Miriam Hopkins almost steals the picture from Chevalier in the final scene, changing before our eyes into a sexy, jazz-playing, irresistible temptress. Part of the film's appeal was in Lubitsch's implication that, deep down in any woman, however straitlaced, lurks a sexual demon, waiting to shed her inhibitions.

While *The Smiling Lieutenant* was still in preproduction, Chevalier asked Walter Wanger to find him an all-purpose American aide with stage and movie experience. Wanger suggested Robert Spencer, a strikingly handsome young actor, dancer, and occasional male model, then appearing on Broadway in a show called *Ballyhoo* starring W. C. Fields. They hit it off. Spencer was put on the Paramount payroll, at minimal salary, Chevalier paying him an additional seventy-five dollars a week out of his own pocket.

During the course of the next few years, Spencer would see a great deal of Chevalier. They were the same height and build, and though neither the official stand-in nor the official dialogue coach, Spencer acted at times as both, also playing bit parts in some of Chevalier's subsequent films. Because *Ballyhoo* started at 8:00 P.M., and Equity rules compelled actors employed elsewhere to be free by 6:30, Spencer quit *Ballyhoo* (which was, in any case, in financial trouble, folding soon afterward) and began working full time for Chevalier, for the duration of *The Smiling Lieutenant* shooting. When Spencer broke the news to W. C. Fields, who remembered him from his old days on the French vaudeville circuit, the latter gruffly told Spencer to "give the old Frog my best."

Spencer recalled Chevalier's unhappiness, on the set, during this period, and his occasional cryptic comments about his problems with Yvonne. "She simply didn't fit into Hollywood," Spencer recalled. "Her English wasn't that good. But the main reason was that she behaved like Chevalier's mother. She would be across the room, and she would watch his every move, he was unable to avoid the gaze of those big, disapproving eyes. 'She's so jealous,' he told me. 'I can't take it anymore. It's bad for my work.' "[3] The secretive Chevalier hardly ever commented on his private life to relative strangers. That he started doing so proved his well-placed confidence in Spencer, who liked and admired him and whom he trusted. It also proved the sorry state of his marriage. Lubitsch recalled:

> I was busy on the set but out of the corner of my eye I would see him sitting quietly in a corner, grave and serious. He never talked much or laughed with any of the others. Then, when I was ready to shoot a scene—before us, in a split second, is the same man. The same man? No,

a very different man, a man of force and sparkle, a very dynamo of a man, whose irresistible personality has captivated millions of men and women around the world.[4]

Back in Hollywood after the "wrap," Chevalier and Yvonne had one of their fiercest confrontations. She packed and left abruptly for Paris on August 7, 1930, first by air to New York, then by sea aboard *The Berengaria.* The studio explained her mother was seriously ill. She was, but Madame Vallée had been ailing for some considerable time.

Her departure immediately dispelled all trace of Chevalier's gloom: The following week, about to leave himself for Europe, he threw a party in the Blossom Room of the Roosevelt Hotel that, Louella Parsons wrote, was the most glittering of the year—and also seems to have been a celebration of his newfound freedom. Chevalier clowned throughout the evening, imitating a series of French and American actors' mannerisms, including—to his guests' huge delight—Mistinguett's. To the staged embarrassment of Douglas Fairbanks, he kissed him resoundingly, Gallic-fashion, on both cheeks, and went on to kneel before Mary Pickford, dubbing her "the queen of Hollywood." He also wittily thanked those present, including Lasky, Zukor, Walter Wanger, and Lubitsch, for having made him a star, ending up, by popular request, singing his own songs to over a hundred guests. The Chevalier party, wrote the *Los Angeles Examiner,* "will go down in film history." In retrospect it was, perhaps, the apogee of his Hollywood career. Never again would he be as popular with Paramount, his acting colleagues, and the press.

Chevalier left for Europe immediately after his party, for another, unsatisfactory spell in La Bocca with a still-aggrieved Yvonne, and more music-hall bookings in France at unprecedentedly high fees.

In Paris he discovered at first hand the enormous resentment his huge success had aroused. At Ciro's nightclub, whose MC was Harry Pilcer, himself a huge star (and, almost inevitably, one of Mistinguett's former lovers) Chevalier provoked a riot when he refused to do an impromptu music-hall turn. It was customary for visiting stars to contribute to the evening's entertainment out of friendship for Pilcer, but Chevalier glumly sat at his table and refused to budge after being introduced. "Ah, well," Pilcer said diplomatically, "maybe I'll have better luck next time." "There were catcalls among the diners," Jacques-Charles recalled. They shouted, "We're not good enough for him. He's used to dollars. We only have francs." Jacques-Charles, then an administrator of the Paramount Cinema in Paris, rose to get Chevalier off the hook. "I happen to know," he told them, "that Maurice has to get Paramount's approval before singing in public or else he's in breach of contract."

"I hadn't the faintest idea whether this was so or not," he wrote (it wasn't). "I only wanted to get him off the hook." Later, Jacques-Charles called on him at his hotel and was hurt by Chevalier's "cold reception" and the fact that he did not even refer to the Ciro's incident. "Like all those in the public eye, he believed all visitors wanted something out of him."* He also agreed to a two-week spell at the Dominion Theatre beginning on December 1, 1930, billed, somewhat to his embarrassment, as "the highest-paid entertainer in the world" at four thousand pounds a week. The arrival at Victoria Station of this "idol of two continents," wrote the *Daily Mail,* was marked by "amazing scenes." "For hours a massed crowd of close on 10,000 had been waiting inside Victoria Station and outside in the rain." There had been nothing like it since Mary Pickford's visit in the 1920s. "You darling," the women screamed, while "outside the station, women clambered all over his car amid 15 minutes of total confusion." Chevalier told the press he regretted the four-thousand-pound "label." "I hate it," he said. "Never again am I going to have a guaranteed minimum. It's not fair to tie a manager down to a definite figure which might involve him in a loss. I hate the idea that all this talk about money may have led people to think I am a 'society' actor. I come from the streets and not for a moment have I forgotten it. I want to please audiences who are my own people, not merely those who can afford to pay big prices."

In the same *Daily Mail*'s real estate section, a large, timbered six-bedroom Oxfordshire mansion complete with acreage, stables, and cottage, was advertised for sale, freehold, for five thousand pounds.

*Jacques-Charles, *Cent Ans de Music-Hall.*

The Chevalier phenomenon aroused the curiosity of George Bernard Shaw, who had never seen any of his films but wanted to meet him. Chevalier had never seen any of Shaw's plays, and, indeed, had never heard of him. The highly publicized encounter was cordial, but left each star baffled by the success of the other.

Yvonne was with Chevalier in England. In the British press, theirs was still considered to be an ideal relationship, and Yvonne's own interviews upheld this view. "How can I be anything but happy and proud?" she told the *Daily Mail.* "What more charming token of his success could I wish for?" She did, however, hint at her isolation in Hollywood. "I have plenty to do as the housekeeper of the little villa we rent," she said, "but I have not many friends there, though sometimes we entertain some of our fellow countrymen. One of our few friends there is Mary Pickford." The need to pretend to an ideal domestic relationship caused Chevalier considerable behind-the-scenes stress. He was not only compelled to display his carefully contrived, cheerful seductiveness charm onstage but also, now that he was a megastar, whenever he appeared in public with his wife at his side—where she almost invariably could be found.

Outside the Dominion Theatre, on opening night, were more huge crowds. They prevented Chevalier from leaving for over an hour, and the small dinner party at the Mayfair hotel, hosted in his honor by Sir Francis Towle, chairman of Gordon Hotels (the Mayfair was part of the group) was endlessly delayed. Guests included several lords and ladies, Sophie Tucker, the playwright Frederick Lonsdale, Seymour Hicks, and Lady Mountbatten, whom Chevalier tried to dance with, but so many couples made for the dance floor to get a close look at them that they were forced to return to their table. Chevalier looked drawn, tired, and bored. Lonsdale turned to a society reporter and said, "I bet all he wants is to go to bed right now."

When the time came for him to return to Hollywood, embarking on the *Île de France* for New York, he was alone. Yvonne would join him later, but not for long. On the first day of the crossing, a strikingly attractive brunette provoked an immediate, irresistible arousal. She was a manicurist in the ship's barbershop. What happened next Chevalier told in the third person[5]:

Recognizing him, she smiled so sweetly, her blue eyes seemed to worship the adored demi-God to such an extent that he was charmed by those resplendent, graceful features; their eyes exchanged so resolute a message that he felt a kind of spasm in his heart.

Her name, he discovered, was Marcelle, and she was unmarried.

Seducer Number One felt his hunting instincts rise. . . . He had been struck by lightning. Apart from her delightful looks, she seemed so fresh, so new, far closer to him than the famous dolls his heart had become entangled with [in Hollywood].

He made an appointment for a manicure, in the privacy of his stateroom, that afternoon, chain-smoking, "nervous as a schoolboy." Marcelle duly showed up and began manicuring his nails. As she did so, she told him how much she admired his films, how she cut out photos and magazine articles about him, keeping them in a special scrapbook. Coming to his stateroom and doing his nails was like a fairy tale, she said—she couldn't believe she was in the same room, seeing him in the flesh. As she babbled on innocently, Chevalier was beside himself. "He reached out his arms and embraced her. Don't be afraid, little one," he said. "Just a kiss."

Her expression changed from enthusiasm to fear. She had seen in his eyes what he wanted of her. "Oh, no, Sir, please . . . Oh, don't do that, you mustn't!" She began to struggle. He became brutal, sought her mouth, thought she was simply being coquettish. The child was begging him: "No . . . No!" she shouted.

The scene must have turned quite violent, for

a piece of furniture was overturned. There were footsteps in the passageway outside. Dazed, he relaxed his hold, while she, adjusting her dress, instinctively made for the door. He stammered excuses. Upset, trembling, Marcelle was now in tears. She didn't want to leave like that.

What happened next revealed the extent of Chevalier's vanity as much as the male-dominated sexual climate of the times:

> She gave him a wan smile. "Oh, I beg you, Sir, you mustn't blame me! You mustn't be vexed. I would have been so miserable! You must understand the way I dream about you; you're unreal to a poor girl like me . . . I can only admire creatures like you. That's all . . . I don't deserve anything else. Otherwise, afterwards, my life would be ruined! For you, it would be just one more [conquest]. Please, Sir, let's leave things as they are. You have paid me such a compliment: you wanted me! Me . . . A nobody! I'll think about it for the rest of my life. It'll be wonderful to follow your career in the papers, at the movies . . . with my little secret love affair! So unsullied!
>
> "I don't love you, Sir, I admire you. . . . I must be loyal to my boyfriend . . . I'm just small fry. Be nice, Sir, don't hold it against me. Let's not part without shaking hands."

Chevalier "took her hands, kissed them gently, tongue-tied, without saying a word. Then gazing at her with a look that showed he forgave her tenderly, he opened the door."

That night, he recalled, he drank several bottles of champagne, at intervals of

> dancing too merrily with a good-looking, classy woman passenger who had been quite indifferent to him on the promenade deck that morning, notching up another victory that night. That would be his fate, he reflected sadly, as long as he remained one of the Hollywood "top ten" . . . and the Marcelles of this world would prove that there were still humble-hearted, pure-minded creatures for whom love was spelt L O V E.

The episode reveals the extraordinarily vulnerable status of women in 1931: Nowadays, Marcelle would have filed charges for sexual harassment, or, at the very least, gone straight to the ship's purser to report his conduct. But one of the most baffling elements in this, one of Chevalier's few straightforward reminiscences concerning his sex life, was his conviction that he was *honoring* Marcelle by showing her that she sexually aroused him. *He* forgave *her* for not wanting him, and included the story in his memoirs because, no doubt, such a rebuff was so unusual.

Years later, making up for their earlier discretion, Paramount staffers would boast that "the only girl Chevalier never got to know in Hollywood was Shirley Temple." This was a wild exaggeration, for Chevalier's passion for secrecy inhibited him as much as Yvonne's jealous, exclusive nature during their first years together in Hollywood. Temperamentally, though sexually active, he was far too career-oriented to be either a rake or a Lothario. Max Ruppa, Spencer recalled, was far more indiscriminate. But Spencer was to play a key role in one respect: Knowing Chevalier's fondness for slight, dark-haired, and preferably blue-eyed young women, he often attended auditions when chorus girls were selected for minor roles in Chevalier films, acting as his "talent-spotter" and, eventually, go-between. Chevalier was so taken with one of them, Muriel Ferguson, that he later found her a job at the Folies-Bergère, where she remained at his disposal during his spells in Paris.

There's no doubt that, partly as a result of his earlier, casual backstage affairs in France, Chevalier had come to expect uncomplicated sex with beautiful women as his due. During his Hollywood years, his real-life sexual partners would find that the real Chevalier did not match their screen expectations. Lily Damita, for one, told a member of Chevalier's entourage that in her experience, he was "a lousy lover." Mistinguett had said the same thing.* Chevalier himself equated sexual prowess with health, perhaps another Ménilmontant working-class inheritance. Many years later, he would shock dinner-party guests of his French publisher, René Julliard, telling them, again and again, about Chaplin, Douglas Fairbanks, Sr., and himself meeting in a men's room and exchanging bantering small talk about one another's sexual activities. Asked how he was doing, Chaplin replied, "I'm feeling a bit soft in the middle these days." Subsequently, every time Oona Chaplin gave birth, Chevalier said,

*In an unusually sexually explicit book about her mother published in Europe in 1993, Marlene Dietrich's daughter, Maria Riva, claimed that Chevalier admitted to Dietrich, shortly after their first date, that a painful cure for gonorrhea contracted at the age of seventeen inhibited his enjoyment of sex for some years.

he sent Chaplin a congratulatory cable, reminding him that for a man who was "soft in the middle" he seemed to be doing all right. The snobbish French dinner-table guests were not amused.

Chevalier would occasionally use the same expression, with close friends, to describe his own sex life in later years, and worried constantly about the real or imagined onset of physical impotence. As Georges Cravenne, a close friend from the late thirties on, recalled, Chevalier believed that in his lifetime, an average male was physically capable of reaching an orgasm ten thousand times, losing all potency after that magic figure. This belief was not part of dimly remembered adolescent working-class lore: Chevalier claimed a famous French physician had told him it was "a scientific fact."

In Hollywood, Chevalier regarded chorus girls as fair game for casual sex, but with his hankering for "exceptional women," he needed more than that. He did not have to look far beyond the Paramount lot for two of the most exceptional women alive: Greta Garbo and Marlene Dietrich.

For all her later reclusiveness, Garbo showed, in her inimitable way, that she was not entirely indifferent to him. On a date with him, she suddenly suggested they go for a swim in the Pacific. It was past midnight, Chevalier said. "So?" said Garbo. "Besides," Chevalier said, "the Pacific is ice-cold [*le Pacifique est glacial*]." A disappointed Garbo never spoke to him again.

His relationship with Dietrich was infinitely more complex, and lasted far longer. In his memoirs, he described at length how fascinated he became with this tomboyish, aloof, and outwardly cold "German princess," who sat alone day after day in the Paramount canteen, reading scripts and seemingly oblivious to the attention around her. In his abridged American memoirs (*With Love*, as told to Eileen and Robert Pollock) he insisted they were merely "good friends . . . for Marlene was an extraordinary comrade, a woman of great intelligence and sensitivity, spiritual, kind, amusingly and charmingly unpredictable in her moods . . . It was simply *camaraderie*, but it was bound to be seized upon by columnists who needed choice items for hungry readers."

Throughout her long, fascinating, intensely emotionally packed existence, Marlene Dietrich, "spotted" by Paramount in 1929 and brought to Hollywood soon afterward, showed a distinct unwillingness to discuss her private life. In her own disappointingly discreet and thoroughly inaccurate autobiography, she mentioned Chevalier only once, as one of the friends who helped guard her Beverly Hills home after a kidnapping attempt on her daughter, Maria, in 1931. In *his* memoirs, Chevalier insisted that, beginning in 1930, when he first caught sight of her, sitting on her own at the Paramount canteen, he was fascinated by her talent, her intelligence, and her highly idiosyncratic life-style, but that—despite Yvonne Vallée's suspicions—theirs was never a physical relationship. This was patently untrue.

From 1931 to 1933, when both were at the very top of their Hollywood careers as Paramount stars, gossip columnists focused far more on Dietrich than on Chevalier, for her relationships with men baffled Hollywood. She was, officially, married to Rudolf (Rudi) Sieber, an assistant director she had met while still an unknown young actress in Berlin. But Sieber remained in Europe while she made films in Hollywood (he would briefly become Paramount's Berlin representative in the immediate pre-Hitler days, then director of the Paramount-owned Joinville studio in Paris). Like Chevalier, Dietrich regularly left for Europe after each film, resuming a cozily domestic life with her family in Berlin. Gossip columnists dropped occasional hints that Dietrich and Chevalier were together a lot, and that this caused Madame Chevalier intense displeasure. But they were far more interested in Dietrich's real relationship with Josef von Sternberg, who had made *The Blue Angel* before moving to Hollywood and was the only director she would consent to work with (at the start of her Hollywood career, she even had this written into her Paramount contract).

Dietrich and von Sternberg were almost inseparable during her first Hollywood year. Disregarding the hypocritically puritanical climate of America—they were, after all, both Berliners, and in the twenties Berlin had been the sexually freest capital city in the world—they did not even bother to maintain "official" separate establishments, living together openly for months in a bungalow in the Beverly Hills Hotel. She admired him, and—especially in her early days in America, when she was still unsure of her English and unused to American ways—was exceptionally dependent on him.

Von Sternberg was a brilliant, eccentric artist who reduced even Dietrich to tears on the set and was hated by all the Hollywood crews he ever worked with for his autocratic, bullying ways. He thrived on conflict, believing that "the only way to succeed is by making people hate you." In 1931, his wife, Risa Royce von Sternberg, even brought a $200,000 suit against Dietrich for "alienating her husband's affections," along with a libel action for allegedly telling a Viennese reporter that Mrs. von Sternberg "made him unhappy." Paramount paid her $100,000, and both suits were subsequently dropped. The case was referred to in guarded terms in the Hollywood press, and was complicated by the fact that when it was brought, the von Sternbergs were in fact already divorced.

The von Sternberg-Dietrich relationship, which began as an intense "affair," very soon became a platonic friendship.* Von Sternberg, like her own husband, "Rudi," regularly accompanied Marlene to parties at restaurants and nightclubs as "beards" when she was actually dating someone else in the group whose identity she wished to protect. One of the most intelligent actresses ever to work in Hollywood, she collaborated with von Sternberg on every aspect of the seven movies they made together, including storyline, editing, and even lighting, helping him as well on films he made, later, without her.

Though Dietrich was, temperamentally, very different from Chevalier, in many ways they were surprisingly alike: Both had an extraordinary stage presence, both were proud of their professionalism, of their endless capacity to fulfill their directors' expectations of them (in a later, whimsical mood, Dietrich described herself as "an obedient actress" in a memorable documentary made about her by Maximilian Schell). Both were attracted to unusual, complex individuals—Chevalier to "exceptional women" and Dietrich to "exceptional men." Both, in later inter-

---

*The Dietrich-von Sternberg relationship has been brilliantly anatomized in two recent books—Donald Spoto's *Dietrich* (Bantam Books, 1992), and Stephen Bach's *Marlene Dietrich, Life and Legend* (New York: William Morrow, 1992).

views and in their respective memoirs, revealed an extraordinary contempt for the truth: They far preferred the convenient fabrications concocted by inventive Hollywood publicists, which showed them leading exemplary, chaste lives of domestic felicity, to the more fascinating but seamier reality. In time, both may well have come to believe that these idyllic if utterly fanciful accounts of their lives and loves devised for their adoring, gullible public by cynical press agents represented the truth—or as much of the truth as either wished to remember. Both were highly secretive about their real private lives, while perfectly aware of the need to appear transparently candid in the mealymouthed, outwardly puritanical yet basically prurient Hollywood of the thirties.

Dietrich, in particular, was extraordinarily successful in concealing her bisexuality from the public gaze—though it became common knowledge in Hollywood soon after her arrival there. And it was not until the Spoto and Bach biographies appeared in 1992, the year of her death, that her countless affairs with famous men (and women) became public knowledge. Earlier books about her, and her own autobiography,* are practically worthless, revealing only what she herself chose to reveal, or to remember.

While both Dietrich and Chevalier were enormous hypocrites, Dietrich had the true Berliner's cynicism. Chevalier would not admit to a single weakness; the picture he painted of himself, in his memoirs and diaries, was that of a highly moral, almost saintly figure, sinned against but never sinning, a Goody Two-shoes of insufferable honesty and virtue. As a corollary to this, both made their high-handed displeasure plain to those journalists and writers who failed to endorse their platonic image of themselves, flattering and rewarding sycophants who did with privileged access and the illusion of familiarity.

Above all, both were prepared to go to almost any lengths to get what they wanted, and were brilliantly effective in the ways of using people, jettisoning them as soon as their usefulness was over. Chevalier's con-

---

Marlene, originally in German (Frankfurt: Ullstein Verlag, 1987) was later translated into English (New York: Grove Press, 1989). Dietrich claimed both versions were worthless because inaccurately translated.

cerns were strictly professional—he demonstrated, in Hollywood, the same perfectionist determination as in his earlier period as an up-and-coming vaudeville star in Paris, cold-bloodedly turning on the famous Chevalier charm and flattering selected Hollywood columnists to achieve his goals. Dietrich used her sexuality, at every twist and turn in her life, not just for careerist reasons but to get whatever she happened to want at the time: As Spoto's biography of her showed, she embarked, in World War II, on affairs with both generals Patton and John Gavin not only because she could never resist "exceptional men," but for highly practical quid pro quos: Patton gave her privileged treatment as a USO star in the European theater of operations, Gavin speedy access to Berlin—and information about her mother, who had remained there, immediately after the end of the Second World War.

Like Mistinguett, what the indomitable Marlene wanted, or felt she needed, she got—and this included, at the start of her career (and strictly for career reasons), not only her music teacher, Fritz Lang, in his early days as a Berlin-based director, then von Sternberg, but later, in Hollywood, not only Maurice Chevalier but also Gary Cooper, John Gilbert, Jimmy Stewart, Michael Wilding, Yul Brynner, and John Wayne ("Daddy, buy me *that*," she whispered to director Tay Garnett after first setting eyes on him), and of course Jean Gabin and Erich Maria Remarque, the German-born writer, to mention only a few of the well-known, handsome, or otherwise exceptionally interesting men in her life. Her relationship with the Spanish-born playwright, socialite, and acknowledged leader of Hollywood's lesbian community Mercedes de Acosta, in 1933, and her subsequent friendships with many other Hollywood stars known for their exclusive lesbianism or bisexuality, both fascinated and shocked the Hollywood gossip columnists, who hinted at her episodic lesbianism without ever stigmatizing it. How could they, with so many attractive men in her life? Her husband's role in her life became increasingly episodic, and eventually they would live completely separate lives, though they never divorced.

For all their mutual coyness, there is little mystery about her friendship with Chevalier. Among the stereotyped Paramount stars, she stood out, in her striking, mannish clothes, even among people who knew nothing about her—for Paramount deliberately postponed distribution of *The Blue Angel* until the highly publicized *Morocco*, her first Hollywood film, had been released. Even Chevalier had not seen it when they first met.

No one in either Chevalier's or Dietrich's entourage believed theirs was a platonic relationship. Walking into Chevalier's dressing room one day, Spencer closed the door abruptly after catching a glimpse of Chevalier making love to Dietrich (as he recalled, Chevalier was on his knees, engaged in cunnilingus). French contemporaries remember Chevalier and Dietrich, in later days in Paris, reminiscing freely about their past, and Chevalier's gently mocking comment that he hadn't minded being supplanted in her affections by Jean Gabin, but minded very much being cuckolded by her women lovers. This, too, was a trait they shared: While insisting, for public consumption, on a highly sanitized version of their lives, both enjoyed scurrilous, frank reminiscing in the suitably discreet company of their peers. At the age of seventy-nine, Jean-Christophe Averty recalled, Chevalier told him repeatedly and gleefully that the only three things he had ever taken seriously were "his love for his mother, his career, and *le cul.*" Though aggressively homophobic where males were concerned, he was in fact tolerant of bisexuality in women, as his later affair with Kay Francis would prove; perhaps it added to their desirability, for they would not hanker after a conventional, "committed," long-standing relationship.

It was not just Dietrich's sexuality, but her remarkable independence and forthrightness, her masculine turn of mind, that fascinated him. Right up to his retirement from show business, at the age of eighty, Chevalier always traveled with an inscribed photograph of Dietrich that he invariably displayed in his dressing room, a talisman that went with him everywhere. Her inscription to him read, *I have always known you were the greatest. But since I invaded your profession, I am on my knees*—which may have been a subtly erotic reminder of their affair as well as an adoringly flattering message. Chevalier did in fact try to discourage Dietrich from becoming a singer, noting in his memoirs that he thought "she is making a mistake." He only encouraged those talents in others that he regarded as no threat to his own career.

Interviewed (by *Newsweek*) in 1958, Marlene Dietrich steadfastly refused to answer any questions about her or Chevalier's personal life during the early thirties, confining herself to the remark that "to me he *is* France. There is a peasant quality about him. He lives a frugal life."

This was true, and more revealing than it seemed. He did have the French peasant's innate secretiveness, discretion, and distrust of strangers. He also showed a talent for telling his interviewers—and his public— only what they wanted to hear, and for remaining aloof while pretending to be frank. "You understand the personal magnetism, mob adoration, gloves split from applause, fan worship, the supreme ability—the genius—that lifted itself above a worthless first picture and made Chevalier an ascending American idol," wrote Dorothy Spensley in *Photoplay* in 1930. "You understand Chevalier as he sits groping for modest words to explain just how the French public feels about him and just how he cannot desert them permanently for perhaps greater glory on the American screen." "Chevalier is democratic in manner, talks with a very slight accent, is genial, alert, intelligent and interesting," wrote a *San Francisco Chronicle* reporter shortly after his much-praised Roosevelt Hotel party. "He bubbles like champagne in his conversation." J. H. Keen, in the *Philadelphia Daily News*, was surprised to find him less couth than expected at close quarters: "He has squeaky shoes . . . the first impression suggests a veterinary surgeon dressed in his Sunday best." He appeared disappointingly "inelegant, persistently picks his teeth, has bandy legs, swings rather than walks." But in the quaint hyperbolic style of the period, the dazzled reporter finds "there is something about this French idol of a devastating holocaust to drive ladies to drink and servant girls to ruin. . . . Much as I have tried I cannot think of a lady vice crusader who would fight more than tepidly for her honor against this fellow." "Chevalier is the new Valentino," the *Los Angeles Record* splashed over five columns.

Adela Rogers Saint Johns was probably the first Hollywoodian to reveal the real Chevalier behind the charming facade. "There is no such person as Chevalier," she wrote in *Liberty* magazine in September 1931.

The brilliant, smiling idol of the screen is as much a manufactured creation as one of Lon Chaney's thousand faces. The chasm between

Chevalier on and Chevalier off the screen is nine times as wide as the Grand Canyon.

In the past fifteen years I have interviewed or known personally every great star of the cinema. Chevalier is the greatest disappointment, the only real disappointment of them all. Inevitably you compare the man you meet with the personality he sells, and the contrast is incredible. If Maurice Chevalier were allowed to be himself, he wouldn't flash that famous smile once a month. The truth about Chevalier is that he is now a French businessman. His stock in trade is charm. We may call him the Charm vendor.

Adela Rogers Saint Johns, though a prolific free-lance writer, was first and foremost a professional scriptwriter, a respected Hollywood insider with the kind of access to sets and studios that no journalist, not even Louella Parsons, enjoyed. She saw Chevalier as only his directors and fellow actors could:

On the set he sits in a corner, talking with someone, or more often alone. He looks sad, tired, puzzled, and not in the least attractive. Seeing him thus, if you didn't know he was Chevalier, you would not have the slightest desire to meet him.

The director calls. The lights go on. The cameras begin to grind.

You behold a young man with a smile that makes your heart leap, with an attraction that instantly stirs your imagination. He is handsome, vital, fascinating. A man of swift grace, of eyes that sparkle with life, of an irresistible swagger . . . Ten years have dropped from his shoulders.

She witnessed the same metamorphosis at Hollywood parties.

A whisper goes about that Maurice Chevalier is coming. Enter Chevalier. The famous smile floods the room. The charm sweeps all before it. Women grow weak at the knees.

Ten minutes, half an hour elapse. The party is in full swing. You look about for another glimpse of that intriguing gentleman. In a corner stands Chevalier. His lower lip is out an inch. His whole body droops. The sorrows of the world seem to be weighing him down. An hour later he has gone home. He has escaped the terrifying business of being Chevalier.

Her assessment may also have been based on George Cukor's impressions after *One Hour with You*, shot after Chevalier's return and only released in 1932, which Cukor directed instead of Ernst Lubitsch, who was still working on *The Man I Killed*. Adela Rogers Saint Johns and Cukor were close friends, and as such would have had privileged access to the set.

One Hour with You was one of Cukor's most unfortunate experiences. After the first two weeks of shooting, Lubitsch returned to the set from time to time, and the two men worked together, though Cukor always insisted that *he*, and not Lubitsch, did most of the directing. When Lubitsch realized he had a potential hit on his hands, he used his considerable influence at Paramount to have Cukor's name removed from the credits. Cukor, then a young and relatively unknown director, refused, and sued Paramount. There was an out-of-court settlement, Cukor's name was restored (but below Lubitsch's) as "assistant director" and "dialogue director," and Cukor promptly left Paramount to go to work for David O. Selznick at RKO.

But some of the unpleasantness of *One Hour with You* had nothing to do with Lubitsch.

First, Cukor was aware of the uneasy atmosphere on the set among the stars themselves. By rights Chevalier should have been more relaxed. He was now free of Yvonne's jealous, censorious gaze, for she was still in Paris. He was openly seen escorting Dietrich around town, and he was also seeing other women, including Lily Damita, a French-Canadian actress who was to star in the French version. He also, at this time, had his eye on several other women: One was Toby Wing, a Paramount starlet, another was Kay Francis, who had attracted him ever since *Paramount on Parade* two years previously, and whom he saw almost daily, for she was hard at work on another film within the lot. Chevalier had hoped that Kay Francis would be chosen to play opposite him in *One Hour with You*, and had done everything in his power to persuade Paramount to hire her for the film. In any case, Lubitsch, who wanted

Jeanette MacDonald, had vetoed Kay Francis, and Paramount made sure she would not be available, putting her to work in no less than six other films that year. Chevalier was furious that Paramount, at Lubitsch's insistence, had rehired Jeanette MacDonald, offering her a new two-picture contract. And he didn't take kindly to the presence on the set of Bob Ritchie, her lover, for the two still quarreled constantly, leaving the actress in tears. She then retired to her dressing room for long makeup sessions. Chevalier, a true professional, was outraged by Mac-Donald's tantrums: After accepting to wait around for four hours to pose with her for a promotional photograph (she was still needed on the set, he had finished for the day), she stormed off, pretexting a party, "stamping her little foot" and telling John Engstead, the photographer: "If Adolf Zukor himself came out here and got on his knees on the ground, I wouldn't make those stills." "She was a bitch," Engstead recalled, "but she was cute as could be with directors, she would be practically kissing their asses."[6]

Then there was the personality problem between Chevalier and Cukor. "I didn't like Chevalier, and he didn't like me," Cukor later said.[7] The fact that Cukor got on very well with Jeanette MacDonald only made matters worse. Cukor's directing style was idiosyncratic and derived from his theater background: He talked and gave advice incessantly, "acting" out the parts exaggeratedly behind the camera during takes. Chevalier found this exasperating "camp" behavior. Cukor's homosexuality was already well known in Hollywood, and Chevalier never lost his innate prejudice against gays. To some extent, this was understandable, part of his tough Ménilmontant working-class childhood legacy. In his music-hall songs, Chevalier never hesitated to introduce a number openly making fun of "fags." Spencer recalled that he was always on the lookout for real or imagined homosexuals, "and warning me about them." When the time came to make *The Merry Widow* (in 1934), Chevalier told the unusually good-looking Spencer to stay clear of Lorenz Hart, the distinguished librettist, "or he'll try and get into your pants."

Despite his incredibly fast rise to the Hollywood "top ten," Chevalier, the congenital worrier, was anxious about his long-term Hollywood

career. He was trying to steer clear of uniformed, Ruritanian Army roles
in kitsch films, but so far his "natural," more popular roles in noncos-
tume period pieces had not worked as well. He was aware of this, all the
more so since he himself had been instrumental in getting *Playboy of Paris*
made into a film in the first place. Though *One Hour with You* was to win
a "best picture" nomination, he now had second thoughts about his part
in it (as a philandering Paris doctor) and about the film itself. And
indeed, though it worked for American audiences, then always ready to
see a film if Chevalier was in it, in France it was a flop: French audiences,
Weekly Variety reported, "find there is nothing to the film. To their taste
it is slow and without punch." Perhaps the fault lay with its hybrid
nature: a Hollywood film with a script derived from a German play (*Nur
ein Traum* by Lothar Schmidt) set in Paris with an unconvincing "made
in Hollywood" decor—and lacking any truly memorable songs.

Chevalier revealed his constant fears and career preoccupations in a
long, bylined piece for *The Saturday Evening Post* (August 8, 1931). "The
worst moment arrives when you are sitting in a theater, waiting for the
public showing of your first picture. You are the show and yet you are
one of the audience. . . . You sit trembling among those people who do
not know even that you exist." The anxiety remained constant, however
popular he seemed with the public:

> With each picture you have a new fear and a new agony. Because the first
> has been successful means nothing to the second. A disappointed audi-
> ence will not say, "Well, Maurice was not so good tonight, but we will
> forgive him because last month or last year he was amusing." No. The
> next time they see my name on a picture they will say: "Oh, here is that
> French bird again! Let's go to the theater around the corner." In Holly-
> wood, "even if you succeed, this is a game where only a very few succeed
> long. I will give you two years."

"I am just beginning to learn something about the business," he said.
The previous December, in London, he had rather grandly told reporters
that he was through with vaudeville, except for occasional star appear-

ances, and that his future was in films, not on the stage. Now he may have regretted this boast.

By any standards, his rise to international stardom had been staggering, but the initial euphoria was gone, and after *One Hour with You* his quest for ideal film roles would eventually turn him against Paramount. Curiously, while the public's adulation was never sufficient to dispel his sense of insecurity, Chevalier never quite came to terms with his limitations either: In his seventies, he would drop hints that his future lay on the stage of the classic Comédie Française theater, for which he was completely unsuited. For all his mood swings, private fears, and complexes, there was a part of him that believed he was as versatile an actor as Gary Cooper or Clark Gable, as talented a songwriter as Jacques Prévert. There was also another, more realistic Chevalier, who intuitively realized that his Hollywood success was part of the thirties' general craze for musical films, and that this vogue would, one day, inevitably end.

CHAPTER 11

"Am I getting old?"

"I Remember It Well,"
from *Gigi*,
sung by Maurice Chevalier

*C*hevalier's customary European summer break was spent more in Paris than in La Bocca in 1931, for professional as well as personal reasons. As part of his contract, he starred in a Spanish language "short" *(El Cliente Seductor)* filmed in the Paramount-owned Joinville Studios.

He was thus in Paris when Jeanette MacDonald arrived there for a booking at the Théâtre de l'Empire. He hid his private feelings on her opening night (September 7) to the extent of striding up onstage and kissing her on the lips, to prolonged, riotous applause. French newspapers immediately assumed there was a romance between them, speculating she was the "other woman" in Chevalier's life, an allegation Madame Chevalier indignantly denied. (Hollywood gossip-writers must have known about the sorry state of Chevalier's marriage, but had so far refrained from writing about it. French papers had no such inhibitions.)

The report caused some merriment in Hollywood, where the two stars' mutual loathing was well known. MacDonald could have done without Chevalier's gesture, for it reminded French audiences who, of the two, was the bigger star.

She had only undertaken her music-hall tour, which also included a week at the Dominion Theatre, in London, to dispel another rumor, also initiated by a French newspaper, that she had been killed in a mysterious automobile crash, and then subsequent stories that she had been hideously disfigured in the accident. Her trip would, unexpectedly, help her career considerably: That summer, she stayed on the French Riviera, where she befriended the Thalbergs, lending her hairdresser (who traveled with her) repeatedly to Norma Shearer, Thalberg's wife. It was part of a conscious wooing process that would eventually lead to an MGM contract, to Chevalier's intense anger.

Chevalier returned to New York, still without Yvonne, on September 24, 1931, and three days later received the supreme show-business accolade, a Friars Club testimonial dinner at the Astor Hotel. At the top table with the guest of honor were Jack Benny, Heywood Broun, Eddie Cantor, George Conan, Jesse Lasky, Guy Lombardo, Edward G. Robinson, Sophie Tucker, Rudy Vallee, Walter Winchell, and New York's notoriously corrupt, publicity-hungry mayor, James J. Walker. The menu was in the tradition of excessive "thirties" banqueting: *petite marmite bourgeoise, saumon de Gaspe à la Renaissance, noisettes d'agneau, poussins d'Écosse, salade Clementine, bombe Frascati, petits-fours friandises.* Sadly, for this was still Prohibition, beverages included only Perrier, tea, and coffee. The waiters and waitresses all wore boaters. A Chicago poll had recently proved what everyone instinctively knew: that in "name recognition" film stars topped the list, followed, in the following descending order, by gangsters, athletes, and—in fourth place—politicians like Mayor Walker. Chevalier's popularity was such that the entire proceedings, including two hours of speeches, were relayed live on the New York radio station WMCA.

In a long, rambling and at times completely incoherent peroration that failed to get many laughs—his mind was on other things; he was fighting creditors and in the final throes of his losing power struggle at

Paramount—Lasky noted "in all modesty" that if it hadn't been for him, Chevalier would not have embarked on a Hollywood career. Eddie Cantor reminded the audience that he had emceed Chevalier's first U.S. stage appearance ever, his Ziegfeld's "Midnight Frolics" opening night in 1929. "I will never have to buy my wife a fur coat or a bracelet," Cantor told the crowd of diners. "She has just danced two nights in a row with Maurice Chevalier. My uncle's in the straw-hat business and tells me that business is back to normal just supplying the imitators of Maurice Chevalier."

Before Mayor Walker's address, George Jessel, the toastmaster, said it wasn't often the Friars tendered their annual testimonial to a foreigner, but Chevalier, apart from his other talents, "is a representative of the only solvent country left in the world" as well as "the most romantic personality France has sent us since the Marquis de Lafayette."

Chevalier responded with characteristic modesty. "I don't believe one thing that has been said about me tonight. Really. The words of friendship, yes, I believe them. But for the compliments, I smile." He regaled the company with his rags-to-riches story, which included a tearful homage to his mother, culminating in "this dinner, with all the great actors of your country and the greatest of all the mayors."

Nearly two months later, while he was working on *Love Me Tonight*, news of his failing marriage belatedly surfaced in Hollywood. Almost certainly, both Louella Parsons and Hedda Hopper had known for months, but, loyal to Chevalier, deliberately missed out on a possible "scoop."

The first mention came in the *Los Angeles Examiner* (November 27, 1931): "The rumor that there has been some trouble between Maurice Chevalier and his wife, like all Hollywood rumors, has circulated fast. The smiling Frenchman says nothing, which is always a wise procedure." A few days later, it ran a further story, in effect a denial:

Another persistent rumor has been absolutely killed by Maurice Chevalier himself. Any report that he and Madame Chevalier have separated or have had any trouble is absolutely untrue. Madame Chevalier arrives the middle of December to spend Christmas with her husband and naturally he does not want her to land in America and have a dozen reporters grab her and ask embarrassing questions. It will be impossible for Maurice to meet the boat because he will be in the middle of his picture, but as for any trouble, that is nonsense. We are very glad to be able to make this announcement. Silence, perhaps in this case, wasn't golden, for if Mr. Chevalier had only spoken in the beginning, these rumors might have died then and there.

On December 26, 1931, a *Los Angeles Examiner* photograph showed Yvonne, and the Fairbankses, arriving in Pasadena by the Santa Fe Chief. Reporters noted that Madame Chevalier "stepped off the train into the arms of her husband." Though only a few close friends of the Chevaliers were aware of it at the time, they did not remain under the same roof for long.

Love Me Tonight, finally directed not by Lubitsch but Rouben Mamoulian and shot in January–February 1932, represented Chevalier's further, and most successful attempt so far, to play a contemporary role more in keeping with his own character. It was undoubtedly far better than either *Playboy of Paris* or *One Hour with You*—one of the chief reasons being the music and lyrics of Rodgers and Hart.

The film, set in contemporary France, has Chevalier, "the best tailor in Paris," tracking down the spendthrift vicomte de Vareze (Charles Ruggles) in his family château, on behalf of a group of Paris tradesmen, to try to extract the huge sums he owes them (including sixteen tailor-made suits made for him by Maurice). The feckless viscount is heir to the immensely rich, incredibly arrogant, *vieille France* aristocrat, the duc d'Artelines (played with his customary hauteur by C. Aubrey Smith.) The panic-stricken viscount pretends that Chevalier is a member of the French nobility. His family, including the duke's daughter, Princess Jeanette (Jeanette MacDonald) believe him. Maurice falls in love with Jeanette, eventually revealing his true identity. Spurned by the princess, he leaves to an uproarious family chorus ("the son of a gun is nothing but a tailor.") But Jeanette pursues his train on horseback, stops it by standing on the track, and shows Maurice, in the most convincing way possible, that she has had second thoughts: He may be an ordinary tailor, but she is still crazy about him, and willing to share his life.

Love Me Tonight is by far the most *modern* of Chevalier's pre–World War II Hollywood movies. Partly this is due to the quality and wit of Hart's lyrics ("I don't give a stitch/If I never get rich") and the immediate impact of Rodgers's music, which gets the film off to an unforgettable start with the deliberately cacophonic, enchanting "Symphony of Paris" ("Each morning like a baby/Paris starts to cry . . . It has taxi horns and claxons/To scare the Anglo-Saxons . . . You'd sell your wife and daughter/For just one Latin Quarter.")

Love Me Tonight is a reminder of what Chevalier's earlier films could have been like if only Rodgers and Hart had been brought in earlier in his Hollywood career. It had its share of Lubitsch-like "double-entendre" innuendo, but it also showed true wit. For the first time in Hollywood, Chevalier seemed genuinely at home in his part, and, because of Mamoulian's high standards, the decor was an improvement on that of most films set in France but actually filmed on the Paramount lot. Chevalier's long "Poor Apache" song ("She is such a treasure/So I am a gentleman of leisure") provides a rare glimpse of the charisma he must have displayed whenever he appeared on the stage in his prime.

Love Me Tonight temporarily restored Chevalier's faith in Hollywood, and was hugely popular, most of all in Europe, with some highly suggestive lyrics that delighted French audiences but were excised from the final Hollywood version. It had, said *The New York Times*'s Mordaunt Hall, a "sort of magic."

One great difference between this and all previous films, as Mamoulian himself later pointed out, was that "songs and lyrics were carefully planned to advance the story line, and their place in the story itself designed before the writers of the screenplay were engaged. The songs flowed from the action sequences and the actors didn't stop to sing a song. This is the way an original musical film should be developed, in my opinion, but it so seldom happens like this."[1]

Unlike Lubitsch, Mamoulian did not allow Chevalier into preproduction meetings. Chevalier threatened to complain to Zukor. But as soon as he read the script, he was enchanted with it, becoming Mamoulian's instant admirer and lifelong friend. For once, the glowing good humor of the film reflected the atmosphere on the set, though Chevalier and Jeanette MacDonald were still hardly on speaking terms.

Lasky was no longer at Paramount to witness its success when the film was released: Bankrupt as a result of Paramount's huge losses and his own real estate deals, he had been eased out of the studio, losing everything ($12 million) in the process, including his million-dollar Santa Monica beach house, his twenty-five-room New York apartment, and his three Rolls-Royces. His—and Paramount's—mistake had been to gamble, correctly as it turned out, but at the wrong time, on the durable success of the new "talkies," and on the continued expansion of the movie industry. As a result, just before the 1929 Crash, Paramount had made huge investments in new, expensive movie theaters all over the United States. But pre- and post-Crash credit terms were very different, and Lasky—and Paramount—could no longer meet the payments due. In April, Paramount had filed for bankruptcy, too, though it was allowed, under American law, to remain in business. Lasky left the studio for good. Harry Warner, co-owner, with his better-known brother Jack, of Warner Bros. Studio, loaned him $250,000 to help him make a fresh start as an independent producer. As security, Lasky handed over all his recently acquired Paramount stock. He had paid $1,550,000 for it. Now, after the Crash, it was worth $37,500. The indomitable Lasky would start again completely from scratch, as an independent producer; he continued to make films, but only became truly rich again nine years later, with *Sergeant York*, a huge commercial and critical success starring Gary Cooper, which he produced against all odds in 1941.

Chevalier remained unaffected by the crash: Max Ruppa, a brilliant but cautious money manager, had not gambled on the stock market, preferring to invest Chevalier's money in French and American real estate. *Variety* noted, in 1931, that Amos 'n' Andy, Rudi Vallee, and Maurice Chevalier had been the only show-business figures to become millionaires since the 1929 Crash.

Perhaps Chevalier's new mood had something to do with the light-hearted tone of *Love Me Tonight*: He knew his marriage was over, for

Yvonne soon returned to Paris. His affair with Marlene Dietrich, now a huge star in her own right, was at its height, and his Hollywood friends both encouraged it and protected the couple from outside intrusion. In marked contrast to their handling of other, similar affairs, both Hedda Hopper and Louella Parsons helped keep it secret in order to remain friends with the two major stars. Only a few months later, when the Chevalier divorce became front-page news, did the news of his "infatuation" with Dietrich leak out, with stories of their joint attendance of beach parties, friendly wrestling matches in the sand, and near-constant companionship on and off their respective Paramount sets. To a surprising extent, for such a cold, career-oriented man, Chevalier's relationships with women determined his moods. "When all was going well in his love affair, he could be very gay," Robert Florey recalled. "He would dance around and hum tunes of some of his earlier songs. But then, when he was unhappy, I would find him despondent and talking about returning to Paris immediately. Charles Boyer has told me he used to witness the same kind of emotional outbursts."[2]

Immediately after the shooting of *Love Me Tonight*, Chevalier went to New York for a series of music-hall one-man shows, including one-night appearances at the National Theater and at Carnegie Hall. His dressing room was besieged by female fans, and during the intermission two "mature" women even used the fire escape to enter through the window, catching Chevalier at his most vulnerable—naked except for his undershorts (he sweated profusely during the show, and with Spencer's help invariably changed into a fresh suit during the break). Chevalier shouted for help, and Robert Spencer called some security guards. One of the intruders shouted, "Don't you dare touch me! I'm the mayor's wife!"[3] After the show Chevalier and Spencer left Carnegie Hall through an underground passage to avoid further huge crowds of fans on Fifty-seventh Street.

Despite the fact that Chevalier's rift with his wife was now the talk of Hollywood, the *Detroit News* ran a major interview with Yvonne Vallée (May 1, 1932) intended to rebut any further rumors about her marriage. "The suggestion that there might be any cause for jealousy brought an amused smile from her," wrote the reporter. " 'How can one find happiness when there is jealousy?' she asked. 'Maurice was someone who stimulates one's maternal instincts and, like a mother, you cannot be selfish. You want to see him have pleasure and be happy. . . . If you are always jealous and suspicious, then the man feels: what's the use? I might as well be bad.' "

Less than two months later (July 2, 1932), the Chevaliers were in Paris, sharing a suite at the Château de Madrid, facing the unwelcome publicity over their divorce hearing with apparent equanimity. Yvonne's lawyers told the judge, and Yvonne later told reporters, that Chevalier had not allowed her back into their Hollywood home after her last visit, but had "put me out of the house almost as soon as I arrived in Hollywood." His lawyer alleged "excessive and unfounded jealousy." Chevalier told newsmen that "my wife exhibited such extreme and unfounded jealousy that it made my life unbearable." The terms, never made public, were generous: Chevalier gave Yvonne four million francs (about $250,000 at their 1931 value), then a record sum for a French divorce settlement, payable in three installments—half immediately, the remainder in two yearly payments due in 1938 and 1939. Written into the proceedings was Yvonne's pledge not to use Chevalier's name to further her own artistic career and to refuse all screen or stage appearances in America for the next two years. Both parties agreed they would avoid "offensive statements" about each other.

Perhaps out of a genuine regard for both, or because of the irresistible lure of free publicity, Mistinguett got into the act, telling French newspapers she intended to intercede with the couple and bring them back together again as man and wife. This irritated Chevalier considerably, leading to further estrangement with La Miss that would last until a final reconciliation in 1935.

Marlene Dietrich's name came up frequently in the press. "Marlene and I are the best of friends, as the world knows, but there is no thought of marriage between us," Chevalier said. "Yvonne and I wish to be friends, but if we had lived together for another two years, we would have become enemies. I don't love anyone else." So secretive was Dietrich concerning her private life that it was not even generally known, in France at least, that she was still married to "Rudi" Sieber.

Despite the impending divorce, which became final only the following January, Yvonne seemed unable to face up to its consequences that summer. Shortly after her court appearance, she was in La Bocca, telling newsmen she was "getting the house ready for Maurice." "Maurice loves only one person—me," she told them. "No wrong has been committed on either side, but we have a particular—and perhaps peculiar—idea of what life means. To me, it means our love could not last under marriage ties, yet divorce doesn't mean complete separation. We will certainly see each other, and why shouldn't we live together? Maurice is my ideal, and I have but one thought—his happiness. Our love will be more lasting without matrimonial falsehoods. We don't need marriage vows to hold each other's love. I won't give up mothering him."

Chevalier did not see things that way, and Yvonne did not remain in La Bocca for long. "Certain words should never be said between two people, for they are too cruel ever to be erased and you can never buy them back," he wrote later. "We spoke such words to each other. And once we had done so our marriage was ended forever. I consulted my attorneys and instructed them to give her anything she wanted."

Later, Yvonne admitted that she had been less than candid in her *Detroit News* interview: "All I can say," she told a Paris-based reporter, "is that Maurice claims I am a 'jealous woman, suspicious that he is doing things that he didn't do.' Well, perhaps I *am* jealous—but isn't that a woman's right?" To another reporter, she said, "When Maurice and I were in Paris, we were as happy as could be. But in Hollywood everything was different. I was alone most of the time. . . . I wasn't jealous of other women, but of the time he spent with others, and when a woman loves a man, she hates to be left alone."

A Hollywood reporter[4] noted that "instead of spending Christmas with Marlene Dietrich," Chevalier attended a Christmas Eve family party at the house of Norman Taurog, the director, who had recently become a proud father. In fact, though his affection for Dietrich remained constant, their affair, by now, was over: Dietrich was openly courting Mercedes de Acosta, and Chevalier was now dating several young women simultaneously, some of them unknown chorus girls (through Robert Spencer), some of them stars in their own right like Merle Oberon, Miriam Hopkins, and Kay Francis.

It was perhaps because his marriage was over at last and he was mentally preparing himself for a new life, including perhaps, remarriage and fatherhood, that he agreed to star in *A Bedtime Story*. This slight, pedestrian, and extremely predictable comedy about a philandering French aristocrat who finds an abandoned, newly born baby in his car, looks after it, and—his paternal instincts aroused—discovers the baby has transformed his whole life, was a further attempt, by Chevalier, to play "contemporary" roles. Enthusiastic at first about the script, he later changed his mind, but by then shooting had started.

Paramount's publicity department exploited the news value of the subject matter to the hilt. Chevalier accompanied Taurog in his search for the appropriate baby star, despite his physician's admonition that this might be harmful to his health. Over a thousand babies were examined, two hundred were given screen tests, and Chevalier personally inspected the one hundred babies on the studio's "shortlist." "They were lined up in cribs as in an army barracks," Spencer recalled. Their decision to select the seven-month-old baby known as Baby LeRoy was unanimous.

"Baby" LeRoy Winebrenner's real life story was more dramatic than most film melodramas. His teenage mother had been hired by a wealthy family to look after their small children. What the media either never knew or decided not to reveal was that she had been the victim of rape, during a walk on the Santa Monica beach. Totally inexperienced—she was only sixteen at the time—and out of a sense of misguided shame, she told neither the police nor her employers, only later discovering her pregnancy. With her employers' help, she was able to deliver the child and put it up for adoption by the Salvation Army, and it was there that Taurog spotted the irresistible, gurgling infant.[5]

Baby LeRoy went on to become one of the youngest stars in history, starring with, and hated by, the cantankerous W. C. Fields. "Anyone who hates dogs and children can't be all bad" arose out of his experiences on the set with the irrepressible, obnoxious child. On one memorable occasion, he got the then-four-year-old Baby LeRoy drunk, then outrageously proclaimed on the set that "anyone who can't hold his liquor shouldn't drink on the job."

The *Bedtime Story* script was hardly original, and no sooner was it filmed than Paramount faced a $525,000 lawsuit for plagiarism brought against the studio, Taurog, and, to his intense embarrassment, Chevalier himself. Jeannette Druce, the widow of Herbert Druce, an English actor, an occasional free-lance writer, and herself a Paramount employee, had written a story called "Oh, Papa," which she had sent to Paramount three years previously. Though the points of resemblance in her story and in the film were striking, she lost her case—and her job—for Paramount had commissioned the screenplay from *another* book, Roy Horniman's *Bellamy the Magnificent.*

Far more serious for Chevalier than these legal disputes was the fact that Taurog was no Mamoulian, and Ralph Rainger and Leo Robin, responsible for the music and lyrics, no Rodgers and Hart. The film moved with painful, predictable slowness, from one stock situation to the next, and though Baby LeRoy's chubby, cheerful antics made him an instant hit, Chevalier had underestimated the strain of acting alongside a baby who, by law, had to be given a two-hour "rest" for every twenty minutes spent in front of the camera. The aftermath of press coverage of his divorce proceedings, as well as the strains of filming with Baby LeRoy and his own growing reservations about the film, explained his increasingly cantankerous mood, reported in *The New Yorker* on February 20, 1932. "Maurice Chevalier isn't always the joyous playboy he seems to those who only know him on the screen," its Talk of the Town reporter wrote.

> He's rather glum, really. He beams mostly just for an audience or camera. His press agents know this and it keeps them worried. One of them had an awful moment one night in Hollywood when Monsieur Chevalier was on the verge of being photographed at a particularly splendiferous opening night—one of those Klieg-light openings full of ermine. The press agent looking at Mr. Chevalier realized, with horror, that Monsieur Chevalier wasn't smiling. He looked positively agonized, in fact. The

press agent rushed over. "The smile, Monsieur Chevalier," he shouted, "the smile." Chevalier looked at him with an expression of increased depression. "The smile," he said glumly, "will be ready when you need it." It was, and the day was saved.

Bedtime Story was only a moderate financial and critical success. Though Louella Parsons, as usual, loyally praised it to the skies, other reviews were decidedly mixed. The *Hollywood Reporter* wrote it was "probably the poorest that has ever been made with this star, and didn't cost much," and *Picture Play* was more scathing still: "The vogue of Maurice Chevalier is fast ebbing, and it is no surprise to find him in a picture that tries hard to provide him with a new role, a different background and more humaneness. The film will hardly recapture the position that was once Chevalier's. His limitations are now too apparent, his charm too worn."

This was even truer of *The Way to Love*, another Taurog film made before *Bedtime Story* was released, with truly terrible lyrics and music that to a large extent destroyed the film's comedy potential. Chevalier, once more in a contemporary role, played the part of a would-be tourist guide caught up in an intrigue with a circus-playing, knife-throwing family. Two Paramount actresses—Sylvia Sidney and Carole Lombard—walked off the picture after reading the inane script, and the female lead went to Ann Dvorak, a relative newcomer. *The Way to Love* may have proved to Chevalier that Paramount, already in deep financial trouble, had also entered into a creative decline. To keep him, the studio needed better material than that provided by Ralph Rainger and Leo Robin, which included a song even Chevalier could do little with:

> "If you want to see the real Paree
> You've got to view it through the eyes of love
> You don't really see—you *feel* Paree!
> So have the one you love beside you
> Have a man in love to guide you
> Then you'll have romance in every store and statue,
> Even gargoyles will be throwing kisses at you

If you see Paree with a lover
You'll be a lover of Paree."

"The poorest of the Chevaliers," *Variety* reported.

Chevalier was, of course, aware of Paramount's financial difficulties: Its woes were frequently mentioned in the press, and by the time he was making *A Way to Love*, a cluster of major Paramount stars—including William Powell and Kay Francis—had already moved to MGM. Jeanette MacDonald, for the second time, was among those "let go" in the wake of yet another Paramount economy drive, though this, paradoxically, may have induced Chevalier to stick with Paramount longer than he might otherwise have done.

Robert Spencer, Chevalier's American aide, was himself, briefly, a victim of the cost-cutting: His $100 a week retainer was arbitrarily reduced to $28 a week or $7.50 a day. Chevalier exploded: "Those sons of bitches! Why, I'm the one making all the money for Paramount!" He promptly took the matter up with Zukor, who apologized and put things right.

His own position there was secure, and Max Ruppa, on Chevalier's express instructions, made sure that his U.S. taxes were promptly paid. Fortunately for him, French tax authorities only concerned themselves with income earned on French soil. Only on one occasion did the IRS question Chevalier's returns, and then only for a paltry $495, in 1931. This was in marked contrast with Marlene Dietrich, who carried on a protracted war with the Internal Revenue Service practically from the moment she arrived in the United States until she settled permanently in Paris some forty years later. In June 1939, when Dietrich was about to leave for Europe aboard the *Normandie*, sailing was delayed six hours while she argued with IRS inspectors who claimed she owed them $248,000 in back taxes; eventually they allowed her to leave, after she agreed to leave her jewelry behind as surety.

Chevalier lived in Hollywood less extravagantly than many of his "top ten" costars, but he never denied himself any luxuries: His stinginess did not include self-deprivation. He now had a male American butler as well as a French cook. Spencer, being the same height and build, often shopped for him, and recalled spending large sums on his behalf for tailor-made cashmere and suede jackets and tweed overcoats (he would order five at a time) and silk underwear, which Chevalier greatly prized. He became a temporary member of the Hillcrest and Wilshire country clubs (Fred MacMurray was his sponsor) and bought custom-made golf clubs worth seven hundred dollars. In private, his opinion of major Hollywood stars was less glowing than in his speeches at parties. When Jean Sablon visited Chevalier in Hollywood in 1933 and asked to meet Gary Cooper, one of his screen heroes, Chevalier replied, "Whatever for? He's just a cowboy."

His thrift in small matters was comical: The "wrap" party after the final day's shooting was—and remains—an invariable Hollywood ritual. Then it was an excuse for stars and directors to show their appreciation to their crews and justify their huge fees by handing out expensive presents. Chevalier usually managed to leave town before wraps occurred. As Jeanette MacDonald put it, "He was always scuttling back to Paris." Roger Wagner, later to become a famous Hollywood-based musician and chorus leader, who worked briefly as a stand-in (and delighted Chevalier with a superb imitation of himself) recalled that when Chevalier tired of speaking French with Adolphe Menjou (he claimed Menjou did all the talking), they would lunch together. Chevalier, at this time, was earning $25,000 a week from Paramount alone, more if his frequent stage appearances were taken into consideration. Wagner, then earning two hundred dollars a week, always paid the bill. Jean Sablon told of a similar experience: Visiting Paramount Studios as a guest in 1933, he was taken on the set of the French-language version of *The Way to Love* and then to lunch. The cast, headed by Chevalier, included Jacqueline Francelle (with whom Chevalier was having an affair) and the portly Émile Chautard, a relatively unknown, poorly paid actor. At the end of the lunch, Chautard settled the bill while Chevalier looked on.

Unlike some of the top Hollywood players, Chevalier never bought a Rolls, but during the filming of *Bedtime Story* he placed a special order with Earl C. Anthony, then Hollywood's best-known car distributor, for a custom-built, gunmetal-gray Packard Phaeton convertible. Because

Chevalier intended taking it back to Paris, and insisted it be delivered at the New York dockside, Earl C. Anthony, as part of the deal, loaned him a Packard limousine free of charge. In September 1933, there was a sneak preview of *Bedtime Story* in Palm Springs. "Can you drive a Packard?" Chevalier asked Spencer. "Sure," Spencer answered, "glad to." "I knew Chevalier wanted to sleep on the way back, so I drank nothing but orange juice at the party afterwards," Spencer recalled. "We dropped Francis Lederer [a Paramount executive]. 'Wake me up when we're there,' Chevalier told me, 'and I'll drop you off.' "

At 2:30 A.M., Chevalier's Packard was heading toward Beverly Hills along Melrose when a souped-up Ford coming out of June Street crashed into the Packard at huge speed. Both cars turned over several times, and so violent was the shock that the engine parted from the Ford car and ended up on the lawn of the Los Angeles Public Library thirty yards away. "I'm in a daze, I can smell gasoline coming out of the wrecked Packard. It's on its side, I'm close to the ground and I'm struggling out of the window," Spencer recalled. "My panic is total for I know that Chevalier's trapped inside and there's no way I can get him out."

An emergency rescue squad prized the semiconscious Chevalier from the wreck. "He just lay there, not speaking, not moving, before the ambulances came," said Spencer. All concerned, including the two young men in the Ford, also suffering only minor concussion and bruises, were taken to the Hollywood Receiving Hospital. "I was able to leave the following morning," Spencer said. "The studio told me, Don't say anything to the news media." They were discharged the following day. Chevalier alone was taken to the Cedars of Lebanon Hospital for further treatment. Zukor was informed of the accident minutes after it occurred, and Paramount kept in touch with the hospital on an hourly basis. There was good cause to worry, for Chevalier remained in shock far longer than his doctors expected, not stirring or uttering a sound for two whole days. "Everyone thought something terrible had happened to his vocal cords," Spencer said. "It turned out to have been nothing more than the aftermath of shock, and a bruised neck. Perhaps Chevalier was unwilling to use his voice until he was certain he could do so without risk."[6] Though the drivers of the Ford were clearly at fault, they were lucky—so lucky, in fact, that they later decided to sue Chevalier for ten thousand dollars in damages, but the matter never reached the courts. Earl C. Anthony, eager to keep his status as car dealer to the stars, gave them another car. A few days later, Chevalier was able to leave for Paris as planned.

Three days before the accident, Irving Thalberg, making his own comeback after a serious heart attack, staged a spectacular press conference: He announced he had finally fulfilled his 1927 "dream," and had lured Chevalier over to MGM to star in his next major project, *The Merry Widow*, filming to start before the end of the year. The studio turned the event into a lavish news and photo opportunity, with a massive Viennese string orchestra (in wigs and court uniforms) playing Lehár's "Merry Widow Waltz" while Chevalier and Thalberg ceremonially signed the contract, later mingling with a hundred handpicked guests before a lavish buffet tea.

Chevalier's decision to leave Paramount was not unexpected. While on the set of *The Way to Love*, he was already in close contact with MGM. But his choice of film came as a surprise to his close friends, for Chevalier had repeatedly said he was through with romantic, period piece "seducer" roles. Charles Boyer, who saw him often, felt that "his career had taken an uncertain turn," and that he was unsure of the image he needed to project to retain his extraordinary popularity.

Chevalier's lifelong concern for money and security made him unusually responsive to MGM, then the richest, most profit-oriented of all the studios, and the only one to remain in profit throughout the Depression. Thalberg had made his approach carefully, lunching secretly with Chevalier at first without Paramount's knowledge. "You come over with me, and there'll be wonderful parts: you'll make the kind of picture you've wanted to make—I will personally see to it," he told Chevalier.[7] The knowledge that Lubitsch would direct—"on loan" from Paramount—was perhaps an added incentive. So was the written pledge from Thalberg, while secret negotiations were taking place that summer (1933), that if Chevalier came over to MGM, he would not have to make any more films with Jeanette MacDonald—a promise MGM promptly failed to keep.[8]

Chevalier's own candidate for the role was Grace Moore, under contract at MGM but only moderately well known in Hollywood. Thalberg pointed out to her that in her contract she was not supposed to go over 135 pounds, and that she had become fat. She denied this. "Come stand on my scales," Thalberg said. She refused. Lubitsch, for all his fondness for ample women, was no fan of Moore, and sided with Thalberg.[9] She was turned down even though she volunteered to play the part for free.[10]

For all his influential friends in Hollywood, Chevalier had an imperfect understanding of the way the major studios worked. He underestimated MGM's reputation as a no-nonsense, ruthless, money-making "factory" under the mild-mannered, soft-spoken but dictatorial Louis B. Mayer. He was also probably unaware that the family-loving, exceedingly moral Mayer was not above using his power for sexual ends, and that two of the stars he most lusted after were Myrna Loy and Jeanette MacDonald herself.

The exceptionally bitter crisis over Jeanette MacDonald broke a month later while Chevalier was still abroad. Even before sailing, he knew that MGM had made up its mind to have MacDonald star in *The Merry Widow* even though, officially, the studio still insisted, to the media, that no final decision had been made and that Joan Crawford and Grace Moore were being seriously considered.

Chevalier used Louella Parsons to tell MGM how he felt. "The debonair Maurice Chevalier was seething with resentment when he left Hollywood," she wrote. "Chevalier, who never before displayed one iota of temperament, growled and showed his teeth when there was talk of putting Jeanette MacDonald opposite him in *The Merry Widow*. . . . His annoyance didn't stop there. He was equally bitter against Ernst Lubitsch."

The "kindly Lubitsch"—who had shown, in his treatment of Cukor, that he could play as rough a game as anyone in Hollywood—immediately retaliated. He, too, sounded off to Parsons, who immediately quoted him in her syndicated Hearst press column as saying:

Maurice didn't tell me to my face that he didn't want me to direct him in "The Merry Widow," but that wasn't necessary. When the newspapers printed stories against me, Mr. Chevalier didn't take the trouble to deny one of them. . . . I didn't do so badly by him. "The Love Parade," "Smiling Lieutenant," and "One Hour with You" were his greatest money makers. I can only think when he was so determined not to have Jeanette MacDonald [in the film] that he was afraid of her great popularity abroad. . . . I know that Chevalier's feelings towards Miss MacDonald are not rumor. I talked with him and, although his reasons for not wanting Jeanette were vague, he emphatically stated that he would not make the picture if Thalberg put her in the feminine lead.

In a further barb at Chevalier, he added that "if MGM intends to keep Lehar's music and really make a musical play, there should be *someone* who can sing."

Chevalier backed down. Since the Thalberg letter had been an informal note, not part of his contract, he could not use it as a pretext to refuse to make the film. From Paris he cabled that "I could never say anything against Ernst Lubitsch or Miss MacDonald. I have the greatest admiration and respect for both of them, personally and professionally, and a deep appreciation of Mr. Lubitsch's work with me."

Thalberg's view, also leaked to Louella Parsons, was mealymouthed as well as hypocritical in the light of his secret letter to Chevalier. He told her that

I am greatly surprised that a swell fellow like Ernst Lubitsch, in an interview, would jump in and issue statements based only on idle rumors and gossip. Jeanette MacDonald is a talented and charming actress with a beautiful singing voice, who has had many successes on both stage and screen. She is being considered, among other players, for the feminine role. The ultimate selection, however, will not be influenced by controversy or backstage intrigue, but will be decided in favor of the person best suited for the success of the production.

Lubitsch scarcely acknowledged Chevalier's surrender graciously, telling the *Los Angeles Times* that

> I wish he [Chevalier] had expressed the same views before, as it would have saved a great deal of embarrassment and would have spared M. Thalberg from giving out a statement that I was basing my information on idle rumor and gossip.

Belatedly, after being worshiped and fawned over by Hollywood, Chevalier was discovering its hidden ruthless side. He was deeply offended both by Thalberg's duplicity and by Lubitsch's brutal, domineering tactics, his Teutonic directness. On a stopover in London on his return to America, on January 2, 1934, he hinted for the first time that he might well be through with Hollywood, telling a reporter that after *The Merry Widow* he intended to make a film in London with Alexander Korda (this project was later canceled) and then "go back to where I started from, the Parisian stage." "Maurice Chevalier is tired of being funny," wrote the *Los Angeles Times*. "He wants to abandon the straw hat and become serious. He is to make a film in England that will depict the character of Lafayette."

Aware that he had lost the battle, and doubtless eager to remain in good standing with two of Hollywood's most powerful men, Louella Parsons revealed that her own loyalty to Chevalier had limits. On January 17, 1934, she wrote that "when Maurice Chevalier gets back today, he will be asked to speak on several important questions. First, why his indignation when a reporter in New York suggested he was engaged to Toby Wing? (a dark-haired starlet he had been seen with frequently in Hollywood.) Second, his version of the 'Merry Widow' squabble which has been going on so long we'd like to have it settled."

By the time shooting started (not as originally planned, by the first of the year but in early March 1934), Chevalier and MacDonald had publicly kissed and made up, for the benefit of the press and MGM's publicity department. In the light of all the recent acrimony, Chevalier was unexpectedly gracious on the set. "He had a terrible temper," Spencer recalled, "but in a good mood he liked to play practical jokes."

One of these jokes was on Spencer himself. At Chevalier's instigation, Louella Parsons had the Hearst press run up a mock column ("She could do anything she wanted at Hearst," Spencer recalled) that included the following item: "Robert Spencer, one of Chevalier's aides, has been seen mixing with male companions, not only off duty but while at the studio, and this is causing Mr. Chevalier great embarrassment."

"Have you seen this?" Lubitsch, also in on the conspiracy, asked him. "I was devastated," said Spencer. "I thought it was the end of my career." Lubitsch told him it was a mock-up, Chevalier's idea of a prank. "When they showed it to me, I said, I'm going to sue this paper for a million dollars, and they got back to me, and said it was a joke, not a real column. But it was a cruel thing to do."[11] Above all, it was a reminder of Hollywood's intolerance and of Chevalier's ingrained homophobia.

The Merry Widow shooting went off without a hitch until the final day's shooting, when the "wrap" party occurred. The target of Chevalier's wrath that day was not Jeanette MacDonald, but, again, the unfortunate Robert Spencer.

"In those days," Spencer said, "studios worked with two crews, the first from six A.M. to one, the second until the director called it a day. This meant a lot of people on the set. A week or two before the shooting ended, Lubitsch told me he and Jeanette MacDonald would be giving a party, for sixty people, 'and we wonder whether Maurice would like to be part of it.' It would be quite expensive. Lubitsch said that with gifts to the crew, it could come to three thousand or four thousand dollars, for cameramen and lighting directors always got expensive presents. Chevalier agreed, and told me to go out and buy some 'little presents.' I got a gold-tipped alligator wallet for the cinematographer, less expensive presents for the others, including premium bottles of whiskey and cigarette lighters with Chevalier's signature on them, but there were lots of them, and all told I must have spent around a thousand dollars.

"Chevalier was in his dressing room, being made up for one of the final scenes being shot on that last day. 'Did you get the little presents?' he asked me. 'I have the bill,' I said, and handed it to him.

"He studied it and went berserk. 'You don't know the value of a dollar!' he shouted. In an uncontrollable rage, he threw a can of makeup powder at me. I was in uniform myself, for I had a small part in the movie [they were shooting the final part of the ballroom scene] and I looked a mess, with makeup powder all over it. I got the hell out of his dressing room. Lubitsch spotted me and said, 'My God, Bob, what's wrong?' "Maurice just threw a can of powder at me, I guess because of the money I spent on presents for the party."[12] Lubitsch told him to get cleaned up. Moments later, Spencer and Chevalier were on the set together—in *The Merry Widow* scene where "Count Danilo" cuts in on the waltzing Jeanette MacDonald, whose partner was Spencer.

To his credit, Chevalier later realized how badly he had behaved. "I've done something terrible," he told Lubitsch. "I've hurt a very dear friend, and I don't know what to do about it." Chevalier apologized to Spencer, and there was an emotional reconciliation. "Chevalier," Spencer recalled, "had never attended a real wrap party in his life and was overwhelmed when member after member of the crew came up to him and told him what a great experience it had been working with him." He was also unaware that expensive gifts to film crews were a tradition, at least when the film involved highly paid stars.

Chevalier's reputation for excessive thrift amounting to meanness gave rise, both then and later, to scores of unflattering anecdotes about him. There was no doubt he had a lifelong ambivalence toward money. In his memoirs, he wrote with pride that he regarded thrift as a virtue, but he carried this to extremes: He was a notoriously mean tipper, never paid taxis himself if he could help it, and always let others reach for bar and restaurant bills. On the other hand, he contributed to major charities in France, both in his lifetime and through donations in his will. He made much on his arrival in Hollywood of his support of the Maurice Chevalier Clinic for Children in his native Belleville—a privately run establishment in the XXᵉ arrondissement—but raised money for it through special galas (mostly film and music-hall premieres) rather than by direct donations. With characteristic shrewdness, shortly after his arrival in Hollywood, he obtained from Adolph Zukor the sum of four thousand dollars for the clinic, arguing that Paramount should make amends for taking him away from his French public. In 1930, he told Hollywood reporters he intended to raise $400,000 "over the next five years" for a home for old and destitute actors in Ris-Orangis, but this was almost certainly an unrealistic figure. Though over the years, gala "premieres" did provide considerable revenue for this establishment, the

As a waiflike comic, Maurice Chevalier was already on the road to stardom at age twelve, but his career was almost shattered when he was taken prisoner in the first week of World War I (inset).

Chevalier was posing for postcards at fifteen (left), but real fame came when top music-hall star Mistinguett made him both her stage and real-life partner. He was twenty-four, she was thirty-six.

Among the innumerable women linked to Chevalier, Yvonne Vallée (above) became his stage partner and his wife; Fréhel, once a teenage beauty (top and above right) was a blowsy alcoholic later in her life. His dislike of his co-star Jeanette McDonald (seen here in *The Love Parade*) was reciprocated. Chevalier's mother, "La Lonque," was, he said, the only woman he ever loved (left).

Clockwise, from right: Chevalier and
Mistinguett made real love on stage in their
infamous carpet scene (top right). Nita
Raya, later a girlfriend (here in 1938), also
co-starred in his shows (right). By this
time, his marriage to Yvonne Vallée (seen
here in a posed moment of domestic bliss in
1927) had ended in divorce and he was
barely on speaking terms with Jeanette
McDonald (here in *Love Me Tonight*).

Chevalier loved walking the streets of his native Belleville, alone and unrecognized.

Bottom: Chevalier grew a moustache as a roué in a
pre-World War II film, *Beloved Vagabond* (1936), but
was more at ease as a gala circus ringmaster in 1937
with Josephine Baker (above) Baker later unjustly
accused him of collaboration when, in 1942, he
performed in German-occupied Paris at a gala for
children of French POWs (top).

Top: Chevalier, here in a rare and unconvincing "straight" role in Siodmak's thriller *Pièges*, in 1939, became embroiled in real-life controversy after visiting his old POW camp in Germany in 1941. He sat out most of the rest of the war in his house near Cannes (right), gardening and milking his cow.

In 1950, at the Gala de l'Union (top left), Chevalier looked a youthful sixty-three, but celebrated his old age and regained stardom in *Gigi* (with Louis Jourdan and Leslie Caron). He turned a protégée, Patachou, into a co-star (right), starred in *Ma Pomme*, became a bestselling author, and turned every birthday into a performance.

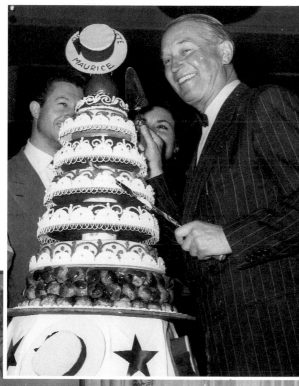

Autographing his last book at eighty-two, Chevalier seemed
cheerful enough, but his periods of melancholic brooding in
his Marnes-la-Coquette mansion worsened in degree,
leading to a suicide attempt from which he never recovered.

At the Casino de Paris in 1939. Chevalier's performance was
virtually the same polished act it had been in 1929—and would be
twenty years later.

bulk of the money from Chevalier came posthumously, as a testamentary donation.

Immediately after the wrap party, Chevalier's spirits were high. He must have been pleased by a backhanded confirmation of his huge popularity in France: Mistakenly, at a recent premiere of Love Me Tonight in his native Belleville, the American version, and not the expected French version, had been shown. A few minutes after it started, there were catcalls, and when the projectionist failed to stop the film, several hundred enraged Parisians in the audience completely wrecked the movie theater.

Another reason for his sunny mood was that he was at last seriously involved with someone he had long had his eye on—Kay Francis. In an interview with Louella Parsons, shortly after the memorable wrap party, he had told her that his "ideal wife" would be "the girl who is domestic, loves a home and her husband and wants children. The girl without the petty vices of 'modernism' is my favorite. I prefer above all the girl of simple tastes." Perhaps he was, as usual, covering his tracks. Perhaps, in his eyes, Kay Francis was one of those "exceptional women" to whom these standards did not apply, for she was hardly a paragon of domestic virtues.

When Kay Francis began dating Chevalier, she was still married to, but in the process of divorcing, her fourth husband, actor Kenneth McKenna. She was also famous, like Dietrich before her, for her bisexuality and intense friendships with women. Friends of Chevalier noted her resemblance to Yvonne Vallée, and so close did they come to getting wed that Newsweek even announced their "impending marriage." Like Chevalier, Kay Francis owed her stardom to determination and hard work: She came to Broadway, and eventually Hollywood, by way of summer-stock theater, earning her living as a stenographer, secretary (for a real estate company), and ladies' companion. Though Elsa Maxwell, another famous columnist, would later claim that "Kay Francis cares only about money," she refused alimony from her four husbands, eventually leaving her considerable fortune to Seeing Eye, an institution that trained dogs for the blind. She herself was humorously deprecating about her career, describing herself as a "glorified clothes horse." But despite her slight but charming lisp and her average acting abilities, she was, at the time, one of Paramount's hardest-worked actresses, making eight films in 1932, five in 1933, and four a year both in 1934 and 1935, many with William Powell, who was (falsely) rumored to be her lover. Chevalier, morose and insecure so much of the time, was irresistibly drawn to strong, secure, fun-loving women, who made him laugh and were able to dispel his "black dog" moods. Kay Francis had this gift, and there's no doubt that their physical attraction was mutual: He was, after all, one of Hollywood's handsomest male specimens around, with a legendary reputation as a "French lover."

Their relationship became public knowledge in France when reporters discovered that Kay Francis was already in Paris when Chevalier, in September 1934, boarded the *Île de France* in New York to join her there. On arrival, he rushed to the Crillon Hotel to be with her. Two weeks later, he was at the Cannes station, to greet her train from Italy. Oblivious of their surroundings, they embraced in what a *Los Angeles Examiner* reporter described as a passionate "real fade-out kiss," before Chevalier whisked her away to La Bocca in his Packard.

Perhaps it was their constant, close proximity at La Louque in La Bocca that heralded the end of the affair: For here, though there was plenty of tennis, Kay Francis experienced little of the Riviera glamour she expected in Chevalier's company. Instead of the round of parties and nightclubbing that was a feature of her life in Hollywood, she found herself presiding over stolid family lunches (for Chevalier's brother Paul was present most of the time) and dull evenings, for Chevalier rarely wanted to leave the house. When he did, it was to meet with old friends like Albert Willemetz, the theater manager and librettist, and other French show-business cronies who either ignored her or treated her with friendly, patronizing contempt. At La Bocca she was not a star, only Chevalier's latest American girlfriend. His French friends not only spoke a language she could not fully understand, their conversation was full of colloquial allusions and focused on events and people she knew nothing about. Their insular "Parisianisme" made her feel inadequate as well as ignored—as out of place in La Bocca, ironically, as Yvonne Vallée had been in Beverly Hills.

Elsa Maxwell, the gossip columnist who, for all her appalling traits, was a shrewd observer of human nature, visited Chevalier in La Bocca that summer and must have witnessed things at first hand. As she later wrote, Kay Francis

> had the opportunity of observing Maurice on his home ground and saw a different man from the one she used to know in Hollywood. There was nothing of the matinée idol or romantic lover about the thrifty shrewd "monsieur" who presided at the dinner table, over the gathering of numerous relatives . . . who seemed to care very little about glamour but a great deal about another helping of roast spring lamb. That was that Back to America went Kay, carrying with her the memory of a beautifully cooked meal.

Though Chevalier and Kay Francis remained friends (she would visit him again in La Bocca in 1935, "to ask his advice" about a movie part she intended playing), the romance was over. Both she and Chevalier issued lighthearted denials there had ever been a question of marriage, Chevalier noting that French newspapermen, who would once never have dared ask him about his private life, were now just as inquisitive.

On his return to New York aboard the *Île de France*, he clasped a silver-plated "loving cup," and proudly explained this was the prize for winning the passengers' champagne-tasting competition; he had correctly identified eight of the ten brands. The runner-up, Jack Pearl, a celebrated New York radio personality, claimed he would have done better still if his taste buds hadn't been wrecked by speakeasy "hooch"— Prohibition had finally ended in 1933. As was his habit aboard the *Île de France*, Maurice Chevalier distributed autographed photographs of himself to cabin attendants and waiters at the end of the voyage, but no tips.[13]

The Merry Widow, first shown in November 1934, got critical raves but was not a commercial hit. It had cost a record $1.5 million, and MGM was later to claim it lost $115,000—not an excessive amount, except to Louis B. Mayer, for whom any loss was unacceptable. It remains one of the outstanding pictures of its genre, a multifaceted example of

Lubitsch's art and artfulness, whether he is circumventing looming censorship problems or Chevalier's own singing limitations. Film historians will probably never tire of enumerating the different ways Lubitsch manages to suggest that Maxim's was really a brothel, or that in his part as Count Danilo, Chevalier's purpose there was sex—even if a languorous Jeanette MacDonald as Sonia, the rich widow who owns half of the minuscule Balkan kingdom of Moldavia, keeps both of her tiny feet firmly on the ground while she's sprawled on the huge damask-covered couch and about to make love to Danilo. Much has been made of the fact that, for the first time in their musical partnership, in *The Merry Widow* Chevalier and Jeanette MacDonald never sing together. In her first song, from her bedroom balcony, she thinks it is Chevalier in the street below, responding to her with the line "Love calls to love and my heart is your own." Her melancholy turns to rapture, and Lubitsch promptly cuts to the wall outside her palatial house where, in fact, the baritone voice, far more melodious than Chevalier's, is that of Count Danilo's orderly (Sterling Holloway.) Danilo (Chevalier) silently directs him, as he would an orchestra. The point made—that Chevalier can't sing worth a damn but doesn't need to—is both Lubitsch's and Chevalier's private joke.

Even before *The Merry Widow* was made, it must have been clear to Chevalier that this type of picture would soon become a period piece. In December 1933, *Vanity Fair* had deplored the typecasting he was forced to endure:

> There are, I imagine, an increasing number of people who find themselves
> tired of Chevalier's movie characterization, and, as for various reasons the
> productions themselves have gone gradually downhill, an equal number
> of people probably feel that the French comedian has run his race.

Chevalier's "rejection phenomenon" went further than that, involving, as it did, "a rejection of the entire world of European naughtiness that Lubitsch's American films generally invoked."[14] Times were changing, the novelty of sound had long worn off, and the escapist vogue was coming to an end. Chevalier was not alone in tiring of films set in minuscule, remote Balkan kingdoms in a bygone age. The American musical film, to be successful, now needed more than the kitsch Ruritanian settings that Lubitsch so loved. The mood was ripe for the still extravagant, but more contemporary musicals of Busby Berkeley, with new stars like Fred Astaire and Ginger Rogers, in plots and situations that a more sophisticated American public could relate to more directly: the Judy Garland–Mickey Rooney hits would soon be inescapably rooted in mainstream small-town America. Even the later, much inferior musical films starring Jeanette MacDonald and Nelson Eddy would have more believable, realistic topics. The real surprise was that the "kitsch" vogue had lasted so long.

Chevalier may not have understood the full sociological and cultural implications of his diminishing popularity, but he did know that, while he was still the epitome of the charming, popular French seducer, his later pictures were not making as much money for Paramount or MGM as the earlier ones. He attributed part of his recent failures to inferior scripts, a paucity of ideas, and the studios' aversion to casting him as a dramatic actor. Even before *The Merry Widow*, he had started complaining about his stereotyped "French seducer" roles. In a long interview, he told the *Pictorial Review* (November 1933), "I'm sick of always being photographed by the side of bed that isn't my own and of standing under a window at night singing foolish songs to a mysterious lady." If women didn't want to see him in "serious," realistic roles, "that's too bad. I'll do it just the same." He wasn't worried, he added, about a "fickle public."

Folies Bergère, his next, and, as it turned out, his last, Hollywood film for a very long time, did give him the chance to show his acting talents, in a dual role. This was a "one-off" assignment for Twentieth Century–Fox, for MGM was still grappling with the consequences of *The Merry Widow*'s unexpected failure and had nothing ready for him. He played both the part of "Baron Cassini," the dour banker, and "Eugène Charlier," the well-known music-hall star who is hired to impersonate him. As a Feydeau-like farce more suited to French than American audiences, the film's effectiveness depended to some extent on the skill with which Chevalier was able to create two very different characters. While his performance as Charlier—himself—was convincing, his depiction of the banker was somewhat wooden and predictable. Still, audiences flocked to see it in France because of the bevy of bare-breasted Folies-Bergère dancers (the scenes were reshot with bras for the benefit of the MPA code) and because Marcel Achard, the well-known French play-wright, and Albert Willemetz managed to inject a light touch into its French-language version. In English it lacked wit (and nudity). In neither version was the music memorable.

Chevalier made his doubts clear, but MGM was in no mood to listen. Despite Thalberg's earlier promises, he had no intention of allowing Chevalier to abandon his "French lover" film persona. *The Merry Widow* had failed commercially simply because it had cost too much. He was certain that *The Chocolate Soldier* (MGM's next film for Chevalier) and *The Cardboard Lover*, more films in the same old genre, would hit the bull's-eye.

Chevalier had been brooding for over a year now on the advisability of giving up Hollywood. After his tiff with Lubitsch over *Merry Widow* casting, he was, at last, more experienced in Hollywood's ways, more aware of the weapons at a star's disposal. Thalberg's word clearly meant little, but contractual obligations were another matter. Chevalier now played his cards skillfully. He no longer directly fought MGM's decision to have him star in *The Chocolate Soldier*. He simply exerted his legal rights to insist that his name be placed at the top of the credits—one of the clauses in his MGM contract. When Thalberg insisted that his new costar's name be placed above his own, he refused, broke his MGM contract, and severed his connection with Hollywood forthwith.

Ironically, the new costar MGM intended to hire was none other than Grace Moore, whom the studio had rejected eighteen months previously for the leading role in *The Merry Widow*. Overnight, she had become a highly desirable property thanks to a film she had made in the meantime, *One Night of Love*. Chevalier had nothing against Grace Moore. On the contrary, he liked her and had done his best to get her the *Merry Widow* part. At the hugely successful premiere of *One Night of Love*, Chevalier had even squired her and been with her in her hotel room when she called her Spanish husband long-distance to tell him the good news. After unabashedly listening in, Chevalier told her, "You know, I've been all over the world, had all the beautiful women I've ever wanted, but I never knew what it is to be in love with anyone till now. No one talked to me the way you talked to Val [her husband Valentin Parera]. You put a wall around the two of you. I felt very much alone." "Poor Maurice," Grace Moore wrote. "He did look desolate but I was woman enough to know that his nostalgic melancholia did not concern me."[15]

Hollywood historians concur that it was pressure from Harry Cohn, Grace Moore's lover, that led Thalberg to offer her top billing. Thalberg did his best to get Chevalier to change his mind: "The important thing is to make a good movie, Maurice, and earn money. Isn't that right?" But Chevalier's pride had already been somewhat hurt when the *Merry Widow* credits had given him and Jeanette MacDonald equal billing, and MGM's almost inexplicable insistence that he play second fiddle to Grace Moore looks, at this remove, like a Machiavellian power ploy to effect a parting of the ways. There may well have been private doubts about a long-term return on Chevalier's huge salary. In any event, MGM delayed making *The Chocolate Soldier* till 1941, and *The Cardboard Lover* was never made at all. The financial settlement Chevalier received from MGM was never made public, though it was substantial. Chevalier told the press he was "losing big money" by returning to Europe: His MGM contract guaranteed him $250,000 per film as well as a percentage of the gross.

Without apparent regrets, Ruppa packed, paid off servants, terminated the lease on his house, and Chevalier informed close friends like Charles Boyer and Douglas Fairbanks, Sr., before the news of his and MGM's parting of the ways became public. Both Chevalier and Thalberg at first maintained the fiction that disagreement over billing was the only issue. Very quickly, however, Chevalier revealed this was only part of the problem. "I'm tired of being pictured in the same role," he said on March 22, 1935, in New York, on the eve of boarding the *Île de France* for Le Havre. "I want to do serious characterizations. I have not been too happy, always being the same old fellow," he told *The New York Times*. "I get no more kick out of doing that. I will just sit in my house and decide what to do." He might have stayed had he been offered another role like that in *Folies Bergère*, he said, for

[t]he critics saw I could do something different. . . . I got a kick out of doing the last picture, and although I did not think I was a great actor, or that the picture was a masterpiece, it was something new and different. I had two pictures signed with Thalberg. They were going to be good, but in them I was the same old fellow. He didn't see my view and I didn't see his, so after a friendly discussion we parted friends.

Chevalier added that "last night I was out with Beatrice Lillie and Fanny Brice and they seemed to think I was right." On their last night on American soil, Chevalier and Ruppa stayed up all night, celebrating, first in his suite at the Ritz-Carlton, then at a series of brief appearances in some of the nightclubs where he was well known. Kay Francis joined them. Everywhere he was given a hero's send-off, with innumerable toasts.

The following day, outside his cabin, forty-two large baskets of flowers were stacked, far more than could fit into his suite, and hundreds of women pushed and shoved to get an autograph and a last glimpse of their idol. Neither they, nor Chevalier, could possibly imagine that it would be more than ten years before he would return to the United States, in very, very different circumstances indeed.

CHAPTER 12

"Does anyone in the room remember a Frenchman with a broad smile, a protruding lip, a straw hat and a cane?"

—*New York World Telegram*, 1937

*B*ack in France, Maurice Chevalier used far less diplomatic language to explain his break with MGM: "I am happy to return to the music hall, my first love," he told reporters. "I belong here and not in Hollywood. I am glad I am finished with pictures. They do not suit my temperament."

Repeated statements like these did not endear him to the Hollywood community he had left behind. "Chevalier is sour," wrote the *Los Angeles Times* (May 2, 1935). "His pockets bulging with money he made out of motion pictures, Chevalier has resumed his music-hall career with some sour remarks flung back at Hollywood. . . . The crooners chased the illustrious Chevalier off the screen. The American public never gets more than a half-scared interest in the mocking satire of Paris. We like songs where love rhymes with dove." He would only be missed, the *Los Angeles Times* added archly, by the girls. "Whenever he fell in love—which was frequently—

he insisted on acting as chauffeur for the precious one, which was a saving."

For all his Hollywood stardom, Chevalier did not find it easy, at first, to resume his career as a full-time music-hall entertainer. Several producers balked at his huge fees. Other, younger men like Saint Granier, Odett, Charpini, and especially Tino Rossi, had blossomed as vaudeville stars in his absence. Charles Trénet, first a protégé, then a rival and finally a bitter enemy, was about to make a name for himself, introducing a completely new genre that made Chevalier's act look singularly old-fashioned.

Chevalier found this out the hard way: Preparing for his comeback at the Casino de Paris, he undertook a tour of the provinces, starting off in nearby Nice. The size of his fee compelled the management of the Eldorado to increase the price of its seats to ten francs, a third more than usual. The theater remained half-empty until the old price was restored. "I was surprised to find," Chevalier noted, "that Hollywood stardom didn't necessarily guarantee a faithful music-hall audience." He showed his customary ruthlessness in appropriating material he felt would improve his act. Fully aware that Jean Sablon intended to include in his repertoire a singularly polished, lilting song by Michel Emer called "*Si Tu M'Aimes*," ("If You Love Me"), he went behind Sablon's back to try to acquire it for himself. To his credit, Emer refused Chevalier's compelling offer. Similarly, a year later, he took over Charles Trenet's composition, "*Y'a d'La Joie*," at first with the author-singer's consent. Trenet, originally part of a double act and only beginning his rise to stardom, was proud that it had attracted Chevalier's attention. But when Chevalier tried to prevent Trenet from using it in his own act, claiming he had acquired full rights to it, relations between the two men soured. For years they were not on speaking terms, and Chevalier's homophobia was such that he seldom lost an opportunity to make fun of Trenet, occasionally imitating his mannerisms onstage.

He did not abandon movies for long: In quick succession, he would make three distinctly unmemorable films, all released in Europe in 1936 (but not seen in the United States for several years).

As soon as he set foot in Paris, Mistinguett approached Chevalier. She wanted him to become her business associate in acquiring a major Paris theater, where they would produce their own shows and become stage partners once more, just like old times. In her usual style, she summoned the press, announcing their new partnership as a fait accompli.

Nothing could have been further from Chevalier's mind. By now Mistinguett was sixty years old, and he recalled her tantrums and other idiosyncracies only too well. Moreover, his feelings for her had cooled considerably. In 1933, while Chevalier was at the peak of his Hollywood career, Mistinguett had conveyed a message to him through a mutual friend. "Tell him I am happy and proud of his success," she had said. Chevalier's response was unexpectedly catty: "That old bag," he said, "that old monkey [*cette vieille guenon*], why *does* she keep at it? Doesn't she know it's time to go?"

They did, however, make up, at least for a while. Shortly after his return to France, she invited him to dinner in her house at Bougival, outside Paris. The other guest was Jean Gabin. Both were gourmets with solid appetites, and, for once, Mistinguett recalled, she stocked up on costly delicacies. Lino Carenzio, her lover and current dancing partner, was staying in Bougival with her. "Well, Micky, are we friends again or not?" she asked Chevalier. "We had never really fallen out, Maurice and I," she wrote of that encounter.

> We weren't seeing each other anymore, that's all. Maybe I'm getting absentminded, but I'm sure I never quarreled with Maurice. I should have remembered if I had. Arm in arm, Maurice and I walked round the seven acres of my property and went down to the river and watched the barges going through the locks. "You see," said Maurice, "you and I are essential to each other." We went back to the house. Suddenly, I felt very happy.

Two months later, after Fraisette, her confidential secretary who had married Marcel, Mistinguett's younger brother, had given birth to a baby girl, she insisted that Chevalier come to the clinic with her to see the child. It was crying.

> "Hear that?" Maurice said. "She's going to be a singer." "And look at her legs," I said, "that's a dancer's leg if ever I saw one." Chevalier lifted up

the baby, and started singing "Valentine" in her ear softly. We left the nursing-home together. Chevalier looked sad. "Why couldn't it have been us?" he said simply, as he left. Well, why? I don't know. He hasn't explained why yet.[1]

Mistinguett undoubtedly let her romantic imagination run away with her, or else there may have been yet another falling out, for later Chevalier's behavior toward her would be strangely formal. Janet Flanner, *The New Yorker*'s Paris correspondent, wrote, in 1938, of a Chevalier concert at the Casino de Paris:

> Chevalier still has more *métier* in his lower lip than any newcomer can offer. Unfortunately, he also still has the knack of offending his Paris devotees, as he did at the Casino's *premiere*, when, having kissed Marlene Dietrich and Grace Moore, who were in the audience, he only shook hands with Mistinguett. His devotees, by their devoted booing, made him kiss her, too.

While Chevalier was still in Hollywood, in 1934, France was buffeted by a series of scandals and political crises that degenerated into street fighting in Paris between the French left and the antiparliamentary extreme right. A year after his return to France, fears of a right-wing coup and mounting social unrest caused by the Depression led to a backlash: The French general election of May 1936 resulted in a distinct swing to the left and a socialist-led government: Léon Blum's Popular Front, a coalition of radicals, socialists, and communists, won the elections, and Blum, the new premier, introduced a series of social reforms that made him, overnight, the most hated man in France, at any rate in the eyes of the staunchly conservative French property-owning middle class. Though Blum was in fact a moderate left-wing liberal, a freethinker and an intellectual, French conservatives (and "Silent Majority" stalwarts) saw him as "the man with the knife between his teeth," a covert "*salon* terrorist" whose left-wing radicalism would destroy traditional French values. French politics, never remarkable for either consensus or tolerance, had become unprecedentedly divisive. Thierry

Maulnier, the well-known conservative political scientist, philosopher, and *Figaro* contributor, wrote that "it is essential for the salvation of the French people that Blum, his government, his regime, go from failure to failure, from defeat to defeat, from humiliation to humiliation."

Blum came to power after two years of increasing political chaos, with "new right" groups like the Croix de Feu and Action Française, many of whose members were disgruntled ex-servicemen. But the deep resentment at what many French men and women felt had been the betrayal of France by its former allies was not confined to veterans, or to the extreme right.

Anti-British and anti-American feeling ran high from the moment British and American political leaders parted company with their French wartime partners over the question of German reparations and the five-year-long military occupation of the Rhine (both Britain and America opposed it). Because the "Great War" had left France's economic infrastructure in ruins, but German resources relatively intact, most French people had supported their leaders' demands for enormous, near-crippling German reparations. It was the only way, they believed, to ensure that Germany would never again be able to threaten France militarily. Successive shortsighted French governments borrowed huge sums rather than raise taxes or devalue the franc—using expected German reparations money as security. But Germany was unable to pay more than a fraction of the huge sums demanded—and since both Britain and the United States had been against the reparations principle, refusing to support what was seen as French intransigence, France responded by defaulting on nearly all her wartime debts. Her main creditor was America—hence the grilling Chevalier received at his first press conference in 1929 while still aboard the *Île-de-France*, and William Randolph Hearst's anti-French speech at his welcoming party in Hollywood.

As a result of these misguided policies, protectionism would become a way of life in America as well as in Europe, restricting markets and leading to economic stagnation, especially after the Great Crash of 1929. As usual, the hardest-hit victims were working-class men and women. Wages, already low in France, fell still further: In 1936, a skilled French worker, putting in long hours, six days a week, earned 35 francs a day—20 percent less than in 1932—while a bottle of champagne in a Parisian nightclub could cost more than 440 francs.

Blum's reforms caused a furor. He compelled employers to give their workers paid two-week vacations, instituted a forty-hour work week, and increased wages and social-security benefits. Until the Popular Front, the quality of French working-class life had not changed very much since Chevalier's boyhood. Now there was a new spirit abroad. Workers flocked to enroll in the Communist-dominated CGT Trade Union in huge numbers, and, inevitably, many became Marxist converts.*

Blum's government collapsed in June 1937 after only a year in office. His successor, Édouard Daladier, a middle-of-the-road radical, did not attempt to put the clock back, which would have triggered a real revolution, though he did abrogate Blum's forty-hour work week legislation.

The Popular Front had a traumatic effect on the French silent majority, now in opposition. It left conservative France with an almost hysterical fear of the "international communist menace" and, indeed, of social change of any kind. It was this, in turn, that would pave the way for French collaboration with the Nazis after the collapse of France in June 1940. The sad fact was that, after the 1936 Popular Front, most of the French bourgeoisie regarded Hitler as a lesser menace to the social fabric than Blum. The consequences of this wretched shortsightedness later explained both the low morale of France on the eve of the Second World War and the zeal with which so many Frenchmen embarked on collaboration with the German victors, with traumatic repercussions that have kept skeletons rattling in French cupboards to this day.

The wave of strikes affected all theater and music-hall box-office revenues. Chevalier, who was starring in a Casino de Paris revue that summer, and had a percentage of the gross, performed for weeks in a half-empty theater. He did not take kindly to the loss; he was also strongly influenced by the two intellectuals he knew best, Sacha Guitry and Albert Willemetz, both staunch conservatives.

*CGT: Confédération Générale du Travail

While Chevalier's huge wealth insulated him from ordinary people's fears, his working-class background should by rights have made him sympathetic to the workers' demands. This was not the case. Some music-hall stars, including Charles Trenet, gave concerts at workers' sit-ins in French factories during the long strikes that were staged before Blum, reluctantly fulfilling his election promises, gave in to their de-mands.* Not Chevalier. Always a great respecter of established law and order, he was as opposed to workers' sit-ins in 1936 as he would be, decades later, to student agitation during May 1968.

At first Chevalier remained indifferent to the turmoil around him. The French music-hall world was extraordinarily inner-directed: The *monstres sacrés* of the French music hall were interested first and foremost in their own careers, petty rivalries, and their continuous struggle to remain at the top. It took a major crisis to distract Chevalier from his career preoccupations. When he *did* become fully aware of what was happening, he showed not just indifference but loathing for politics and politicians.

His reaction both to events in France and to the growing threat of Nazi Germany—Hitler had become chancellor in 1934—was an ostrichlike "plague on both your houses." It was, perhaps, the under-standable response of someone brought up in an underprivileged envi-ronment, for whom politics was simply irrelevant. Chevalier felt that ordinary people should not indulge in polemics or get involved in current affairs. It was pointless; far better to leave everything to compe-tent specialists, and just try to do one's job as well as possible. Politics was a mug's game, and self-interest the only real motivating factor. This would also be his attitude during the war, only a couple of years hence.

Writing, as usual, in the present tense, he described his feelings at the time (1937–38) as follows:

I, who have never been interested in politics, start reading the newspapers and listening to the radio. I try and understand what is going on. But how

*Recently conscripted into the French Army, Trenet got into considerable trouble, going AWOL several times to entertain the strikers.

boring it all is! As though—apart from those who make their career out of [politics]—people didn't already have enough on their plate, whether trying to earn a living or indulging in affairs of the heart?

What [the politicians] are really saying is: "if you think as I do, you can die for me. If you don't, you bastard, you swine, you piece of dirt, you deserve to be hung, drawn and quartered." Above all don't make the wrong choice! It's so much more pleasant to enjoy a round of golf!

He was enjoying more than golf. During the heady months of the Front Populaire, he fell in love, and his lightning courtship revealed an unexpectedly endearing, schoolboyish, romantic side.

One night, in 1936, he went to the Théâtre Saint-George to see a show. He realized when he got there that he had made a mistake—the theater was "dark." On the spur of the moment, he went to the nearby Théâtre de la Renaissance instead to see *Broadway*, the French adaptation of the popular U.S. musical-comedy-thriller written by Philip Dunning and George Abbott. A young actress called Nita Raya fascinated him from the moment she came onstage. Hers was only a small role; she played Ruby, the chorus girl, the same role that had launched Marlene Dietrich on her stage career in the play's German version in September 1927. After the final curtain call, Chevalier went around to the stage door and waited. When she emerged, he introduced himself and asked her to have dinner with him.

"I was immensely flattered," Nita Raya recalled, "but I turned him down. He was there again the following night. This time I said yes. He took me to Maxim's. We saw each other constantly after that, and a few days later, when the show came to an end, he asked me to come and stay with him at La Bocca. I had been hired to appear in a revue that Mistinguett was starring in, but I said no to Mistinguett and yes to Chevalier."[2]

Nita Raya, still extraordinarily poised and handsome in 1992, did not fit the pattern of those women he was usually attracted to. She was neither dark-haired nor blue-eyed and looked a little, a contemporary recalled, "like a lithe and lissome Betty Boop."[3] Like Kay Francis, however, she had an independence of spirit and an inner strength that

Chevalier admired in women. Also like Kay, she could make him laugh.

"I was caught up in an irresistible whirl," Nita Raya said. "It sounds corny, I know, but Chevalier simply swept me off my feet. I was barely eighteen, and was just starting out in the theater. He was extraordinarily handsome, a megastar. His charm was overwhelming, though his somber side was always apparent. I was the one who brought fun and laughter into his life, and that, perhaps, was why he fell for me in the first place."

When he met Nita Raya, Chevalier was a semipermanent resident of the Crillon Hotel, having sold his apartment on the Boulevard Pereire. She moved in with him. Later they would stay at the Georges V. When not appearing, for forty minutes nightly, at the Casino de Paris, Chevalier was on the move, either appearing in shows in the provinces and in other European capitals or making films in London. Everywhere he went, Nita Raya would soon come too.

"One day he said, 'Why don't you learn a few songs, then you can be part of my show?' I took singing lessons, worked hard, and soon after that, whenever he was booked anywhere, I was hired, too, as part of the show." They traveled all over Europe, vaudeville royalty, staying in the best hotels, besieged by fans. "In Stockholm, Maurice really was treated like a king," she recalled. "They even brought the Royal Guard out on parade for him." Every three months, they went to London to take in the shows. "Maurice never relaxed, he was always trying to learn something, watching other people perform," Nita Raya recalled. Perhaps to erase memories of his earlier trip with Mistinguett, he insisted they stay not at the Savoy but at the Dorchester.

"Maurice needed someone to be a buffer between him and the outside world," she said. "I was part mistress, part secretary, part public-relations assistant." He consulted her about his choice of songs. "I learned never to say, 'It's terrible,' she recalled. "I would say something like: 'Do you think it really suits you?' " Chevalier was very conscious of the thirty-year age gap between them (he was forty-eight when they met), "but Maurice could be quite childlike at times: I was the strong one, reassuring him all the time. He was the worrier."

They went house-hunting together. "I liked the look of an apartment on the Boulevard de Courcelles," she recalled, "and Maurice bought the

whole six-story building." He wanted to move into the top-floor apartment, which had an impressive balcony overlooking the Parc Monceau,
but the sitting tenant there refused to move out, so he had to make do
with the smaller third-floor balcony. It was a source of constant resentment that, though he owned the building, he could not move into the
apartment of his choice.

Chevalier's contemporaries all liked Nita Raya and felt she was the
ideal woman for him—neither a fortune hunter nor an aggressively
career-oriented potential rival. "She charmed everyone," Pierre Galante
later recalled, "At La Bocca she was the perfect hostess. I was never aware
of the slightest stress between them. They never quarreled."

Though Chevalier, after an uneasy beginning, soon regained his status
as Europe's most popular music-hall star, the same could not be said of
his film-star status. None of the films he starred in, after returning to
France, were particularly successful, commercially or critically. All
seemed to confirm only one thing: that after leaving Hollywood, he was
no longer a major star, that the legendary Chevalier movie vogue was
over. Neither *L'Homme du Jour, (Man of the Day)* directed by Julien
Duvivier, nor *Avec le Sourire, (With a Smile)* made by Maurice Tourneur,
nor *Beloved Vagabond* directed by Curt Bernhardt (all distributed in 1936),
nor even René Clair's *Break the News* (1938) made the kind of impact he
had hoped.

Graham Greene, then supplementing his still-meager literary income
as a London *Times* film critic, was kinder to *L'Homme du Jour* than most.
"A charming comedy about an electrician (played by Maurice Chevalier)
who becomes famous for a day after he has given blood to save the life
of a tragic actress," he wrote,

> May not be vintage Duvivier but is admirable "vin ordinaire." In the
> electricians' boarding-house, among his friends, there is only jealousy, the
> mean, middle-aged passion to taker him down a peg. And so we get in
> this airy ridiculous comedy, one of Duvivier's saddest episodes—bogus
> letters that arrange an assignation between the electrician and a flower-
> girl who secretly and hopelessly loves him, while the hideous inhabitants

of the boarding-house sit in the evening light sniggering over their cruel joke.

In *With a Smile*, Chevalier indulged himself in the kind of serious role he had craved while in Hollywood, as a crafty, scheming Iago-like character who works his way up from doorman to theater owner through a series of dastardly intrigues, only to find that his underling, another show-business Iago, is about to supplant him. Chevalier, as the smiling, charming villain, gave a credible, polished performance, but the scenes were static—the script, by Louis Verneuil, was an overfaithful adaptation of his successful stage play, with undistinguished music and lyrics.

Even less successful was *The Beloved Vagabond*, despite music by Darius Milhaud, one of France's most famous composers, and one hit song, "The Reason Is You." Chevalier stepped in after Cary Grant had bowed out, rejecting the inane script about a French architect who gets involved with a Gypsy minstrel family after falling in love with a Gypsy girl. It remains memorable for film buffs because it was one of Margaret Lockwood's first major film roles, as the girl Chevalier (the architect) falls in love with. Both English and French versions failed dismally. After its London "premiere," *Variety* wrote:

> Absent from American screens for about three years now, Maurice Chevalier returns in an English-made [film] which gets release on this side by Columbia. It will not hasten his return to Hollywood, in case the French singing star is interested, and in all probability will not encourage further American release of anything he does on the other side. . . . It is rather shoddy entertainment and will have difficulty grabbing more than passing notice on double bills. Chevalier does okay with the weak material handed him. He is deserving of much better.

The *New York World Telegram*'s William Boehnel, once a great fan of Chevalier's, was equally scathing:

> Since this department has pleasant memories of earlier Chevalier films, nothing would please it more than to write cheerfully of "The Beloved

Vagabond." But the bitter truth compels me to report not only has M. Chevalier been unhappy in the script he has chosen for his return to the cinema, but also that M. Chevalier is only a shadow of his former self.

But most discouraging of all was the rejection, on both sides of the Atlantic, of *Break the News,* a comedy with a plot similar in some respects to *Ishtar,* that record-breaking flop of the eighties. Set both in an imaginary revolutionary Balkan state and in Britain, *Break the News* was the tale of two obscure music-hall comedians (Chevalier and the British screen and stage star Jack Buchanan) who fall foul of the publicity-mad star of their revue and are fired. To gain publicity and a name for themselves in show business, Chevalier pretends to murder Buchanan, who actually leaves for the Balkans. The plan is for Buchanan to make a last-minute London courtroom appearance to exonerate his partner. But a revolution prevents him from returning, and Chevalier is only saved from the hangman's noose in the nick of time.

Quite apart from its mediocre, predictable script, and the fact that musical films were not René Clair's forte, its intrinsic flaw was that audiences could not believe in Chevalier or Buchanan as failures any more than later audiences could accept the same premise with *Ishtar*'s Dustin Hoffman and Warren Beatty. *The New York Times*'s Bosley Crowther, already reviewing movies, felt "there is little to suggest the old René Clair wit and humor. . . . Buchanan and Chevalier go about their merry-making with little cheer and the one song by Cole Porter lacks the spark." Chevalier's last pre–World War II film, directed by Robert Siodmak, *Pièges (Personal Column)* distributed in 1939, represented a further attempt by Chevalier to star in a noncomic role. He played the part of a wealthy show-business entrepreneur, suspected by the police of being a serial killer, saved from the guillotine at the very last moment when the girl he loves lays a trap for the real murderer. Despite a glittering cast that included Pierre Renoir, Erich von Stroheim, and a startlingly attractive newcomer called Marie Déa, this, too, failed to make its mark. Audiences could not possibly believe in Chevalier as a suspected murderer, especially in the role of a sexually ambiguous, unsympathetic character. In the American version, only seen in a handful of theaters long after its European release, extensive censorship (on the grounds of obscenity) by the Hays Office made the plot incomprehensible.

Try as he might, Chevalier was not cut out to be a character actor, though he himself never admitted this. Hollywood had cast him in the only role he could play convincingly—himself, or, rather, Chevalier as he projected himself onstage. In *Pièges* he was hopelessly miscast. As Graham Greene wrote in the *Times*, "Chevalier seems a little out of place as a rich impresario—he can't help looking like a waiter or a chauffeur of immoderate charm—but there's Pierre Renoir and a lovely new actress, Marie Déa, and all sorts of admirable minor parts."

Chevalier could no longer blame Hollywood set-piece casting or "kitsch" Austro-Hungarian musical-comedy revivals for his successive failures. All his films, after his return to Paris, were contemporary stories firmly rooted in everyday life. He monitored their preproduction details carefully, even getting a writing credit in *L'Homme du Jour*. Nor were those responsible for lyrics and music necessarily at fault. Not only Cole Porter (admittedly cruelly misused in *Break the News*) but some of the outstanding French composers (Darius Milhaud, Vincent Scotto) and lyricists like Willemetz and Michel Emer (who would later become famous for the haunting songs he wrote for Edith Piaf) worked on them. As the highbrow *Les Nouvelles Littéraires* wrote in 1937, "There is a Chevalier problem."

"How come," it asked, "he has never really made it? He almost succeeded several times. He never quite scored a goal. There was always something missing." The answer, it said, was that his stage personality had been indelibly imprinted on audiences even before he became a film star. "People wanted to see him as they had known him onstage. They were disappointed if he played a different part." This led to a dilemma: "Either the producers cast him in a stereotyped role, or they were bold enough to move away from the stereotype, and the public didn't follow." In the course of his film career, "trying to avoid these twin hazards, both Chevalier's talent, and the public's curiosity, has been blunted."

Though this analysis of the "Chevalier dilemma" was unusually perceptive, it was valid only for France. Very few Americans had seen

Chevalier onstage before Hollywood turned him into a star, and the ease with which he became America's heartthrob for young and middle-aged American women almost overnight, retaining his place as a "top ten" Hollywood star for five years, baffling as it is, rests on the handful of American musical films he starred in between 1929 and 1934. Had he remained in Hollywood, Chevalier's decline, as a film star, would probably have been more dramatic, speedier, and more noticeable than was the case in Europe, for Hollywood was a ruthless, pitiless Moloch, quick to discard those who failed to please. As it was, the Chevalier myth faded in America long before his European crop of films was cruelly savaged by critics.

"Does anyone in the room remember a Frenchman with a broad smile, a protruding lip, a straw hat and a cane?" asked the *New York World Telegram* in 1937. "I visited him in his dressing room," the reporter wrote, and

> backstage he denies any bitterness about the fickle Americans who made a fuss of him over seven years and then dropped him like a ton of bricks. Remember the Chevalier imitations? No mimic's act was complete without one. And three years ago any schoolboy could have told you the name of the owner of a straw hat, a swollen lower lip and a malacca cane.

When American newsmen did refer to him, it was in nostalgic, elegiac terms, treating him like an almost-extinct species, comfortably outliving his legend. "He seems happy and affluent enough in his native France," wrote the *New York Herald Tribune* on February 19, 1939.

Billy Wilder once remarked that "one of the strange things about Hollywood was that French accents like Chevalier's were as much of a plus in the early thirties as they would become a drawback after the Second World War." Perhaps the answer could be found in changing American attitudes toward France in general. When Chevalier became an overnight Hollywood star, in 1929, France earned considerable respect as a major European power, the country that had borne the brunt of the fighting, destruction, and casualties of the "Great War." By the time his post-Hollywood European films were distributed in the United States,

France's prestige had vanished: Overrun by the Germans in 1940, it had ceased to count as a nation.

There would soon be more valid reasons still for reporters to concentrate on the present rather than the past, and to forget the glamour that had surrounded Chevalier at his Hollywood apogee. Four days before Hitler invaded Poland, Chevalier was still trying to convince Charles Boyer, then visiting him in La Bocca, that there would be no war. On the day it broke out, Chevalier had called on the Duke of Windsor, a neighbor and frequent visitor, with whom he had a date for golf.

As Chevalier recalled in his memoirs:

> "A newscaster's voice, high-pitched and intense, was announcing that Germany had invaded Poland. . . . We listened, so stunned by the impact of this news that we didn't notice a man whispering in the Duke's ear that George VI of England was on the phone from London to his brother, the former king.
>
> When the Duke returned, his face was taut with strain, but he smiled gravely at me. "Monsieur Chevalier," he said, "I think golf is out of the question now. I'm sorry."[4]

The game was canceled, but Chevalier stayed for lunch. Afterward Nita Raya hastily packed, and within hours both were on their way back to Paris.

CHAPTER 13

"Et tout ça fait d'excellents Français!" ("They're excellent Frenchmen for all that")

—sung by Maurice Chevalier, 1939

The Second World War means different things to different people: One crucial distinction is in its very time frame. For Britain it was a long haul, almost six years of exhaustion, drudgery, and increasingly severe rationing, while British casualties mounted and the once-proud, increasingly punch-drunk British Empire embarked on a fatal decline. But the heroism of the Battle of Britain pilots, the increasingly effective RAF raids on Germany, the stirring reports of the progress of the war from Tobruk to Anzio to Normandy as the tide changed from near defeat to imminent victory, all contributed to a sense of exhilaration, a collective adrenaline flow, that is impossible to convey to those who did not experience the war directly.

Americans experienced neither bombing nor shortages on anything like the British scale. There was some rationing, imposed in 1942, of food, clothing, and gasoline, but compared to spartan

British allocations, quotas were on a generous, even lavish, scale. Another major difference was that for Americans, the war itself was shorter by almost two years, beginning on December 7, 1941, the "day of infamy" of the Pearl Harbor raid, by which time the worst was over, in Britain at least. The sense of exhilaration, of participation in an event of cosmic importance to the future of humankind, was, however, comparable.

The situation was entirely different in France: For the French, the Second World War really consisted of two, entirely separate, wars: the war of 1939–1940 and that of 1944–45. The first ended disastrously, less than a year after it began, with a humiliating armistice and the German Occupation of most of France. Then followed three years during which most of civilian France remained, technically speaking, at peace. There were, to be sure, gallant commando and sabotage raids on German targets by Resistance fighters, and hundreds of hostages were shot in retribution; Allied bombing of military targets on French soil, with French civilian casualties, occurred on an increasing scale from 1942 on, along with deportations of Jews and Resistance members. There were also short but sharp military engagements by French units loyal to Vichy against British forces in Syria and Madagascar, and other French Army units (sometimes those very veterans of the earlier clashes against the British) fought bravely alongside the Americans and the British in Italy from 1943 on. But it was only in the wake of the D-Day landings in June 1944 that France went to war again as a full-fledged nation under General de Gaulle's inspiring leadership.

At the start of the war, Chevalier gladly responded to official requests to help the war effort, whether touring the Maginot Line with Josephine Baker to entertain the troops or being filmed (by Pathé News) donating his car for scrap, clowning, bussing it, and shedding a mock tear as it was torn apart. (It was the old Packard he had brought back from the United States in 1933—not the luxury sporting two-seater he had more recently acquired). He opened in a new Casino de Paris revue, but audiences dwindled, and in May 1940, after the start of the German blitzkrieg, Henri Varna closed the show.

Maurice Chevalier fled Paris in the last week of May 1940, heading south as the German Panzer divisions hurtled through northeastern

France on their way to Paris. In his Bugatti, with Nita Raya doing all the driving, he joined the huge column of motorized refugees and ended up in a small village in the Dordogne called Sainte-Meyme.

His hosts were "family," Myrio and Desha, a couple of former Casino de Paris hoofers he had known for years. The house was small and hideously crowded—for Chevalier liked to surround himself with a small, deferential court, and had asked Joe Bridge, his World War I stalag companion, to join him, along with another, small-time, show-business couple: Félix Paquet, a music-hall comedian, and his wife, Maryse Marly. In the twenties, before his rise to stardom, they had all been on the same music-hall circuits.

Conditions were primitive: There was no electricity, gas, or running water. "We used the garden hose to take showers in the open air," Nita Raya recalled. "Maurice felt it was all rather fun. He enjoyed the sudden contrast in our life-style." He put himself in charge of the cooking stove, gathering firewood, taking a break for a quick trip to nearby Bordeaux. It was crowded out, he noted at the time. "Refugees from all over the place. Jews. Well-known actors. Industrialists. The atmosphere of a Tunisian 'souk.' "

Compared to Britain or even the United States, life in wartime France—for all its hardships, dangers, and crises—was clearly very different, and it is impossible to understand Chevalier's own conduct during those years without a constant reminder of the fact that, for over three years (1940–43), most of civilian France remained in an odd, peacetime, Pétainist limbo.

Philippe Pétain, the new head of state, was one of France's most distinguished soldiers of World War I. The silver-haired, white-mustachioed, exquisitely turned-out old roué was brought out of semiretirement; he had been French ambassador in Madrid, where his close friendship with the Caudillo had been something of an embarrassment to French liberals. But no longer. Franco and Pétain had a great deal in common: Both worshiped the old-fashioned values without which, they believed, neither country would have become great, and which would shortly be embodied in Pétainist France's new slogan, taking the place of *Liberté, Egalité, Fraternité: Travail, Famille, Patrie* (Work, Family, Fatherland). Both believed that rootless *métèques*, sinister Marxist agitators, and Freemasons were responsible for their countries' ills, and that only authoritarian rule, and the restoration of old-fashioned corporatist values, would lead their countries out of the mess they had got themselves in. The transformation of republican France into Pétainist France (of the 666 deputies and senators present, only 80 voted against, 569 voted in favor of Pétain's accession as head of state and 17 abstained) was a measure of the disarray—amounting almost to a national nervous breakdown—that engulfed France as the prospect of rapid military defeat became a certainty.

Pétain's headquarters, in unoccupied France, was Vichy, a medium-sized spa town chosen largely because of its profusion of hotels, easily turned into ministry buildings. There was no conscription, after 1940, and the Germans allowed Pétain to retain only a small standing army (itself reduced to little more than a ceremonial Guard of Honor for "Monsieur le Maréchal" after the North African landings of November 1942) but ironically, Vichy reflected, in defeat, a militaristic culture that republican Frenchmen—and women—would normally have derided. It echoed to the sounds of bugles, the clatter of elaborate changing-of-the-guard rituals. There were some 1.5 million Frenchmen in prisoner-of-war camps, a figure that did not include those later conscripted (or volunteer) civilian workers assigned to German factories. But despite all this, despite the constant front-page news of the war, suitably tailored to the diktat of the all-powerful German *Propagandastaffel*, despite the growing food shortages and the flourishing black market, despite the presence of German uniforms on the streets of Paris, life somehow went on "normally"—in marked contrast to the heady, aggressively belligerent mood so apparent in London.

Perhaps one of the most insidious successes of the German Occupation authorities (and their "collaborationist" French allies running the media and Vichy propaganda generally) was to instill, in French minds, the notion that all those unwilling to settle down and accept Pétain's leadership—all those, in short, who spoke up against Nazi Germany, or attempted to resist, via sabotage, tract distribution, or the gunning down of uniformed Germans on the street and in the métro—were not only unpatriotic but were not French at all, puppets manipulated by stateless "Jewish-communist-anarchist" criminals beyond the national pale, alien "terrorists" who deserved to be handed over to the appropriate authorities by "patriotic" citizens.

This was, of course, untrue. It was, however, at least during 1941 and 1942, a notion that prevailed among a majority of French men and women. For most French families, the war, at any rate between August 1940 and 1943, was not something they were directly involved in, though its attendant hardships—food and gasoline shortages, the continuing detention of French P.O.W.'s in Germany—were of immediate and lasting concern.

Outsiders tend to forget this fundamental difference, not least because the figure of General de Gaulle has so dominated French history for the last half-century that it is almost impossible, at this remote vantage point, to differentiate myth from reality. In our consciousness, the war, at least where France is concerned, bears his indelible imprint. We tend to think in clichés here: that wartime France consisted of "good" and "bad" Frenchmen. On the one hand, there were the collaborationists, evil, opportunistic politicians like Pierre Laval and senile ones like Marshal Pétain, who believed that a Franco-German entente was the only possible path to French recovery, as well as a minority of villainous French officials and policemen who assiduously followed Nazi directives, rounding up Jews and even, in their zeal, going beyond what the Germans expected of them. On the other hand were the Gaullists, active or biding their time. We tend to forget that the vast "Silent Majority" of France—especially in 1941–42—was neither Gaullist nor collaborationist, but "Pétainist" and passively dependent on events beyond French control.

So strongly did the personality of de Gaulle and the myth of wartime Free France possess us in later years that the Occupation period evokes, through a plethora of films and books, an exceptionally heroic period, a time when all self-respecting, patriotic Frenchmen joined in the struggle against a cruel, alien Nazi foe. Despite scholars like Henri Amouroux, Robert Aron, Herbert Lottman, and Robert Paxton, we tend to think of France during those years—if we still think of that period at all—as a time of heroic, artfully cunning derring-do, an amalgam of films like Truffaut's *Last Métro* and René Clement's *La Bataille du Rail,* which commemorated the heroism of France's railroad workers who risked their lives sabotaging German convoys.

The truth, of course, was very different, and the wartime behavior of Maurice Chevalier, who saw himself as the quintessentially "good Frenchman," can be understood only if we rid ourselves of such clichés and turn to reality, to Maurice Chevalier's France as it really was on the outbreak of World War II, and as it remained until, by the end of 1943, Germany's defeat appeared, at last, inevitable.

Chevalier was no political animal. His ignorance of world affairs was both astonishing and self-serving: He was incapable of sophisticated political analysis, seeing everything through a highly personal spectrum. Because his career was the only thing in the world that really mattered to him, his reactions to world events were inevitably shortsighted and self-centered. At the same time, as a popular artist, sensitive to his audience's response to his songs at any given time, he was also—his popularity depended on it—at all times profoundly, instinctively in tune with the successive moods of France. And even Chevalier, indifferent as he was to outside events unless they impinged on his career, was aware of the critical events leading up to France's collapse in June 1940.

One of its deep-seated reasons was not only the crushing superiority of German Panzer divisions and German military strategy but the low morale of French troops, and of France generally. Long before professional pacifists and Fifth Columnists began spreading rumors of "perfidious Albion's" determination to "fight the war against Hitler down to the last Frenchman," Germany had embarked on a brilliant propaganda exercise, a perfectly executed disinformation campaign to convince the French, especially members of Chevalier's generation, who had experienced the carnage of the First World War and were now at the helm, that nothing on earth was worth a second sacrifice of that order again. As Otto Abetz, Germany's ambassador to Paris during part of the Occupation years later pointed out, in his self-serving memoirs,[1] from 1934 on Franco-German friendship celebrations and conclaves, between French and German veterans, developed so successfully and revealed a spirit of such comradeship that this came as a pleasant surprise to Hitler himself. Georges Lebecq, the head of the French Veterans Organization, who disagreed with this new Franco-German entente cordiale, lost the presidency of the Union Nationale des Combattants, the largest of the ex-servicemens' unions (it boasted a 900,000 strong membership) in 1934 because he was among the small minority who distrusted German motives in making such advances. The Comité France-Allemagne and the Deutsche-Franzozische Gesellschaft—ex-servicemen's organizations both that spared no effort or expense to bring French and German veterans together—were not marginal, extreme rightist organizations but respectable, mainstream associations that capitalized on the memories of the wasted lives on both sides in World War I. Hitler himself, in a headline-making interview with the famous French writer and journalist Bertrand de Jouvenel in February 1936 (in *Paris-Midi*) coined the much-quoted lapidary phrase: *"Lasst uns Freunde sein"* ("Let us be friends"). And even after the August 1939 Russo-German Pact, the conventional wisdom of much of middle-class France, at the time, was that fighting Hitler made no sense, for Nazi Germany was the best possible bulwark against encroaching Soviet-style communism. One must remember, too, that the French Parliament that had ratified France's declaration of war, in 1939, was the same, deeply suspect, left-inclined National Assembly that was held responsible for the advent of the 1936 Popular Front. This attempt to turn France into a "welfare state," with the threat of a still more radical social revolution to come, had shaken conservative bourgeois France to the core.

All this explains why there was simply no mistaking the surge of joyous if shamefaced relief when Pétain announced over the radio, shortly after noon on June 17, 1940, that the government he had formed the night before was seeking an armistice[2] and why de Gaulle, in his own memoirs, bitterly recalled that "not a single public figure raised his voice" to condemn the humiliating terms of the armistice. There was uglier proof still of war-weariness and unwillingness to fight: in the crowd at Vierzon that turned on the gallant French tank officer who wanted to hold the bridges and lynched him, in the French troops who "fragged" their own officers who wanted to break out of the Maginot

Line. It was no pro-Nazi firebrand but General Maxime Weygand himself, briefly France's commander in chief, who wrote that the 1939–40 encounter was "a war where the interests of France are not at stake but only those of international communism." In the summer of 1940, the overwhelming French consensus was that "the war was over and Germany had won."[3]

For all his distrust of politicians, Maurice Chevalier, if only as an occasional newspaper reader and assiduous filmgoer (for Pathé newsreels were part and parcel of all film shows), was aware of all this. In his memoirs, his brief, ambiguous comments on the events leading up to war reflect apprehension but also irritation: Once more, for reasons that escaped him, stability, which he prized above everything else, was being threatened. For the second time in his life, politicians were about to jeopardize his glittering career.

Chevalier's own attitude toward the war, and toward the military in general, was ambivalent. He was extremely proud of his World War I Croix de Guerre (not for any single feat of bravery, but an award handed out to almost all those veterans who had been wounded and captured) and of his Legion of Honor, awarded the previous year (1938) for his "cultural services" to France. He had been deeply affected by the memories of the carnage of the First World War, and, from 1917 on, like so many surviving World War I veterans, had become a lifelong admirer of Marshal Pétain, the one commander who did his utmost not to waste French lives in hugely costly frontal attacks on the German trenches. To the end of his life, Chevalier would defend Pétain's reputation, and memory: "Let no one say that he was a traitor to his country," he repeatedly told Janie Michels, his constant companion from 1953 until 1968. "The man was a patriot and a hero."

Chevalier was also eager to maintain his image as the working-class *gosse de Ménilmontant* who had made good—and the French working class was traditionally antimilitarist. In 1914, Chevalier had greeted the war with singular sobriety, in striking contrast to the warlike hysteria of the time—understandably so, since he had already wasted six months of his life as a conscript when it broke out—and his memories were conditioned by the fact that the twenty-six months he had spent as a prisoner of war had almost ended his career. If he had any archetypal sense of the French military at all, he probably regarded them with suspicion. In Chevalier's youth, there were still memories of the army as a "class weapon of the wealthy." The Commune uprising of 1871 had left its imprint—especially in Communard strongholds like Ménilmontant and Belleville. Only twenty years before Chevalier's birth, the MP-elect for Belleville, Chevalier's constituency, had voted in favor of the suppression of the standing army, as Clemenceau (himself MP for Montmartre) would thirteen years later. When Chevalier was a child, the army was still being used as a strikebreaker. To the Belleville-Ménilmontant poor, two-year army conscription (instituted in 1905) was an unavoidable calamity, since conscripts were virtually unpaid and became dependent on their parents for even minor comforts during their stay in the army.

The French Army itself was an object of derision: Indeed, in his youth, some of Chevalier's early numbers had been in the *comique troupier* vein, those song-and-dance acts ridiculing army life and the stupidity of French officers and NCOs. On the stage, one of the greatest pre-1914 hits (originally a novel) had been Georges Courteline's *Les Gaietés de L'escadron (Squadron Frolics)*—a bitter, devastating farce about army life that was constantly revived thereafter.

Shortly after the outbreak of the war, in 1939, Chevalier launched his topical, highly popular *"Tout ça Fait d'Excellents Français"* ("They're Excellent Frenchmen For All That), a lighthearted but barely disguised antiwar ditty ridiculing the muddled unreadiness—and the disgusting physical ailments—of a cross-section of an average conscript battalion, from colonel to private soldier. The song ended with a reference to the need to "all pull together" so that "we can live peacefully ever after," but it was perceived, correctly, as reflecting the lukewarm enthusiasm of most Frenchmen for war. Typically, having struck out in one direction, he struck a balance with another song, the stirring, chauvinist "Victory" ("It's the colonel's command! It's the nation's cry!"), a song specially composed for a series of morale-building concerts (undertaken with Josephine Baker) for French and British troops during the early months of the "phony war"—itself an adaptation of a much earlier song ("*La Madelon de la Victoire*") Chevalier had sung, briefly, immediately after the end of the First World War. Its jingoism had nauseated him, and he had only performed it a few times.

Understandably, by July 1940, "Victory" had disappeared from Chevalier's repertoire. In May, shortly after the German offensive on Holland, Belgium, and into northeastern France, Varna had closed the Casino de Paris. By the end of June, not only had France sued for a separate peace, but anti-British feeling was running high: On Churchill's orders, the Royal Navy, in what was seen, all over France, as an unprovoked and unjustifiable attack, had sunk most of the French fleet off the Algerian coast, at Mers-el-Kébir, to prevent it from falling into German hands. Over a thousand French deaths resulted from this action.

Mers-el-Kébir provided the French with a convenient rationalization for Pétain's humiliating unilateral armistice request, justifying the anti-British propaganda campaign that marked the Pétain regime from the start, and led to a drastic reduction in the size of de Gaulle's Free French forces in Britain. The figures were staggering: In July 1940, there had been thirty-five thousand French officers and men stationed in Britain (among them the remnants of the ill-fated expeditionary force to Narvik and other units that had embarked for Britain at Dunkirk). In October 1940, the number had shrunk to seven thousand—and this level was to remain substantially the same for the next two years. The Free French Navy was the most affected by the Mers-el-Kébir tragedy: There had been five hundred naval officers and eighteen thousand naval ratings in Britain in June 1940. After Mers-el-Kébir, only fifty officers and two hundred naval ratings chose to remain in Britain.[4] The sad truth was that—of all the French forces in Britain at the time of the separate armistice, all but a hard core of Gaullists chose repatriation to France.

The mood of France was not only anti-British: With very few exceptions, the French view of the war differed completely from Britain's. As Robert Paxton wrote:

For France the war had already been decided on in the battlefield of the continent. If peace could be made before all parties sank into total exhaustion, France would eventually recover the leading European role decreed by her geographical position and resources. This hopeful possibility was greatly enhanced by the survival of her fleet and the French Empire.[5]

The anti-British mood was compounded, in September 1940, by de Gaulle's unsuccessful attempt (with British Army and Navy backing) to seize Dakar. Newsreel films of the French defending Dakar were shown again and again all over France, and Chevalier, always an avid movie buff, must have seen them too.

Viewed today, the magniloquent bombast of those newsreels, with their absurdly jingoist commentaries, is richly, sadly, absurdly comical. But in the fall of 1940, making up for the humiliation of recent events, they struck a chord. The subliminal message was that Vichy France was far from finished. It could repel aggressors. It had a leader, a government, an army. Despite appearances to the contrary, it still counted.

For the mood of France by the fall of 1940 had become not simply pacifist, both anti-British *and* anti-German: It was above all, in various degrees, Pétainist. In their overwhelming majority, the French put their faith in the man who had pledged to bring France back from the brink of appalling disaster and return it to *la normale.* And Maurice Chevalier, ever sensitive to the national temper, had found additional reasons for his own, ardent *pétainisme,* remaining a Pétainist for a long time, according to those who saw him regularly from 1940 to the end of 1943. As François Vals, his confidential private secretary and business manager in the postwar years, recalled, Chevalier respected Pétain's aims and the "trim, clean, dignified figure" of the impeccably groomed old marshal of France.

Shortly after his return to La Bocca, two recently demobilized French journalists phoned Chevalier, suggesting the three meet at the open-air terrace bar of Cannes' Carlton Hotel. Pierre Galante and Georges Cravenne had covered the show-business scene in Paris before the war, and Chevalier had been friendly and forthcoming. Both had an ulterior purpose in mind. Galante hoped to resume his career in Nice, as a free-lance contributor to a local paper—the hope turned out to be very short-lived, for his passionate Gaullism made him unemployable, and he soon became active in the local Resistance; Georges Cravenne was broke, and while waiting for Chevalier, wondered aloud whether he dared ask him for a small loan.

Chevalier showed up on a bicycle, as friendly as ever. Cravenne, who was Jewish, knew that he was in for a hard time, rightly suspecting Jews would be prevented from working as journalists (this became law three months later). Aware of Chevalier's thriftiness, he decided not to raise the question of a loan. Chevalier listened to the journalists' war experiences, asked them about their future plans, commiserated with both of them, and after forty-five minutes or so glanced at his watch and said, "Well, I've got to go." Looking at the bill, he said, "Let's split this, shall we?"

"It was an unconscious reflex," both Cravenne and Galante recalled. "He simply was not used to paying bar or restaurant bills himself. By splitting it, he probably thought he was doing us a favor."

Galante, who later saw Chevalier at odd intervals from 1940 to 1943 (and was eventually, after the war, to marry Olivia de Havilland) was adamant about Chevalier's *pétainisme.* In December 1940, he interviewed him for a local paper, *L'Éclaireur de Nice.*

"I've never understood anything about politics," Chevalier told him.

> But since we are lucky enough to be able to venerate a man [Pétain] and fully understand what he expects of us, I involve him privately in all the decisions I'm compelled to make. I ask myself: what would he say if he were in my shoes? How would he behave if he were beneath my straw hat? That's why, for the coming year [1941] I can only make the same wish that our Great Man among the Greats would make. . . .

"We had lots of arguments," Galante recalled. "Chevalier made the point, again and again, that Pétain had saved France, that if we were able to live at peace in Cannes in the Unoccupied Zone, without any Germans around, this was his doing. He remained a Pétainist until the end of 1943. He knew I was a fervent Gaullist, and at times I felt I had won him around. But he only had to listen to the other side to revert to his earlier views."[6]

Galante added that Chevalier was certainly neither pro-German nor anti-Semitic, but that his general attitude, especially in 1941–42, was perfectly in tune with that of the majority of the French people—themselves, immediately after the 1940 armistice, overwhelmingly Pétainist, desperately anxious to return to "normalcy" and confidently expecting Pétain to make this possible.

It was a craving both the German masters of Occupied France and the French Vichy authorities exploited to the hilt. The quicker the return to normalcy, the less fear there was that Frenchmen might be tempted to join de Gaulle to continue the war abroad, or that internal unrest might lead to a social revolution (the other Vichy obsession in those first few months following France's collapse).

The motives of those who flocked back to Paris after the traumatic May–June exodus were complicated and contradictory. "Vast public events brought their own individual physiological agony but I wanted to become a *person* again, with a past and a future of my own," wrote Simone de Beauvoir of her own mood as she returned to Paris to teach in a girls' school for the fall 1940 semester.[7] Chevalier, had he been as articulate, would probably have said the same thing.

The French authorities were determined to make a show of normalcy in the occupied capital—and succeeded beyond their wildest dreams. By August–September 1940 most Paris theaters and music halls were open again and doing a thriving business. As Otto Abetz, about to become German ambassador to Paris, put it, "given the important role of art and science in the life of the French capital, the embassy intervened so that theatrical and musical life, conferences and exhibitions, be resumed, normally and as quickly as possible. I managed to get the permission of the [German] General Staff to reopen the Sorbonne and all higher educational establishments."

An even more eloquent testimony was that of René Rocher, who headed the Odéon Theater in Paris from 1942–44:

As soon as they entered Paris, the Germans, for understandable propaganda motives, strove to give the capital a normal life. With this purpose [in mind] they encouraged and facilitated to the greatest possible extent the reopening and reorganization of all places devoted to public entertainment.[8]

Paris theaters, in the early months of the German Occupation, came briefly under the direct control of the German *Propagandastaffel*, but in February 1941 authority was invested in a prestigious committee of actors and theater personalities working hand in glove with the German authorities. This committee consisted of Gaston Baty, (1885–1952, one of France's most inventive and renowned theater directors), Charles Dullin (1885–1949), Louis Jouvet[9] (1887–1951), both distinguished actor-managers, and Pierre Renoir, the actor-director (and elder son of Pierre-August Renoir, the world-famous painter). This group had the full confidence of the German Occupation authorities, Rocher wrote,[10] and enjoyed the support of another committee of prominent French intellectuals and theater-world personalities unambiguously labeled "Collaboration." One reason, Rocher pointed out, why the German Occupation authorities were so keen to get the efficient Paris métro going again was to enable Parisians to go to the theater. Because of the curfew, performances now began earlier (7:00 P.M.)* In Rocher's view, "The theater in France during the German Occupation was at least as prosperous as it had been in the preceding years," possibly more so. Music halls and theaters were packed, and the speed with which the theater and music-hall world reverted to *"la normale"* surprised everyone.[11]

The *Théâtre de l'Oeuvre* was the first to open (July 11, 1940) with a comedy, *Juliette*. The Paris Opéra, Opéra-Comique, Comédie Française, and Odéon theaters opened in August–September, under new French management, compelled to furnish the *Kommandantur*, without charge, a large quota of the best seats daily; the Palace music hall opened on July 16, 1940, followed shortly afterward by all of Chevalier's old haunts— the Concerts Mayol, the Lido, and the Casino de Paris. Paul-Louis

---

*By the time Chevalier performed in Paris in 1941 and 1942, the opening time had reverted to 8:00 P.M.

Derval's Folies-Bergère gave its first postwar show by the end of 1940. Three quarters of the audience were German. Most theaters and all music halls played to full houses practically from the day they opened, responding to the expectations of a German clientele anxious to glimpse nudity on the stage and the legendary spectacle of "*les petites femmes de Paris.*"

The French film industry, after a brief hiccup in the first half of 1940, enjoyed a boom during the Occupation years it has never equaled since: In 1939, 75 French films were produced, seen by 6 million people; from 1940–44 there were 225 French films made, seen by 250 million. From December 1941 on, no American films were shown, and German films, though heavily publicized, attracted almost no French audiences.

On the literary front, too, leading members of the French intelligentsia outdid one another, at least at first, in their attempts to prove to France and to themselves that the new collaborationist regime of Marshal Pétain was all for the best, and almost certainly preordained. French publishers, with only one or two exceptions, decided of their own accord to stop publishing authors who might conceivably offend German susceptibilities. Hundreds of thousands of banned books were burned, and several publishers went out of their way to print arrantly anti-Semitic books such as René Dumont's *La France Juive.* In Dumont's lifetime, he had failed to find a publisher and had brought the book out at his own expense.

In the immediate aftermath of the *débacle,* André Gide, by 1940 probably the grandest of France's men of letters, Teilhard de Chardin, France's leading Christian philosopher, Maurice Rostand, the famous playwright, Paul Claudel, the diplomat turned writer, moralist, and Academician, all indulged, at any rate at first, in embarrassingly fulsome Pétainist panegyrics. (To his credit, Gide, after praising Pétain's "admirable" behavior in 1940, quickly turned against the Vichy regime, and spent most of the war in Tunisia, refusing to listen to leading collaborationist writers like Drieu la Rochelle and Jacques Chardonne who tried to persuade him to return.) Sacha Guitry, the most flamboyant actor-manager of all, one of Willemetz's closest friends, was a fearful snob, and flattered the new masters of Paris considerably: His play, *Le Bien-Aimé*, a historical romp nominally about the "beloved" court of Louis XV, was in fact a thinly disguised piece of pandering to the new German Occupation authorities, the thrust being that the "new Germans" were the "new kings," as popular as the old and as capable of leading the French nation. An inveterate partygoer, Guitry was unable to resist the blandishments of the suitably deferential Abetz and the *Propagandastaffel*, duly attending, among others, a lavish party staged by Abetz for the premiere of a propaganda movie called, unambiguously, *Hitler Youth*.

As Paris gradually "returned to normal," the threat of the social revolution that Pétain and his government feared above everything else receded. In a meeting with Otto Abetz in January 1942, Hitler would note, with considerable surprise, "France's baffling goodwill towards Germany."[12]

Such was the prevailing climate, in the arts, when Maurice Chevalier returned to his Hollywood-style ranch at La Bocca, near Cannes, in early July 1940. In his urge to return to show business, his only durable love, "Momo" behaved not unlike millions of other Frenchmen. But he happened to be a hugely popular, internationally known show-business figure, and his failure to realize this difference would later almost cost him his life, cast a slur on him that exists to this day, and leave him with a lifelong sense of grievance and resentment.

To Chevalier, in July 1940, the disastrous ten-month war had been an unfortunate hiatus in his career. From his home in the Unoccupied Zone, this lifelong worrier was concerned, first and foremost, with his own show-business career. In those brief pages in his memoirs dealing with this period of his life, and in his "as-told-to" autobiography, *With Love*, Chevalier was economical with the truth. To hear him tell it, he spent most of the war in his house at La Bocca in voluntary idleness, giving a few scattered small shows, here and there, in the French Unoccupied Zone. He described in detail how he was blackmailed by French officials—acting on behalf of the *Propagandastaffel*, who came to see him and obliquely threatened him (and Nita Raya) with dire penalties unless he performed on the Paris stage once more—thus providing the ultimate proof that everything in Paris was back to normal since the quintessentially Parisian superstar himself was back onstage.

This is how he told it in *With Love*:

> Two "important theatrical men from Paris" showed up unexpectedly at la Bocca in July 1940. "Hide, darling," I told Nita, who was Jewish.
>
> "The Germans admire you, Maurice," one of them said. "But if you don't come back, they could get annoyed, even irritated, if you know what I mean."
>
> "As a matter of fact I don't," I said carefully. "Why should my staying here in my own house upset anybody?"
>
> "Look, Maurice," the other one said with a winning smile, "Paris has to start living again, we all know that. . . . Paris made you what you are, the people wouldn't understand it if you stayed away."
>
> I rose to my feet. "I'm afraid they'll have to, gentlemen. I'm staying right where I am."
>
> Their smiles faded, and moments later they left. I turned back inside the house with an odd sense of foreboding that would not go away.[13]

In his memoirs, Chevalier never divulged the names of these two "well-known" show business visitors, and Nita Raya herself, astonishingly sprightly in 1991, cannot recall any such visitors, or being told to hide. "I *do* remember Henri Varna showing up several times," she recalled. "He was very insistent, desperate to bring Maurice to Paris. The theater and music-hall boom was in full swing from the end of 1940 onward, and Varna felt that without Maurice at the Casino de Paris he was losing out on it."

Henri Betti, the well-known French composer who became Chevalier's pianist and almost constant companion from July 1940 until 1945, also cast doubt on Chevalier's reluctance to perform in the Occupied Zone. Born in Nice in 1917, Betti was twenty-three years old when a chance meeting there changed his whole life.

A housepainter's son, like Chevalier, he had been called up at the outbreak of war into the somewhat curiously named 72nd Alpine Fortress Battalion, in Briançon, a garrison town near the Italian border. Betti, a brilliant Paris Conservatoire music student and gifted pianist, spent most of his time during the "phony war" months there either moonlighting in local bars, cafés, and nightclubs or else performing at officers' private parties, playing after-dinner Chopin, Ravel, and Debussy selections. His official duties seem to have been light: He welcomed the official spells he put in as garrison telephone operator because this enabled him to put through limitless calls to his girlfriend in Paris at the army's expense.

He had been a civilian for less than two weeks when, in early July 1940, he and Roger Lucchesi, a professional guitarist and songwriter, met on the Promenade des Anglais and Lucchesi dragged him over to see Maurice Chevalier in La Bocca. Lucchesi wanted Chevalier to hear a song he had just written, hoping he might take it up, and he needed Betti, he explained, because a piano accompaniment sounded more impressive than a guitar.

The two men took the train to Cannes, hired bicycles at the station to make their way to La Bocca, about three miles distant, and were let into the La Louque estate, which Betti found "palatial." A maid showed them into a large sitting room, "furnished Hollywood-style." They could see Chevalier playing tennis with friends in the garden outside, which boasted a large swimming pool, also being used by guests. Shortly afterward, Chevalier, wearing white and sweating profusely, made his appearance. "I've brought a pianist," Lucchesi said, not even mentioning Betti by name. "And why not?" said Chevalier. He settled into an armchair and motioned them to start.

Nervously, Betti started playing the introductory bars on Chevalier's Steinway concert grand. From the start, he felt he was under his intense scrutiny. Chevalier turned down the song—but not the pianist. "I don't feel it's my thing," he told Lucchesi. "Hope you have better luck elsewhere." Then, to Betti, he said, "But *you* interest me a great deal." Betti's piano-playing, he added, was more than competent—it showed considerable style. He asked Betti about his musical experience, and was impressed to hear he had won a scholarship to the famed Conservatoire.

"My regular accompanist for the last ten years has been called up, and I have no idea where he is, or even if he's still alive," Chevalier said. "Will you fill in for him?"

Betti was speechless.

"I need a quick answer," said Chevalier. "My impresario is arranging a two-month series of concerts for me in the Unoccupied Zone, starting almost immediately. After that, in October, I'll be making my comeback in Paris, at the Casino de Paris, in a big musical spectacular Henri Varna [the Casino's owner] will be staging there. So I need to know soon so that I can look for someone else if you're not interested in my pro-posal.[14]

"But first of all," Chevalier said, drawing him aside, "I need to ask you some personal questions. Are you married?"

Betti shook his head—no.

"Are you liable for call-up?"

Betti mumbled that he was only just getting used to being a civilian again.

"Now, please excuse me for an indiscreet personal question, but there's a war on," Chevalier said. "We'll be going to Paris, to the Occupied Zone. So I must ask you this: Are you Jewish?"

Betti said he came from a poor Italian-Catholic immigrant family.

"In that case," said an elated Chevalier, "it is heaven itself that sent you here!" ("*C'est le ciel qui vous envoie.*")

Betti asked to think things over. He was hoping to resume his studies at the Conservatoire, which was about to reopen, and had already made plans to return to Paris. The prospect of working with France's top singing star, however, was irresistible: Two days later he became Cheva-lier's official accompanist.

CHAPTER 14

"I've seen you in your mad days
And some of your bad days"

—from *The Love Parade*,
Maurice Chevalier's opening
song about Paris

*C*hevalier's first concert, with his new accompanist at the piano, took place in Nice. On this and every subsequent show, Betti received a flat 250-franc fee (about $50). "Chevalier made the rules very clear from the start," he said. "I was only paid for the actual performance, and, of course, traveling expenses when we were on the road. There was no retainer, and no remuneration for often lengthy rehearsals. To his credit, Maurice, who always stayed in the best places, always booked a room for me in the same hotel." At the first few shows, Betti read from the sheet music provided. Very quickly, however, he memorized everything, which impressed Chevalier considerably. "At first he worried that I might not remember the notes," Betti recalled. "Then he got used to it. 'You're the first pianist I've worked with who can do that,' he said."

Chevalier was known for his remarkable talent-spotting powers. While still a Hollywood star on one of his many trips to Paris, he had encouraged Louis Leplée, the owner of Gerny's on the rue Pierre Charron, to take on the troublesome but awesomely gifted Edith Piaf, telling him cold-bloodedly: "Try her out. The 'natural' bit could work." (*Ça fait nature*) But he was not invariably prescient: Betti recalled listening to an unknown *fantaisiste* singer in Maxim's nightclub in Nice, early on in the war, perhaps in 1941. "I was hugely impressed by his original style and repertoire, he said, "and told Chevalier about him. 'I want to see his act,' Chevalier said, so I took him there a few nights later. Throughout his performance, Chevalier looked glumly disdainful. Afterward, he told me: 'That protégé of yours, he'll never get anywhere.' " The beginner's name was Yves Montand, and Betti believes that Chevalier deliberately put him down because, though generous in helping some careers (invariably, Betti felt, "people who would be no threat to him"), he was deeply suspicious, and hugely jealous, of all potential rivals.

Betti and Chevalier traveled everywhere in overcrowded buses and trains. Gasoline was scarce, and Chevalier didn't want to draw attention to himself by requesting a special gas allocation from the Nice Préfecture, which he would almost certainly have received.

At these shows, booked for him by his Egyptian-born agent, Max Ruppa, Chevalier appeared only after the interval. The first half was given over to lesser acts—obscure *chanteurs de charme*, jugglers, conjurors, stand-up comedians. The notion of a one-man show was unknown in France: Only after the war, in Lyons in 1945, would Chevalier inaugurate this genre.

Almost everywhere he went, in both occupied and unoccupied France, Chevalier was lionized, feted, wined and dined. Some of the places he performed in, he noted later in his memoirs, "were so small I'd never even heard of them." He sang in church and town halls, for only the larger towns boasted cinemas or theaters. "He would never have condescended to appear there in normal times," Betti recalled. After the show, there would usually be a party organized by the local dignitaries—the mayor, *sous-préfet, conseilleurs généraux,* local landowners or factory owners. "Things were pretty boring then in provincial France, and Chevalier's arrival in their home town was a huge event," Betti noted. "They had usually planned their reception for us months in advance.

"Looking back on those years, in many respects the happiest and the most satisfactory in my whole life," Betti recalled with an ironic twinkle in his eye, "it's weird that what I remember most about them, at a time when most of France was suffering and going short of everything, are the good times and the marvelous meals."

After 1940, there were severe shortages of almost everything (the Germans requisitioned most of France's food supplies), "but you'd never know it from the banquets that were laid out for us: There was foie gras [goose liver], lobster, even sometimes caviar, and great wines, to the point where I couldn't take it anymore and wanted to bow out. But Chevalier wouldn't let me. 'We have a duty to perform,' he would say, 'we're on parade'—and it was obvious that an evening with Chevalier was the high point in the lives of our hosts. There were times when all I wanted, after several consecutive nights' sampling all that rich food, was to retire to bed with an apple and a glass of water."

When Chevalier performed in the evening, he had a very light lunch, or nothing at all, "so he was able to do ample justice to it all," noted Betti. And the fact that he was almost invariably invited for dinner, he added, appealed to Chevalier's inordinately developed sense of thrift. Night after night, Chevalier would hold forth at the dinner table, name-dropping and reminiscing about his career and his Hollywood years, his deferential hosts lapping up every word. He had always needed docile listeners to bask in his glory. Now he had a different audience every night.[1]

The year 1941 marked the lowest point in Franco-British relations. Papers were full of accounts of British "piracy and acts of savagery" (such as seizing French cargo boats containing "bananas for French children"). General Fernand Dentz, the former commander of the "Levant Army," which had fought against the British troops in Lebanon and Syria in 1940, gave a lecture (October 13, 1941) to army veterans that was widely reported in the press. He called Britain "the secular enemy," representing "all the things which had almost destroyed us: democratic-masonic politics and Judeo-Saxon finance." At dinner parties with representatives of la France profonde—most of them, by the nature of their jobs, members of the Vichy "establishment"—it is likely that such subjects of conversation were not lacking and that they did nothing to shake Chevalier's faith in Marshal Pétain. As Nita Raya recalled, Chevalier had "an innate respect for established authority"—the same respect for rules and regulations that made him shun the thriving black market and rely on their official rations, at least in his own home. The household was better off in this respect than the average French family: Chevalier turned his lawn into a vegetable garden, fed chickens and rabbits on food scraps, and even bought a cow for milk, which was kept in a shack at the bottom of the garden. "The gardener was the one who benefited most from the cow," Nita Raya recalled. "We all supposed he was selling the surplus milk somewhere, but Maurice didn't mind."

In his memoirs, Chevalier commented on the large numbers of Jews in Cannes, noting that his friend the writer Tristan Bernard, himself a Jew, felt the town ought to be respelled "Kahn."* Chevalier also noted that, increasingly "in the unoccupied zone, Jewish performers were being hooted off the stage by gangs creating havoc in the audience," and that theater directors did nothing in the face of such growing anti-Semitism. "I myself," Chevalier added (writing in the present tense), "deliberately show myself in public places in the company of known Jews, despite sharp reactions and violent criticism."

His oblique reference to the plight of French Jews (Nita Raya, and many of his friends, were Jewish) implied that, for all his busy schedule and self-centeredness, Chevalier was well aware of their plight. But— and here he was no different from millions of other Frenchmen—in his mind, he seems to have disassociated the anti-Jewish legislation promulgated by Vichy from Pétain himself: The marshal, in the eyes of many French people, at least in the early days of the Vichy regime, could do no wrong and was not held responsible for some of his ministers' servile pro-Nazi behavior.

The truth is that—while yet under no compulsion from the Germans to do so—one of the first things Pétain's Vichy government did was to draw up its own anti-Jewish laws, promulgating them well in advance of

---

*Tristan Bernard had written *Le Petit Café*, made into Chevalier's Hollywood film, *Playboy of Paris* in 1930.

the German anti-Jewish measures in Occupied France. The artisan of these Vichy laws was a notorious anti-Semite, Interior Minister Raphael Alibert. Jews were banned from public office (with certain exceptions for war veterans and cases "at the discretion of the Council of State"), *numerus clausus* ceilings for Jews were introduced in the liberal professions, and Jews were totally excluded from employment in the press, the radio, the theater, and the movie industry. In 1941, Jacques Copeau, the famous theater director and chief administrator of the Comédie Française, insisted that the male *sociétaires* display the proof of their noncircumcision to him. One of its women members, a leading actress called Marie Ventura, of Romanian origin, in a letter to Copeau, bragged not only of her own, but of her mother's anti-Semitism in her native Romania.

Xavier Vallat, another well-known anti-Semite who became France's first commissioner for Jewish Affairs, wrote, "in this way the law fulfilled the highly correct idea that Jewish saturation was not merely to be feared by the state as far as the administration was concerned, but was also to be regarded as a danger when it reached certain liberal professions like medicine or banking. . . . It was very clear that any racial group or political party which in any way controlled the majority of the newspapers, the cinema, the radio stations, would have no need, in order to hold true power, to include officials in its ranks."[2] (In 1941, the list was extended massively, to include cattle-trading, art, antique dealing, and real estate, except for "subordinate and manual labor" in these professions). The German-promulgated anti-Jewish laws, which became law shortly afterward, were, of course, to be even tougher. There were, at the time, some 315,000 French Jews in France out of a population of around 40 million—with another 350,000 in Algeria, Tunisia, and Morocco, then all under French rule.

One of the absurdities of the Vichy regime was that Pétain himself was known to intervene on occasions to save Jews personally recommended to him from arrest or deportation, always begging his entourage, "don't tell Ménétrel." Bernard Ménétrel was his personal physician, with a highly influential role at the Vichy "court." The absurdity was compounded by the fact that Ménétrel himself was not only maniacally anti-Semitic, but also hated the Germans almost as much. In the later stages of the war, he kept a rucksack packed in his quarters, next to Pétain's own, always on the brink of joining the French Resistance—which he never did, the real reason being, his friends said, that he was afraid of meeting too many Jews there.

The obsessive anti-Semitic tone of the French press in 1940–41 comes, even now, as a surprise. Mass-circulation papers like the Nazi-controlled *Le Petit Parisien* and *Paris-Soir* systematically indulged in racist attacks that outdid anything in the German media—or even in Hitler's *Mein Kampf* itself. In the light of the bloodcurdling series of articles in *Paris-Soir*, it is strange, to say the least, that Chevalier allowed this mass-circulation daily to sponsor his various gala appearances in Paris in September–October 1941, for in the French press published in Paris under German control, not a single opportunity was ever missed to stimulate the hatred of the French people toward the Jews. Here, for instance, is a *Petit Parisien* reporter describing the French Riviera on August 30, 1941 (four days before Chevalier left La Bocca for Paris): After noting that the place had become, in 1941, the paradise it must have been in 1900, devoid of noise, cars, gasoline fumes, or crowds, he wrote:

> The only people these days ostentatiously spending as if there were no tomorrow, spattering you with the filth of their luxury and their jewels, are the stateless Jews driven to the Mediterranean by war and exodus. Their insolence is a provocation for all the poor and the deprived.

As an anonymous witness put it, "You can't imagine what things were like last year."

> Those who were here still speak of 1940 with a catch in their throat. The Jews set themselves up as though in conquered territory. Many Jews trying to leave the country were fleeced by other Jews. This is under-standable for nothing gives a Jew more pleasure than swindling a fellow Jew. Even when assigned to villages far from the Riviera coast itself, they buy up everything at any price, sending prices sky-high, but luckily some of them have been sent to concentration camps.

The increasingly strident anti-Semitism of the Vichy government, and the October 1940 meeting between Hitler and Pétain, at Montoire, do not seem to have made any significant inroads in Chevalier's esteem for "Monsieur le Máréchal." Like so many French men and women at this particular time, he wore mental "blinkers," was able to ignore the hateful aspects of Pétainism, the virulent anti-British, anti-Semitic tone of the French press, and the unspoken implication—that France was, step by step, being enrolled in a pan-European crusade under the Nazi banner. It seemed, in 1941 (and there were of course incredibly brave men and women who felt and acted otherwise), an acceptable price to pay for peace and "normalization."

For all Chevalier's later claims that he only went to the Occupied Zone under duress, Betti remembers him saying, shortly after they first started working together, that there was no earthly reason why he should restrict his audience to the Unoccupied Zone. "As long as our travel permits, our 'ausweiss' passes, were delivered, we were all set," he recalled. "Our conscience was clear."

To some extent, Chevalier's behavior could be condoned: Paris papers were not readily available in La Bocca: The newspapers and magazines on sale in Cannes were those published in the Unoccupied Zone, and these were somewhat less stridently anti-Semitic; and in this precassette, pre-CD, pre-television era, there were only two ways for an entertainer of Chevalier's caliber to remain in the public eye: to perform live and on the radio. Chevalier did both, indefatigably, from 1940 until mid-1943. "We were on the go practically all the time," Betti said, "though there was a lot of time spent in distinctly uncomfortable bus and rail travel."

From the moment he began working with Chevalier, Betti came under his spell. "He was like a father to me," he recalled, "always giving me advice. 'Never try and do too many things at once,' he would say, over and over again, 'always concentrate on one thing, always try and improve whatever you're engaged in, try and go beyond your natural capabilities.' He had a favorite catchphrase he used again and again: 'You must hang in there.' ['Tiens bon la rampe.']" Soon, Chevalier set aside a room for him at La Bocca, and Betti became a semipermanent houseguest. At first he worried about his interrupted Conservatoire studies, but gradually stopped thinking about them. Chevalier's relations with Betti became avuncular, but he deliberately maintained his distance. Months after they started performing together, Chevalier told Betti that since they got on so well, he should call him "*tu*" (instead of the more formal "*vous*") and "Maurice," "as my friends do," instead of calling him "Monsieur" and addressing him formally at all times. Moments later, a somewhat embarrassed Chevalier changed his mind. "Since the difference in our ages is so great," he said, "it might be better after all if you were to go on calling me 'vous.' But you can call me 'Monsieur Maurice.' "

Betti's most anxious moments had nothing to do with the war: "Whenever we hit a new town, the first thing I'd do was try out the piano," Betti recalled. "Often it was in appalling condition, and I was always complaining, but Chevalier didn't seem to worry about that too much." To keep his hand in, Betti would play classical music on his own in the mornings, whenever the state of the instrument allowed.

"One day, I heard a voice at the back of the hall shout 'Bravo.' It was Chevalier. He hadn't recognized the piece—he knew nothing about classical music. He asked me, What's that you were playing? I said, Chopin's first ballad in G-minor. He said, Do you mind playing it again? When I'd finished, he said, That was great. I have an idea, how about playing that in public at the show tonight? I said, No way. I'm not bad, but I'm not Cortot, I'm not Horowitz, I don't want to look ridiculous. But shortly afterward, in Neufchâtel, he played a trick on me. In the middle of his act, in front of an audience of two thousand people, he turned to them, and said, 'And now I'd like to introduce this young man at the piano. His name is Henri Betti, and he's going to play you'—he made a show of consulting his memory—'a Chopin ballad'—more fake concentration—'in G-minor.' Under his breath, he hissed at me, 'Got you there, didn't I?' Then he put his straw hat on the piano, leaning on it in rapt attention while I played, just in case there were any hecklers who might start shouting, 'We came for Maurice, not for a piano-player.' But no one ever did. My own piano 'intermezzo' became a regular feature of Chevalier's show. I always got a rapturous reception, and his introduction onstage was what counted, for sometimes the sounds coming from those pianos were appalling."

Increasingly impressed by Betti's skills, Chevalier, only a few weeks after hiring him, asked him to compose some music for some new songs, to enlarge his repertoire. "It got so that during the course of the evening, during the latter part of the war, Chevalier would sing fifteen songs, and fourteen of them would be mine," Betti said.

One of the first songs Betti composed for Chevalier, which he first started singing in early 1941, was called *"Notre Espoir"* (*"Our Hope"*). In an oblique, strangely effective way, it expressed Chevalier's own war-weariness and frustrations, an accurate reflection not only of his mood, but that of 1941 France as a whole. The idea came to Chevalier, says Betti, after a night's insomnia, and at the piano, at La Bocca, Betti and Chevalier quickly hammered out a completed version the following day.

I used to sing about love, about happiness, the song begins, but what on earth is there left to sing about now? Only this: "Tra la la la la la et tsing pa poum"—a series of meaningless onomatopoeic sounds sung to a typically lilting Chevalier-type tune. The lyrics underline the futility of using any real words, the danger inherent in doing or saying anything at all, the constant risk of labeling oneself as dangerously controversial if one expressed an opinion of any kind out loud.

Its message was less of hope than of patience—a form of passive resignation, the song implied, was essential if one was to survive. It had the widest possible appeal: The French public immediately perceived what Chevalier was trying to convey, for increasingly, in France itself, people were inhibiting their true feelings, fearful they might lead to trouble.

But an even more popular song, and one that made Betti a moderately wealthy man, for, again, he composed its music and got a share of the royalties, was "The Bricklayer's Song," (*"La Chanson du Macon"*) with words by Maurice Vandair, written and composed just before Chevalier's Casino de Paris engagement, in September 1941. Vandair, himself a cheerful anarchist, a colorful show-business personality who had chosen to remain a card-carrying Communist, neatly, or perhaps with cold-blooded opportunism, tailored the lyrics to the prevalent Pétainist French mood.

The song tells of a bricklayer on the roof of a house in a small French village, humming a tune to himself. The melody is taken up by others, growing in intensity until eventually, from one end of the country to the other, all those at work all over France are inspired by the song to new efforts to "make houses grow like mushrooms."

In the last verse, in a barely disguised appeal to the values of *Travail, Famille, Patrie,* Chevalier sang:

> "And the thought came to me
> And you can make of it what you want
> That if we all sang like that,
> If everyone put their backs into it,
> We could rebuild our house,
> It would become God's own house,
> And our song would be beautiful,
> The most beautiful tune in the world
> And when the good times came
> We would be millions of builders
> Singing away on the rooftops of our houses."

The metaphor—"house = France"—was obvious. From the start, the Vichy government had stressed the need not only to "rebuild" France's war-damaged infrastructure, but to introduce new moral values in France, to rid the country of the sinister aftereffects of the pleasure-loving, decadent, prewar Third Republic, whose vices, in the eyes of Vichy propagandists, had been the root of all evil, the very cause of its defeat. Chevalier sang "The Bricklayer's Song" at the Casino de Paris, also recording it on Radio-Paris. At first he intended to jettison his straw hat and assume the cement-stained garb of a mason, even going so far as to brandish a trowel as well, but just before the first night he decided against it: The song didn't require any props after all. "The Bricklayer's Song" immediately became, with *"Notre Espoir,"* one of the hits of the year.

Nobody but Chevalier himself really knew the extent of the pressures he came under while in Cannes and later in Paris, but given the way he concealed his motives, in his memoirs, and later, in Hollywood, for performing in Paris in the first place (understandably, he also failed to mention his admiration for Pétain), it is a little difficult to exonerate him entirely.

His was the *Mephisto* syndrome—as portrayed in Istvan Szabo's Hungarian film. Based on Klaus Mann's novel, it told the story of a compulsively hardworking, gifted, and ambitious actor in Nazi Germany (played with hypnotic skill by Klaus Maria Brandauer) who subordinates everything—love, friendship, political convictions, and, eventually, his soul—to his one real passion: the theater. When writing the book, Klaus Mann may actually have had Chevalier's erstwhile Hollywood friend and colleague Emil Jannings in mind. Certainly, Chevalier never "collaborated" as Brandauer did in *Mephisto* and Emil Jannings in real life. Nevertheless, the parallel was there: For Chevalier, all audiences were equally deserving, and since his aim was to give pleasure to the greatest number, he felt he could not afford the luxury of choosing his public. It chose him. He was blameless. This explains why, later, he was utterly baffled by the reactions of the French Resistance, and the analysts who monitored the German-controlled Paris newspapers and Radio-Paris. For Chevalier, these were simply essential tools to enable him to remain in the public eye.

It was virtually impossible for anyone living in France, even someone as self-centered as Chevalier, to be totally unaware of the role of Radio-Paris, the main Paris radio station, the only one with sufficiently powerful transmitters to be heard throughout northern and central France as well as in the Paris area. It was the principal radio vehicle for Nazi propaganda. Its staff, all French except for a handful of German supervisors who never appeared directly on the air, were handpicked by the German *Propagandastaffel* not just for their "collaborationist" reliability, but for their anti-British and anti-Semitic virulence and polemical skills. In London the station was monitored closely by Gaullists, the BBC, and British Intelligence services alike for the clues it revealed concerning German propaganda strategy. Its often indigestible, hysterical propaganda would not, in itself, have commanded large audiences. But Radio-Paris program controllers, under German supervision, made large audiences a certainty by broadcasting songs of France's best-known crooners, comedians, and top entertainers. The propaganda—like advertising on TV—was effective because its programs were popular and entertaining. Chevalier's failure to perceive its role is baffling. No French songster, however naive, could ignore this aspect of Radio-Paris.

Chevalier compounded his error by accepting Radio-Paris's sponsorship for a number of concerts, including a matinee at the Théâtre des Champs-Élysées, in October 1941. And it was to be Chevalier's relationship with Radio-Paris—more than his stage appearances in Paris—that would eventually attract the attention of London-based Gaullists, getting him into serious trouble.

As his conversations with Betti in July 1940 showed, Chevalier went to Paris of his own accord when on September 2, 1941, he boarded the train to Paris for an eight-week appearance at the Casino de Paris, and a series of radio and record-making sessions of his new songs. He may well have felt that he was taking out a form of insurance for Nita Raya and her parents by showing he was ready to perform in Occupied Paris. There was also the strong urge to make money. At war's end, a prominent French Nazi propagandist with close Radio-Paris ties, Jean-Herold Paquis, later shot after his trial for treason, would claim in court that Chevalier received sixty thousand francs for his appearance at the "Gala des Ambassadeurs," as much as he—one of the heads of Radio-Paris—earned in a month.[3] Another attraction was that Radio-Paris fees, for noted artists, were not only princely but tax-free. In his Hollywood years, Chevalier had taken on nightclub assignments between films, often to the surprise of studio heads, aware of the huge sums they were paying him each week. His obsessive thrift went hand in hand with a totally irrational fear of poverty.

The attraction of Paris was overwhelming for other reasons. After so many seedy venues, with out-of-tune pianos and unsophisticated, provincial audiences, it was essential to test himself in front of his favorite public. There was also his awareness that he was missing out on a great deal, for the Paris theaters and music halls, in 1941 and subsequently, were playing to unprecedented, capacity audiences. (The daily "take," at the Casino de Paris, during Chevalier's spell there, was fifty thousand francs). In the music halls and cabarets, the clientele was, to be sure, overwhelmingly German, but most of Chevalier's colleagues (and to Chevalier, every fellow performer in the same line of work was a rival) were uninhibited by this. The top show-business figures—Mistinguett, Suzy Solidor, Lucienne Boyer, Charles Trenet, Tino Rossi, George Guetary, and André Dassary (famous for his ode to Pétain called "*Maréchal, Nous Voilà*," which became the Vichy equivalent of "Hail to the Chief") had never been busier.[4] As Ninetta Jucker, a British journalist married to an Italian who spent the Occupation years in Paris noted, the "charm onslaught" of the Germans "was too much for the vanity and weak judgment of most theater folk. With a few notable exceptions, they succumbed to the flattery and gastronomic attentions of the besiegers." A typical "high society" party—given considerable coverage in the German-run Parisian press—followed the "premiere" (on March 6, 1941) of a film unambiguously titled *Hitler Youth*. It was attended by an impressive number of leading stage and screen stars, including Alice Cocea (Chevalier's costar in *Dédé*), Marie Bell, Janie Holt, Corinne Luchaire, and the ubiquitous Sacha Guitry.

Similarly, flattery and the lure of VIP travel caused a group of famous French artists—including Dunoyer de Segonzac, Kees van Dongen, Othon Friesz, André Derain, Vlaminck, Landowski, and the sculptors Maillol and Paul Belmondo—to embark on an extended tour of Germany in 1941 to visit fellow artists, museums, and art galleries and "exchange cultural experiences."[5] Some prominent writers and intellectuals, like Céline and Pierre Drieu la Rochelle, needed no convincing— their obsessive anti-Semitism made them converts from the start. The extraordinary success of the German *Propagandastaffel*'s public-relations exercise, where French artists and intellectuals were concerned, was also due to the careful choice of staffers working in the commandeered building on number 52, Avenue des Champs-Élysées. High-caliber intellectuals themselves, many were genuine Francophiles, all spoke fluent French, and those whose task it was to win over the French artistic and intellectual establishment were often lukewarm Nazis or even closet democrats. As Pierre Drieu de la Rochelle, one of France's most baffling writers—an unabashed pro-Hitlerite who had also been one of the most promising novelists of his generation—wrote, "The comedy of 'collaboration' was perfectly human: [it consisted of] Germans with insufficient belief in Hitler indoctrinating Frenchmen who believed in him too much."⁶

The lure of the Paris stage, during the Occupation years, was irresistible to practically all French show-business performers. Later on in the war, in February 1944, Yves Montand himself would have no qualms about performing in Paris, at the famed ABC Theater, acquiring instant fame. Montand, then an up-and-coming performer but by no means a star, came from a working-class family of Italian origin with strong Communist affiliations, and was himself on the run from the French authorities, having torn up a "movement order" to report to a German factory as an STO "conscript worker."* Every night, in the métro or on the streets, walking back to his hotel room after his ABC performances, he risked arrest and immediate deportation. It was a risk he had been prepared to take in order to make it in Paris.⁷

And in 1941, the most prestigious literary and theatrical figures were still, in their overwhelming majority, in favor of Pétain. The bylines of Colette, the historians André Castelot and Alain Decaux, and the famous gastronomic writer Curnonski appeared regularly (they were not, of course, writing about politics or international affairs) in the most arrantly collaborationist, anti-Semitic, and pro-Nazi newspapers and magazines under direct German control, like *Paris-Soir* and *Le Petit Parisien.* Presumably they felt immune from criticism because they stayed away from "controversial" subjects—a mind-set Herbert Lottman has aptly referred to as "Occupation colorblindness."

From early 1941 on, Raimu, Fernandel, Pierre Fresnay, Lucienne Boyer, Alice Cocea, Yvonne Printemps, the aging Cécile Sorel, Paul Meurisse, and other top-ranking film actors resumed their activity in French films, most of them financed and supervised by an official, specially established German production company, La Continentale.

The smiling faces of several popular French show-business figures of stage and screen—among them André Préjean, Suzy Delair, and Marie Marquet—were seen in the Vichy and Paris press, waving to cameramen

*STO: Service du Travail Obligatoire

at the Gare de l'Est as they set off for a trip to Germany to perform before German audiences. With some justification, as Chevalier pointed out, in his memoirs, "I was one of the last well-known artists to show up in Paris," where Henri Varna anxiously awaited him. Edith Piaf, already a major star, and Charles Trenet had made their acclaimed debuts to packed theaters months before, in February 1941, Tino Rossi in June.

Postwar judgments so long after the event need to be tempered by an understanding of the climate and mood of wartime France—a mood almost impossible for non-French people to grasp. What is striking, among the reminiscences of French show-business figures who wrote, later, about their experiences, either to exonerate themselves or as a brief chapter in their autobiographies, is the absence of any kind of guilt. What was an artist, a writer, a performer, to do under such circumstances? With Gide as with Chevalier, as indeed with Sartre and Simone de Beauvoir, the prevailing impression is of passive detachment—this was simply not their war. Their own lives, literary careers, and introspective ratiocinations came first.

A handful, to their eternal credit, remained silent. Jean Guehenno, the elderly novelist and essayist, refused point-blank to have anything to do with any of the French publishing houses during the war. (All of them, rather than go bankrupt, agreed to refrain from publishing "subversive," "decadent," or "Semitic" writings, including a fairly extensive "blacklist" of banned authors.) Some actors (like Jean Gabin) fled to Hollywood, then joined the Free French Forces. Others (like René Clair) sat the war out in America, and Louis Jouvet eventually left Paris, joining him there. From Hollywood, from July 1940 on, Charles Boyer repeatedly wrote Chevalier, urging him to leave France.

Chevalier never even considered this. He felt, he wrote later, that "this would be letting the side down." This was a highly creditable attitude. But it's also true that Chevalier's departure from Hollywood, in 1935, had been abrupt, and his subsequent criticism of the Hollywood film industry had infuriated the tycoons who claimed, with some justification, that they had "made" him. Chevalier's pride was at stake, and a return to the United States, especially in the wake of the French collapse, would have been a delicate undertaking for someone with such a colossal ego.

It was this ego that led to a vicious attack on him in the weekly arts magazine *Comoedia*, shortly before his arrival in Paris to star, at last, at the Casino de Paris. Despite the fact that *Comoedia* was published in German-occupied Paris, it had less of a collaborationist stigma than other papers because it dealt, exclusively, with arts subjects, and its contributors included Jean-Paul Sartre, and, eventually, Albert Camus, neither of whom, by any stretch of the imagination, can be seen as pro-Vichy. In a *Comoedia* article entitled "Tell us, M'sieu Chevalier" (June 28, 1941), Serge Weber wrote:

> So Momo has remained in the Nono Zone.* He will be returning at the end of August to make a film and introduce his new repertoire of songs. In a recent interview, he announced that he would, in future, be writing all his songs himself, because his lyricists were too weak, too mediocre, and because one is never better served than by oneself. Perhaps this revealed a somewhat ungrateful attitude toward those like Jean Boyer and Van Parys who had provided him with outstanding successes like "Mi-mille," "Appelez Ça Comme Vous Voudrez" ("Call It What You Want") and "*Tout Ça, Ça Fait d'Excellents Français.*" He said he had received a couple of songs from them and had turned them down. That was his absolute right. For this reason we were waiting for his new personal crop with a certain amount of impatience. So it is our luck to be able to offer in advance to our readers the text of his first oeuvre, "Our Hope."

The text that followed, largely composed of meaningless *"tsa tsa tsa tzing poum"* sounds, without any explanation of their content, made little sense and was clearly intended to ridicule him. Chevalier assumed this was an indirect attack on him inspired by those officials desperate to have him return to Paris—an example of the kind of blackmail they routinely practiced. He seems to have overlooked the possibility that the "leak" may well have come from his irate erstwhile songwriters, for even

---

*"La Zone Nono" was the colloquial term for "*Zone Nonoccupée*"—the Unoccupied Zone of France.

his old friend and close collaborator Albert Willemetz had been hurt by Chevalier's remarks.

Two months after the *Comoedia* article appeared, Chevalier, wearing a smart dark suit and polka-dot bow tie, and "looking fit and tanned," arrived at the Gare Saint-Lazare in Paris on September 3, 1941, to find not only a large crowd of fans, reporters, and a mobile Radio-Paris recording van waiting to greet him, but also an impressive and unexpected welcoming committee from the show-business community. It reminded him, he told them, of his 1927 Hollywood arrival.

Heading the group was a radiant Henri Varna, surrounded by Casino de Paris minions; Lucienne Boyer, the well-known singer, the powerful French movie producer Jean Paulvé, and the French film star Marie Déa, who kissed him on both cheeks and presented him with a huge bunch of flowers. Her presence, and Paulvé's, was part of a publicity gimmick: They were there to promote the film Paulvé was financing, which she and Chevalier would star in after his Casino de Paris stint.

"*Bonjour, Paris,*" he shouted. He was immediately asked for his impressions. "Let me first rediscover *Paname,*" said Chevalier. He was wheeled to face the Radio-Paris microphone. "I will be making *The Two Crowns,* a film with Marie Déa to be directed by Marcel L'Herbier," he told reporters.* Turning to Henri Betti on the station platform, after kissing Marie Déa for the assembled photographers, he said, "Let me introduce my new pianist, who has composed my latest songs." (In the *Petit Parisien* account of his arrival, Betti's name is misspelled—Beth—presumably on the basis of Chevalier's pronunciation.)

On the train, Chevalier had asked Betti where he intended staying in Paris. Betti said he had unrivaled knowledge of Paris's cheaper hotels. Chevalier suggested that Betti should stay with him in his Boulevard de Courcelles apartment. "You can use the Chinese room," he said. A few minutes later, he had second thoughts. "I understand a young man's needs," he told Betti. "You may feel certain constraints at being under

---

*Though Chevalier made several trips to the Joinville studio before his Casino de Paris performances began, the film was never made, and there is no mention of it in Marcel L'Herbier's exhaustive autobiography.

my roof. Why don't you stay a few days, and find yourself a good room?" Privately, Betti was relieved.

There was a car waiting to take him to his new apartment on the Boulevard de Courcelles. A voice in the crowd shouted, "You taking a taxi, Maurice?" Chevalier said, "No, old boy, I already know that nothing beats the métro." The car left, loaded only with his suitcases. "Paris and Chevalier have found each other again," wrote the *Petit Parisien. L'Oeuvre*, another German-run newspaper, reported that a young Parisienne in the crowd asked him about his life down south. He gave her a brief description of his idyllic life on the Riviera. "You should see my rabbits, my chickens," he told her.

For *Paris-Soir*, the paper organizing his various galas, Chevalier had a special message. A sunburned Chevalier, the *Paris-Soir* reporter noted, said, "Here I am—bringing the sun with me." He felt "a great deal of happiness, especially at the thought that I will be doing some good immediately on arrival," thanks to the Gala des Ambassadeurs, a fund-raising evening for various charities, including a fund for prisoners of war, the home for indigent actors at Ris-Orangis, and a medical dispensary.

"He deliberately let the car go" a reporter for *Comoedia*, the weekly literary magazine, wrote, "taking the métro, so impatient was he to see Parisians at close quarters."

In his memoirs,[8] Chevalier gave a somewhat edulcorated version of his arrival, with no mention either of Marie Déa, the film *The Two Crowns*, or *Paris-Soir*'s role. He claimed he was taken completely unawares. "A *Petit Parisien* reporter asked me, at the station: 'what do you think of Marshal Pétain?' he wrote.

> I had not expected that. How to get out of this? I zigzag. I must look like a performing bear attempting to dance.
> "The Marshal? . . . The Marshal? . . . Well, as for myself, I happen to be against war, you understand, like everybody else . . . and I think it would be better if there was more understanding between peoples."

That night, tuning in to Radio-Paris, he heard a French editorialist vituperating against "the indecent reception for a strutting actor who not so long ago had performed in front of England's king and queen." But Chevalier's run-in with Radio-Paris could not have lasted long: On September 13, he was interviewed by a Radio-Paris reporter (there is no record of what he said), a month later he was the star attraction of a Radio-Paris concert at the Théâtre des Champs-Élysées widely reported in the French press, and Radio-Paris would interview him again after his return from Germany.

On September 15, *Le Petit Parisien* carried a front-page, banner-head-lined interview with Chevalier, claiming he was in favor of Franco-German collaboration. Years later, in his memoirs, Chevalier claimed that his off-the-cuff remarks at the Gare Saint-Lazare had been deliberately and maliciously distorted, and that the entire article had been concocted by German propagandists. The headline (CHEVALIER, THE POPULAR ARTIST, IS IN FAVOR OF COLLABORATION BETWEEN THE FRENCH AND GERMAN PEOPLES) may well have been a piece of creative editing, but Chevalier's disclaimer is not supported by the facts, for the *Petit Parisien* story was based not on statements made at the time of Chevalier's arrival, but on an "exclusive interview" he gave the paper on September 14, over a week later, in his apartment on the Boulevard de Courcelles.

The interviewer described the red blinds filtering the sun, and the splendid view from Chevalier's windows onto the Parc Monceau. "Did Maurice Chevalier, the Parisians' idol, have some secret motive for not returning to our zone? Was this absence, which some regarded as overlong, the result of his believing that there were two Frances?" *Le Petit Parisien* asked.

It is ten A.M. He is an early riser, and has already made a large number of phone calls, dictated his correspondence, conferred with his pianist, Henri Betti. "For professional reasons," he tells me, "I have often deserted 'Paname' and it is perhaps because I have been away so often that I have kept the public's favor. After each return, I felt more affection, more tenderness for Paris. Need I say that I have never been as moved as I am today. In the past, when I returned to Paris, it had gone on with its everyday life. This time, after staying away for two years, so much has happened!"

Chevalier told the reporter he needed to walk the streets of Belleville and Ménilmontant, to rediscover the sights, sounds, and faces of his youth. He described how a young woman with a small child had asked him for an autograph, and how a war-blinded veteran, on a walk with his wife, had touched his arm and said, "Good luck, Maurice." "All this explains why one cannot stay away from Paris and why I am so glad to be back."

Asked whether he was in demand abroad, Chevalier said, "I have had at least twenty offers to go and perform in America, but it is too easy to shout 'Long Live France' from abroad. There are not two Frances, there is only one, where each and every French man or woman has a duty to accomplish to the best of their abilities."

"In a grave tone of voice," wrote the reporter, Chevalier went on:

Please understand me: I have never been involved in politics. The artist's mission is, above all, to entertain the public, whatever this public may consist of. Song is an admirable instrument to bring people together. When I was in America, I did my best to make the Americans love France. Now I'm in France, and in Paris, I follow the Marshal [Pétain] blindly, and I believe that whatever can bring about an understanding between the French and the Germans must be attempted. That is what I meant when I spoke yesterday on the radio.

"A few moments later," the *Petit Parisien* reporter wrote, "Chevalier is in the métro. People smile at him. How can he go unnoticed? And how can he be unaware of the gratitude of those for whom he sings Paris, I love you. It is indeed love without a cloud."

Chevalier later claimed that, appalled by the *Petit Parisien* story, he summoned the reporter, who admitted that his own initial, and innocuous, article had been rewritten by the editor after consultation with German officials who routinely supervised the contents of all Paris-based French newspapers. In *With Love*, Chevalier wrote he protested to no avail to the *Petit Parisien* editor. "Luckily," he wrote, "I had friends who enabled me to put the record straight in *Comoedia*, which simply commented on the exaggerations of the press concerning unnamed top stars who were playing in Paris and went on with a specific quote from me to the effect that I was just a singer who was uninvolved in politics and had nothing to say on the subject."

A front-page interview with Chevalier did indeed appear in *Comoedia* two weeks later, but in no way could it be said to "put the record straight." Though never mentioning Pétain by name, most of it was an extravagant paeon of praise to him, on the lines of the interview granted to the *Espoir de Nice* the previous August—but far more fulsome. The *Comoedia* reporter, Jean Rollet, wrote that Chevalier told him, "over a drink on the boulevards," that "there are some people here who irritate me. I am here to sing and only to sing. I have never been involved in politics and I don't need to start now. Since my arrival here," Chevalier went on:

I've seen a lot and understood a few things. What I have discovered is that if everyone stuck to their jobs, and tried to carry them out as well as possible, without useless argument where competence is so often lacking, things would go far better, as far as the health of that grand "Old Lady" [Paris] is concerned.

What has struck me most is that if destiny has dealt us a blow with one hand, in its remorse it has also caressingly rewarded us with the other, since it has miraculously enabled Him* who has the admiration and esteem of the whole world to obtain what no other leader has been able to secure from the French people—unanimity.

So how best to behave to be in harmony with one's heart, one's head and with the future in mind?

In my small way, this is how I have solved my particular problem: With all the respect and adoration I bring to Him, I say to myself: If He were in my shoes, in this case or that, how would He react? What would He say or do? And immediately the solution comes, clear and luminous. Of course: *This* is what He would say. *That* is what He would do. If one patterns oneself on His common sense and honesty, decisions come easily. One marches straight ahead, and that's it. One prays that his marvelous health will continue and allow him to fullfil his purpose. We

*All capital letters as in original French text

must observe Him, follow Him, with all our heart, we must help Him with all our soul.

Each particular problem can be resolved as follows: how would He behave if his name was Maurice Chevalier? The answer comes easily. He would be content to sing his best, in his own country, and lessen as far as possible, the sadness of the times. And he would be content to let the One who already has the aura of the greatest French names in history act and decide on his behalf.

It was this flowery, almost hysterical panegyric that would later get him into serious trouble with the Resistance, for his accusers, later, were adamant that on at least one occasion, during his first stay in Paris, he delivered the same message on a Sunday lunchtime program of Radio-Paris, as a preamble to his new repertoire, and that it was retransmitted, again and again, on the radio station that was rightly regarded as the most reliable German propaganda weapon.

Chevalier's arrival in Paris was singularly ill-timed: The following day, a much publicized exhibition opened at the Palais Berlitz, on the theme "The Jew and France." At the entrance, a specially commissioned statue symbolized "the new France extricating herself from the Jewish influence." The same papers that heavily publicized Chevalier's return wrote at length about it. "More than one person must have shivered at the discovery of the deep-seated evil that was eating into France and leading to inevitable degradation" wrote the *Petit Parisien.* "If you want to learn how to differentiate a Jew from a Frenchman, and witness the deep-seated infiltration process whereby the people of Israel, throughout French history, thanks to careful planning and some lucrative deals, have been able to leave their disgusting ghetto and set themselves up in luxury, one must go to the Palais Berlitz." And Chevalier's gala sponsor, *Paris-Soir,* wrote: "neatly emerging from their native ghetto, arriving on this soil, so hospitable until lately, like a cloud of locusts, here is the slow and skilled invasion of Israel. . . . Here is no passionate, partisan exposé but the most complete documentary fresco so far on the pernicious activity of the people of Israel." Huge lines formed outside the exhibition, the French press duly reported. Eighteen thousand tickets were sold in the first five days, proceeds going to the Secours National, the equivalent of the French Red Cross. The 100,000th visitor, in November, coincidentally a former P.O.W., newly released and unemployed, received a cash prize of ten thousand francs from the organizers. Chevalier's Gala des Ambassadeurs was also in aid of the Secours National, an institution under the direct patronage of Marshal Pétain.

By an unfortunate coincidence, a *Paris-Soir* article showing Maurice Chevalier playing with his gardener's son in La Bocca, on September 12, with an accompanying story reporting a complete sell-out of the Gala des Ambassadeurs for the following evening, appeared on the same page, juxtaposed next to a "scoop" by André Chaumet, the paper's in-house Jew-baiting reporter. Astonishing even by *Paris-Soir* standards, its title read, "I have been the privileged observer of these Jewish millionaires, once celebrities of the Paris Bar, inside their internment camp near Paris. Everything is perfect here," he wrote:

> The fate of these imprisoned Jews is no more tragic than that of our beloved prisoners-of-war, except for the fact that the latter happen to be innocent. Here are the celebrities of the Jew-tainted Bar [*le barreau enjuivé*]. What an equitable turn of the screw! One of them confirms he has never been ill-treated. Never did such an absolute truth fall from Hebraic lips. But why not put them to work? Make them restore used clothing donated through the Secours national? Israel at work for the good of the community? Believe me, that would be their worst punishment.[9]

Why they had been interned in the first place was never explained in the story.

Before Chevalier could perform, his songs had to be "vetted" by a German censorship committee, whose office was in the requisitioned *Propagandastaffel* building, on 52, Avenue des Champs-Élysées. Chevalier himself refused to be present. Instead, he sent Betti, who ran through the words and music and had some difficulty convincing a particularly thick-headed German official that the "tra la la la la" part of "Our Hope" "was not a subversive, secret code—and that 'bing tsa boum' was not a disguised reference to an RAF bomb."[10] Other, later censors would be less suspicious. One of them, a French-Canadian citizen with Nazi ideals, later "passed" all of Montand's songs (in 1944) even though they dealt with the "Far West," cowboys, and New York in highly sympathetic terms.

The Gala des Ambassadeurs organized by *Paris-Soir* raised 700,000 francs for its various charities. A gold cigarette lighter donated by Chevalier, with his initials on it, was auctioned for almost half the total proceeds (300,000 francs), acquired by an anonymous "American philanthropist," who may well have been the socialite Florence Jay Gould, the American heiress residing in Paris who was on the best of terms with both top French government and Occupation authorities.

Paris-Soir had also organized two gala performances for Chevalier "at popular prices" at the Folies-Belleville, a local music hall seating five hundred, before his Casino de Paris season began. Proceeds from this gala went to the *Entr'aide d'Hiver du Maréchal* (Pétain's personal charity fund), French prisoner-of-war relief, and the XXᵉ arrondissement soup kitchens. "I haven't sung in this place for twenty-five years," Chevalier told a *Paris-Soir* reporter. The public, *Paris-Soir* noted, "was not always an easy one," clamoring for encore after encore.

What the paper failed to mention was that his appearance onstage there led to a not entirely adulatory uproar. Étienne Léandri, then the manager of an American-owned cosmetics factory in Paris and a personal friend of Chevalier's, who was there, recalled the commotion— catcalls and insulting remarks, almost all coming from the cheaper balcony seats. They had been provoked, Léandri felt, by Chevalier's remarks in *Le Petit Parisien* about Pétain and collaboration. A furious Chevalier turned on his detractors. "That's enough," he shouted from the stage with considerable aplomb. "When I have something to say, I say it. You shouldn't believe anything if you've only read it in the newspapers, and if you haven't actually heard me say what I'm supposed to have said." There was applause, and no further heckling.[11]

Many years later, reading Chevalier's memoirs, Léandri was amused to note that Chevalier had pointedly written that, after greeting his fans at the Gare d'Austerlitz, he returned to his Boulevard de Courcelles apartment by métro—thus establishing that—as at all times during the Occupation—he refused to apply for privileged status.

"We had made an arrangement," Léandri recalled. "As a businessman and factory manager,[12] I was entitled to gasoline coupons. The ever-cautious Chevalier did not want to accept any official favors. He could, like other prominent actors, have received unlimited gasoline coupons, but didn't want that. He asked me whether he could use my car—I had two—and of course I agreed. So when he first arrived at the Gare d'Austerlitz, he took the métro, but got out at the Hôtel de Ville station, where Louis, my driver, was waiting for him in my green convertible Simca to drive him home. The Simca, with Louis, was his for as long as he needed them in Paris." Betti confirmed that he and Chevalier used a car that day, noting their surprise and consternation at the "heavily Gothic" German street signs.

Chevalier, Léandri recalled, was "instantly recognizable" in Paris. Apart from the fact that his face was by now an unforgettable one, he habitually wore, that autumn, a distinctive green loden coat and Tyrolean hat. (In an interview with a *Petit Parisien* reporter, Chevalier had stressed his preference for old, shabby, "comfortable" clothes, adding that his underprivileged childhood had left him indifferent to luxury in this domain. It was an innocent fib, explicable under the circumstances, but typical of Chevalier's need to present a perfect public image to the world at large.) Léandri and Chevalier often lunched in well-known black-market restaurants, invariably at Léandri's expense. "He was a particularly good trencherman, and he had two or three favorite places," Léandri recalled. One was Chez Nine, on the rue de Douai. Another was Alexis, a fish restaurant on the rue Notre-Dame de Lorette. How the "patron," Alexis, obtained large quantities of fresh fish, shellfish, and lobster at a time of increasingly scarce gasoline and wretched railroad communications remains one of the war's best-kept secrets. At least once a week, when he was in Paris, Chevalier, a great gourmet (especially fond of fish) sat down with Léandri to *loup flambé* or *loup au beurre blanc* and, occasionally, bouillabaisse. The prices, Léandri recalled, were, in real terms, roughly what a three-star Paris restaurant would charge today.

Another of Chevalier's favorite wartime haunts was Chez l'Ami Louis, still going strong today, which has deliberately preserved the decor of a World War II black-market restaurant to such a caricatural extent that at any moment one expects uniformed German officers to stride in with their French mistresses in cloche hats. The standards of these wartime black-market restaurants were such, noted Ambassador Otto Abetz, that "many Germans were convinced that in the Occupied Zone, in 1941–42, France lived better than Germany," some German gastronomes even claiming that "one eats even better in France than in peacetime"—an extraordinary example of German blindness, or indifference, to the plight of ordinary French families unable to afford black-market prices.[13]

At these lunches with Léandri, Chevalier would talk with a great deal of nostalgia of his Hollywood days. He also talked about money, but with one important reservation: "He was very eager to boast about his fees, about how much he had made, per film, or per concert. But he'd never say what he did with all the wealth he had accumulated," Léandri said.

Chevalier was anxious about Nita Raya's safety, and at one lunch asked Léandri whether he knew of any German contact who might intervene in an emergency. Léandri was a useful man for someone like Chevalier to know in Paris in 1941: an exceptionally good-looking, free-spending, tough young Corsican, immensely attractive to women, equally at ease with American socialites and members of the French underworld, Léandri was on friendly terms with prominent show-business personalities like fellow-Corsican singing star Tino Rossi and Léon Volterra, also mingling with Germans on the General Staff—including members of the Gestapo. One of them was a political officer of Czech origin called Roland Nozek, almost certainly working for the Gestapo in an intelligence capacity, whom Léandri promised to contact if ever Chevalier were to need help.

Later, it transpired that Léandri's contacts with the Germans and the French underworld may have been closer than Chevalier suspected: On the one hand, he saved the lives of a number of Jews, including Georges Cravenne, whom he hid in his home in Antibes for several months. On the other, his links with French underworld figures, some of whom had Gestapo connections, led to his precipitous departure from France in 1944; he remained abroad until it was safe to return.

Unusually for Chevalier, who very seldom discussed his private life, he frequently referred to his love affair with Nita Raya. It was clear, said Léandri, that he was faithful to her. In those heady Paris days, Chevalier could have had any number of lighthearted affairs. Léandri got the impression, from Chevalier's own cryptic remarks, that, for the time being at any rate, he was uninterested in sex.

But in common with many show-business personalities, Chevalier could not resist an occasional visit to the One-Two-Two, the most luxurious brothel in Paris, "more club than bordello," as its ex-owner, Fabienne Jamet, later claimed.[14] Whether he went solely to meet his show-business friends, who patronized the place regularly, or for a more active purpose, she did not reveal. Probably the former. Chevalier, "like Mistinguett, who only showed up when she was invited, hated to pay for anything," Jamet wrote. Unlike most brothels, women were welcome at the One-Two-Two, which got its name from its address—122, rue de Provence—but they came either as guests of male friends, or else as clients, hiring the girls for sex themselves.

Cole Porter's "Anything Goes" could have been the One-Two-Two's signature tune: Every room had a different decor. There was a funeral parlor, a torture chamber, a ship's cabin, and a Deauville beach hut. The One-Two-Two's clientele, throughout the war, was decidedly mixed: entertainers and film stars, industrialists, journalists, and black marketeers rubbed shoulders with gangsters, Gestapo officers, top German officials like General Schaumberg and Radecke, and even—for a brief while—a Canadian airman on the run after being shot down.

Unlike most French brothels, clients at the One-Two-Two were equally welcome if they remained at the bar (only the best champagne was served) or if they took the girls of their choice to the fourth floor, where the bedrooms were, using the elegant wrought-iron art-nouveau elevator.

Clients could also dine in its black-market restaurant, called Le Boeuf à la Ficelle. A contemporary photograph shows a shapely waitress, naked except for a short, frilly apron, serving a customer an unmistakably phallic-shaped piece of beef. The restaurant was also famous for its omelette Norvégienne, by all accounts the best Baked Alaska in town. When it was brought to the darkened dining table, the only light came from the waitresses, who discarded their aprons for the occasion, wearing only tiny tinkling lights, fore and aft, in strategic places.

Though he himself seemed unaware of it, the German *Propagandastaffel* exploited Chevalier's presence in Paris in every conceivable way. The Gala des Ambassadeurs audience, for example, had included large numbers of handsome, uniformed German officers, some of them bandaged or in wheelchairs. From photographs appearing later in German and French "Occupied Zone" magazines, it looked as if Chevalier had been performing exclusively for them.

On the opening night of *"Toujours Paris,"* Chevalier noted with satisfaction that, as far as he could make out, only a quarter of the audience happened to be German. "I felt the best thing was to ignore them, to look through them without ever making eye contact, or saluting them. They are just not there!"[15] Chevalier's assessment of their numbers may well have been on the optimistic side, for off-duty, many Germans wore civilian clothes. Throughout the Occupation, Germans made up to 80 percent of the audience in some music halls and all Paris nightclubs, to such an extent that, at the Folies-Bergère, program notes were in German as well as in French.

Only a few days before his Casino de Paris season opened, and the day after his second Folies-Belleville gala, a front-page alert in all French newspapers in the Occupied Zone warned that the military governor of France, General Stülpnagel, was taking collective reprisal measures to punish the French for noncooperation with the authorities following the killings of uniformed Germans. On August 21, French Resistance men had gunned down two German soldiers in the métro. "I was compelled to take hostages," the Stülpnagel communiqué read. "I warned they would be shot if there were any more killings. I was forced to carry out these executions. Now that there have been more killings I am compelled to take further measures that will disrupt the daily lives of the entire population." As a punitive measure, all existing curfew passes were canceled, and from September 20 to 23, "all movement is banned from nine P.M. to five A.M., and all cinemas, theaters, restaurants and other places of entertainment are to close at eight P.M. Those apprehended disobeying these orders will be arrested and treated as hostages." Two days later, the Germans announced that two Frenchmen had been shot as hostages, and on September 22 the names of twelve more Frenchmen—variously labeled "Jew" or "Communist"—shot the day before, were released. "I draw your attention to the fact that if there is any repetition [of the killings] a far higher number of hostages will be shot," a further Stülpnagel communiqué added. There were emotional appeals from the prefect of police, and from Pétain himself, begging French citizens to abstain from violence, cooperate with the authorities, and turn in all suspects. *Paris-Soir* proudly noted, in a front-page story, that a "patriotic Frenchwoman" had passed on vital information to the police about a suspected terrorist after reading the warnings and editorials in the newspaper. It wrote, "*Paris-Soir* is proud to have been the intermediary between the judiciary and this witness whose loyal act may throw fresh light on events."

The curfew ended on September 23. Chevalier's Casino de Paris debut began four days later—on September 27. He himself did not appear until after the interval. The first half of the program consisted of standard music-hall acts, including a dance number by Myrio and Desha, whose hospitality he had enjoyed in the Dordogne. Before beginning his act, Chevalier introduced Henri Betti, as he had on his provincial tours, and Betti duly played a Rachmaninoff prelude.

Critics praised Chevalier's "tender, irresistible, comic directness." The *Petit Parisien* critic, Morvan Lebesque,* said the new songs were "somewhat banal" but "Chevalier himself emerges greater than ever from the experience. He is incomparable." Chevalier's closing song, "*Ma Pomme,*" brought the house down. "Because everyone knows the words, thanks to the radio, everyone sings along. . . . The Parisian audience gives its Maurice—who has rediscovered Paris and in the process acquired some pretty solid material advantages inherent to the capital of his heart

*Later a postwar *Le Monde* drama and literary critic

[Lebesque was almost certainly alluding to Chevalier's large theater and radio fees.]—a triumph." But it was Jean Cocteau, in the weekly arts magazine *Comoedia*, whose column must have pleased Chevalier most.

"He doesn't emerge from the wings," Cocteau wrote,

> but from all the wings of the past. Glory, habit, destiny propel him on stage. He enters the stage as he would enter his home, escorted by success, carried by a robust sea, and his skill as swimmer enables him to move with a minimum of gestures. From that moment on, you will say, he can behave according to his whim. Not so. His freedom to behave according to his whim is the result of a secret science he has mastered and which it is only right he should keep to himself. One follows him as one would a regiment, and just as those who follow a marching body of men become soldiers themselves, imbued with a sense of heroism, so those who follow Maurice Chevalier feel proud to be Parisian.

Cocteau did not call on Chevalier in his dressing room after the show "because I wanted to write this, and follow the crowd, which found its identity again in the cloakrooms, with a loudspeaker relaying his bantering voice. They picked up the tune of the song which is as exalting to them as the trumpet calls at a bullfight are to Spaniards."

Chevalier's decision to allow *Paris-Soir* and Radio-Paris to sponsor his gala appearances had been unwise. More foolish still was his decision (in October) to grace the Corporatist Paris Press Festival with his presence at the Vel d'Hiv, the huge sports stadium. Its two presiding patrons, both present, were Jean Luchaire and George Suarez (both later executed for collaboration) and there was a large contingent of senior German officials from the *Propagandastaffel* and high-ranking German officers and German embassy staff. The "Paris Press Festival" was Parisian only in name: All Paris dailies, by this time, were run by Germans (*Paris-Soir* by a German former elevator operator with appropriate Nazi party connections) and the Vel d'Hiv audience consisted almost entirely of the collaborationist "smart set"—large numbers of whom, like Luchaire and Suarez, would eventually pay a heavy price for their ideology—or their opportunism.

The Radio-Paris–sponsored concert took place at the Théâtre des Champs-Élysées on November 9, and two weeks later, after his last Casino de Paris performance, came the announcement (in *Le Petit Parisien*) that "Maurice Chevalier will go to Germany to sing before the prisoners of war." A brief article in *Paris-Soir* also gave advance notice of Chevalier's impending trip to Alten Grabow. "I'll sing 'Our Hope,' and our hope of seeing them back here soon among us, helping the Marshal to build a new France," he was quoted as saying. The Casino de Paris revue was uninterrupted, except for two days' rehearsals, Mistinguett taking over star billing for the next five months. (During the entire Occupation period, there was rarely a month when she was not performing in theaters or cabarets).

As Betti recalled, Chevalier's decision to go to Germany "was very sudden. A delegation from Vichy called on him at the theater, and, after they had left, Chevalier summoned me and said: 'I've been asked to do something, but I can't force you to go along with me. I was told,' Chevalier went on, 'you were once a prisoner of war at Alten Grabow. You came back, you became a star, you're earning a great deal of money. Right now, in this very same camp, are prisoners of the same age as your sons would be, if you had any. We want you to go there to give them some hope, to tell them to hang in there.'"

Chevalier went on to tell Betti that there would be no fee for either of them for the trip, which would begin immediately after their last Sunday matinee performance. They would take a train to Berlin, spend the night in a hotel there, get up early on Monday morning (Monday was in any case closing day for all Paris theaters) go to Alten Grabow, some seventy-five miles south of Berlin, spending another night in Berlin before returning to Paris the following day. Betti agreed to go along.

"We won't see a single German," said Chevalier, "and we'll be speaking French on the train." This turned out to be not strictly true. Chevalier did meet the Alten Grabow camp commandant, and there was at least one German liaison officer on the trip. But the whole journey came under the supervision of the permanent French Military Mission in Berlin, a liaison group composed of senior officers dealing with prisoner-of-war affairs, and in Chevalier's compartment, there were no Germans.

As soon as he arrived in Berlin, however, Chevalier must have realized the perils involved: He came under pressure to extend his stay. There was a message delivered by a German colonel from Emil Jannings, the famous German actor who had provided him with valuable advice during his own first few days in Hollywood. The unforgettable "Professor Unrath" of *Blue Angel* fame, now an influential Nazi film executive as well as one of Hitler's favorite actors, was keen to get Chevalier to prolong his stay, promising him a large fee if he would only perform at the La Scala Theater in Berlin for one night. Other intermediaries, Chevalier wrote in his memoirs, sounded him out on his career in France. Could his songs not become a little more political? Chevalier was able to deflect all such requests by pretending a busy schedule.

For Betti, who mistakenly believed the Berlin trip came during a Monday break in schedule (it actually occurred *after* Mistinguett replaced Chevalier at the top of the bill in "*Toujours Paris*"), the most memorable part of the Berlin journey was not the concert itself, but his own glimpse of Hitler, making an unscheduled appearance at the Hotel Europa on the Unter den Linden, where they were staying. "He strode into the hotel, surrounded by *Sieg-heiling* uniformed officers and a bevy of bodyguards," Betti recalled. "A civilian brutally shoved me out of the way in the hall. I asked the concierge, who spoke French, 'Who was that thug manhandling me just now?' and he said, 'Oh, that was Herr von Ribbentrop.' "

Chevalier, Betti, and an escort of uniformed French officers from the French Military Mission were driven, by bus, to Alten Grabow, near Magdeburg. "On the way they gave us cartons of Gauloises and Gitanes cigarettes to give to the troops," Betti recalled. The concert took place in the open air, on an improvised stage, in front of some three thousand prisoners. Among the songs Chevalier sang was "The Bricklayer's Song," and, Betti recalled, "tears came to my eyes as the entire audience took up the words, singing along with Chevalier. Afterward, I asked one of the French soldiers how come they knew it. 'We hear it on the radio all the time,' he said."

After the applause had died down, Chevalier gave them all a pep talk. "You guys may know I was here myself once, in World War One, a prisoner like you," Chevalier told them, deliberately adopting the *faubourien* tone of the working-class boy from Belleville. "The place hasn't changed. I hung in there, and got home. If you hang in there, you'll make it too." Chevalier was mobbed by the French soldiers, handed out the cigarettes, and the party quickly returned to Berlin, taking the train back to Paris.

Chevalier had gone to Alten Grabow on two conditions, he wrote later in his memoirs: that ten P.O.W.'s from the Belleville-Ménilmontant district be released, and that there should be no publicity. Either he was misled, or his memory failed him: In the first place, various Paris newspapers had announced his impending trip to Alten Grabow *before he actually went there;* despite his earlier run-in over the subject of collaboration, a *Petit Parisien* reporter was on the station platform in the murky early-morning darkness when the train drew in on Sunday, November 30, 1941.

In an interview, published on December 1, Chevalier told him, "They sang along with me. I spoke to them like an old pal. I've known that same sadness, that same nostalgia, those same blues. I told them to have faith in the future, and that, once free, they would discover, as I had, their courage and reason for living." A French Army chaplain, a Dominican priest called Dubarle, had made a welcoming speech on the prisoners' behalf, Chevalier told *Le Petit Parisien.* "We couldn't believe it when we first heard the news," the chaplain had said. "Now that you're here, we seem to be breathing the same Paris air. Believe me, the prisoners of '41 will be worthy of the older generation. We all steadfastly await the day when, back in France, we will start rebuilding our house"—another allusion to Chevalier's "The Bricklayer's Song." "I only sang at the stalag itself," Chevalier said. "In Berlin I was received by Oberleutnant Bentmann, the father-in-law of Ambassador to France Otto Abetz, by Mr. Lienenthal, representing M. von Ribbentrop, and (on the French side) by Captain Dunand, representing the French ambassador in Berlin. There was no publicity. Everything was very discreetly handled. My sole mission—as I tried to explain on the radio yesterday [he had also been interviewed on Radio-Paris on his return] was to entertain my prisoner comrades. What I said, what I sang, was recorded and will be rebroadcast in other P.O.W. camps. I am happy to have fulfilled the most satisfying assignment any artist could hope for in the present times."

The magazine *Je Suis Partout*, the most arrantly anti-Semitic and pro-Nazi of all French papers, carried a short piece by its anonymous in-house columnist writing under the nickname of "Denys de Syracuse." In its December 1941 issue, the columnist wrote:

So Maurice Chevalier went to sing, giving two recitals to French P.O.W.'s while airing his latest songs at Radio-Paris—including "The Bricklayer's Song," which is an act of faith in the future. It was fascinating to hear him last Sunday [on Radio-Paris] soberly explaining the purpose of his trip. "I thank the German government," he said. Coming from a son of Ménilmontant, that phrase had grandeur.

In *Le Petit Parisien*, Chevalier was also quoted as expressing "my very great thanks to the German authorities for displaying such an understanding of this sentimental pilgrimage," adding that "I was very hospitably received by German artistic circles." Even granted the tendency of the collaborationist press to put quotes in people's mouths, it is unlikely that either interview was wholly imaginary. They also made nonsense of Chevalier's later claim, in the American version of his memoirs (*With Love*) that

five days after my return I was walking the streets of Cannes when I saw my name staring up at me from a newspaper stall, and stunned I looked at simultaneous editions of the Paris papers and those of the free zone, each with a long story on my visit to Alten Grabow. The Germans had not kept their word after all, I was thinking bitterly, but the bitterness became shocked anger as I read each report, for none of them pointed out what had really happened—that I had visited one single camp, that this one had been the prison where I had spent more than two years in captivity myself, and that my price for this attempt to bring a message of hope to the men of Alten Grabow had been the release of ten prisoners.

In fact both the Occupation and Free Zone press carried accurate stories of his trip, the only difference between their version and Chevalier's being that they had him giving two concerts (in the same camp, on the same day) while he claimed only one. And Chevalier could not possibly have seen copies of both Vichy and Paris papers in Cannes on the same day: Paris newspapers were never on display on the simultaneous day of publication alongside those of Vichy France. And no French paper, either Paris- or Vichy-based, had actually alleged that he had given concerts in Germany for gain.

The only picture released to the French press showed Chevalier in the company of French uniformed troops. Goebbels himself, three days after Chevalier's return to Paris, did exploit the trip in characteristic fashion in the *German* media, announcing that Chevalier had completed a concert tour of Germany—without specifying that the P.O.W. camp concert had been Chevalier's only show there.

Shortly after his return from Alten Grabow, Chevalier learned that ten French P.O.W.'s from Belleville and Ménilmontant had indeed been freed. He was extremely proud of this, but, aware that he had fallen into a propaganda trap, later recorded a version in his memoirs at variance with what really happened. By claiming that he had been victimized, he sought to deflect criticism for his *pétainisme,*—not once mentioned either in his French or American memoirs. Prisoner releases were, of course, a favorite German reward for favors received: After the unsuccessful Dieppe raid by British and Canadian forces in 1942, for example, the German High Command would release over seven hundred French P.O.W.'s from the Dieppe area to reward the local Dieppois for their "correct behavior"—at no time did the civilian population join in an uprising, as the British planners of the operation had hoped they would.

Despite his naive vanity, Chevalier could not have been completely unaware of the way his behavior on this, his first season in Paris, had been exploited by the *Propagandastaffel*, the Paris-based collaborationist authorities, and Vichy. He chose to claim, later, that he returned to La Bocca convinced that he had acted wisely, oblivious, until much later, that his ill-advised trip had branded him as a traitor in the eyes of innumerable fans in Britain and the United States. In fact, he was to find out very soon, though this, curiously, would not prevent him from returning to the Casino de Paris in September 1942.

CHAPTER 15

"When you do something wrong, you must do something right,
and I'm doing all right tonight."

—from *The Merry Widow*,
sung by Maurice Chevalier

Until November 7, 1942, Maurice Chevalier's home base,
at La Bocca near Cannes, was probably the most congenial place
in France to sit out the war. Under the 1940 armistice terms, there
were no German troops in the Unoccupied Zone. The Occupation
troops were Italian, delighted not to be fighting the British Eighth
Army in Africa and enjoying the good life on the French Riviera
far too much to take Il Duce's orders seriously. Chevalier's journalist friend Pierre Galante, later to become active in the French
Resistance, remembered them with affection. "The officers were
mostly pro-monarchist and anti-fascist, and regularly provided
French restaurants with ingredients at a time of increasing shortages," he recalled. "In particular, there was a pizzeria near the
Negresco Hotel in Nice that was pure heaven. . . . As long as the
Italians remained on the Riviera, life was tolerable."

But with "Operation Torch," the Allied invasion of French

North Africa, all this came to an end. Hitler ordered his troops to move into the hitherto Unoccupied Zone: German troops replaced the Italians on the Riviera, henceforth the Nazi writ ran everywhere in France, and in the wake of the German forces, increasing numbers of informers and French security officials working for the Gestapo flocked south.

Even before the North African landings, there had been an element of risk for all those daring to speak up at all against the Germans or Vichy, a fear perceptively illustrated by Chevalier's own song *"Notre Espoir."* The French Riviera remained, throughout the war—despite the orchestrated newspaper campaign against them—a haven for refugees of all kinds, including a large contingent of French and foreign Jews, though a hard core of local French fascists compelled them to keep a low profile, live warily, and hide, especially in the later stages of the war. Alexandre Trauner, France's greatest contemporary film-set designer, worked throughout 1943 on the sets of *Les Enfants du Paradis* without ever leaving his hiding place in Vence, not once visiting the Studios Victorine in Nice, where it was made. The dangers were considerable. Jacques Doriot, an ex-communist turned fascist, one of the pro-Nazi leaders of the Party Social Français, was active in Marseilles, his local power base, and Nice was the hometown of Joseph Darnand, an equally rabid fascist leader of the Service d'Ordre Légionnaire, who recruited local "Niçois" and "Cannois" into his Praetorian Guard of thugs and bullyboys. Both Doriot and Darnand felt that Pétain's Vichy regime did not go far enough in its "collaboration" with Germany, and used their private armies to terrorize recalcitrants into submission.

Shortly after Chevalier's trip to the Alten Grabow stalag, the London *Daily Mail* published a story alleging that he had performed in Germany, without specifying that he had only sung for French P.O.W.'s, adding "he has become a Nazi supporter." This was probably based on monitored German news agency reports. Chevalier heard about it, dismissing it as of no importance. Like so many megastars before and after him, he displayed a certain amount of paranoia where the press was concerned. "The media and journalists have already played such tricks on me throughout my career that I do not take this tragically," he wrote in his memoirs, "convinced as I am that the public will reestablish the facts of its own accord."

This was wishful thinking, for his once-devoted American public was turning against him too. Even before his Casino de Paris stint, a refugee conductor, Oscar Straus, had told *Variety* (in October 1940) that "Chevalier has the free run of France because he is well liked by the Germans"—presumably on the basis of sheer gossip and Chevalier's appearances in the Unoccupied Zone. Four months before "Operation Torch," a far more devastating article appeared, this time in America, that was to have lasting consequences.

Life, in its issue dated August 24, 1942, ran a long piece on the French underground, written by *Time-Life*'s former Paris correspondent, Richard de Rochement. Accompanying the piece, which was based on an interview in Washington with an anonymous visiting French underground leader referred to simply as "Pierre Durand," whom de Rochement had known before the war, was a full-page spread headed "Black List." "These are some of the Frenchmen condemned by the underground for collaborating with Germans: some to be assassinated, others to be tried when France is free," read the caption beneath a large photo of "Pierre Durand" (with his back to the camera) and some uniformed "Free French" officers facing him.

The odd *Life* list included top pro-Nazi politicians like Admiral Jean-Louis Darlan, Marcel Déat, Jacques Doriot, and Pierre Laval, arrant collaborationist Vichy ministers and senior officials like Fernand de Brinon, Pierre Pucheu, Xavier Vallat, and Joseph Barthélemy, collaborationist publishers like Jean Luchaire and Horace de Carbuccia, but also a painter, André Derain, two playwrights, Marcel Pagnol and Sacha Guitry, Georges Carpentier, the former boxing champion, Mistinguett, and—last on the list—Maurice Chevalier.

Nowhere in the *Life* article was the rationale for the selection explained. While the inclusion of Pétain, Laval, Darlan, Doriot, Pucheu, Vallat, and others with policy-making responsibilities was understandable, there were surprising omissions—and equally surprising inclusions. Among the "blacklisted" collaborators on the list was Jean

Prouvost, described as "owner of *Paris-Soir*." This was not the Paris-published *Paris-Soir*, the German-controlled pirate version of the original, but the paper that continued to publish out of Lyons (and would fold in November 1942 after the Germans moved into the Unoccupied Zone). Prouvost had indeed, very briefly, served as Vichy's first information minister, but by no stretch of the imagination could he be considered a leading collaborationist. He very quickly resigned his post after the French collapse, and at war's end would resume publication of the highly popular mass-circulation *Paris-Match* without having to face a "Purge Committee." André Derain's name was there presumably on the grounds that he had visited German artists in Germany in 1941. A prewar disciple of the noted German sculptor Arno Brecker, Derain had done little more than respond to an admired colleague's pressing invitation—as had Kees van Dongen, Dunoyer de Segonzac, Othon Friesz, Landowski, Vlaminck, the sculptors Maillol and Paul Belmondo and others—who were not on the list at all. Marcel Pagnol, creator of the famed Marius series of plays about working-class life in prewar Marseilles, was presumably included because he had continued making escapist, nonpolitical films (admittedly financed by La Continentale, the German production company) after the French collapse of 1940, but he was no collaborator in the true sense of the term.

Sacha Guitry was a special case. Often compared to Noël Coward, this lifelong rake, snob, opportunist, wit, and cultural gadfly, as well as talented writer and actor, was almost as much of a social butterfly as he was an egotist—and his ego was, even by French standards, enormous. The son of the famous actor Lucien Guitry, a contemporary and favorite of Sarah Bernhardt, Sacha was attracted to young actresses and married several. This may have been for show more than anything else, for the self-centered Guitry was incapable of showing real interest in anyone but himself. ("Stiff at last," said one of his numerous ex-wives, after his death in 1957). He had indeed put on plays after August 1940 that could be construed as being pro-German. Guitry found parties given by powerful people irresistible and was incapable of turning down festivities organized by *Propagandastaffel* officials, especially when his hosts were "respectable" German intellectuals on their best, pro-French behavior, suitably briefed to flatter him outrageously. Göring had once summoned him "for a friendly chat" while in Paris, and Guitry had immediately made himself available. (Sacha Guitry's only comment: "The coffee was undrinkable.") But his political views were singularly naive: He genuinely believed that de Gaulle and Pétain were in secret collusion, and that both would emerge in postwar partnership. Like many French socialites who mingled with the German Occupation cultural aristocracy, he also, on occasion, did his best to help his Jewish friends—saving, among others, his friend and colleague Tristan Bernard from possible deportation. Guitry's reaction to the *Life* piece was in character: "To call oneself *Life* and ask for death is rather odd, don't you think?"

Even more than Guitry, it was the appearance on the list of Mistinguett and Chevalier that caused the greatest stir. The absence of any detailed explanation of the grounds for their inclusion only provoked unverifiable rumors, all of them darkly magnifying their alleged collaborationist roles.

Mistinguett, like Chevalier, was a Casino de Paris star, performing far longer in Paris than he. Like him, she was incapable of letting up: Her need for applause and adulation was, if anything, even greater than his, and so was her legendary greed. (As the war continued, she began demanding, onstage, donations in kind, like wine, butter, and goose liver, as tributes from her audience, thus accumulating a fantastic reservoir, which she hoarded preciously.) But unlike many other music-hall performers and leading actresses (who did not figure on the *Life* list), she had not performed in Germany, though she had had a succession of German lovers. ("*Ça, c'est différent,*" she later told a prosecuting attorney, "*Ça, c'est l'amour.*")

Needless to say, the *Life* story had considerable impact throughout the United States. Just about the only newsman who expressed doubt was columnist Louis Sobol in the *New York Journal,* quoting Ernest R. Bauer, a New York–based Free French journalist on the staff of *La Voix de la France,* who thought, Sobol wrote, "that German and Vichy pressure may have subdued him or that just plain nostalgia for the city he loved so dearly enticed him back. . . ." Bauer, who admitted that most Frenchmen did not agree with him, "still believes that Chevalier is loyal to the France that was."

As far as Mistinguett, Chevalier, and Pagnol were concerned, the *Life* list seemed based more on wild hearsay and malicious gossip than on any factual evidence of actual ideologically motivated collaboration. One likely source for such rumors, at the time, was thought to be the French actress Françoise Rosay, who had settled in Hollywood and may simply have been motivated by jealousy of stars more successful than she.

That Chevalier was aware of the *Life* article very soon after publication is beyond dispute, for he told Albert Willemetz about it, asking him to warn Guitry of its contents, adding, "Tell him not to go to Vichy."[1] Nita Raya cannot recall his mentioning the article to her, but then he may well have kept the news to himself on purpose, to avoid alarming her.

Nevertheless, in the light of the *Life* piece, Chevalier's decision to go to Paris for the second year running to appear in a Casino de Paris revue, which opened in October 1942, was baffling. One can only guess that Henri Varna made him an offer he couldn't refuse, and that, needing the audience's approval like a drug, he simply couldn't sit still. "When, for any reason, he was not working, he was miserable," said Nita Raya.

In his memoirs, he simply notes, cryptically:

A second six-week spell at the Casino de Paris. My life has become impossible. All sorts of traps and obstacles. "They" are trying to compromise me in every way.

Had he turned down Henri Varna's offer, and stayed in La Bocca in the first place, he would have avoided the "traps and obstacles," and, perhaps, the harassment to come.

This time around, he was careful to give no interviews. In any case, newsprint was now in such short supply that all dailies had drastically reduced their size, cutting out entertainment sections almost entirely. During his Paris stay, his name cropped up only once: *Paris-Soir* announced his presence at a special gala under the paper's patronage "for the children of prisoners of war," attended by Fernand de Brinon,* the chief French liaison official to the German Occupation authorities. There was a *Paris-Soir* photograph of Chevalier, holding aloft a singularly thin, ill-nourished, and rickety child.

His new show, "*Pour Toi, Paris*" was, however, exceptionally well reviewed, both in *Le Petit Parisien* and in *Comoedia*. Many of the songs were new, and Chevalier, for the first time, took to addressing his audience half in song, half in a spoken monologue, as he had in earlier appearances in the United States.

One of France's best-known critics, *Comoedia*'s Gustave Fréjaville, who had followed Chevalier's career from the start, noted his "inventive, unexpected parodies" in his new material. "His personality defies classification," he wrote. "In the second part of the program he provides us with a medley of old songs, but Maurice Chevalier wants to be contemporary, and, without ceasing to be himself, refuses to allow himself to be a prisoner of his past successes. This is surely the best way of staying alive and young despite the passing years."

While Chevalier was starring at the Casino de Paris, Félix Paquet was performing at the smaller Théâtre de l'Étoile. And it was while they were both in Paris that "Operation Torch" occurred, provoking the end of the "Zone Nono," the Unoccupied Zone. *Paris-Soir's* headline announcing Hitler's total occupation of France was comically euphemistic: "Hitler orders his troops to ensure the protection of the Mediterranean coast and of Corsica."

Chevalier's second year's stint in Paris was even less satisfactory than the first. Not only was the earlier euphoria missing, but it was becoming clear that Germany was in the process of losing the war. This did not improve the morale of the German-controlled Paris media, which had made such a huge fuss of Chevalier on his previous visit, though *Le Petit Parisien* gave him an exceptionally favorable write-up: The show's finale, its theater critic wrote, "has considerable emotional content, in the colors of France, led as it is by Chevalier singing the widely known refrain, "*ça sent si bon la France* [France smells so good]."

*Later shot by firing squad

It was the kind of flag-waving, subliminally Pétainist number that almost all French variety shows indulged in, if only to keep the Occupation authorities and the *Propagandastaffel* censors happy. National pride, even of the most misplaced kind, was also an antidote to the daily humiliations, the bankruptcy of Pétainism, for, reading between the lines, most French people following the war news closely, even in its censored form, now knew that the tide was changing at last and that Nazi Germany was bogged down on both the North African and Russian Fronts; those who had enthusiastically welcomed Pétain as their savior were becoming aware that they had backed the wrong horse. Chevalier almost certainly realized, when his Casino de Paris season finally ended, in December, that both his Paris trips had been a mistaken career move. He later wrote:

> I end my Casino de Paris engagement in early December and take the secret decision to cease performing for Radio-Paris or on stage in the capital until the resurrection of France. I insist on the date: December 1942. In early 1943, after a brief concert tour in the former non-occupied zone, I decide to stop performing at all and cease all artistic activity until the country is freed.[2]

Again, his memory was at fault. In 1943, Chevalier's concert tour was not simply to the "former non-occupied zone." He was in Charleroi, Belgium, for a concert in 1943 the day a Belgian Resistance squad blew up the town's power station.

By this time, Félix and Maryse Paquet, with whom he had stayed in the Dordogne after the 1940 debacle, had become permanent houseguests in La Bocca—the beginning of a long-standing relationship that would end only with Chevalier's own death. Félix, a sallow small-time music-hall comedian, had worshiped Chevalier for years: a deferential listener and straight man, he flattered Chevalier constantly and professed total devotion to him. Later, Chevalier would write that he "reminded me of a French Eddie Cantor"—though this opinion was not shared by any of Chevalier's friends and acquaintances. Maryse, who from 1942 on, with only intermittent gaps in the fifties, was to run Chevalier's household until his death, proved a formidable organizer. It made sense for Chevalier to ask them to come to La Bocca. Nita Raya recalled that "the four of us were very close during those years (1942–44) and had a great time together." Paquet, said Janie Michels, another, later companion of Chevalier's who knew him well, "was a highly intelligent man who did his best to conceal his brightness. He made sure everyone knew of his admiration for Chevalier, which some-times reached embarrassing proportions." As later events would show, this hero worship was not entirely disinterested.

There were still, in 1942 and 1943, occasional, formal luncheon parties in La Bocca, especially after Maryse Paquet took over the man-agement of the household; Chevalier liked to entertain local dignitaries, but this, too, was becoming increasingly difficult—for when in La Bocca, Nita Raya recalled, Chevalier would not allow his housekeeper to buy anything on the local black market, and refused to apply for gasoline "tickets." So feeding the Chevalier household was a constant problem. Betti recalled one party attended by the local prefect and other "notables." During the meal, Betti was rash enough to suggest that while Chevalier was world-famous, part of his fame would die with him, for the reputation of performers was short-lived, whereas the achievements of composers, writers, and poets survived. "I was very young, and wanted to take part in the conversation," Betti said. "I immediately realized my gaffe, but was too far gone to stop. I could see Chevalier looking at me with a mixture of quizzical irritation and disbelief," said Betti. "After I'd finished, Chevalier said pointedly, 'Well, thank you, young man, thank you very much, I'll remember that.' "

When Chevalier and Nita Raya first arrived in La Bocca in the summer of 1940, they had found an apartment nearby for Nita Raya's parents, who, as Jews and Romanian immigrants, were obvious targets for the French police and Gestapo. By early 1944, Chevalier decided their lives were too much at risk: Through a trusted intermediary, and with the complicity of an understanding official in the Alpes-Maritimes Prefecture, he found them a discreet apartment in Nice—and false identity papers.

He also made plans to leave La Bocca; until mid-1943, he had been a familiar figure on the Cannes Croisette, taking long walks or bicycling back and forth. Now the risks were too great. Though, in his memoirs, he claimed the French Gestapo was his greatest threat, because Nita Raya was Jewish and her parents were living close by under a false name, he also knew that the French Resistance had decided he was a legitimate target. He had been warned by a friendly neighbor and Resistance member, René Laporte, that his Radio-Paris songs and broadcasts, together with United States and British newspaper allegations, had brought him to their attention.

In the American version of his memoirs, Chevalier mentioned a further blackmail attempt on him by the French Gestapo, headed by the same French official who, Chevalier maintained, had been one of the two hard-faced men who had "persuaded" him to perform in Paris in 1941—this time threatening to initiate an investigation into Nita Raya's background, to be carried out by the dreaded French Commission on Jewish Affairs. If so, she herself had no knowledge of it at the time.

That same spring—Nita Raya could not recall the exact date— Chevalier decided to make a break. Abandoning the luxury of the La Louque estate in La Bocca, the entire household moved back to the house in Sainte-Meyme in the Dordogne, the primitive farmhouse belonging to Myrio and Desha. In his American memoirs, Chevalier claimed he went into hiding because the French Gestapo was closing in on him and Nita Raya. According to local contemporaries, including Henri Betti, they left because Chevalier feared possible "uncontrolled action" against him by trigger-happy Resistance groups.

Chevalier had found the simple rural life in the Dordogne amusing during the summer of 1940—but it was less fun during the first winter months of 1944. There was still no electricity, gas, or bathroom, but there was a fireplace, and Chevalier foraged for wood, becoming an expert with an ax and handsaw, enjoying the hard physical work involved. It all reminded him of the primitive living conditions of his early childhood in Ménilmontant, and anything that brought his beloved mother to mind redeemed even the most painful experience. Nita Raya's parents also left Nice and found a hiding place near Sainte-Meyme. The Dordogne then was one of the most backward provinces in France, with narrow country roads and poor communications, and this, Chevalier later wrote, made it a safer place than the Gestapo-infested Riviera.

In his memoirs, he claims that he did not move to the Dordogne until shortly before the D-Day landings—June 6, 1944. Nita Raya, however, is certain that the four of them (Chevalier, Nita, and the Paquets) left much earlier—with her parents following soon after.

On February 2, 1944, *Variety* had run a small piece on Chevalier, reviving the earlier *Life* story about him. "Free French sources and French-language newspapermen have received no further word on any change in Maurice Chevalier's status as a collaborationist," it wrote. "René Haugh, the managing editor of the French language paper *France-Amérique* [published in New York] said that when last heard from Maurice Chevalier had gone to Berlin to appear in shows and had performed before German occupation troops in Paris"—a distressing distortion of the facts, but one widely supported by German propaganda and the German press. *Variety* also reported the strange discovery of a letter, purportedly written by Chevalier to the giant American Borden milk company, asking it to donate milk for French children. The letter was signed by "Captain Maurice Chevalier" (in the army, he had remained a private), but someone who claimed to know authenticated the handwriting as his. "The letter," wrote *Variety*, "can only be passed off as an attempt to get him back into the good graces of the United Nations." The true circumstances of the background to this letter were never elucidated.

A few days later, in a Free French radio program called *"Les Français parlent aux Français"* ("The French speak to the French"), transmitted by the BBC and beamed to France, came the bombshell that was to smear Chevalier's reputation for the rest of his life: His name was included in a list of "arrant collaborators" deserving the death penalty.

The actual speaker on the BBC-beamed Free French radio network was a well-known prewar French *chansonnier*, Pierre Dac, who had fled Occupied France in 1943, spending several months in a Spanish jail before ending up in London. Its producer was Maurice Van Moppès, a well-known lyricist and early Free French volunteer, who wrote all the material of the nightly satirical broadcast. Its main thrust was against

French collaborators of all kinds, parodying the Radio-Paris call sign with the words, sung to music: *Radio-Paris ment, Radio-Paris ment, Radio-Paris est Allemand* ("Radio-Paris lies, Radio-Paris lies, Radio-Paris is German," to the tune of "*La Cucaracha*"). "I found him very amusing" Chevalier wrote in his memoirs,

> at least until that night in February 1944 when he fingered members of his own profession, the artists who had chosen to remain in France, and described them as bad Frenchmen. They have collaborated with the enemy, he decreed in his characteristic hollow voice. They will be punished according to their responsibilities. [I asked myself] is he sentencing all of us to death?

In an earlier broadcast (which had not mentioned Chevalier by name), Pierre Dac had warned that collaborators mentioned on his program were "identified, catalogued, labeled. You'll be taken away, and a few days later all that will be left will be a small pile of garbage. Wherever you may be, you'll be hunted down, to face a firing squad, a hangman's noose, or the guillotine." On that February 1944 night broadcast, Dac even sang a pastiche of Chevalier's own 1939 song "They're Excellent Frenchmen for All That," with the words changed to "They're Rotten Frenchmen for All That."

By this time Free French broadcasts on the BBC had a huge audience in France, and Chevalier knew that millions of people must have heard Dac's program. In his memoirs, he claimed that he listened to it in his house in La Bocca. Nita Raya is adamant that they never actually heard it, but learned about it only after they had left for the Dordogne. If so, Chevalier's memoirs are at variance with the facts, for in his book, Chevalier went on to describe how, after the Pierre Dac broadcast, everyone in Cannes was aghast: "They were all aware of my lack of activity. People from the Resistance seek me out. 'Maurice, what does it all mean?' they ask. . . . That guy can't be aware of the facts. . . . We'll let him know that we guarantee your true feelings." Since he was in Dordogne at the time, all this can only have come to him as hearsay.* But the Riviera neighbor, friend, and authentic Resistance leader René Laporte, who earlier had tipped him off about the danger he ran, did send a radio message to London to warn Pierre Dac that the charge was unfair, and the Chevalier parody ("All This Makes Rotten Frenchmen") was not repeated on the air.

Even worse was to follow. In a May 27, 1944, United Press story datelined Algiers, his former costar Josephine Baker "denounced her pouting colleague as a Nazi collaborationist."

> "Maurice Chevalier is to the stage what Laval is to diplomacy," she said bitterly. "Maurice Chevalier is doing for the Germans what I am doing for United States soldiers. His type of propaganda, trying to put Nazism over to the French people, is worse than a speech by Hitler. After the beginning of the war Chevalier and I performed together in a show designed to whip up the Anglo-French spirit. Today he's helping Goebbels keep up Nazi morale. He has even performed in Berlin and other parts of Germany, to say nothing about all he has been doing on the radio, and in the music halls of occupied France, for the Nazis."

By this time, though Chevalier had no inkling of this, a special tribunal, had met in Algiers and sentenced him to death *in absentia.*

In later years, Chevalier, who rarely referred to those pre-Liberation months, would make an exception where Josephine Baker was concerned, recalling how he had helped her become a star in earlier times, implying that her venom had been sexually motivated, a clear case of personal revenge because he had once spurned her advances. (Another show-business star who adamantly, and repeatedly, charged that he had collaborated was the opera singer Lily Pons: Unlike Josephine Baker's, her path had never crossed Chevalier's.) The Josephine Baker attack, full of innuendos, half-truths, and total falsehoods, was widely reproduced in the U.S. and British press. No one questioned its veracity.

The charges against Chevalier reflected the insuperable gulf between

---

*In *With Love,* the Pierre Dac episode occurs in the Dordogne; in his French memoirs, it occurs while he is still in La Bocca.

countries like the United States and Britain, formally at war but never occupied, and a defeated country like France under German Occupation. At the height of the war, any German—in British or American eyes— automatically became the enemy, and a target for annihilation. Under the Occupation, especially in Paris, the Germans were everywhere, and all French performers, whether Chevalier, Charles Trenet, or Yves Montand faced audiences that were at least part German. Chevalier *had* allowed his songs to be broadcast on Radio-Paris, but the notion that he had acted as a Nazi propagandist, "putting Nazism over to the French people," was ludicrous: Chevalier was far too cautious ever to allow himself to be drawn out on his political views, except for his emotional odes to Pétain—and here he only reflected the views of millions of French people, at least until 1943.

Even before the spell of enforced idleness in Sainte-Meyme, Chevalier had started writing his memoirs. He noted that just before D-Day, he took a quick trip to Paris to see his doctor, obtaining a certificate to prove he was too ill to perform. He also turned down a large fee to be the guest star of the March 1944 French Film gala the *Nuit du Cinéma,* somewhat naively mentioning the size of the fee he turned down (200,000 francs) as proof of his sacrifice; that a major film gala could occur in the first place in the spring of 1944, at a time when the Germans were on the run in the East and expecting an Allied landing in the West, was yet another example of baffling French "normalcy" in show-business circles.

It was in Sainte-Meyme that Chevalier and his "family" heard the news of the Normandy landings (June 6, 1944) and monitored the progress of the Allies from BBC broadcasts. A month and a half later, on August 27, 1944, a German News Agency story announced that Chevalier had been seized by French Resistance fighters on a Paris street, taken to a cellar, and shot for collaboration. The DNB report, datelined Belfort, eastern France, included a heartfelt tribute to Chevalier as "the most charming of all Frenchmen . . . a man who was completely disinterested in politics." The language was curiously similar to that used later by Chevalier himself to justify his actions against "collaboration" charges:

He had set himself [said DNB] the task of placing his popularity and his gift of entertainment at the disposal of the hardworking men and women of the Parisian population living, as it did, in the shadow of a lost war and in the uncertainty as to the country's future. The establishments in which Chevalier performed were solely places of entertainment visited by Parisians and hardly ever frequented by Germans.

The dispatch added that the Maquis (the Resistance) had sent him a warning in February, "but he did not allow this threat to deter him." Even his last moments had been mythic: "He was bludgeoned with cudgels, fists and kicks until he collapsed covered with blood. Shortly afterward he was found by two women college teachers and breathed his last in their arms."

All the major news agencies—Reuters, AP, UP—picked up the story. A few hours later, it was front-page news all over the world. FRENCH REPORT CHEVALIER SLAIN FOR COLLABORATING WITH GERMANS was *The New York Times* headline, its article quoting both Reuters (for the death) and AP in London. The AP reporter had talked to a Free French HQ spokesman, who said there was "no confirmation," adding that, if it were true, "we would be very much surprised, because orders were that any suspects were to be arrested for trial, not shot immediately."

CHEVALIER SLAIN AS FRENCH TRAITOR said a *New York Herald Tribune* headline. The *London Daily Express* ran a bolder one:

How the Paris F.F.I. liquidated the peace-time idol of the boulevards
CHEVALIER TRIED AND SHOT IN THE CELLAR OF A HOUSE

Only later did correspondents find out that the German News Agency had heard that a Frenchman called Chevalier had indeed been executed. He turned out to be the collaborationist mayor of a small French town.

All papers expressed doubt about his actual death; the versions differed, one being that he had been stoned to death. There was, however, a broad consensus as far as Chevalier's alleged wartime activities were concerned. The *New York Herald Tribune* said he was "long tagged for 'punishment' because of collaboration with the Nazis . . . Earlier in the war French underground leaders put up the numbers of this quartet of former idols [the others were Guitry, Mistinguett, and Georges Carpentier] who had sunk deep in the mire of treason." "There was little doubt of his collaboration with the Germans," wrote *The New York Times*, adding that he had broadcast for the Occupation authorities, quoting *Variety* as saying that he had not only gone on the radio to urge Franco-German collaboration but "repeated it in press interviews widely printed in the unoccupied zone." The *Daily Mail* somewhat fancifully alleged that "he was seen at the Adlon Hotel in Berlin in 1942 in the company of P. G. Wodehouse," and that he had taken refuge in Germany "after his house was bombed in May 1944." In America, only a handful of close friends, most prominently Charles Boyer, Marlene Dietrich, and René Clair, came to his defense. "I cannot believe his alleged allegiance to the Nazis and can't pass judgment," said Clair. "He never expressed any such views to me." Completing her autobiography at the time, Grace Moore wrote, "I have thought about this blithe Frenchman often and wondered about the stories which put him on the poltical blacklist. But like all his friends, I can only hope the tales are not true."

The motives of some at least of the later recruits to Free French units were highly suspect. As German Spoken signs disappeared from French shop windows, innumerable scores were being settled, often by those belatedly anxious to prove their patriotism. *Newsweek* war correspondent Al Newman reported that "the courtyard of Chartres Prefecture was an almost solid mat of hair clipped from mistresses and wives of Germans."[3] "As to prominent collaborationists," he wrote,

> you can get any opinion you want from colleagues of such famous French as Georges Carpentier, Chevalier and Mistinguett who have been accused of playing too closely with the lads across the Rhine. I had been assured by many that Chevalier would never survive the march of Allied troops into Paris but would be shot first by his indignant countrymen.

Chevalier quickly became aware of reports of his own death, and decided to stay put. When he was not chopping wood, or making notes, or listening to the BBC, he went for long walks. One afternoon in September, this probably saved his life.

While Chevalier was out for a long walk with Félix Paquet, and Maryse Paquet and Nita Raya were on another, shorter walk on their own, three armed French Maquisards showed up at the house and demanded that Maurice Chevalier be turned over to them. An aged housekeeper, Louise, said she knew nobody by that name. "No problem," their leader said. "We'll be back." They looked very determined and threatening, Louise told Nita when she got back, and it was immediately clear to her that these members of the Maquis had come to make good Pierre Dac's threat.

"We realized straight away it would be dangerous for Maurice to return to the Paquet house," she said. "We set out to meet him on his way back from his walk and, happily, stumbled across him. Maurice was very calm, but surprised. We decided he should leave immediately, without returning home, for a place called Cadouin, about ten miles away, where we knew some friendly farmers, called the Dellemares. Maurice and an already exhausted Félix Paquet immediately started walking across the fields to Cadouin. We returned to the Paquet house, fearfully waiting for the Free French Maquis men to return. None came, and the following morning Maryse and I decided to join Maurice in Cadouin. We packed rucksacks, got on our bicycles, and headed for Cadouin. There, we found everyone safe and sound, though Félix Paquet was still tired out by his long walk. The Dellemares had a huge farm, and we thought we would be completely safe there. But then, three or four days later, we got a nasty surprise: Lots of French Maquisards showed up. We all hid in our rooms. The Dellemares told us the local 'Maquis' had decided to make the farm their headquarters. It was clearly impossible for Maurice to leave the room, and equally impossible to stay indefinitely like this. So I decided to go to Toulouse, where René Laporte now was, to warn him of the situation, and—hopefully—extricate Maurice from this mess."

Showing considerable courage and initiative, she walked out of the farmhouse unnoticed, went to the station, eventually found a train to Toulouse, located René Laporte, the newly appointed local head of the Free French–controlled radio there, and explained Chevalier's predicament. Using his Resistance connections, Laporte was able to make arrangements for a car and a military escort, to take Chevalier from the farmhouse in Cadouin to Toulouse, where, thanks to Laporte, he would be safe. These various steps took at least four days, and when Nita Raya returned to Cadouin in the car provided by Laporte, Chevalier had quite a story to tell.

Somehow, the French Resistance had become aware of his where-abouts, and, shortly after Nita Raya left for Toulouse, a car with three armed men in it showed up at the farmhouse. Chevalier was driven to Périgueux under guard. There, inside the town hall, taken over by the Resistance as an operational headquarters, he learned that a Free French Court in Algiers had sentenced him *in absentia* to death for collaboration, and that he was requested to undergo cross-examination, and sign a statement, in preparation for his trial.

The news of his arrest quickly spread. A sizable crowd gathered outside Périgueux town hall, and inside the building, too, people came and stared at him. "They seemed to be more curious than hostile," Chevalier wrote later.

> Some even asked me for autographs. One of them said: "I'm sorry, it's come to this, Monsieur Chevalier." But my heart sank when I heard another say: "To think that I once heard him sing in Toulouse! I prefer to leave, or I'll be tempted to kill him."

Chevalier wrote later that he was scared but determined not to let it show.

The first Free French Maquis official who questioned Chevalier was from Ménilmontant, "and I had the gut feeling he didn't want anything bad to happen to me," Chevalier noted. But he was then passed on to the chief local prosecutor, a giant of a man nicknamed "Double-Mètre," (double meter) because he was so tall. This was a Polish-born Commu-nist called Urbanovitch, and while Chevalier waited in an anteroom for him to arrive, he heard people in the building talking about Double-Mètre with awe. He clearly had a fearsome reputation.*

---

*"Urban" later established himself as a successful art dealer and gallery owner in Paris.

Urban, as he preferred to be called, was not nearly so accommodating. "Two months ago, we would have had great pleasure in arranging for a firing squad for you," he told Chevalier. "But now all cases have to be referred to Paris." Again Chevalier stated his case: He had *not* given any concerts in Germany, other than for the Alten Grabow stalag P.O.W.'s. He had *not* been paid a fee for this, but had requested that ten of them, from Ménilmontant and Belleville, be released, and this had occurred, in due course. He had never performed for exclusively German audiences. Luckily for Chevalier, his accuser did not appear to be aware of his Parisian Press Gala appearance in October 1941 at the Vel d'Hiv. Chevalier said he had never applied for special privileges of any kind, not even gasoline coupons. René Laporte, in Toulouse, could vouch for his sympathies for the Resistance.

Chevalier disliked Double-Mètre intensely. "He is too tall, too fat, too pale," he wrote. But it was also clear to Urban, as the cross-examination proceeded, that, whatever his personal feelings, Chevalier's case was so special that Urban was aware that he needed to tread carefully. At the end of the day, he decided that Chevalier need not be kept under arrest and could return to Cadouin, "but must remain available for further questioning." Urban had him stand against a wall to be photographed. In the background were framed pictures of Stalin and de Gaulle. Urban refused to provide a car for Chevalier to take him home, telling him to make his own arrangements, but another, more accommodating Resistance leader found one for him.

In *With Love* (but not in his original French autobiography) Chevalier claimed that Laporte had recruited him, during the Occupation years, as a "letter box" for the local French Resistance in Cannes. Laporte died suddenly in 1954, and—owing to Resistance compartmentalization—it's unlikely that anyone else knew of this. Surprisingly, Chevalier never mentioned the fact to Urban or other, later Resistance "Purge Committee" members when he was at his most vulnerable (August–October 1944). Had he done so, and had Laporte testified to that effect, all charges against him would have been dropped immediately. He did, however, tell his accusers that he had contributed to the survival of several French Jewish families in the Cannes area throughout the war, using his influence to get them false papers and residence permits. Here he was almost certainly telling the truth; he did help out Nita Raya's parents, who emerged from the war unscathed, and may have acted similarly for others in a similar predicament.

Back in Cadouin, Chevalier faced the prospect of sitting things out and waiting for a decision from a higher Free French authority—and possible rearrest. Luckily for him, at this point, Nita Raya showed up with the car and escort. Chevalier left forthwith for Toulouse. The escort's travel document stated that the identity of the person in their charge was not to be divulged, and this enabled them to pass through a number of self-important Maquisards manning checkpoints. Laporte found a comfortable "safe house" for Chevalier in Toulouse, and Nita Raya joined him there shortly afterward. Chevalier's morale was low, though he realized how lucky he was to be out of Urban's clutches.

Back in Toulouse and living with Laporte, Chevalier knew that he would almost certainly have to appear before a Purge Committee before being allowed to perform in public. Now Pierre Dac himself got into the act.

Showing up unexpectedly in Toulouse, he told René Laporte he would be able to sway the committee into being "lenient" with Chevalier. "I didn't want to see him," Chevalier wrote in his memoirs. "Laporte persuaded me to do so. 'He says he can get you out of this mess. If he retracts his charge, he can do a lot for you.' "

They finally met, and shook hands. Chevalier wrote:

My heart, my pain, my shame led to a feeling of nausea. I cannot utter a word, for I would burst into tears. I have to leave the room. I then make an effort to control my emotions, and gradually I am able to explain exactly what had happened.

Pierre Dac's version of the meeting (in a book he wrote twenty-six years later, and published the year of Chevalier's death) differs considerably:[4]

He fell into my arms, weeping copiously, in front of his charming companion, Nita Raya, who was also deeply grieved. Naturally I did everything in my power to see to it that nothing serious would happen to him. We got the "Purge Committee" to whitewash him completely. . . . Years later, reexamining the whole affair in its necessarily detached perspective, he responded by dragging me in the mud, without once mentioning my name (but he didn't have to) in the third volume of his *Memoirs*. Of course, I have since forgiven him his ungrateful behavior but have never forgotten it.

Nita Raya did not recall meeting Pierre Dac in Toulouse, either alone or in the company of Chevalier, "and Maurice wasn't the kind of man to cry on anyone's shoulder," she said. Both accounts may have been equally self-serving: Chevalier, in *his* version, did admit he was close to tears but was careful to give a "manly" account of the meeting, while Dac clearly milked the encounter for all it is worth. By this time, Dac knew, as he put it, "that certain Resistance comrades had been a little excessive and exalted" where Chevalier's alleged collaboration was concerned.

The proliferating Purge Committees, which displayed considerable, and sometimes misplaced, zeal as far as writers, journalists, and show-business figures were concerned, did so for one very simple reason: These were the only professions where there were ample public records— thanks to press interviews and articles that enabled prosecutors to flesh out charges of collaboration. Conversely, in the police, the diplomatic service, and the French civil service generally, records were not available, and nothing like the same purge was taking place. A discreet veil was drawn over the past activities of all French civil-service and government personnel. As a result, after the Liberation, the French judiciary remained virtually intact, only a few heads rolled in the various police departments, and over half the French diplomats who had continued to serve the Vichy regime to the bitter end remained at their desks, and in the same jobs. Where purges within the administration *did* occur, vacancies were filled from below, and very often the record of the beneficiary of a sudden promotion, replacing an embarrassingly prominent advocate of wartime collaboration, differed hardly at all from that of the man he replaced. In some cases, those appointed to head "Purge Committees" (*comités d'épuration*) had unsavory records themselves. It became a matter of some hilarity that the very same president of the French publishers' association, René Philippon, who in 1940 had issued the blacklist of decadent and anti-German publications that had to be withdrawn from circulation and burned, was the same man who, after the Liberation, drew up blacklists of firms that had published collaborationist material.

This state of affairs provoked a great deal of ill-feeling, ranging from disgust to cynical rejection of the "Liberation" myth. Georges Bernanos, a leading philosopher (and former contributor to the underground "Resistance" press) wrote, "There were collaborators—but collaboration was a lie; there were Resistance fighters, but the Resistance was another lie; there was victory, which, out of a sense of decency, masqueraded as Liberation—and this was the biggest lie of all."

Purge Committee activities also provoked the anger of the scores of writers, actors, and music-hall performers, and of their defense counsel, who felt their clients were being singled out as scapegoats. Arthur Honegger, the composer, was bold enough to air his own case in the post-Liberation French press. "We write music which can have no political significance," he said. Some of his work, he pointed out, had been used as background music for German-approved newsreels and documentaries. The same music had been used in London by the Free French documentary unit (France-Libre-Actualités). In other words, there had been "the same music for Pétain and de Gaulle, and the same music can be cursed or glorious." As Herbert Lottman pointed out,[5] writers and entertainers were treated far more harshly than those who had "materially contributed to the Nazi war effort." Jean Paulhan, the Gallimard editor who had also contributed to underground Resistance papers during the Occupation wrote, "Engineers, industrialists and construction executives who were responsible for the "Atlantic Wall" are all at large, perfectly free and busy building new prisons for those journalists who were unwise enough to write that the "Atlantic Wall" was a good example of French construction know-how."

For in the aftermath of Liberation, scores of show-business personalities, writers, and journalists were being rounded up for real or alleged collaboration, and "Purge Committees" were being set up for different categories—journalists, playwrights, film producers, directors, actors, music-hall comedians, and so on. The Comédie Française had its own in-house Purge Committee to look into the past activities of its members. French stars used to the public's adulation simply could not begin to understand the motives for their prosecution—any more than Chevalier could understand why the Maquis had wanted to arrest him. Henri Jadoux, Sacha Guitry's biographer, reflected this bafflement: "Willemetz is busy and appalled," he wrote.

> He too had simply lived like everyone in show business. He was a "bourgeois" if by that one means someone with money, a comfortable apartment, servants, who wore smart suits when he dined in restaurants. The turbulence of the liberation had taken him by surprise.

What Jadoux failed to mention was that Willemetz had been a pillar of the French theatrical establishment throughout the Occupation, had managed both the Bouffes Parisiens and the Athénée theaters and had contributed to a theatrical monthly (he was also one of its editors) that, in one of its articles, had provided a cogent rationale for the French laws banning Jews from theaters and other places of entertainment.

The day after the false news of Chevalier's death hit the newstands (August 28), Sacha Guitry was arrested and taken to jail, followed, a few days later, by two of his ex-wives, Yvonne Printemps and Yvette Lyses. Also arrested were Germaine Lubin, the opera star, Mary Marquet, Mireille Balin, Léo Marjane, Georges Guetary, and Tino Rossi, all well-known film or music-hall stars as well as Paul Meurisse, Raimu, Fernandel, Michel Simon, Danielle Darrieux, Gaby Morlay, and Arletty. Some were held for only a week or two, others for several months. Because they had praised Pétain after the 1940 *débacle*, the celebrated writer Jean Giono and Pierre Benoît, writer of pulp best-sellers, were also summoned to appear before the new Purge Committees, as was Pierre Fresnay, France's best known *jeune premier*, for having acted in films financed by La Continentale (though neither Giono nor Fresnay were arrested).

Fresnes Prison became, briefly, a green-room annex, full of some of France's top stars of stage and screen. The stagestruck warders made little attempt to enforce usual prison discipline on such illustrious charges. Edith Piaf was also questioned, for she, too, had been to Germany to entertain French P.O.W.'s. But she was able to convince her accusers that she had tried to provide fake identity cards for some of the prisoners, should they attempt to escape. She was congratulated for her patriotism.

Max Ruppa, Chevalier's business manager, now contacted the London *Daily Express* war correspondent, Basil Cardew, who flew to Toulouse, at the end of September in a USAAF plane, to interview him. "Chevalier is alive," Cardew wrote. "We met in a small house in the suburb of a southern French town. I have agreed to keep it secret until his story is placed before the world."

To Cardew, Chevalier gave the fullest account so far of his version of events: "I want to swear to you," Chevalier said:

> That I have never taken a penny from the Germans, that I have never made a film for them, that I never accepted a thimbleful of petrol from the Huns. Never have I given my services for any political purpose that would help our enemies. In four years I sang only 16 weeks in Paris and I sang for the French people. . . . I am from the streets of Paris and it was because of this I would not leave France. The Germans tried everything to get me to appear before them. They offered me the life of a king. They wanted to make propaganda out of me as a symbol of an ordinary Frenchman. They trapped me and I will tell you how.

Chevalier went on to explain his trip to Alten Grabow. "The Germans came to my hotel. I said no to everything. I would not see anyone. And three days after my return Goebbels broadcast the false news that I had toured Germany, giving shows."

> I say to you that I had to fight all the time. The Germans were always after me. The Gestapo was always ready to pounce on me if I showed I was hostile to them. Most of the time, I spent at my villa near Cannes. With me was Mlle Nita, and her mother and father, and they are of the

Jewish faith. I tried, and I think I succeeded, in protecting them from the German purge. I helped twenty other good Jewish families who never fell into the hands of the Gestapo. I earned a twentieth of what I could have got had I chosen to leave my people and accept offers from America. Twelve times I sang on the Paris Radio, but I never made any political reference in these broadcasts. But people were always trying to push me into corners and ask me what I thought of Pétain's politics. I say to you that my life was always a hell.

"For nearly four hours," Cardew wrote, "Chevalier gave me chapter and verse of his movements. Often the Germans offered him a thousand pounds for a single performance of four songs. He said he would come back to Paris just as soon as his story is known. 'I would come now, if you would take me,' he said. 'But there might be some hot-headed person who might attempt to shoot me and then regret it.' " Chevalier did not refer to his paeon of praise for Pétain in *Comoedia*, and Cardew, of course, was unaware of it. Nor did he explain why, after his 1941 experience of Gestapo manipulation, he had agreed to return in 1942 for another season at the Casino de Paris.

After the *Daily Express* story appeared, Paramount News wanted to do a filmed interview with him in Paris, and this time Chevalier decided to return. The military flight arranged for him had to turn back a first time, because of bad weather, but on landing, Chevalier, who by now had moved to a new, smaller apartment on the Avenue Foch, found that he still attracted crowds of well-wishers.

On October 6, shortly after his arrival, he had an emotional reunion with Marlene Dietrich, one of his few staunch American defenders. She was in uniform, entertaining GIs, and asked Chevalier to appear on her show. This, he explained, would be difficult, at least in the near future, because of the charges still pending against him. On October 11, 1944, *Variety*, in an interview with him, quoted his indignant response to them. "Collaborate? Never. The Germans offered me large sums of money to tour the Reich, but I refused. During the past four years I have earned only a fraction of what I could have earned in Britain or the United

States. I want the people of Britain and America to know the truth—I never collaborated." "Of course," wrote the satirical weekly *Le Canard Enchaîné*, in one of its earliest (October 11, 1944) issues:

> that was not the real Chevalier, putting us off our food on Sundays at one P.M. no matter how hungry we were, blathering away about Marshal Pétain being a marvelous old man, who had to be obeyed unquestioningly. It was an "ersatz," a German fabrication. How was it we never spotted that the Belleville accent was really German?

In those first few weeks in Paris, Chevalier was instantly recognized on the streets. "Most people look at me with sympathy," he wrote. "Others are transfixed, staring at me as if I were a kind of ghost. They thought I was dead. Occasionally their looks are hostile, but there is no insult or untoward gesture that requires me to react."

His scorn for the "superpatriots" and "supercops" *(superflics)* who indulged in such "persecution" was understandable, but there was also a paranoid streak in his comment that

> in the last resort those who are against me now are the same who were against me before the "events" and will also be against me in 25 years time, if I'm still alive.

His stardom may have provoked some bitterness among a handful of less successful vaudeville rivals, but to argue that the hostile mood he sensed in the crowd around him stemmed from either jealousy or rejection of his artistic worth was an absurd rationalization.

Though Chevalier was unaware of it, his case was attracting the attention of the powerful French Communist party. "His background was a very suitable one, said René Andrieu, later a veteran member of the Central Committee, and a leading member of the Communist-inspired Resistance, the FTP.* "He was extremely popular with the masses, and in any case there was the feeling that he had been unfairly

*FTP: Franc-Tireurs et Partisans

singled out. So many music-hall stars had behaved much worse than he."
(Tino Rossi, for one, had appeared at a gala for the League of French
Volunteers (LVF)—the French, but German-uniformed, contingent
raised to fight the Russians on the Eastern front.)

Leading the fight for Chevalier's rehabilitation within the French
Communist party was the celebrated ex-surrealist French poet Louis
Aragon, who had been a prominent member of an "intellectual resistance
movement" called "Les Étoiles" (the Stars) and—at the liberation of
Paris—became hugely influential within the party executive committee
as one of the leading members of its "intelligentsia." Aragon was married
to Elsa Triolet, the Russian-born daughter of a former Soviet ambassador in Paris and herself a noted writer. The outspoken, shrewish,
strong-minded Elsa Triolet, whose considerable influence over her husband was no secret, happened to be a great fan of Chevalier's. "There
was a nickname for Chevalier," Andrieu recalled. "Inside the party, we
called him 'le Chevalier d'Elsa.'" Word of the Aragons' interest in him
quickly spread throughout the party, and very shortly afterward the
influential Variety Artists Trade Union, affiliated to the Communist-
dominated Confédération Générale du Travail (CGT), expressed its
wholehearted support for Chevalier.

This was crucial, for the Purge Committee invariably consulted it on
individual cases under review. Aragon's tolerance was markedly one-
sided: His campaign in favor of Chevalier did not prevent him from
making virulent attacks on André Gide, who had tired of Pétain relatively early, in 1941, and, from Tunisia, refused his friends' pleas to
return to the capital—partly on the grounds that if he did so, he might
be "corrupted" by a young, and irresistibly attractive, Propagandastaffel
officer. Romain Rolland was also a prime Aragon target. So was Colette,
bitterly attacked in Aragon's literary weekly, Les Lettres Françaises, for her
Petit Parisien columns that had never mentioned politics, and even François Mauriac, whose mild pétainisme had not lasted more than a few
weeks.

In Chevalier's case, no official party directive was required, for the
Communist party's "line" was clearly indicated in a front-page article in
the pro-Communist daily, Ce Soir, on October 8, 1944. Under a huge

picture of a smiling Chevalier, an article headlined MAURICE CHEVALIER IN PARIS stigmatized "the calumny which did not spare this great artist who has been deeply pained by it."

A vested-interest propaganda which he was unable to refute led people to believe that his conduct could be construed as gravely reprehensible. These are accusations he intends to destroy today. Not only does this most popular of artists have nothing to be ashamed of, but he is eager to spell out what he has been accused of, in order to demonstrate the bad faith of his accusers.

In a lengthy interview, Chevalier spelled out the circumstances of his trip to Alten Grabow. "They wanted me at all costs to meet Emil Jannings," he said, "but I always refused to take part in anything organized by the Germans and my heart was heavy indeed when I read in the Paris press that I was 'resolutely collaborating with them.' "

"What Chevalier does not say," *Ce Soir* went on,

is that it was of the greatest import for the media to let Parisians believe that the great artist was in cahoots with the enemy. . . . Maurice Chevalier was a prize recruit. He was annexed into the clan and since they knew full well he would be unable to refute these allegations, they gave full vent to the apparent truth [of his collaboration]. "But no one believed any of this for a minute," says Maurice Chevalier. "For all the provincial and foreign press rumors and amplified stories, I was convinced that all my friends kept their faith in me. Up to the end of 1942, it had still been possible for me to stave off pressing invitations of the Germans or their accomplices, but when, around this time, I was asked to make a clear choice, I decided to stop performing. I settled in Cannes in April 1943 and, pretexting ill health, only rarely returned to the capital where my attitude had become suspect to the authorities."

"I will not dwell here on Chevalier's attitude in Cannes," the anonymous *Ce Soir* interviewer wrote. "He met with intellectuals of the Resistance, and had been in touch with them since 1942. Neither will I mention the services rendered to a good number of friends." The fact that Aragon and René Laporte were close friends was of immense importance to Chevalier. Later, as part of a brilliantly executed campaign to exonerate himself more completely, Chevalier would spread the word, to the American media, that he had himself played a role in the French Resistance, and been an active member of the "Stars" group.

Nevertheless, for all the considerable help from the French CP, Chevalier was brutally cross-examined about his wartime career by a French journalist, at a press conference organized by Aragon, and left the room "totally emptied, exhausted, dried out."

A few days later, a huge (150,000 strong) march was staged at the Père Lachaise Cemetery to commemorate the deaths at German hands of those French intellectuals "who died that France may live." Expressly invited by Aragon and Elsa Triolet, and linking arms with them at the head of the procession, Maurice Chevalier eclipsed everyone else, including Picasso. His appearance caused a clamorous ripple of approving comment mixed with applause. "I'm the one everybody was looking at," Chevalier wrote later, "not at all disapprovingly, either." Though he failed to mention it in his memoirs (he may not even have realized its political significance at the time), the demonstration was one of the French Communist party's first muscle-flexing, head-counting exercises. Chevalier and Jean-Paul Sartre apart, all the other prominent leaders of the procession were either seniormost party leaders—Marcel Cachin, Jacques Duclos, Benoît Frachon, André Marty, Colonel Rol-Tanguy, and Charles Tillon—or else leading communist intellectuals like Aragon, Picasso, and the film director Louis Daquin (the party's titular leader, Maurice Thorez, had not yet returned to France from Moscow). Aragon's invitation had been a deliberate ploy to indicate, in the most unequivocal way possible, that Chevalier could rely on Communist support.

The irony of the situation was not lost on the *Canard Enchaîné.* "Accused of taking part in a Judeo-Marxist demonstration, Chevalier claimed he had only acted under duress and had concealed his real feelings. He will shortly take part in a gala in memory of those French members of the Gestapo killed in the line of duty" (November 22, 1944).

Some of Chevalier's earlier friends were now an embarrassment to him. In *Combat* (October 18)—there was no mention in *Ce Soir*—a short item read:

> Commissioner Clot, investigating the Bony-Lafont affair,* has sum-
> moned Maurice Chevalier to the Quai des Orfèvres [police HQ] to
> question him about a number of curfew passes and permits obtained by
> him thanks to a friend of Lafont's.

The "friend" in question was in all probability Léandri, in hiding in Italy. Chevalier was doubtless able to explain everything, for the matter was never raised again.

By this time, Chevalier was in constant demand for galas of various kinds, appearing alongside Marlene Dietrich, to entertain British and American Army audiences, also singing at galas for the FTP and for the French Foreign Legion at the Paris Opéra—where General Pierre Koenig, de Gaulle's top-ranking representative and military governor of Paris, was guest of honor. The Purge Committee had not yet examined his case but, exceptionally, allowed him to perform. François Périer, the veteran French actor, remembers the occasion well. He was asked to act as master of ceremonies, and approached the assignment with some trepidation. A promising young actor, but not yet a star, he had not been the organizers' first choice: This had been the veteran music-hall comedian Saint-Granier, who had indignantly refused to have anything to do with Chevalier. This was a typical example of hypocritical behavior on the part of French show-business stars, pathetically eager to display their brand-new patriotism, for Saint-Granier had performed in Paris music halls and nightclubs throughout the war, far more consistently than Chevalier, and had indeed been part of the cast at the Casino de Paris during Chevalier's first show there. There was a strange symbolism about the date of the gala, Périer recalled: It took place the very day Pétain was escorted back to Paris under armed guard to stand trial for treason.

---

*Bony and Lafont were French gangsters hired by the Gestapo who blackmailed, swindled, tortured, and executed French suspects "fingered" by the Germans. Both were executed after a highly publicized trial in 1944.

Chevalier's arrival onstage was greeted with rapturous applause, and one of his most vociferous fans turned out to be none other than Madame Koenig herself. Chevalier's business manager and impresario, Max Ruppa, had had the foresight to pack the upper balcony of the Opéra with American servicemen, who gave him a delirious welcome. *Variety* noted that "Chevalier is wildly acclaimed by GIs when he entertains them at their Riviera playground, as their rest center in Nice is called."

Pierre Dac now asked him to make a full statement, for the record, "expressing his regrets" for having taken part in Radio-Paris broadcasts. "He tells me he will read it on the radio, personally, to restore the public's affection for me," Chevalier noted. By now he was sufficiently confident of the outcome to dismiss Pierre Dac as an insignificant little publicity hound. After the *Ce Soir* article and the Père Lachaise demonstration, he wrote Dac, there was no point. "I think that to rehash it all on the radio would only be a repetition of everything that has already been said and that there are more important things to talk about than the renewed explanations of an artist who has nothing more to say."

There were still some doubting Thomases, he noted.

Some journalists intensify their attacks. Daily, I am stabbed in the back. What am I accused of? Of things which, I believe, are of no concern to real Frenchmen. That I believed in Pétain at the beginning of his reign? And who didn't? I ask you, since the American, and even the Russian, ambassador, saw him every day. That I sang eleven times in four years on Radio-Paris?—when they wanted me to perform every week! What would have happened had I refused categorically? You know as well as I do. A dawn visit. I and my little family sent God knows where!

He must have known some of these arguments were specious: Nita Raya never felt her life had been in any particular danger; though Chevalier only took part in eleven recording sessions at Radio-Paris, these had been broadcast with extreme frequency; ambassadors do not necessarily approve of the heads of government they have to meet with officially—and Chevalier's appearances at *Paris-Soir*, Radio-Paris, and

Presse Corporatiste Parisienne galas, unmentioned even by his official accusers, undoubtedly conveyed the notion that he approved of their policies at the time, even though personal acquaintances knew better. Chevalier may well have been in the mind of Jacques Debû-Bridel, the noted Catholic writer (and Resistance member), who wrote after the war that[6]

> some, without getting involved in the enemy's insidious maneuvering, felt it was all right to collaborate in papers and magazines created by the Germans or their accomplices. The harm they did was magnified by the fact that they were famous, and that their contributions appeared to be neutral, exclusively literary. They provided public opinion and the propagandizing overtly pro-enemy agents, with the surety of recognized and admired talent.

There was another aspect to real or alleged "collaboration" that baffled non-French outsiders: As so often in France, personal friendships and affinities cut across ideological barriers. Thus, Pierre Drieu la Rochelle, an arch-collaborationist, not only remained welcome in Malraux's home in 1942 and 1943, lunching there several times, but also "protected" Jean Paulhan, the senior Gallimard editor (who ran an underground magazine). (After the war, both Paulhan and Malraux tried to intercede in his favor before he committed suicide in 1945.) Joseph Kessel, the writer active in the Resistance, did his best to help the pro-Nazi editor and Radio-Paris spokesman, George Suarez, (shot for treason in November 1944) who happened to be a prewar friend. Sacha Guitry, to his credit, saved Tristan Bernard from possible deportation; Simone Signoret's father, Maurice Kaminker, an outstanding League of Nations interpreter, tried to intercede in favor of Jean Luchaire, the arch-collaborationist editor-publisher whose film-star daughter Corinne was one of *his* daughter Simone Signoret's closest friends. The "Purge Committees" were always aware that powerful Gaullist or Resistance figures might be secretly challenging their decisions behind the scenes.

So when, months later, after the *Ce Soir* article and the undisguised weight of the French CP lobby in his favor, Chevalier went before the

Purge Committee, he was asked only a few perfunctory questions. He was told a formal decision would be made only after Pierre Dac's testimony. Dac duly appeared before the committee, alone, and shortly after that, an official report to the Fine Arts Ministry exonerated Chevalier of any wrongdoing.

Though severe penalties (including death sentences) were handed out to some (but by no means all) leading collaborationist editors, journalists, and writers, most actors and members of the music-hall profession got off lightly: Punishment ranged from a reprimand to a one-year ban on public appearances, and even these were in almost all cases reduced to a few months. Fernandel, Michel Simon, and Edith Piaf were given a clean bill of health. Mistinguett was "reprimanded." A few performers (Suzy Delair, Léo Marjane, Tino Rossi, and Suzy Solidor) were put on a "blacklist" that was sent to the Pathé-Marconi recording company, but this did not prejudice their careers for long. Georges-Henri Clouzot and André Cayatte, excluded from the French Film Directors Association and thus unable to work, were making films again from 1946 on. Charles Dullin was exonerated, despite the fact that he had worked closely with the "Collaboration" group and changed the name of the Théâtre Sarah Bernhardt (a Jew) to that of Théâtre de la Ville—still its current title. Jean Cocteau, who had written profusely in collaborationist papers, slipped through the Purge Committee net entirely. Georges Simenon was held, briefly, under house arrest but never formally charged. One of the hardest-hit in the entertainment world was Sacha Guitry, who remained in jail until 1947, never recovering either his morale or his health.

Chevalier's first concerts were marked by hecklers. After one show, at the Folies-Belleville, where he had appeared under the auspices of *Paris-Midi* in 1941, the *Chicago-Tribune* correspondent, who was present, wrote that "underneath the cheers was a wave of boos, which soon ceased. After a song a woman in the balcony turned loose a stream of abuse . . . but she was shushed by the crowd."

The ordeal scarred him, however, more than outsiders realized. Perhaps the most humiliating snub was Britain's refusal to grant him a visa to perform in London. Jack Hylton, the well-known impresario, had signed him up for a two-week one-man show, but Britain (in March

1945) was still at war, and all foreigners had to obtain visas. The British Foreign Office explained that "visas were only granted to persons likely to contribute to the British war effort and it has been decided that Monsieur Chevalier would not come under this category." There was no doubt, in the eyes of the British press, that the ban was imposed because of his wartime record.

For the rest of his life, Chevalier would convince himself that his problems had been exclusively caused by a minority of small-minded, envious colleagues, out to destroy his reputation and career. Many years later, meeting Jean Sablon (who had spent the war years in America) at a party in Paris, he said, emotionally, "You at least never said anything bad about me." Sablon told him he never met anyone who had.

The ordeal affected him far more than he implied, even in his memoirs. "He never fully recovered [from the collaboration charges]," said Georges Cravenne. "They would haunt him for the rest of his life."[7]

CHAPTER 16

"I'm glad I'm not young anymore."

—"I'm Glad I'm Not Young
Anymore"
from *Gigi,* sung by
Maurice Chevalier

His troubles with the Purge Committee over at last, Chevalier was determined to make up for lost time and become the first French music-hall artist in France to have his own "one-man show." Traditionally, until 1946, the top-billing star, in France at least, appeared only after the intermission—the first half was invariably given over to lesser acts. Chevalier chose Lyons as the ideal place to inaugurate what French theater owners, impresarios, and performers alike regarded as a revolutionary, somewhat risky innovation, though they would soon welcome it for its additional profitability. The inaugural concert went well, a "one-man show" at the Théâtre des Champs-Élysées followed—but his favorite pianist was not there to share in Chevalier's success.

During Chevalier's anxious months from August 1944 until the end of the war, Betti, who no longer had any plans to take up his Conservatoire scholarship, had stood by him, and believed Chevalier, too, looked forward to their continued partnership. Then, suddenly, after a gala performance with him at the Palm Beach Casino in Cannes, only a few hours before both were due to catch a train for Paris for a series of nightclub and theater engagements, Betti "felt a sudden hideous pain, like being stabbed in the back," collapsed, almost died, and was rushed to the hospital for an emergency lung operation. For years, without realizing it, he had suffered from tuberculosis, and it had finally caught up with him. "It was nearly the end of me," Betti said. "They had to remove a lung, a risky operation in those days, and I was told I would have to remain in a sanatorium for at least a year, probably more." With French social security in its infancy and no private health insurance, Betti knew that the prolonged costs of his illness would wipe out all his savings. "But Chevalier was like a father to me, nothing bad could happen to me as long as he was around. I asked him for a loan."

Chevalier agreed. During the war, the star had made friends with two young French tailors who lived together in Cannes and moved into La Bocca as caretakers whenever the house was empty. He sent one of them around to see Betti in the hospital in Nice shortly before his operation. "That was my first nasty surprise," Betti recalled. For "with some embarrassment," the emissary told him that Chevalier needed some security for the loan. He then asked Betti to sign a document he had brought along, prepared by Chevalier and Max Ruppa. This legally binding agreement was designed, in the event of Betti's death, to transfer all his royalties to Chevalier for the next five years. "Chevalier must have felt that because he had taken me up in the first place, he had more right to the music I had written for the songs we had composed together than I did. But by this time I was supporting my aged parents, and if anything happened to me, I wanted *them* to have the royalties. So I refused to sign."

The second unwelcome surprise was that from that day on, and until 1954, when they met accidentally on a Paris street and went through a form of reconciliation, "Chevalier behaved as if I no longer existed. He never wrote, never bothered to pick up the phone once, never took the trouble to find out how I was doing. Nothing." Chevalier's "betrayal" provided Betti with an incentive to work with others, "for I couldn't stand the thought that perhaps I owed what success I'd had so far to him alone." Betti would eventually become famous in his own right, composing the music for many of Montand's songs, but the memory rankled. He often wondered whether Chevalier cast him off because he refused to turn over his royalties, "because I was no longer useful to him," or simply because of an irrational fear of sickness in any form.

There is no mention of Betti's illness in Chevalier's memoirs. But he did allude to another parting—from Nita Raya. "She had become very edgy," he wrote.

> There were sudden, astonishing sparks, invariably provoked by her. Our mutual tenderness was now too often disturbed by her new, all-consuming ambition to become a music-hall star. . . . Instead of the extraordinary grace and clear, tender cheerfulness she had displayed during our strange life together during the Occupation, she revealed another side of herself. We were no longer in harmony.
>
> Young and spirited, she could no longer restrain herself, she was champing at the bit, while I needed to gather up what was left of my physical and mental powers to stay afloat, so saddened and sickened by the bill I was being made to pay simply because of my mistake in allowing Paris to choose me. We were drifting apart. . . . All my sorrow, my anger, my resentment, all that remained of my combativity translated into a thin-skinned impatience and tenseness.

This was another example of Chevalier's capacity for omission and self-deception. He *had* been unfairly singled out as a "traitor" by London-based Gaullists and American journalists who had relied overheavily on public rumor. But had he examined his own past lucidly, he should have recognized that he had not been wholly blameless either. The *Paris-Soir* and Radio-Paris galas, the paean of praise for Pétain in *Comoedia*, the second Casino de Paris season, the numerous concert tours with Betti all over France from 1940 on had not been imposed on him by some mysterious fatality. The compulsive need to perform, the thirst for an audience—and of course the fear of poverty—explained, and to a large extent excused, his behavior. The self-image he now sought to impose, increasingly successfully with the passage of time, as a passive victim of circumstances beyond his control, did not entirely correspond to the facts. But as his memoirs showed, again and again, Chevalier was incapable of admitting that he might ever have lapsed, even in a minor way, either in his professional or personal life.

In *With Love,* Chevalier claimed this conversation with Nita Raya in Paris in 1945:

> I felt my heart move towards her in that old protective way and I kissed her lightly and gently. "Now, what's the problem? is it work?" She shook her head. "Everything's fine. I've been talking with the Folies-Bergère. There could be a spot for me soon."
>
> "Good."
>
> "It's something else, Maurice." She hesitated, then took a deep breath and the words rushed out. "There's a man, he's very rich, and I think he's in love with me. I've been seeing a great deal of him and I thought you should know."
>
> I looked at her with surprise. "Well, Nita, I'm pleased and happy for you. . . ."

Nita Raya herself remembered things very differently. She was not contemplating marriage. "In 1945–46," she said, "what Chevalier really wanted was for me to become his full-time secretary and personal impresario, and I had my own career to think of." The Folies-Bergère had asked her to star in its forthcoming revue, and Chevalier had insisted she refuse. This, in fact, was what had caused most of the scenes between them. Although still very fond of him, she was now more mature, more lucidly critical where Chevalier was concerned, also less willing to put up with his neurotic fear of poverty. "He would buy me a diamond bracelet for Christmas," she said, "but wouldn't give me a métro ticket, complaining about small, insignificant expenditures, saying things like, 'It's perfectly obvious it's not *your* money that's being spent.'" As if to emphasize the need to economize, he moved out of his large Boulevard de Courcelles apartment (which he rented to Mitty Goldin, a leading French impresario) and into a smaller walk-up on the Avenue Foch. "Mama" Delpierre, one of the elderly lady ushers in a Paris vaudeville theater, agreed to work part time as his cook and housekeeper. "He didn't pay her very much," said one close acquaintance. "Chevalier always believed that serving him was privilege enough."

Though it was apparent, immediately after the Liberation of France, that Chevalier had lost none of his prewar popularity with European audiences and GIs alike, resuming a busy traveling schedule that extended to Scandinavia and, eventually, even Berlin, he was perfectly aware that in France at least, in the new postwar music-hall medium, competition was becoming unusually fierce. Mayol and Dranem were no longer around, Trenet had become as much of a legend as Chevalier himself, but there was a crop of new postwar talent: By 1948, Piaf, Henri Salvador, Philippe Clay, Juliette Gréco, and Mouloudji were already well known, while Gilbert Bécaud and Charles Aznavour were just starting out on their careers. Chevalier's main challenger, however, was the "beginner" he had dismissed out of hand in 1941 — Yves Montand, thirty years his junior, whom he now praised as "the best talent of his generation."

In some respects—their stage mannerisms, their determination to turn every song into a self-contained, carefully rehearsed yet seemingly spontaneous act, a *show*, using dance, body language, mime, and mimicry to retain the audience's attention—they were alike. But Montand, in 1946, made no secret of his left-wing, *engagé* commitment, and his often ironic subject matter, with mocking, satirical overtones, culled from everyday events and recent films (including westerns, now being seen in France for the first time in four years), was in perfect accord with the mood of French youth. Understandably, because of the Occupation, this postwar generation, rebellious and distrustful of authority, had few prewar role models. The postwar young were idealistic, and overwhelmingly left-wing: in the words of poet Paul Éluard (himself a Communist) they expected as a right "*des lendemains qui chantent*" ("tomorrows that sing"). Perhaps influenced by Sartre's novels, they were also imbued with a Manichean streak, determined to wreak vengeance on *les salauds*, a term that cropped up constantly in Sartre's books and plays and referred indiscriminately to former collaborationists, ruthless plutocrats, or simply anyone whose views failed to coincide with his own.

After the Soviet invasion of Czechoslovakia in 1968, Montand and his wife, Simone Signoret, made their dramatic break with Communism, campaigning ceaselessly, in the seventies and eighties, for the rights of the Kurds, the boat people, and individual "prisoners of conscience" whether in gulags or in Western jails, without ever losing their "radical chic" aura. While the causes they championed after 1968 made them the bane of the much-weakened, neo-Stalinist French Communist party, their capacity for moral indignation—which had fueled their Communist commitment in the first place—weakened not at all.

Chevalier, the music-hall artist who went back to the pre–World War I Belle Epoque, was a completely different species. Though he sought out the company of intellectuals, he was not one himself, and affected to despise their—to him—largely incomprehensible jargon. Abstractions meant little to him. For all his wealth and fame, he retained the underdog's distrust of politicians, tempered by an innate respect for established order and rigidly hierarchical scale of values. He was also, in the world of vaudeville, a quite remarkable survivor. Already, as far back as 1917, Jacques-Charles, the Folies-Bergère director, had dismissed him as a has-been; his music-hall colleagues had privately rejoiced in his fall from grace in Hollywood in 1935; in the intervening years, he had enriched his repertoire with songs from his prewar Hollywood hits, but did not—and could not—change his style, or, except in minor respects, the nature of his songs. For someone who had already become a legend in his lifetime, it would have been absurd, as well as counterproductive, to give up the image of the girl-ogling, pleasure-loving boulevardier who invariably looked on the bright side of life. The few attempts he made, at the end of the Second World War, to deliver a message—as in "*La Chanson du Populo*," a mawkishly sentimental patriotic song with left-wing undertones—was disastrous, the mediocrity of the lyrics underlining the flatness of his delivery.* His foremost asset, as he well knew, was his

---

*"*Les coeurs sont pleins de chants nouveaux*
Apres le boulot, c'est des chansons qu'il nous faut!
Écoutons chanter le populo."

"Hearts are full of new songs.
It's songs we need after the shift!
Let's listen to the working man!"

formidable stage presence. "I have no voice," he constantly told report-ers, with undisguised self-satisfaction. "I sing from the heart."

Willemetz, Chevalier's favorite songwriter, shared his distaste for *engagé* songsters. In a preface to a book of photographs of Chevalier, Willemetz wrote that

> [t]o maintain the note of happiness, he has methodically ousted all the themes which today, alas, are beloved of our "dismal Desmonds": mist, fog and the bitterness of rebels. Even when he portrays a down-and-out he is never gloomy or sad. "Ma Pomme," [the song about the happy tramp] reveals the cheeriness of Daumier's boozers and the derisive banter of Gavarni's weary Willies.
>
> His repertoire is free of all political allusions, believing that it is not for an actor to take sides, since his job is to create unity in feeling among people often at variance, and his aim is to cause individuals of different outlook to be swept by the same gust of laughter or emotion.[1]

It was indeed this last characteristic that had been responsible for his traumatic months during and after the Liberation. The Parisians who had lionized him in 1941 and 1942, flocking to his Casino de Paris shows, were the very same people who had turned against him two years later, conveniently forgetting the brief, lighthearted respite he had given them during those grim Occupation years. Chevalier would never forgive them, just as he could never forgive his countrymen for putting him through his Purge Committee ordeal. By 1946, he had reestablished himself as a top performer, resuming his concert tours not only in France but throughout Western Europe with considerable success, but he could not and would not change his genre, while the new up-and-coming music-hall stars were delighting French audiences with a completely different kind of show.

Remembering his days as a megastar, Chevalier sensed the new post-war mood: He still attracted large crowds, but his audiences were on the whole considerably older than those that came to hear Montand and Bécaud. It was more important than ever to reestablish himself in the country that had made him a megastar—America. Here, consecration was still possible. Even in the darkest days, at the height of the "anticollaborationist" frenzy, he had been careful to remind Louella Parsons of his existence, sending her an autographed copy of one of his theater programs in February 1945. The emissary who delivered it reported that "he has gone very gray, looks very much older and seems anything but happy." But even Louella, his staunch ally, could not entirely avoid a reference to his recent controversial past, noting (in a March 31, 1945 column) that Lily Pons, the famous singer, had refused to appear in the same program as Chevalier at the Stage Door Canteen, the entertainment center of Americans on leave in Paris.

There was even talk that America, like Britain, might declare him persona non grata, but he did make one brief, unpublicized trip to New York, in the company of Nita Raya, just before their separation. They traveled as man and wife, confirming gossip-writers' suspicions they might be secretly married. Chevalier's purpose was to examine a number of offers from American film companies, and talk to his new U.S. agent, Arthur Lesser, who was confident he would soon resume his glittering prewar career there. And while Lesser worked on a possible schedule for him, Chevalier resumed his film career, this time in a René Clair film, *Le Silence Est d'Or (Silence Is Golden)*, uniquely tailored to his age and acting potential.

François Périer, his costar in the film, then a young, up-and-coming *jeune premier*, remembers Chevalier's unfailing courtesy, punctuality, and professionalism on the set. "In real life as in the film, he really was an avuncular figure," he said. He made no reference to his recent ordeal, or to his growing personal problems with Nita Raya. *Silence is Golden* prefigured the later *Love in the Afternoon* and *Gigi*—offering Chevalier a role that suited him perfectly. He looked his age—he had turned fifty-eight by the time it was released—and clearly enjoyed the part René Clair devised for him, as the debonair, bohemian film-studio head at the very beginning of the movie era (the film was set in 1906), who, though himself in love with the young actress he has selected, encourages her idyll with her shy, tongue-tied partner (Périer). The film, as well received in the United States as in Europe, with ecstatic reviews in *Life* and the *Hollywood Reporter* ("as smooth as a fine liqueur, as bubbly as good champagne") was the perfect preamble to his return. So was his much-acclaimed visit to the first postwar Cannes Film Festival, in 1946. Both he and Charles Boyer, appearing together, received a standing ovation.

He was flattered, too, by the attention French literary critics gave, that same year, to *Ma Route et Mes Chansons*, the first of what would eventually be eight volumes of his memoirs, which he had been working on since 1943.* French publishers were not in the habit of handing out vast advances even for potential best-sellers, and he never made more than a modest income from his writing (though he did work out a lucrative prepublication deal with *France-Soir* thanks to Pierre Daninos, the well-known French essayist, who was then one of the paper's senior editors.) His publisher, René Julliard, himself the epitome of French radical chic, staged a series of well-attended promotional parties for him, introducing him, for the first time, to distinguished literary figures like François Mauriac. He frequently attended dinner parties given by the French writer André Maurois and exchanged several letters with André Gide and the French historian Henri Guillemin. Autographing his book in crowded stores, he was mobbed by crowds. Even inside the Julliard offices, the staff ogled at him from behind glass doors. Though he constantly expressed demure, self-deprecating surprise at his success as a self-taught writer at the age of fifty-eight (his first book sold over 100,000 copies in France, subsequent volumes much less), it was clear that from 1946 on, he began taking his new occupation seriously. In a detailed questionnaire submitted to him by a French magazine, which included the question "What is your favorite occupation?" He replied "to write." (His favorite historical hero, it revealed, was Marcus Aurelius; his favorite composer Henri Christiné, and his favorite literary heroes "the defenders of the oppressed." He also revealed the lingering bitterness he felt toward those who had accused him of wartime collaboration. To the question: "What is, in your eyes, the crowning misfortune [*le comble de la misère*]?" he replied, "to be unjustly despised.") In his old age, he seriously hoped to be elected to the Académie Française, and toyed with the idea of lobbying some of its forty members, as all

---

*The ninth, "*Bravo Maurice*," was nothing more than a "digest" of the previous volumes.

candidates must. Fortunately for him, he was never aware of Académician Marcel Achard's cruel comment: "We might have elected him if only he'd never written anything."[2] In fact, the first three volumes of his autobiography, although blatantly self-serving, are well written, albeit in a somewhat flowery, old-fashioned style, and some of his letters to his friends are stylish, and even amusing, whenever Chevalier is able to forget that they are being penned by a living legend. The later "diaries" are, however, trite and tedious in the extreme.

Ma Route et Mes Chansons was by no means his first writing experience: From 1937 on, he had contributed occasional travel pieces and diary extracts to *Paris-Soir*. Immediately after the war, he had tried his hand at sports reporting (on the Tour de France bicycle race for *Paris-Presse*). He had had a writing bug ever since he began catching up on the education he had never had. As Charles Boyer used to tell a multitude of friends, Chevalier had come to him for advice while in Hollywood in the thirties, asking him to draw up a list of some twenty essential books that would improve his mind. These he had assiduously read.

He had always been a prolific letter-writer, first as a teenager, writing to his mother, then to mistresses, casual friends, and acquaintances. He invariably wrote to those concerned to express his appreciation of plays, books, and films he had seen. After reading Oscar Levant's *Memoirs of an Amnesiac*, for instance, he wrote him, "wishing you to be able to go on laughing at your miseries for a long, long time." He received a considerable amount of mail from strangers. Demands for money apart, he answered all his fan mail, usually with a brief acknowledgment, but occasionally with a much longer letter. Anything relating to his love of America, or to his mother, provoked an instant response. When an amateur poet, George M. Gillespie, sent him a "personalized poem," Chevalier responded effusively: "Dear versemaker, thanks a lot to include me in the talented lot of your favorite people. I have been in love with America since I was a boy and every time I feel that your great country has taken me to its heart is a reason for me to rejoice. The idea that you spent so much time and thought for writing that friendly poem about me makes me infinitely grateful." A letter from a Chicagoan, Elaine Fallon, whose mother, a lifelong fan, was terminally ill in 1959, led to the following reply: "Your letter," he wrote Elaine from the Waldorf-Astoria, "is one of the most touching I have ever read. I have—also—had such a strong love for the Saint that my own mother was, and I understand totally how you feel." Chevalier wrote Elaine's mother a long letter, and then several more, at regular intervals, even though she was too weak to answer them. After her death, he wrote Elaine: "That aching emptiness will, in time, become a warm and constant presence wherever you will be. You will talk to her in defeat and success. She has left your blood life but is, and always will be, right in your soul. Be sure of that. Bless you, Maurice Chevalier."

When on tour, he spent hours in his hotel room, covering page after page in his bold, highly idiosyncratic handwriting. After the publication of his first book, he cultivated a somewhat ornate style, but the contents of his letters seldom varied: Most were progress reports about the size and acclaim of his audience in the city he was writing from, the terms of praise used by critics and important people he had met, the relentless work discipline involved, and his wide-eyed, incredulous wonder at the durability of such an exceptional career.

The letters were virtually interchangeable, becoming increasingly self-congratulatory as he got older, for he seldom mentioned private doubts, unfavorable reviews, or patchy performances—and, inevitably, there were some. Those who knew him best after the war—Patachou, the nightclub singer, and Janie Michels—still have hundreds in their possession. Most make somewhat disappointing reading, containing little that is not already known about his life; in his letters he seldom unburdened himself, or referred to any of the real emotional or artistic crises in his life. As Daninos (to whom Chevalier wrote at length on his first postwar American tour) noted, "though his letters were always about himself, there was nothing either self-revelatory or spontaneous about them—he remained, to the end, an extraordinarily secretive man."

His memoirs, after the third volume, gradually became almost indistinguishable from his letters, mostly diary jottings larded with frequent name-dropping references to the rich and famous, along with highly predictable reactions to current events in the world at large. Increasingly, in the later volumes, he referred to himself, in a curious rhetorical style, as "you"—addressing himself as though he were another person. By 1947, he saw himself as a legend, a mythical French figure, though he had no illusions about the impermanence of his kind of artistic fame. About to leave for his second postwar trip to America, he wrote, in the manner of an elder statesman at France's helm: "Let's hope nothing unfortunate happens to my country while I'm away!"

Very much in demand socially, he was as averse to "celebrity" parties as he had been in Hollywood—with one exception: He never turned down an opportunity to meet famous French writers and intellectuals. Introduced to Jean-Paul Sartre at the gala opening of a new Paris satirical *boîte*, La Rose Rouge, in 1952, he noted that "I found him as sympathetic as his young disciples. I must read his books for I want to understand their outlook. They cannot be entirely wrong, given the way the world is going." He was particularly elated when Sartre asked him for signed copies of his books. Though he dearly loved meeting Belgian, British, Dutch, Monegasque, and Scandinavian Royalty—appearances before the British royal family were "the high point of my life," and they were as charmed with him as he was with them—he was quick to perceive real or imagined slights. "A real working-class type," he wrote in his memoirs, "can never really be understood by socialites. They are too blasé, too sure of themselves and of their tastes, nothing astonishes or moves them. For these people, artists are clowns, puppets at their beck and call, whom they either languidly reject or on whom they set their seal of approval."

Both letters and memoirs reflected a total self-absorption and an almost childish craving for reassurance: As François Vals, his later aide and business manager noted, "he was always susceptible to the grossest forms of flattery." Though he mellowed somewhat in his old age, those who came to know him well, like Nita Raya, Patachou, and his later companion Janie Michels, while at first bowled over by his charm whenever he chose to exercise it, soon realized that, with the exception of his dead mother, the only person of genuine interest in Chevalier's life was Chevalier himself.

In 1947, he did have a serious preoccupation: his transatlantic image. On the eve of his return to America after a thirteen-year absence, and the wartime slurs on his character, what would be the reaction of American audiences? The impact of the Holocaust had been greater in the United States than anywhere else in the world (Israel would not come into existence for another two years). The full story of the fate of Jews in France under the Occupation had not yet been told, and the distinction between *pétainisme* and collaboration was difficult to explain—and is still not fully understood outside France. So rumors concerning Chevalier made a deep impression among leaders of the American film and theater community, many of them Jewish, and these had not entirely been dispelled by the findings of the Purge Committee.

Long before he actually set foot on American soil (March 1947) Chevalier's new American business manager, Arthur Lesser, and a press agent, Carl Erbe, worked hard to set the record straight. They succeeded beyond all expectations.

The notion of fair play means a great deal in America, a profoundly legalistic country, where the ritual of success, so often followed by the ritual of humiliation, can also have a happy end, through the ritual of redemption. One possible reason for Chevalier's extraordinarily thorough rehabilitation was that leading American media personalities, aware that Chevalier had been unfairly mired from 1942 on, were so determined to be fair that they did not mind if, in the process, they leaned a little in the opposite direction.

Edwin A. Lahey, a syndicated columnist working for the *Chicago Daily News*, was one of several journalists who called on Chevalier in Paris shortly before his New York opening "to inquire about the accusations in part of the Paris press that he had been too friendly with the Nazis during the Occupation of France."

> There was none of the accustomed banter in his voice as he insisted that the newspapers that attacked him after the liberation were Socialist and attacked him because of a suspicion that he was sympathetic to the Communists. . . .*" All these attacks did was to make me more loved,"

---

*At the time, the pro-American Socialists and Stalinist French Communists were bitter political foes.

he said. "I appeared in Paris in November 1944, immediately after the liberation, after being silent since 1942, and the people gave me the biggest reception I ever had. . . . Any Frenchman who accuses me should first have the Croix de Guerre, and a bit of shrapnel in him, then we begin to talk business," the actor almost barked.

To the International News Service agency (INS), Chevalier was even more forthright. "I stayed out of Paris for nearly the four years the Germans were there. I refused to sing on every pretext. I sang only for French prisoners of war when they paid my 'price' of liberating ten prisoners. I didn't get a cent."

American Weekly, in June 1946, gave a somewhat one-sided account of his troubles: "The most determined of all his enemies was a jealous actor who managed to get on the purification committee," wrote Charles Robbins, in an article entitled "Chevalier Sings Again" syndicated in the Hearst press. *Liberty* magazine went a step further:

> Otto Abetz, the military commander of Paris [sic] insisted Chevalier appear in Germany to entertain French conscripted workers there. Maurice refused on the grounds that such an engagement would imply an approval on his part of the conscription of French labor. He was later given no choice in the matter, but told he must perform for French prisoners in Germany.*

This news item probably originated with an advertisement paid for by Lesser in the New York *Daily News*, in the form of a show-business column written by Walter Shirley: "During world war two, Chevalier was asked to perform for the French conscripted laborers in Germany at his own price."

The French Foreign Ministry's Information Department, on the eve of his return, backed Chevalier's version of events to the hilt: In a press handout summarizing his career (dated February 27, 1947), it said that

---

*In 1941, the enforced conscription of French factory workers to Germany had not yet begun.

continued successes in London and Paris were interrupted by the war. M. Chevalier spent the greater part of the Occupation in retirement in Cannes. He appeared only once without fee before the French P.O.W.'s at Alten Grabow. The Purge Committee of theater artists exonerated him of all collaboration charges.

Later the William Morris and Universal Studios releases would draw on this to state that "during the second world war, Chevalier worked only 12 weeks in four years," and Chevalier himself, in later life, went even further: "In three years, I gave only 17 performances," he told the *Los Angeles Examiner* in 1958. He may well have forgotten the embarrassing *Paris-Soir* and Radio-Paris galas, but the thought arises; Might not his sudden jettisoning of Henri Betti have been part of an unconscious wish to rid himself of an unwelcome witness of his wartime past? His conduct had certainly been no worse than that of most other French vaudeville stars, and in many respects compared favorably with that of his peers, especially Mistinguett and Tino Rossi. What perplexed and amused those in the know in France at the time was his determination to prove that it had been no less than perfect.

As with the hype surrounding the circumstances of his "escape" from the Alten Grabow P.O.W. camp in 1916, efforts were made to make his record even more palatable: Billy Rose, the well-known columnist ("Pitching Horseshoes"), songwriter, and nightclub owner, wrote somewhat imaginatively that

I was in Paris last November [1946] and did a little poking around on my own. I talked to Maxine de Biex, Paris correspondent for a fine show business paper called *Variety*. For three years Maxine had been hiding in friendly peasants' barns by day and working with the Underground at night. I asked him how Chevalier rated with the fighters of the resistance. He told me the boys who had to know counted Maurice as one of them. He may have played pattycake with the Nazis, but he worked with the right guys in the right cellars. . . . I talked with other members of the Underground whose names I can't even spell. I quizzed taxi drivers, bartenders and bellhops—the people who know about everyone's dirty linen. I think I got the straight story. To them, I was just another little geezer in a blue suit and there was no reason to give me the double shuffle. As far as they were concerned, Maurice was still the big boy of the Boulevards.

The Billy Rose column was decisive, influencing almost all subsequent pieces about Chevalier: In *Coronet*, some years later, Laurence Lader would even claim that had had been a member of the French wartime Resistance, "in a group called 'Les Étoiles.' " This was the Aragon-led section, consisting exclusively of French intellectuals, that had distributed underground pamphlets and banned literature. By no stretch of the imagination could even such a fan as Elsa Triolet have claimed that Chevalier had been one of them.

By 1947, his visa problems over, Chevalier returned to London for the first time since 1939 on his way to America—a public-relations operation to exorcise the memories of those unfortunate 1944 press reports. Jack Hylton and C. B. Cochran staged parties for him. London was in worse shape than Paris, he noted: Postwar shortages were such that when he visited Locke's, the famous hatters, he was told they could not make him a felt hat—they had no felt. From Southampton, with some trepidation, he boarded the *Queen Elizabeth* for New York with Max Ruppa and Ruppa's wife, Yvonne.

Chevalier's anxiety over collaboration charges was understandable, and he instinctively understood that attack was the best form of defense. "I have never been so popular with French crowds as I have been since the Liberation," he told *The New York Times*. Even more preoccupying to him was the expected reaction of the New York public to an act that had not basically changed since his arrival there in 1927. As Chevalier candidly put it to Lucius Beebe, in the *New York Herald Tribune*, "I want to find out if I'm still any good. I want to find out if I have any hold at all on the American public, or any claim to prestige in the country that I am never able to forget gave me my greatest acclaim and popularity."

He need not have worried. On March 7, 1947, the day of his arrival in New York, photographers jostled one another as frenziedly as on his first visit as he clowned on deck for their benefit with a straw hat and cane. "It doesn't seem like thirteen years," he told them with a grin. The only minor false note had nothing to do with the media: Chevalier had never met Carl Erbe, the youthful-looking agent who had done so much behind-the-scenes work for him. Singling him out, Chevalier told Lesser, "Tell that kid to take care of my baggage." A disappointed Erbe, who had himself invested ten thousand dollars in Chevalier's show at the Henry Miller Theater, did as he was told. "Later, when the luggage was brought into Chevalier's hotel room," Erbe recalled, "Chevalier took one look at it and started to bawl me out because the leather was scuffed."

Newspaper and magazine critics of his show were almost all uniformly enthusiastic after the first night of "An Evening of Songs and Impressions," as his show was called, though *Time* felt that "a whole evening of Chevalier is a bit too much." His stage presence was as compelling as ever, and the admittedly somewhat elderly but glittering first-night audience eager to share in a nostalgic experience. The twelve-hundred-seat theater was full, the considerable "first-night gala" proceeds (at fifty dollars a ticket) raised a sizable amount for the American relief Fund for Aid to France, and Chevalier himself was suitably modest and deferential, addressing his audience like an old flame who has to be wooed all over again. "I've brought you all my best French songs, and every night I will polish my work a little more and try and understand you a little better," he told them. Mary Pickford had him to tea, Ruth Gordon and Garson Kanin to lunch; Barbara Stanwyck and Robert Taylor came to his show. In all sorts of ways, Chevalier realized that his reputation was, after all, intact. His one-man show was as well received in Boston and Canada as it had been in New York. To celebrate, he ordered a new Pontiac station wagon to be delivered to him in France.

There was an emotional reunion with Louella Parsons. He thanked her profusely for her support of him during his "dark days," but it must have been clear to him, from her tone, that his status, in her scale of values, had undergone a considerable change. She wrote:

"They want me in Hollywood," the onetime film idol said. "I'll go there around Christmas time. I have four offers and haven't decided which one to accept."

"I am very enthusiastic about Chevalier's return to the screen," Louella Parsons went on,

for there's never been anyone who could fill his place or has his ingratiating charm and spontaneous gaiety. He's older, it's true, and sadder—and I think probably wiser than in the days when he was on top. . . . Now Maurice's art is his life. He doesn't smoke or drink. he works so intently that nothing else seems to matter. He goes out very little socially and has given almost no interviews because there's much that must be left unsaid.

She noted, with disappointment, that he had not brought Nita Raya with him, correctly surmising their affair was over at last. Neither Chevalier nor Nita Raya had made their split public: Even a year later, in 1948, with his new American career in full swing, *The American Weekly* insisted the two were about to marry, quoting Chevalier himself ("Nita offers me what I seek most: understanding, companionship and sincerity. I have a better chance of making success of marriage with her than with someone I don't know so long. Love is love—but love is life!") "We have a tender feeling for each other," Nita Raya told the magazine's Joan King Flynn. "It was Chevalier who discovered me, launched me. I owe him everything and he is the center of my life. To speak to you about me is to speak about him." By now Nita Raya was the star, the *meneuse de revue*, of the latest Folies-Bergère show; they no longer lived under the same roof or saw each other often. She had also learned to emulate Chevalier and cover her tracks. There was another reason for pretending they were still lovers: She wished Chevalier well and knew that his second American career would be better served if the American public believed they still had an ongoing, steady relationship.

Chevalier's relations with the media remained ambiguous: Though he complained throughout his long career (but always in private) that the press was invariably out to get him, he was, under a veneer of gruff, bluff innocence, shrewdly manipulative. "Nita plans to leave the profession entirely. She wants to give up her work and try to be happy with me," he told *American Weekly*. He must have known that at the peak of her music-hall career and reveling in her new fame, Nita Raya had no intention of giving up the Folies-Bergère.

The impact of the 1947 American tour was such that from then on, Chevalier decided to resume his prewar routine, spending almost half his time in America with intervals of filmmaking and concerts in Europe. He was in fact now more acclaimed in America than in France, where his popularity was flagging slightly, not because of his recent troubles, but because of the lure of a bevy of new stars. Jean-Christophe Averty, the jazz specialist and director, who would later work closely with Chevalier, remains convinced he avoided France deliberately—to get even for the treatment meted out to him in 1944.

He returned to the United States for another tour seven months later, arriving on the French liner *De Grasse*, staying for several months, appearing in a different town every week. In New Orleans, immediately after the show, plainclothesmen closed in on a smartly dressed woman whom they were arresting for organizing a prostitution ring. Unfazed, she turned to them as she was being escorted out of the theater and said, "Wasn't that Frenchman marvelous?"

In Los Angeles, he stayed with the Boyers, who threw a Christmas party for him attended by Ronald Colman and Arthur Rubinstein, the concert pianist. The following day, early in the morning, he made a pilgrimage to Marlene Dietrich's old house on Roxbury Drive. It looked exactly the same, he noted, with understated nostalgia.

His next trip to the United States was in 1948, for a short season at the Golden Theater. The show opened, hardly coincidentally, around the time of Chevalier's sixtieth birthday. "It was not quite as great a success as he himself later made out," said Jo Siritsky, a prewar friend and French cinema owner. "I had to rush around and make a lot of phone calls to get people to attend." In 1949, he was there again briefly, this time with his latest love. She was Jacqueline Noël, a dark-haired, strikingly beautiful aspiring actress, forty-one years his junior, whom he had met, by chance, at a dinner party, and dated the following day—very much as he had begun his affair with Nita Raya.* In his diary, Chevalier charted the rise and fall of his latest affair candidly and sometimes even explicitly, but, as usual, without mentioning her name, leaving most of the story untold.

An early entry read, "She's twenty-two. What can I do about it? I'm only going along with this because I think the kid is perfectible, sweet and loving. I need to protect someone and she seems tameable." He himself had raised the age-gap issue with her, only to be charmed by her "adorable, naive" rejoinder that "with the right make-up I can look at least ten years older." Addressing himself in his usual style, he made it clear that the initiative to seduce him had been hers: "You're not raping her. Far from it," he wrote.

As usual, he was determined to mold his new companion in his own image: "Who knows whether this love, originating in a mixture of feelings where sex is the least important element, won't result in a wee human being who will become a kind of child for you?" The age difference was bound to shock, "but what kind of a person do you think you are" he asked himself, "to stave off such adorably tender advances? Some people get attached to dogs, cats, parrots. What I'm attempting seems to me to be akin to adoption. It would be wonderful to succeed. And if it worked out, I'd be helping other men of my age, proving that one should no more despair in the affairs of the heart than in one's professional life."

He was strongly smitten, and his claim that "sex was not important" fooled no one, for he had seldom been more sexually active, even in his youth, archly noting that "My friends say: what's the matter? You look tired." His vanity was appealing in its naïveté, and some entries could have been written by a teenager: "The kid says she's fallen in love for the first time in her life. I represent all that she has always dreamed of in men (or so she says). I like her so much I've decided to enter this handicap race."

A few weeks later, he wrote, "I still don't quite understand what's happening to me. The little one is so agreeable and interesting that I feel

*In *With Love*, Chevalier calls her "Françoise."

I'm on a magic carpet. I've not yet lost control but my surprise grows from discovery to discovery. She is physically adorable and I'm already in love. But her thoughts and judgments reveal such an instinctive intelligence that I am, sometimes, speechless. . . . For the last two weeks we have been discovering each other."

He made no attempt to conceal his new liaison. "The kid's in love," he wrote, "and I like her so much that the fear of ridicule doesn't even begin to affect me. . . . I only feel awkward when, along with the kid, I happen to come across a woman I once knew when she was young and beautiful and who has become less so."

Soon, however, the tone of his diary changed, with a series of tantaliz ingly cryptic entries: "A cloud, and then another, major one, on the blue horizon," he wrote a few months later. "I reacted like a typical male. The kid couldn't believe it." He was still infatuated, though. In La Bocca, in her company, "hours go by like minutes."

Jacqueline Noël was now his constant companion, and wherever she went, Chevalier noted, men's heads turned. "I realize my jealousy to-wards all the men who are attracted by the kid has taken on morbid proportions," he wrote. A few weeks later, he confessed that "she is an adorable little sun but from time to time she gives me sunstroke."

Finally, toward the end of 1949, came the following enigmatic but unmistakable entry: "The dream has turned into a nightmare. I've just been stung, in my most vulnerable place, by a little bee with a honey-dipped sting. . . . At 61, one can't play the passionate lover anymore."

It was not just "morbid jealousy" that led to the end of the affair. He had discovered that his latest companion had been somewhat economi-cal with the truth about her own past, that he was by no means the first man in her life—and his pride had been hurt. But there were other reasons: It was Jacqueline's goal to move into his house in La Bocca, assuming the role of *maîtresse de maison* once held by Nita Raya. Perhaps she overestimated her physical hold on him. In any case, rightly or wrongly, Chevalier began detecting a predatory streak in both Jacqueline and her ubiquitous mother, who moved into an apartment in nearby Cannes to be closer to her daughter.

Max Ruppa had always viewed this particular idyll with considerable concern, for he felt Chevalier's career was in possible jeopardy. He now played a considerable role in ending it. The final break came after a heart-to-heart talk with Ruppa, who revealed that Jacqueline had dropped hints that she was expecting his child—she was not—and that Paris gossip was that Chevalier would soon marry her.

The end of the affair left Chevalier depressed and emotionally drained: At sixty-one, and nearing old age, he was aware that his sexual drive remained as vigorous as ever—he was as physically attracted to young women as he had been in his youth—and this resulted in mingled self-satisfaction and embarrassment. Well into his sixties, in a moment of unusual candor, he wrote that the sight of a beautiful young woman "makes me shake with lust, like a reformed alcoholic with a bottle at his elbow." Above all, he realized that this susceptibility made him exceptionally vulnerable to fortune hunters of all kinds, and he later hinted that he had had a narrow escape. Though able, in time, to joke about his predicament and claim that it no longer bothered him (Alan Jay Lerner would brilliantly exploit this aspect of him in the *Gigi* song "I'm Glad I'm Not Young Anymore"), he never really came to terms with it: The tragic last few months of his life would be proof of that.

As was his habit, he tailored the facts somewhat. He would later (February 20, 1957) tell *Variety*, "There have been seven women in my life and I have been able to walk away from all of them. When a man falls in love with a woman, it is so easy to become a prisoner of the flesh. It is that which ruins most entertainers, especially singers. A singer must ask himself: with whom do I want to be a hit—my wife or my public? I have always chosen the public." He told his French publisher, shortly after he turned sixty-two, that he had taken a birthday vow to give up sex altogether, as he had given up smoking years before. However, many years later, when several of the female acquaintances who had known him well in his later years were reminded of this vow, they burst into raucous laughter.

While the affair with Jacqueline Noël was drawing to a close, concrete Hollywood proposals still eluded him, though he made much, to the press, of his preliminary talks with producers. One possible reason for his failure to break back into the Hollywood film community may have been Chevalier's reluctance to accept scaled-down fees reflecting his postwar status. This may not have been the only issue. Though never stated, his wartime record may also have been an unspoken factor: It was certainly discussed when tentative plans to film his life story were made—and shelved—in the early sixties.

Chevalier did resume a film career in France in 1949–50, but the earlier success of René Clair's *Silence Is Golden* would not be repeated for a decade: *A Royal Affair*, a period-piece farce more suited to the prewar Hollywood era, did poorly at the box office in both Europe and America when it was released in 1949. His next film, *Ma Pomme*, released in 1950, was an even greater flop. Both were written and directed by Marc-Gilbert Sauvageon, a highly predictable, old-fashioned filmmaker whose chief quality, in Chevalier's eyes, was his extreme deference to the star.

Ma Pomme had been the title of one of Chevalier's best-known songs about a happy-go-lucky hobo, that archetypal, universally popular vaudeville character, but Bosley Crowther, of *The New York Times*, wrote, "it is sad to behold the old favorite playing a wistful and aging bum in a drab little bit of French flim-flam." *Cue* scored the "dull writing and plodding direction" and *Newsweek* the "unfunny ballast" and inferior music. Soon, but for very different reasons, Chevalier would wish he had never had anything to do with it. For at the closing wrap party, the head "grip" on the set, a member of the Communist-dominated CGT, produced a piece of paper and said, "Will you sign this along with us, Maurice?" He was told that the document, called the Stockholm Appeal, had the backing of most of France's leading artists, scientists, and intellectuals, that most of the cast of *Ma Pomme* and all of the crew had signed, that "there's nothing political about it, absolutely nothing. It's just about whether you like the atom bomb or not." Chevalier scrawled his name at the bottom of an eighty-five-word manifesto he didn't even bother to read. In his diary, he wrote, "I felt I was not doing wrong in adding my name to the list."

Without realizing it at the time, he had signed away his right of entry into the United States, becoming a prohibited alien in the one country, outside France, that mattered most to him, professionally as well as emotionally.

CHAPTER 17

"Fewer people come to see me."

—Maurice Chevalier
Ma Route et Mes Chansons, Vol. 5

The Stockholm Appeal was probably Communism's most successful propaganda operation of the entire Cold War. It stemmed from Stalin's recognition that, despite the quality of physicists like Sakharov and the KGB's successful quest for atomic secrets, the Soviet Union would continue to lag behind the United States for years to come. From this position of weakness, the logical course, in 1949, was to exploit to the hilt the worldwide revulsion against nuclear warfare. It was only four years since Hiroshima, and in the "Cold War" climate, the threat of nuclear warfare was brandished, from Moscow, as a distinct possibility. Until such time as the Soviet Union itself acquired a nuclear arsenal, it made sense to encourage fervent, worldwide peace campaigns against nuclear war. The Korean War gave the campaign additional credibility, for European Communist parties, at Moscow's instigation, depicted it as a dress rehearsal for the real thing.

Stalin's propaganda machine went further than that: The Soviet line imposed on the docile leaders of European Communist parties (with the exception of Tito) was that the United States was not only arming itself and forcing its allies to follow suit, but was secretly preparing for an imminent showdown against the USSR that would involve a nuclear holocaust, already decided on by top-level reactionary circles in Washington.

Few Europeans (including European Communists) really believed this to be the case, and the irony was that, by 1949, at the very time the "international Communist threat" was becoming such a high-priority issue in the eyes of the U.S. Congress, the credibility and influence of Marxism-Leninism was already on the wane in Europe. Only in China, where Mao was winding up his war against the discredited Chiang Kai-shek, was Communism actually gaining ground. Elsewhere, and especially within the West European Communist parties, the rot had already set in: Many cardholders found the imposed Stalin personality cult grotesque; among the USSR's East European satellites, especially in East Germany, Czechoslovakia, and Poland, Stalin's ruling puppets relied on deportations, millions of informers, and the systematic use of physical and psychological police-state terror to keep those trapped behind the Iron Curtain suitably cowed.

But while Stalin failed to stem this downward slide, he won a series of major propaganda victories in 1949–50, and of all his ideological weapons, none was more effective than the Stockholm Appeal.

Ironically, the unveiling of the "peace" campaign occurred in New York itself, in 1949, with an American-organized Scientific and Cultural Conference for World Peace, followed soon after by similar conferences in Paris, Stockholm, and Warsaw. These rallies were only part of a brilliantly concerted whole, involving the mobilization of trade unions in France and Italy to disrupt delivery of arms to America's allies in Western Europe, and a more classic diplomatic offensive conducted by Soviet diplomats all over the world, and especially at the United Nations, where the Soviet delegation ceaselessly lobbied for the nonrearmament of Japan and Germany, the abolition of nuclear weapons, and a friendship and nonaggression pact among the "Big Five."

Two permanent bodies coordinated the Peace Partisans' activities: the World Federation of Democratic Youth, and the International Democratic Federation of Women, with headquarters in Paris (until banned by the French government). Both movements were Communist-subsidized, though many of its members were simply idealists, either unaware or ready to overlook international Communism's role in the "higher interest" of world peace.

The "Peace Partisans" immediately attracted the attention of the media: Queen Elizabeth of Belgium, the mother of King Leopold, became one of their sponsors in March 1949. Perhaps not entirely coincidentally in the light of what would occur later, Chevalier had been her dinner-party guest the previous January. In America the movement was endorsed by well-known left-wing intellectuals like Howard Fast, the writer, Dr. W.E.B. Du Bois, the educator and champion of black rights, and elicited favorable initial responses from Arthur Miller and Charles Chaplin. Paul Robeson, the famous black singer, became a committed advocate, performing at most Peace Partisan rallies throughout the world.

In France the movement was spearheaded by Frédéric and Irène Joliot-Curie, France's most famous atomic physicists, both actively committed Communist party members, but supporters included not just leading artists like Picasso and Jean Lurçat with Communist affiliations, but also many leading judges, parliamentarians, and members of both the Académie Française and Académie Goncourt with no Communist links whatever. Louis Aragon, then editor of *Ce Soir*, was a frequent Peace Partisan orator.

Britain's peace activists were less glittering members of the intelligentsia. Leading British figures included the maverick left-wing MP Konni Zilliacus, Iver Montagu, a not very well-known film director, and, inevitably, Hewlett Johnson, the "Red Dean" of Canterbury. Though the Vatican remained hostile, many European Protestant clerics rallied to the cause.

Shortly after the New York conference, the Peace Partisans staged a four-day convention at the Salle Pleyel concert hall in Paris in April 1949: The poster commemorating the occasion was Picasso's celebrated green-and-white lithograph of a dove bearing an olive branch. On opening day, there was rapturous applause when a French Communist MP announced that Picasso had just fathered a daughter—and that, in honor of the Peace Partisans, he had decided to call her "Paloma"—dove.

By this time, because of its simple, straightforward language, the Stockholm Appeal had become the Partisans' chosen recruiting instrument. Canvassing for signatures followed a standard procedure, designed to hook the unwary and the politically naive. The French CGT, like other Communist-led organizations, was instructed to approach potential signatories with such leading questions as: Are you in favor of war or peace? Do you approve of the use of atomic bombs against women and children? The document Chevalier signed on the set of *Ma Pomme* read as follows:

1—We demand the absolute banning of the atomic weapon, arm of terror and mass extermination of populations.

2—We demand the establishment of strict international control to ensure the implementation of this banning measure.

3—We consider that any government which would be the first to use the atomic weapon against any country whatsoever would be committing a crime against humanity and should be dealt with as a war criminal.

4—We call on all men of goodwill throughout the world to sign this appeal.

In March 1950, Picasso and the Red Dean made headlines all over the world when they were denied visas to come to the United States to present a similar petition to Congress. The State Department called it "a major Soviet instrumentality for propaganda and political pressure." At this remove in time, the fuss seems absurd, but in 1950, because of Korea, the Cold War, and the considerable fear inspired by Communist parties and Communist-dominated Trade Unions in Western Europe, the Stockholm Appeal was an extraordinarily potent symbol. "The fear of possible retaliation if the Communists happened to come to power induces many to sign, although they mistrust the

aim of the appeal," noted the Associated Press. The mounting numbers of signatures (5 million in France alone by June 1950, 20 million
in Western Europe, soon rising to 50 and even 100 million—though
such figures were unverifiable and almost certainly inflated, for whole
towns were deemed to have signed) alarmed the U.S. State Department. The Stockholm Appeal proved extremely difficult to counter in
propaganda terms: All the Truman government could do was point
out that its four points were identical with those advocated by official
Soviet policy and that, "read more attentively, the expression of moral
indignation at the idea of atomic bombing must be seen as an attack
on U.S. policy and a plan for atomic control on Russian terms"—
hardly a compelling debating point. As the *New York Herald Tribune*
wrote during a second Peace Conference in Paris, June 1950, "Something has gone wrong, it seems safe to say, when a plea for peace can
be regarded only as a communist catchword."

Chevalier's conduct, admittedly, was extraordinarily naive: By 1950 it
was generally known that the real instigator of the Stockholm Appeal
was the Kremlin. Leading French intellectuals of the non-Communist
Left, led by Albert Camus and Jean-Paul Sartre (who by this time had
distanced himself from the Stalinist French CP) even staged a diversion-
ary demonstration at the Vel d'Hiv stadium in Paris to protest its
one-sided "peace *à la Russe*" during an "official" Peace Partisans rally. All
this was front-page news in all French newspapers, and it is highly
unlikely that it escaped Chevalier's attention.

Because of the hysteria induced by the Cold War, the official American response to the Stockholm Appeal was to regard all signatories not
simply as idealist dupes but as conscious agents of world Communism—and by the summer of 1950 steps were being taken, in secret, to
bar, under the Internal Security Act sponsored by Nevada's maverick
Democratic senator Pat McCarran, all those who had signed from
entering the United States.

This act, banning not only pro-communists, but also prostitutes,
polygamists, paupers, stowaways, and lepers, was to be followed by an
even harsher measure—the McCarran-Walter Act, which President

Truman vetoed in 1952, but which Congress passed anyway. (It would only be scrapped thanks to amendments introduced by Senator Patrick Moynihan thirty-five years later.)

By 1950, J. Edgar Hoover's FBI had entered the anticommunist witch-hunt with glee, defining the World Peace Council (the permanent body that eventually assumed the task of counting signatures) as "a worldwide Soviet-oriented communist front whose primary object is to discredit the United States," and Senator McCarthy, shortly afterward, would base his entire sleazy political career on anticommunist hysteria. The purge of real and suspected Hollywood Communists, encouraged by veterans like Cecil B. de Mille and Chevalier's old friend Adolphe Menjou, was further evidence of this new American obsession. Some of its manifestations would be richly comical: Two young McCarthy aides, Roy Cohn and G. David Schine, became a laughingstock in 1953, when they toured United States Missions in Britain, searching U.S. government funded libraries for traces of anti-American books and other disguised forms of Communist propaganda. Other symptoms of the sickness were more ominous: At home and abroad, Americans suspected of being "soft on communism" were tricked into surrendering their passports, condemned in some cases to unemployment and semipermanent exile.

Chevalier was aboard the *Empress of Canada* in May 1951 with Patachou, the French singer, and her new husband, Arthur Lesser (Chevalier's American business manager) when he heard the news that he had just become persona non grata in the United States. Patachou, an up-and-coming music-hall star whose career Chevalier had begun promoting, would share in his music-hall bookings for the next few months, and remain a close friend until a major fallout a few years later. Hélène Gougeon, a Canadian journalist working for *Weekend* magazine, an insert in some twenty-five Canadian dailies, went to see Chevalier at Her Majesty's Theater in Montreal. He did not seem too distressed by the news, and her lasting memory is of her amazement that Chevalier, already in his sixties, "could do back flips so gracefully and without pratfalls." She wondered then whether he was more than Patachou's patron or mentor, and as she recalled, "the fact that her husband/manager was along on the trip didn't convince us they weren't having a romance."

After his Canadian tour, Chevalier was due in Hollywood for talks with Billy Wilder, who wanted to make a film with—and perhaps about—him, a trip that would now not take place. Chevalier did of course appeal the decision, under a provision of the "Communist control" law that allowed the attorney-general to make special exceptions. But Dean Acheson, who approved of the McCarran Act, favored Chevalier's exclusion, his spokesman accusing Chevalier not only of signing the peace petition, but of taking part in "pro-Communist entertainment, singing for a group which turned its receipts over to a Communist affiliate." Though technically correct, such a charge was grotesque: The reference was to Chevalier's presence at a gala, shortly after the Liberation of Paris, to raise money for widows and orphans of members of the Franc-Tireurs et Partisans (one of the largest, most active of all French Resistance groups), who had died in the Maquis while fighting the Nazis and members of the French Gestapo. Admittedly, the FTP had been under Communist control. Then still under investigation by the Purge Committee for alleged collaboration, and befriended by Louis Aragon, himself a leading Communist, Chevalier could scarcely have refused.

With considerable dignity, Chevalier expressed his baffled surprise. He had only done "what millions of Frenchmen had done," he said. "Someone asked if I was against the A-bomb. Well, nobody likes the bomb. I sing about l'amour, work, life. I leave to others the task of deciding what is right and what is wrong. I sing to make people forget things like politics."

Chevalier was only one of the prominent victims of this anticommunist frenzy; over the years, those denied American visas would include Graham Greene, Dario Fo, Jorge Amado, Carlos Fuentes, Gabriel García Márquez, and Pablo Neruda. Many more artists and intellectuals simply failed to apply for American visas because they knew they would be turned down.

The U.S. State Department, itself suspected of being soft on communism, was in no mood to defend Chevalier in 1951, cravenly acknowledging that his entry into the United States would be "contrary to the best interests of the United States." News of the ban, though widely reported, triggered surprisingly little adverse comment. For sheer nastiness, few rivaled the "Cholly Knickerbocker" column of May 15, 1951: "To those who know Chevalier well," he wrote,

> it seemed incredible that he could ever be a Communist sympathizer. For the talented Maurice has the typical mentality of the middle-class Frenchman—he loves money and he's parsimonious to the point of stinginess. . . . And if there's anything the Communists hate it's a bourgeois. But then, how can you explain Chevalier's action? Well, if you remember, Maurice had been accused of collaboration with the Nazis during the war. So the day France was liberated, Chevalier grabbed a Red Flag and started waving it. You see, it was a good way to avoid getting shot. . . . But otherwise there isn't one single person who really knows Chevalier who is not ready to testify that the famous Parisian star is no more a Communist at heart than he is a Nazi. Let's just say he's a fool.

In fact there is no evidence that the French CP put any special pressure on him. It is far more likely that the usually cautious Chevalier simply decided that if Queen Elizabeth of the Belgians, whom he admired, could sign the Stockholm Appeal with impunity, then so could he.

In private Chevalier criticized French diplomats in Washington and Cabinet ministers in Paris for failing to protest the measure against him. Arthur Lesser, active on his behalf in America, assured him it would only be a matter of months, if not weeks, before he was allowed back. But Dean Acheson proved surprisingly intractable.

Meanwhile, Chevalier carried on: Instead of America, he toured Argentina and Brazil, then returned to Europe. There were short appearances in a distinctly unmemorable Italian film.* His vaudeville career

---

*Cento Anni d'Amore (1954), produced and directed by Lionelle de Felice

slowed down, though the tours continued. A revue with the French singer Colette Marchand, at the Théâtre de l'Empire, in 1952, was a distinct flop: For the first time in his career, to keep the show going, he was compelled to take a 50 percent cut in his fee. A young actress, Odette Meslier, was given a small part in the show, appearing onstage with him during his "Valentine" number. His contemporaries recall that he had a very brief fling with her, but that she left no lasting impression on him.

His disappointment at the Théâtre de l'Empire flop didn't last, for a highly successful engagement in London soon followed. A monthlong London Hippodrome booking was extended by another three weeks. He was also one of the stars of a Variety Command Performance at the London Palladium attended by the queen and Prince Philip, and mingled with the royal family again at a private dinner party staged in his London house by Douglas Fairbanks, Jr. Chevalier sang for the royals for forty minutes, Queen Elizabeth and her entourage joining in the chorus of his songs with evident delight.

He and "Lady Patachou," as he nicknamed her, continued their European tours together, on terms of "affectionate friendship." He also used some of his unexpected leisure time to rearrange his own life-style: Willemetz had moved to a large house in Marnes-la-Coquette, west of Paris, and urged Chevalier to move there too. He did so, acquiring a splendid estate there, formerly owned by the millionaire philanthropist Sir Richard Wallace. Chevalier's older brother Paul, recently widowed, moved in with him, also accompanying him to La Bocca. Shortly afterward, however, he donated his La Louque home on the Riviera to the SACEM, the French artists' and writers' copyright and welfare association. Inevitably, there were those who said he only did so because he found it too expensive to run, but it was a valuable gift for all that. Willemetz was then a member of the SACEM board, and Chevalier gifted the house on the understanding Willemetz would turn it into a leisure center for "deserving" SACEM members. Chevalier even added that, the way things were going, he might end up there himself one day, as a "deserving poor" SACEM pensioner.

Ruppa had been seriously ill with leukemia for several years, and died in 1952. Chevalier's new French business manager, François Vals, with his wife, Madeleine, would became over the years part of the Chevalier "family," and remain with him almost constantly until shortly before Chevalier's death. A lifelong admirer, Vals was only twenty-two and knew nothing of show business, though he had a grounding in business management and accountancy. Chevalier picked him on the spur of the moment, after Vals had called on him in his dressing room during a concert in Bordeaux, to ask him to autograph his memoirs.

It was an inspired choice: Vals not only mastered the intricacies of show business with surprising speed but also provided Chevalier with unfailingly good advice. He was one of the few members of Chevalier's "court" to speak his mind to him on all occasions. Their relations at first were curiously formal: After moving into his palatial new estate in Marnes-la-Coquette Chevalier was surprised, and at first somewhat offended, when the Vals refused the offer of a luxurious, rent-free house inside the Marnes-la-Coquette grounds, preferring to stay on in their small house in suburban Sèvres.

He told Georges Cravenne, shortly after moving into his palatial Marnes-la-Coquette house (also named La Louque in memory of his mother) that the gatekeeper's cottage might come in handy one day, "if I fall on hard times and have to let the property." His friends were used to such talk: It was all part of his continued neurotic fear of financial insecurity that went hand in hand with childish enjoyment of his considerable wealth, for immediately after referring to his possible plight "in old age," he would itemize, in letters to friends, the huge size of the fees he still commanded. In Lausanne, Switzerland, with Patachou, around this time, he looked up at a street sign and said, "I think I own some buildings on this street but can't remember which."

One guest who did move into the Chevalier estate with her two small children was Janie Michels, a talented painter and protégée of Matisse, whom Chevalier had met during his final months in La Bocca. Divorced from a French aristocrat and in her midtwenties when she first met Chevalier, she fell into the category of his "exceptional women." Strikingly good-looking, with impeccable social and artistic credentials, she was responsible for turning Chevalier into a discriminating collector.* Under her guidance, he started accumulating the works of Utrillo, Van Dongen, Matisse, and Vlaminck.

They had first met in 1950, on the Riviera: even before his exclusion from the United States, she recalled, he had been in a "suicidal" mood, unable to overcome the humiliation of his arrest and what he described, again and again, as a "smear campaign" masterminded by less successful show-business rivals. He had also not entirely recovered from the end of his affair with Jacqueline Noël. "I think he was attracted to me because I wasn't overawed by him, and was able to make him laugh," she said. "He unburdened himself to me, told me all about his finicky little domestic problems." Though she staged several exhibitions in the United States, which Chevalier attended, she never accompanied him on any of his tours, and was seldom seen at his luncheon parties, invariably excusing herself on the grounds that she needed to work in her studio. "I got to know his moods and habits well," she said. "He was a complete workaholic, rehearsals were never fun: The reason he liked to walk so much every day, in the huge park near Marnes-la-Coquette, was that he could run through his songs as he walked, without being disturbed. I sometimes went with him on these long walks, but knew better than to interrupt." In August 1954, Chevalier was officially informed that he was welcome in the United States once more, but did not return there for another year. By this time, Janie Michels had become even more important to him, for his "affectionate friendship" with Patachou had just come to an abrupt end. This talented singer had become not only the star but also the director of the Théâtre de l'ABC, one of France's top vaudeville theaters, producing and presenting shows there. She got Georges Brassens, the reclusive singer-poet, to perform there, and he immediately became a star. Chevalier reacted pettily. He was still, as in his youth, neurotically insecure, especially when directly challenged by a male *"fantaisiste"* singer. He got Vals to deliver a letter informing Patachou that since,

*In *With Love,* Chevalier calls her "Nicole."

by selecting Brassens, she clearly intended to slight him professionally, he never wanted to see her again. She wrote back that he might be a great artist, but was a singularly small-minded person. Patachou consistently refuses to discuss the role Chevalier played in her private and professional life. Her deep hostility to him, right up to the present day, is understandable: Arthur Lesser, her husband, was to be involved in a protracted lawsuit with Chevalier. Lesser had played an important part in Chevalier's initial postwar American music-hall comeback. When Chevalier became persona non grata in America in 1952, Lesser worked hard on his behalf to try and get the State Department to overrule the ban. But Chevalier assumed that his long absence from the United States released him from any contractual obligations he might have toward Lesser, and when he did finally return to America, in 1955, he dispensed with his services altogether. Lesser sued Chevalier for breach of contract, demanding $285,000. The case was settled out of court, but until his death Lesser bitterly complained of this "betrayal."

Chevalier's 1955 American season—his first in seven years—was only partly successful. Though a distinctly minor Franco-Italian film, "J'Avais Sept Filles" (My Seven Little Sins), he had made in 1955, released in the United States shortly before his arrival, got surprisingly favorable reviews, proving he was far from forgotten ("Nobody, but nobody in all the world, grows old as gracefully, slowly and waggishly as M. Chevalier," wrote Jesse Zunser in Cue magazine) his one-man show at the Lyceum Theater was only partly successful. He got a rave review in The New York Times. Lewis Funke wrote, "Has there ever been a more ingratiating, more infectious performer than this Maurice Chevalier, this symbol and personification of all that is meant by the phrase 'gay Paree'? Has there indeed ever been anyone more indomitable?" But the Lyceum Theater was never sold out. Danny Kaye, Dietrich, Sophie Tucker, Jimmy Durante, and other Hollywood veterans did their best to publicize his show. The public, however, at least at first, gave him a lukewarm reception. As even Funke felt compelled to add, "for all the gusto and good fellowship, there are inescapable thoughts: the world is not quite what it used to be when M. Chevalier first began making his imprint upon us. Behind the frivolity there is a lurking hollowness, a sense of great effort to get off the ground."

Exceptionally, Chevalier himself noted the fact in his published diary. "Fewer people come to see me," he wrote. "The one-man show is anemic." Danny Kaye advised him to change its format entirely, introducing dancing girls and complementary acts. Not until Chevalier began performing at the Waldorf-Astoria's Empire Room did he get into his stride. He then went to the Dunes Hotel, Las Vegas, for the Christmas season. It was there, in December 1956, that he learned that Mistinguett had had a stroke. He sent her an affectionate telegram, but she was unconscious by the time she received it, dying a few days later, on January 5, 1957, at age eighty-two. The night after her death, with genuine emotion, Chevalier dedicated his performance to her.

He returned to Paris somewhat depressed, openly contemplating either retirement or a completely new departure—a season at the Comédie Française. He had been offered the lead in Molierè's *Bourgeois Gentilhomme*, but was reluctant to commit himself to a yearlong contract, and eventually turned it down. Robert Manuel, a leading member of the Comédie Française at the time and later one of Chevalier's best friends, felt that the very offer had been a mistake: Chevalier, he said, for all his stage experience, was not a trained actor: "It would have been a disaster."

It was a singularly bleak period in his life. At the wedding reception of Georges Cravenne, now a leading impresario (marrying French film star Françoise Arnould), Chevalier noted with some bitterness that "about 25% of the guests, the older ones, that is, greet me with great consideration, while the rest of those present ignore me." He had had no part in any film since *My Seven Little Sins*, apart from a voice-over title song in the equally slight *Happy Road* (1957, produced and directed by Gene Kelly). Even the fact that the Alhambra music-hall theater had been renamed the Alhambra–Maurice Chevalier Theater did not restore his morale completely. He hinted that he would have preferred to have had his name associated with the more prestigious Théâtre des Champs-Élysées.

His recent American tour was, however, to have spectacular consequences: Having seen Chevalier perform at the Empire Room, Billy Wilder believed he would be perfect for the film he was planning to shoot in Paris, *Love in the Afternoon.* It was this—and *Gigi,* which followed soon after—that would lead to yet another comeback and turn him, once more, into an international star of the highest order.

CHAPTER 18

"Look at all the captivating,
Fascinating things there are to do."

—"It's a Bore," from *Gigi*,
sung by Maurice Chevalier

Love in the Afternoon, shot in Paris, was an ideal vehicle for Chevalier. Though by no means a masterpiece (Billy Wilder himself rates it as a "pleasant movie in a minor key"), this classic romp about a private detective (Chevalier) whose daughter (Audrey Hepburn) falls in love with one of his clients (Gary Cooper) had already been the subject of two films, a silent version in 1926 and one starring Elizabeth Bergner in 1933. But Chevalier's part in the Wilder and I.A.L. Diamond script had just the right mix of avuncular bonhomie, wit, and humor to once again charm moviegoing audiences around the world.

Gary Cooper, though in 1957 slightly past his prime, was still a "bankable" star, his presence alone ensuring both worldwide distribution and wide American interest. Wisely, Chevalier accepted a name billing below both Hepburn's and Cooper's. Always the complete professional, he jumped at the chance of working with an internationally renowned director for the first time in a decade. He must also have realized that here was his possibly last chance of making a major comeback after several difficult, unrewarding years.

He was indefatigable, and his enthusiasm, infectious cheerfulness, and energy led Hepburn to comment afterward that the film would have been even more credible had Cooper and Chevalier switched roles. She meant it as a joke, but it was a cogent point: Gary Cooper had always been more at ease as a strong, silent he-man: As a philanderer, in the kind of part that Chevalier had played to perfection in earlier days, he was somewhat unconvincing, and it showed—while Chevalier, under Wilder's direction, gave an ebullient, truly memorable performance. "He was like a child," Wilder recalled, "a collector of autographs of famous people still, with a perfect elocution and amazing discipline and energy—the acting equivalent of a wonderful vintage Rolls-Royce." By now his English was so good that Wilder found himself asking Chevalier to be "a little more French, please"—he could turn his accent on and off like a tap. On some nights, during the final stages of the shooting, Chevalier went straight from the Boulogne Studios to the Alhambra Theater, where he was appearing nightly, "a routine," said Wilder, "that would have exhausted an athletic twenty-year-old."

His old failing now provoked more amusement than resentment. "Traditionally," said Wilder, "the French crew staged a 'miniwrap' party every Friday evening. One or other members of the leading production team would host a party for all those on the set. Invariably, Chevalier managed to wriggle out of it when it came to his turn, pretexting a headache or a visit to the dentist."

Love in the Afternoon was a hit, Chevalier's first since René Clair's *Silence Is Golden* in 1947. "The oldest member of the cast seems the youngest—the most unchangeable, the most interested, the wittiest, the most interesting—Maurice Chevalier!" wrote Courtland Phipps in *Films in Review*. "Chevalier is a triumphant personality, giving besides a superior performance—a complete departure from the old days," said Edwin Schallert in the *Los Angeles Times*. The *New York Times*'s Bosley Crowther was equally enthusiastic: "The pedestal on which the reputation of Ernst Lubitsch has been sitting all these years will have to be relocated slightly to make room for another one. On this one we'll set Billy Wilder."

Chevalier was entranced by Audrey Hepburn, and the film enabled him to heal his rift with Henri Betti completely, for Chevalier introduced Betti to Wilder, who hired him to compose one of the film's songs. Royalties from Betti's song, "*C'est Si Bon*," would in time make him exceedingly wealthy. *Love in the Afternoon* also provided Chevalier with a badly needed new repertoire of English-language songs for future use. The comeback had begun.

Gigi, shot soon afterward in 1957, at first in Paris, then in Hollywood, completed his transformation into a major star. The man most responsible for this metamorphosis was Alan Jay Lerner, the famous *My Fair Lady* librettist, whom producer Alfred Freed had hired to write the screenplay and lyrics, in close association with his partner, the composer Frederick Loewe. As Lerner recalled:

> One of the reasons that musical films have all but disappeared from the screen is because there are no more great entertainers who can set the film's musical style. One never had to explain why Fred Astaire or Gene Kelly danced, or why Judy Garland or Bing Crosby sang. The fact of their presence automatically meant "a musical."[1]

Not only was Chevalier in this category, according to Lerner, "but he had been an idol of mine ever since every little breeze started whispering Louise." Some of Chevalier's most memorable songs in an already long career ("Thank Heaven for Little Girls," "I'm Glad I'm Not Young Anymore," "I Remember It Well") arose out of the unique Lerner-Loewe partnership, but as much as the music and lyrics themselves, it was Lerner's sense of plot and character, and his brilliant use of the Chevalier stage persona, that gave *Gigi* its special fluid quality. Meticulously directed by Vincente Minnelli, the film's shift from spoken dialogue to song and back was so natural, so effortless, that audiences were almost unaware of the transition: *Gigi* is one of those rare musical films where the narrative unfolds with such seamless grace that artifice becomes reality, and fairy-tale, turn-of-the-century Paris as familiar, and as believable, as the street where we live.

Audiences were not aware that Lerner's relentless search for perfection drove him to bouts of agonizing insomnia, depression, and despair. But finding the lyrical *mot juste* was not his only skill. *Gigi*, Colette's minor masterpiece, is about the innocent granddaughter of a scheming, irrepressible *cocotte* (Hermione Gingold) who tries to get Gigi (Leslie Caron) to follow in her own footsteps as a French "geisha," in order to become the mistress of the jaded millionaire Gaston Lachaille, (Louis Jourdan) and thus provide her impoverished family with lifelong security. In lesser hands, it could well have been a standard period-piece cliché in the manner of Chevalier's more recent films. Lerner's genius was to convey innocence, lust, nostalgia, cynicism, depravity, and greed with the lightest, most impressionistic of touches. In Colette's original story, Chevalier's character, Honoré Lachaille, uncle to Jourdan's jaded millionaire, was a minor, uninteresting figure. Lerner turned him into the equivalent of a Greek tragedy chorus. In this way, Chevalier not only set the film's style but gave it a dramatic intensity, depth, and nostalgic flavor the original Colette novel, and the subsequent Anita Loos play adaptation, lacked.

Lerner and Loewe called on Chevalier in Marnes-la-Coquette ("His house," Lerner wrote, "was less of a residence than a museum of Chevalier memorabilia") to play through some of the *Gigi* songs they had just composed together.

He listened politely, thanked us, and took the music and departed. Fritz and I had no idea if he liked them or not. The next morning he called and asked if he could come and see us again at three o'clock. I said to Fritz: "Oh, Christ! What's wrong?"

As the clock struck three, in he came. "I love the songs so much," he said, "that I worked on them all night." He turned to me. "But," he said, "Alan, would you sing the middle part of 'Thank Heaven' again for me? I like the way you phrase it better than I do."

Belying his miserly reputation, Chevalier hosted a lavish dinner party for cast and production team aboard a *bateau-mouche* on the Seine. "It was a great party, and Chevalier was in great form," Leslie Caron recalled. "I still remember the asparagus."

Lerner became even more of a Chevalier fan as time went on. The night before the first day of shooting, another party took place. "Arthur Freed, the producer,

> gave a launching party upstairs at Maxim's. Everyone in the cast was handed his script for the first time. I could not help but notice that only Maurice took his and immediately found a quiet corner and began to read. Everyone else put the script aside and continued with the festivities. The next morning the only actor who called to tell me how much he liked the script was Maurice Chevalier.

Similarly, when the time came to film in Hollywood, the cast was given eight days off for traveling and relocation.

> They were all grateful for the time and disappeared. All but Maurice. The day after the shooting closed down, he flew to California and bright and early the next morning he called Fritz and me to begin work on "I'm Glad I'm Not Young Anymore." Naturally.

On the set, Chevalier was invariably well rehearsed, and always deferred to Minnelli. After the first day's shooting, Chevalier wrote to the director: "Were I a homosexual, I would have fallen in love with you." But the loving charm he displayed toward Leslie Caron in the film was hardly matched in real life. "In her, I never found any warmth towards me," he wrote later. Leslie Caron found him aloof. "His attitude seemed to be, 'You know me on the screen, but you don't really know me at all,' " she said later.[2] "One time I saw him with some fans at a Hollywood premiere. He answered their greetings very sharply, and they seemed to irritate him. I thought they behaved rather well. He seems to resent any intrusions into his private life. In a hotel, I witnessed a French waiter calling him *"Mon petit* Maurice" as he greeted him like a long-lost friend. It sort of annoyed Chevalier. He was extremely hurt. He resented being treated with familiarity."

She was not alone in noting Chevalier's regal attitude, his imperious demands, the off-handedness with which he treated the deferential François Vals; one member of the cast recalls Vals kneeling before Chevalier in front of a small crowd on the set to tie his shoelaces. "He was grumpy," a member of the crew recalled. "He made his demands—whether for a chair in the shade, a sandwich, or a glass of water—imperiously. He never acknowledged the existence of the crew."

Film crews are quick to size up the actors they work with, quick to respond to their moods, quirks, and susceptibilities. Shooting a film, as François Truffaut later showed in his own masterpiece about movie-making (Day for Night) is an intensely emotional, claustrophobic experience. It's the nearest thing to being trapped aboard a small boat for days at a time in the company of strangers who become, by stages, more familiar than one's own family. The inevitable stresses and strains on the set act as a litmus paper, revealing weaknesses, but also individual strengths, compatibilities, and camaraderie—a mood that outsiders, who have never taken part in the essentially crazy sport of filmmaking, can never experience. Leslie Caron, who looked eighteen but was, in reality, twenty-six and a major star, hated the trappings of stardom. In the British acting tradition, she felt very strongly that teamwork, on the set and off, was an integral part of filmmaking, and of the theater. Chevalier, in his regal aloofness, was unlike any of her previous film partners. Temperamentally, she saw no reason to defer to him, to become part of his deferential court. Chevalier must have resented this. He did, however, ask her for an autographed picture. "He had a huge, almost childish respect for anyone who had become a star," she recalled. "At the same time, it was clear he regarded himself as being on a completely different plane. There was a contradiction between his Olympian demeanor, his off-the-set aloofness, and his endless willingness to submit uncomplainingly to take after take."

The critics were unanimous: Gigi was great—and the greatest thing about it was Chevalier's performance. "Chevalier is superb as the cheerful old rip," wrote Bosley Crowther, "Indeed his performance as this tireless boulevardier who views the whole scene of shrewd connivance within full approval and joy is a rare gem of comedy acting—suave, subtle, sensitive and sure." "Chevalier is the scene stealer," said *Variety*. "It is the old master showman, Maurice Chevalier, who steals *Gigi* lock, stock and barrel," wrote the *Los Angeles Examiner*'s Kay Proctor.

Gigi made history the following year, winning nine Academy awards—for Best Picture of 1958, Best Director, Best Screenplay, Best Color Cinematography, Best Song, Best Scoring of a Musical Picture, Best Design, Best Art, and Best Set Direction. Chevalier himself received a special Oscar for his "contribution to the world of entertainment for more than half a century."

In almost all his subsequent shows, Chevalier included the *Gigi* songs in his repertoire to the unfailing delight of audiences worldwide. After *Gigi*, his career was to be an almost exclusively international one, mostly in English-speaking parts of the world (including a highly successful Australian tour.) Henceforth, he restricted his appearances in France to prestigious galas and concerts he could scarcely turn down. In May 1959, as one of the guest stars of the Gala de la Chancellerie de la Légion d'Honneur (in the company of Yul Brynner, William Holden, Cary Grant, and Sophia Loren), he got the tone-deaf General de Gaulle to join in, lustily if tunelessly singing "*Ma Pomme*" along with the rest of the audience. His only other French appearances, until his final retirement tour in October 1968, were twenty-three recitals at the Théâtre des Champs-Élysées in September 1963 and a gala for the French Foreign Legion in Toulouse in 1965. He also continued staging galas for the veteran artists home in Ris-Orangis (including a fund-raising dinner at Maxim's for the premiere of *Gigi* at forty dollars a head.) Visits there filled him with melancholy. "All these old people!" he noted in his diary, "I knew them all when I was just starting out at fourteen."

The huge popularity of *Gigi* meant that several generations of Americans who had never seen his old films now became aware of Chevalier's existence, and his sheer longevity was celebrated in the media wherever he went. The late fifties and early sixties also happened to be golden years for a number of aging Hollywood stars who, like Chevalier, had become legends in their lifetime. At the 1958 Academy Awards, noting the presence of Gary Cooper, Mary Pickford, Ronald Colman, Clifton Webb, Frances Dee, Joel McCrea, Jack Benny, Fredric March, Groucho Marx, George Burns, Ginger Rogers, and Rosalind Russell, Chevalier drew considerable laughter and applause when he told the audience, "The thing that amazes me most in Hollywood is that after twenty-two years, the stars who were tops when I was here are still tops."

His new celebrity delighted him, whether he was breakfasting with President Eisenhower, or entertaining the American Press Club gala dinner in February 1958 (also attended by Eisenhower), meeting Pablo Casals, the world-famous cellist, in San Juan, or making one of his numerous TV appearances with Ed Sullivan and Bob Hope. He was now, with de Gaulle, America's best-known Frenchman. But whereas de Gaulle's anti-American pinpricks irritated and offended, Chevalier was the quintessential Frenchman for whom mainstream America could feel nothing but love and affection. His accent, his charm, the hint of naughtiness about his past, his reputation as a lover, all contributed to his popularity—to the point where he could do no wrong.

Chevalier, while actually making *Gigi*, did not anticipate its huge success. "I am sixty-nine," he told *Newsweek*. "As soon as I finish it, I will prepare a one-man show, a farewell tour. When it's over, that will be the end of my long career as a live entertainer. . . . Recently, I told myself, 'My God, I can't go on doing that for the next half-century!'" In the years ahead, he saw himself as a character actor on films and as a TV talk-show host. "I will be 70 on September 12," he told the *Los Angeles Examiner* (in 1958), "and in motion pictures I am starting a new career as a player of paternal roles. When I was here before, I was never a character, always a personality. But in my one-man show, I am my old self, with new material."

The huge impact of *Gigi* made him change his mind. There was no more talk of a farewell tour. On the contrary, he was on the road more often than ever, becoming, in the process, especially in the United States, almost as popular, and certainly as well known, as he had been as a Hollywood megastar in the early thirties.

For Chevalier, from *Gigi* on, these were halcyon years. In Washington, he stayed, almost by right, at the embassy residence of French Ambassador Hervé Alphand, himself a brilliant mimic, occasional performer (at intimate parties), and devoted Chevalier fan. Conscious of his image, Chevalier, for all his thrift, consistently turned down a succession of hugely lucrative offers to appear in TV commercials, privately expressing his disapproval of those stars who did so. (He made only a few exceptions throughout his career—one for Dubonnet, because he was exceptionally fond of this aperitif and one for cherry brandy, another favorite drink.) Otherwise his bizarre stinginess still baffled his friends. As Cravenne recalled, "I saw him once slip a wad of notes from one pocket to the other, while we were in a cab together. On arrival, he said, 'I seem to have left my money behind.' On another occasion, he asked me for tickets for a Coupe de France soccer final. They were almost impossible to get, and he wanted three—for François and Madeleine Vals as well as himself. After infinite trouble, I managed to get three. 'They're a hundred-fifty francs each,' I told him. Later on in the day, he said, 'You know, I don't think I'll go after all.' "

He exploited his new fame shrewdly, scheduling his road shows to avoid exhaustion, using Marnes-la-Coquette as a base to rest up and recharge his batteries. "When he was on the road," Vals recalled, "all he could think about was his garden, his house, his 'family.' But almost as soon as he settled in there, he was raring to go again, and couldn't wait to get started." Hardly coincidentally, his American tours took place just before his (September 12) birthday, and, following *Gigi*, every birthday became a news event—a celebration and an opportunity for Chevalier to reflect on his past, his present, and his seemingly boundless future.

There's no doubt that these were the happiest years in his life. Not only was he able to put the traumatic Liberation episode behind him and forget the professional rut that had marked the early fifties, but he rejoiced in his new role as father figure to a whole new generation of singers like Jacques Brel, Sasha Distel, and Mireille Mathieu, a young singer compared to Piaf (whom she consciously imitated) whose career Chevalier furthered to such an extent that rumors spread that they were lovers—which was not the case. He was attracted to her because she was a mirror image of himself in his youth. Like Chevalier, Mireille Mathieu came from a tough, working-class background and had had to struggle to become known.

"I have had everything beautiful in life," he told reporters in 1959, "and there comes a time when your reason must be stronger than your instincts, a time to renounce some of the things that were beautiful when you were young." As the *Los Angeles Herald* wrote (headlined BLITHE MAURICE STARTS NEW CAREER AT 70), "Today, quite suddenly and spectacularly, after an absence of more than two decades, he is back riding the crest of Hollywood success."

He also acquired the nearest thing to peace of mind, and a family. Whenever he was in Marnes-la-Coquette, René, Paul's son, regularly came to see him on Sundays with his family; Chevalier bought him a suburban butcher's shop. He also acquired a small knitting factory, which he pledged to his personal aide, François Vals, after his death. The presence of Janie Michels and her two small children in Marnes-la-Coquette, the growing esteem and friendship he felt for François and Madeleine Vals and *their* small daughter, gave him a sense of security, of companionship, that had previously eluded him. He played with Janie Michels's small children almost every day. When at home in Marnes-la-Coquette, his routine seldom varied: He spent the morning in bed, his chinchilla bedspread littered with newspapers and correspondence; for an hour a day, always in bed, he practiced his English, reading aloud from the *International Herald Tribune,* his favorite newspaper, and both *Time* and *Newsweek.* After a light lunch, sometimes brought to him on a tray in his book-lined bedroom, he went for a five-mile walk. Once or twice a week, he gave somewhat formal luncheon parties, choosing his guests carefully, welcoming a guest of honor at the end of the meal with a ceremonious speech. Invariably, there would be a mix of show-business celebrities and socialites. "He behaved almost regally at his parties," recalled his American agent, Sol Schapiro. "He was the somewhat condescending king."

He was in huge demand at opening nights of all kinds, a celebrity ensuring the media's attention for almost any event. He basked in the admiring company of up-and-coming stars like Sophia Loren and Brigitte Bardot, with whom, he repeatedly told newsmen, he would love to make a movie. "She is one of the reasons I am proud to be French." The company of beautiful women still caused the adrenaline to flow, instantly transforming him into a younger man. On most afternoons and evenings, he went to movies or to the theater. Suitably briefed movie-house managers on the Champs-Élysées invariably provided him with complimentary tickets, as did the Paris theaters. He did not like to go on these outings alone, and whoever accompanied him tipped the *ouvreuses* (seating attendants). It would probably be wrong to see this solely as penny-pinching; it was more a matter of pride. Like Mistin-guett, Chevalier felt demeaned if asked to pay for a seat or a restaurant meal. It was all part of the perks of being a star, also reflecting his singularly old-fashioned view of society and his hierarchical sense of values. In the old "Belle Epoque" days, such had been the trappings of rank and status.

Practically his only concession to age was to wear light makeup on stage and reading glasses at home. He owned a dozen pairs, for he was always losing them. He still kept the house lights on during his perform-ance, "in order to be able to observe the audience," and insisted that his dressing-room walls be draped in dark blue, to protect his vision (his eyes were ultrasensitive to spotlights). To reporters, he never tired of expounding his homespun "philosophy of love" ("The men of today," he told reporters again and again, "worry so much that they do not know how to live—to love. They forget a man must be a man to his woman.")

Every succeeding birthday, reporters marveled at his youthful appear-ance. When he turned seventy, *Newsweek* ran a cover story on him, calling him "the century's most personable international institution." He him-self acknowledged he had never felt younger, or more active. "What counts is not to spoil the wonderful story which my life has been," he told *Newsweek*. "My ambition still is to become a little better every day. I want the end to be perfect. . . . I still have to throw some girls out of my dressing room sometimes," he boasted.

There were tributes from show-business figures from the remote as well as the more recent past, though some were less glowing than others. "He oozes charm, he has the most warm, wonderful personality, if you're a woman he treats you as if you were the only woman in the world," said Hermione Gingold. The published comments of Jeanette MacDonald and Leslie Caron were more muted. "I really couldn't say [working with him] was exciting," said MacDonald. "He has a faculty for turning on his personality before the cameras. The moment the scene was over, he was the Maurice Chevalier we knew." "He turns his personality on and off like an ignition key," said Caron. "Throughout the whole of *Gigi* I thought he didn't like me." "He talks a lot but he's reticent too," Mary Pickford said. "He's a darling," said Claudette Colbert, "but he's not the gay comedian offstage. He is very serious, very nice. You know, it's a funny thing, but you never hear about Maurice unless it's connected with his job. I don't believe he's had a happy marriage or love affair, ever. I don't think he's had a happy private life."

Sadly, Chevalier never again made a film with the likes of Wilder, Minnelli, or Lerner and Loewe, or remotely as good as *Gigi*. His next, *Count Your Blessings*, (released in 1959) though based on Nancy Mitford's sprightly novel *The Blessing*, suffered from a dull script and a thoroughly pedestrian director (Jean Negulesco.) *Can Can* (1960), though star-studded (Frank Sinatra, Shirley MacLaine, Louis Jourdan, as well as Chevalier), remains chiefly memorable for the fact that Nikita Khrushchev, then Soviet premier, while touring Hollywood, was taken onto the set (and later declared the film "immoral").

After watching Khrushchev on TV, Chevalier wrote with considerable prescience that soon, in America at least, actors would become presidential material, for, as he put it,

American politicians can learn an important lesson here. Before too long the candidate seeking office who shows an interest in the performing arts, and can perform himself—especially on television—will be the one who is the most successful. Inevitably, all political campaigns will be exercises in acting with the best performer getting the most votes.

In his next film, *Black Tights*, with Cyd Charisse, he sang four songs but did not otherwise appear; this was followed in quick succession by *A Breath of Scandal*, a Ponti-produced piece of kitsch filmed in Vienna, with

Chevalier in the improbable role of Sophia Loren's father. He had a cameo role in *Pépé* (1960), a vehicle for Cantinflas, the Mexican comic actor—a critical and box-office disaster. Even *Fanny* (1961), the Josh Logan–directed American remake of Marcel Pagnol's tragicomedy set in Marseilles (with Leslie Caron and Charles Boyer), was not entirely satisfactory. Chevalier played Panisse, the elderly "bourgeois" who marries the pregnant Fanny (Leslie Caron) after her lover has run away to sea. In the Pagnol version, Panisse had been a roly-poly, sympathetic but essentially comic buffoon. When he was turned into a noble-minded figure, some of Pagnol's intended effects were lost. Many of Chevalier's friends, the Comédie Française veteran Robert Manuel among them, felt he should never have accepted the part in the first place. But Chevalier enjoyed the experience: Charles Boyer was one of his oldest, most faithful friends, and he welcomed the opportunity of spending evening after evening with him. Boyer himself, though he liked and respected Chevalier, was fully aware of his foibles. Later, he often recalled how, at the end of a fairly lavish meal in their Cassis hotel, while on location in Marseilles, Chevalier drew his platinum fountain pen and marked his room number—and the exact level of the liquid—on both wine *and* mineral-water bottles.

Other, later films were far more forgettable, and Chevalier's motives for making them can only have been financial. The one assignment he craved, and referred to, in interviews, again and again, eluded him: Fellini had promised him an important cameo role in *La Dolce Vita* and then, as was so often the case with the Italian director, changed his mind. Instead, Chevalier accepted parts in films he should by rights have turned down: Jean Negulesco's *Jessica* (in which he played a Sicilian village priest), the Disney-produced *In Search of Castaways* (1962), *A New Kind of Love* (1963)—of which *Time* wrote, "The Lunts in their heyday could not have saved this one"—*Panic Button* (1964), which had no major U.S. release, *I'd Rather Be Rich* (1964)—"Actors like to keep busy and who can blame them?" wrote *The New Yorker's* Brendan Gill—and (also in 1964) the part of another village priest in *Monkeys Go Home*—another Disney production.

But no amount of indifferent moviemaking could affect his morale:

"There is nothing sad about growing old, he told the *Los Angeles Examiner* on his seventy-first birthday, on the set of *Can Can*. "What is happening to me now is really much higher than anything I could ever dream of." "Chevalier is 72 years young," wrote the *Daily Mail* at the time of his seventy-second birthday.

He had reached the stage where his sheer longevity, together with his virtually unchanged, inimitable but much imitated style and youthful vigor made him such a legend that criticism of his act was irrelevant. And for the first time in his life, his real-life image came to resemble the public persona he had carefully projected for so long.

A visit to Chevalier's home, wrote an AP reporter on his seventy-third birthday, "is like a journey to the training camp of a championship prizefighter. You recognize the same self-confidence, the devotion to physical fitness, the awareness of past triumphs and future challenges, the ability to speak of himself as a startling phenomenon, almost a third person."

"Me lonely?" Chevalier scoffed. "Never. I have had everything a man could want. No family? I have my own, one I collected around me, not one I could not choose. I am a happy man."

François and Madeleine Vals, who had won his trust and affection, were to a large extent responsible for his new, serene mood. They knew that for all his halfhearted protests that he was getting too old, Chevalier lived for applause, that his entire well-being depended on the continued adulation of an adoring public. "He sometimes said, this is definitely my last tour!" said Sol Schapiro, his William Morris agent in the sixties. 'I'm sick, I'm quitting the business.' Then he would change his mind. 'I think I have one more trip in my system,' he would say." The crowds of well-wishers and autograph-hunters may not have realized the extent of the strain on him. A limousine invariably waited at the stage door after the show to take him to his hotel—even if it was just across the street—to enable him to cut the autograph sessions short.

François and Madeleine Vals, for whom he became an avuncular figure, were conscious of his dark side, his mood swings: petty, inconsequential matters—an incompetent gardener, suspected pilfering by the hired help, a less than perfectly cooked *gigot* at a dinner party, even a missing pair of reading glasses—sent him into a lasting tantrum, provoking a black mood quite out of proportion to the original irritation. "Small things affected him much more than major setbacks," said François Vals. "He could become extremely cold, and—though he displayed it very rarely—he had a terrible temper." At such times, Chevalier threatened to sell his Marnes-la-Coquette mansion, including his Renoirs, Picassos, and Vlamincks, get rid of all his staff, and move into a small service apartment or hotel suite. Outsiders seldom saw this side of him, and such moods never lasted long.

What they did see was a prodigiously alert, articulate, physically fit man in his seventies who looked at least fifteen years younger, and had lost none of his legendary charm onstage—or off, whenever he wished to make an impression on a newcomer. The image may have been contrived—it required effort, constant discipline, and a strict diet (he now sniffed rather than drank wine)—but it was certainly impressive. He had acquired a near-perfect mastery of English, and was secure enough to bask in his grandfatherly image, belatedly realizing, at this stage of his life, that he no longer had any real rivals. He also felt secure in his private life: His long-standing relationship with Janie Michels worked. They were friends as well as lovers, and she understood him well enough to keep his "black dog" at bay.

In 1963, he embarked on one of the longest, most strenuous North American tours of his entire career. Though he was playing everywhere to capacity crowds, reviews were not uniformly good. He got rave notices from veterans like *Variety*'s Hobe Morrison ("after more than 30 years, the effect is still irresistible"), but some of the younger critics were less kind: "He is an acquired taste, like snails or the Eiffel Tower," wrote the *Toronto Daily Star*, "Having anticipated hearing all his old songs, we were offered far too little. An audience deserves more than nostalgic banter for a full evening," wrote *Cue*. Radio reviewers, perhaps targeting younger audiences, were more scathing. "A tremendous disappointment," said WNEW's John David Griffin of the *New York Daily Mirror*. "He talked too much, joked too much, mugged too much and sang too little." But NBC's Leonard Probst didn't agree. "The best moment is not a song at all. It comes when Chevalier, in a lengthy monologue, talks about his life." Hobe Morrison, in *Variety*, noted the "incredible spell" he cast. In an "unpretentious sketch called 'Stations in Life' Chevalier mentioned the familiar sensations of being twenty, then forty, then sixty-five, and finally seventy, "in each case adding small, amusing observations. At the end, almost as if it were an afterthought, he remarks, "And then you're seventy-five—as I am." The ensuing applause, Morrison wrote,

> is automatic, of course, for what the star has used is an old, old vaudevillian's trick, like a singer holding a full-throated high note at the finale of a song, or a performer waving the American flag as he exits. The notable and touching thing about the incident in this case is the warmth and intensity of the audience response, the long-standing affection the applause obviously expresses.

Inevitably, there were some bad days: One sweltering August evening, before a huge capacity audience at the open-air Greek Theater in Los Angeles, he faltered in midsong, shortly after the beginning of his one-man show. There was a deathly silence. "I am troubled, I am confused, I cannot go on," he said, and walked off the stage. There was anxious whispering among the audience, but no catcalls. François Vals remembered the incident well. "He could not remember the sequence of his songs," he said. "He was not feeling well. He had insisted on taking long walks, as was his custom, to rehearse the text of his songs, despite our warnings that the heat and smog of Los Angeles would be bad for him."

"We rallied round," Vals said, "we hugged him. I told him, 'I know you can do it.' He paused, pulled himself together, concentrating briefly, then strode out onstage, the jaunty warrior once more." During the intermission, Vals recalled, Chevalier suddenly looked very old and was almost in tears. "I can't go on again. How can I ever face them? I'm too old. I should give it all up."

The rest of his performance was flawless, and he received an emotional standing ovation.

Back in Paris, General de Gaulle invited him to lunch. As was his habit, Chevalier asked him for an autographed portrait. A few days later, he received a photograph. De Gaulle had written on it: "for Maurice Chevalier, a very great talent, a very great effort, a masterly success, Yours, cordially, Charles de Gaulle."

On his next American tour, in 1965, Chevalier obtained the most enthusiastic reviews of his entire career. "There was much love at the Alvin Theater last night," wrote the *New York World Telegram*'s Norman Nadel. "The contact of the heart is an almost tangible presence as this everlastingly charming gentleman from Paris entertains. To be embraced in that kind of affection is worth more than the theater ticket costs."

His show, "Chevalier at 77," actually anticipated his birthday. "He will not be 77 till September," ran a piece in *Cue*, "but he fears age so little that he has the habit of making himself older than he is. When he was 74 he claimed to be 75. Actually he looks 50. He would of course say 51."

"Maurice Chevalier is noticeably growing younger," wrote Walter Kerr in *The New York Times*. A few years previously, he *did* look seventy, but "Last night he looked like a winning infant with white hair." Kerr continued:

It started me thinking: What—all along—has been the real basis for the man's appeal? Sophistication? The fact of the matter is that he's not very sophisticated. . . . Naughtiness, downright devilishness, the candid wink behind the breezy *boulevardier*? Well, of course, M. Chevalier does possess these qualities, or at least pretend to them for all he is worth. . . . But take away the tilt, in fact take away the hat, take a long look at his face while he is producing all of his most celebrated expressions, and what do you get? You get a baby in a playpen at its most devastatingly charming, which is to say at its most aggressively intense. Put the smile to one side—which the performer often does, way over to one side—and you will suddenly notice that his face is earnestly fierce.

I never realized until last night how often he scowls, how often he growls, how much his pout is like the pout of an alert and injured tot who wants his puppy back. . . . More than hope is possible. Miracles are still possible, and M. Chevalier will have one, thank you. In a way, he is one. . . .

Jacqueline Kennedy, with Lee Radziwill and her husband, "Stash," came to hear him sing. As so often when famous women were present (he had used the same, highly effective trick with both Princess Margaret and Queen Elizabeth herself), Chevalier drew attention to Mrs. Kennedy's presence and dedicated "You Must Have Been a Beautiful Baby" to her to the noisy approval of the delighted audience. Chevalier usually returned to his hotel suite immediately after his act was over, but on this occasion he, the Radziwills, and Jackie Kennedy celebrated at the El Morocco nightclub till past midnight with caviar and champagne.

In Hollywood that October for a cameo role in a Disney picture (the distinctly unmemorable *Monkeys Go Home*), he answered a Hedda Hopper questionnaire at length, in longhand, in near-perfect English with only a few words crossed out. He was still the inveterate flatterer. To a question, "Should women have the vote?" he wrote, "Definitely. Some women are much more intelligent and full of courage than certain men. Have you heard of a certain Hedda Hopper?" His answers, relatively frank, invariably modest, self-deprecating, and serene, conveyed the impression of someone well aware of his age, fully accepting the limitations it imposed on his life. "As for girls," he wrote, "I still take them out but not in. I won't recommend it because I know some very old men who seem to be some kind of bulls. They are lucky . . . or are they?" He admitted his indifference to pop art ("It is for the very young or those who refuse to accept their number of years"), his fondness for blue jeans ("A pretty girl has even more sex in blue jeans—it adds a little something. For the girls who are not pretty, it does not help at all"), his assessment of himself: "I was never such a big record-seller, I am more a personality who must be seen. I am like a man who shows the shoes he has been making to another shoemaker." To a question: "Are you sentimental about the past?" he replied: "Terribly. I forget the ugly but think very, very often of the beautiful moments." Hedda Hopper's assessment: "Chevalier will never retire unless it is to make way for an older man."[3]

Like a vintage Bordeaux, Chevalier appeared to be improving by the year. Jean-Christophe Averty, who directed several TV shows with him from 1964 on, noted that, as he got older, so his voice became richer, more mellow, and his pace and timing onstage slowed down not at all. "He could swing, he had an extraordinary sense of rhythm, recording sessions with him were a delight," he said. "He even tried his hand at the Beatles' "Yellow Submarine" and managed to bring it off quite creditably." By now he was so well known that people grinned and clapped when he walked down Fifth Avenue, as he did almost daily, before taking an afternoon nap before the show. *The New Yorker* interviewed him at length about his working routine, his diet, and his astonishing energy. In 1966, Averty filmed a Chevalier special for ABC, partnering him with Diahann Carroll, and in 1967 he was back in America again.

"On two counts the news is good this morning," wrote Robert Alden in *The New York Times*. "The Empire Room at the Waldorf-Astoria has reopened [after a two-year closure]. . . . Secondly, Maurice Chevalier—grand old Maurice—now a glorious 79 years, is back in town with his straw hat, bow tie, Gallic charm and mischievous smile. Perhaps not all, but a good part of what General de Gaulle has done to wreck Franco-American relations in the past decade is repaired by M. Chevalier in the course of one glorious evening." Introducing his show at the Empire Room, he invariably brought the house down with the remark that his life was an example of "how to succeed in show business without really trying to be young anymore." His sole concession to age was to give a single show nightly, instead of the customary two. A musicians' union strike was in force during part of his scheduled performance there. On the first day, Fred Freed, his pianist, accompanied Chevalier, but the usual spotlight arrangements were lacking—the house electricians, in sympathy with the strikers, had not shown up. On the second night, things were even worse: Fred Freed himself refused to cross the picket line, for fear of forfeiting forever his right to perform in New York. Undeterred, Chevalier went through his act alone, without any musical accompaniment whatever. As Frank Wangemann, then a senior Waldorf-Astoria executive, recalled, "He had the audience in the palm of his hand." "Many patrons," Arden wrote, "had come prepared to love Mr. Chevalier even if he was but a shadow of his former self. But there was no need for any temporizing. At 79, his act is as good as it ever was and that is very, very good."

He was in demand all over the world. Time seemed to stand still for him, and there was no recurrence of his earlier lapse at the Greek Theater. Only the indomitable old trouper himself knew the physical strain involved. In South Africa, he told the *Natal Daily News* (in February 1967) that this tour would probably be his last—but he was not taken seriously, for he had said that so many times before.

On his seventy-ninth birthday, celebrated quietly at home, he took part in a telephone phone-in, broadcast live on French radio, answering listeners' questions—and emotionally basking in their praise for several hours. On Europe Numéro Un radio station, eighty stars, including Marlene Dietrich, Yves Montand, Eddie Fisher, Sammy Davis, Jr., Charles Aznavour, and Juliette Gréco, performed some of his best-known songs and reminisced about him. Probably, the tribute that meant most to him came from Josephine Baker, exorcizing as it did the ignominy of his 1944 arrest and erasing the memory of her accusations against him.

A few weeks later, he was on the road again, starring in the "Expo 1967" show at the huge Automotive Stadium in Montreal, filled to its 25,000 capacity, performing from the four-meter-high platform at the top of a small tower, his act relayed on a gigantic screen. Jean-Christophe Averty, who directed him, found him once in tears during rehearsal. "I can't manage it," he said, "I'm too old. I can't run up those steps." There was something incongruous about his presence in a spectacle that included more circus acts than vaudeville, for before Chevalier came on, in the second half, it was given over to sway-pole teams and helicopter trapezists.

It was then that Chevalier confirmed, to François Vals, that he would do one more series of shows, in 1968—and then retire from the stage for good. "He did not want to tempt providence," Vals recalled. "He wanted to quit with an unblemished record, at the peak of his fame and his powers."

"We tried to talk him out of it," said Vals. "We did not want him to overtax himself. At the same time we knew that without the applause, the adulation, the discipline, of the nightly performance, his life would not be the same. I suggested that he keep his options open, do the occasional show, and make no irrevocable retirement announcement that he might live to regret. But his mind was made up. Perhaps he recalled the unfortunate spectacle of other aging players, like Mistinguett, who had gone on for too long."

He was, at this stage of his life, not at all perturbed by death, though the deaths of others—Piaf and Cocteau in 1963, Willemetz in 1964—brought him to tears, and he did develop an interest in religion. Though never a practicing Catholic, he sought out the occasional company of two fashionable French priests, Father Pierre Boulogne and Father Alain Carré, a noted intellectual whose parish was the French entertainment industry. As he told them, his worship for God was subsumed in the posthumous devotion he felt for his mother. He had had her remains reburied at the Marnes-la-Coquette cemetery, where he intended to be buried in due course in the same massive marble grave. Addressing his mother directly, as he frequently did in his diary entries, he wrote (in 1966), "One day, little Louque, I'll come and find you at last. . . . If paradise exists, we will be well received. If there is nothing of the kind, well, little Louque, once again we'll be together, as in the past, in the shade, as we were once in the sun. We'll get on well together, won't we, little Louque?"

Chevalier was convinced that, even if he stopped performing onstage, his career as a showman was far from over. He saw himself in the role of a French Ed Sullivan, the TV talk-show celebrity who had interviewed him several times. He also believed he would be in considerable demand as a film actor, writer, and—why not—*Immortel*—as the forty-strong members of the Académie Française were called. He was wrong on all counts, and the consequences would be unbearable.

CHAPTER 19

"What counts is not to spoil the wonderful story which my life
has been. I want the end to be perfect."

—Maurice Chevalier,
to *Newsweek*, 1959

As François Vals began planning the series of concerts throughout Europe and both North and South America that would mark Chevalier's irrevocable farewell to the stage in the year of his eightieth birthday, one key member of his household knew that this would also have considerable repercussions on his own life.

Chevalier's majordomo, Félix Paquet, the former vaudeville comedian who, with his wife, Maryse, had been Chevalier's house-keeper-companion during most of the Second World War, had had a checkered career after 1945. There had been no need for a permanent staff in La Bocca (the two Cannes tailors were only too glad to move into the house while Chevalier was away, and their usefulness ended when he turned it over to the SACEM in 1952). Paquet had attempted to make a comeback in show business, but times had changed, and his act had not.

There had also been a serious falling-out: Chevalier expected to be kept abreast of all show-business news and gossip, but Paquet had failed to inform him of Nita Raya's marriage (to Louis Barrier, Piaf's manager) and an infuriated Chevalier, learning about it belatedly from another source, and unable to forgive this treasonable lapse, severed all connections with him for several years.

Then, in 1958, in dire straits, Paquet wrote Chevalier a pathetic letter. He told of his undying admiration, love, and affection; their years together during the war had been by far the most memorable in his life. If there was anything he and Maryse could do, *anything*, they would gladly enter his service again, in any capacity. Maryse could cook and run a household. Maybe he needed a driver?

It so happened that Chevalier had just fired his chauffeur—a former racing driver—after a trivial dispute over money, and was not entirely happy with his existing household arrangements. Maryse and Félix called on Chevalier at Marnes-la-Coquette and were hired—Maryse as chief housekeeper, Félix in an unspecified capacity. His duties included chauffeuring Chevalier, but he also, in due course, became his dresser, social secretary, ADC and occasional press spokesman, screening telephone calls and keeping unwelcome callers at bay. Above all, he fulfilled a function once required of Yvonne Vallée, Nita Raya, and all Chevalier's subsequent companions: He listened.

His ostentatious veneration for Chevalier was such that he never tired of hearing Chevalier tell—for the umpteenth time—of his triumphal appearance at the Alcazar in Marseilles that had set him on the road to stardom, of his rise to fame with Mistinguett, of the jealous schemers who had almost wrecked his career in 1944, of his meetings with leading statesmen, of his comeback as actor and stage star in America after the Second World War, and the international esteem he had acquired as a writer. In turn, Paquet, whether out of genuine awe or a courtier's calculated subservience, flattered Chevalier outrageously. No one, he told him, neither Montand, nor Aznavour, nor Jacques Brel, came anywhere near him as an artist; as a songwriter, he equaled Jacques Prévert; as a film actor, he was the greatest. There was nothing that he turned to that he could not master—his memoirs were proof of that.

Paquet kept a close eye on press cuttings, encouraging the visits of those who wrote in suitable terms about Chevalier, drawing his attention to the occasional less effusive piece—those responsible would be duly kept at arm's length.

Soon, the Paquets became "family" again. When there were no guests, they dined at Chevalier's table, watched TV together, listened to Chevalier's comments about current events, invariably agreeing with his point of view. Of course, times had changed: Chevalier's bookings were handled by the highly competent François Vals, who had an office in one wing of the main building. Paquet deferred to Chevalier somewhat unctuously. There was a regular feminine presence at Marnes-la-Coquette: Janie Michels lived in a villa inside the La Louque compound with her two children and also joined Chevalier and the Paquets for dinner when they were alone. The Paquets had comfortable quarters in another, slightly smaller villa on the estate.

They were expected to be in constant attendance at Marnes-la-Coquette, but their duties, until 1968, were intermittent and fairly light, for with Chevalier away on tour a great deal of the time, the Paquets had little to do but keep the estate in good shape, forward his mail, and record his messages. It was an ideal existence.

With hindsight, it is tempting to portray Paquet as a vaudeville Iago, but this would be unfair. He may have been a cynical court intriguer, but he was not envious—his admiration of Chevalier was genuine. He was the perfect servant, reveling in his confidential status. Always impeccably dressed, he was equally at ease waiting tables at a formal luncheon party or making small talk with the guests, especially if they had a similar vaudeville background, for he had no illusions about his own small talent, and seemed to harbor no resentment at the success of the more famous show-business guests he had once known on more equal terms. But in the back of his mind, quite naturally, was an anxious preoccupation about his own future: Chevalier was childless, his elder brother Paul in extremely poor health (he would die in 1969), and his nearest family, apart from his nephews René and Paul, and *their* families, were Janie Michels and her two children, Madeleine and François Vals, and the Paquets themselves. This small "family" would clearly inherit Chevalier's considerable fortune; he himself had indicated as much. Whereas Janie Michels, a highly successful painter, had some private means, and François Vals was clearly able to earn a substantial living on his own, the Paquets had no resources whatever, and were utterly dependent on Chevalier. Inevitably, for them, the inheritance issue assumed a huge importance. The unspoken question in Paquet's mind was: Who would get what?

Long before his retirement announcement, Chevalier had thought about its consequences. In his last years as a performer, he had joked about his longevity. At the Royal Command performance, he had expressed the hope he would be there to entertain not only Queen Elizabeth's children but *their* descendants as well. At the same time, he was telling Vals, "I can't keep this up forever." He knew his life would be different, that he would miss the thrill of performing, that the adjustment would be costly. In a diary entry, during his final tour, he wrote, "Will I ever learn to adjust, to live differently?"

In interviews, he never expressed any such doubts, stressing instead his anticipation at the joys of undisturbed leisure in his idyllic Marnes-la-Coquette setting, and his longing to catch up with his reading and writing. He did not realize quite how much he would miss the excitement of travel, the discipline of his daily rehearsals, the anticipation of the evening deadline, and, above all, the nightly applause and adulation. He was so conscious of his unique status as the ageless grand old man of vaudeville that he could not imagine, for an instant, that his image might ever be affected by retirement. He would always be Chevalier.

The impression he projected in his interviews in his last years on the road was that of a simple, plain-living man, content with his memories, a few old clothes, his books, and his friends, whose only real pride was that he had brought some innocent pleasure to huge audiences throughout the world. The real Chevalier was someone quite different: Few show-business figures, with the exception of the Fairbankses, both Junior and Senior, enjoyed such impeccable social connections, but he had very few real, intimate friends in whom he could confide, especially after the death of Albert Willemetz. Nor was he quite as plain-living as he liked newsmen to think. A meticulous dresser who chose a different pen-and-pencil set (either platinum or gold) to match the color of his suits, he reveled in his star status, his Mercedes (which Paquet drove, Chevalier was the ever-cautious backseat driver with a tendency to nag him as in *Driving Miss Daisy*). Though he happily spent hours, every day, meticulously rehearsing and running through his act, his intellectual attention span was relatively short. He didn't really enjoy reading Montaigne, Sartre, or Marcus Aurelius, except for very short stretches of time. He needed his almost nightly performing stint more than he knew. His problem was not all that different from that of many people of his age facing retirement after a hyperactive life: Physically and mentally, he was unprepared for it.

His predicament resulted from inner contradictions. For all his endless talk about spiritual love—for the public, "those wonderful people out there all over the world," for his saintly mother, for all his wide-eyed innocence and somewhat syrupy, oversentimental prose—he had not really changed. He was still the tough, career-oriented performer Colette had described in *La Vagabonde*. Those who knew him well, and shared his life, accepted the gulf between the public Chevalier—capable, like his stage persona, of hypnotic charm, disarming modesty, self-deprecating humor, and gentleness—and the private Chevalier, who was cold, aloof, secretive, often cruelly dismissive. Marlene Dietrich had noted that he had many French peasant qualities, and in his dark, depressive moods, his suspicious peasant nature came to the fore, causing him to question the motives of all those around him. This in turn explained his lifelong, unrequited longing for "true love," for the ideal, elusive figure who would truly "love me for myself." Apart from his revered mother, no human being had ever fulfilled this role to his satisfaction.

For as long as Chevalier spent only part of his time in Marnes-la-Coquette, Félix Paquet was the perfect foil. Chevalier enjoyed his jokes, his malicious show-business gossip, and Paquet was perfectly attuned to his master's moods and needs. But apart from his fawning charm and chameleonlike ability to mix freely in any kind of gathering, Paquet was not an intellectually stimulating companion: Inevitably, Chevalier would soon get bored with his company.

There was another side to Paquet: Before becoming a professional comic, Paquet, eighteen years younger than Chevalier, had been a *danseur mondain*, a semiprofessional dancer hired out by the dance in *thés dansants* attended mostly by lonely middle-aged women. Janie Michels even alleged that, in his youth, he had been something of a pimp. He certainly made himself indispensable to Chevalier in all sorts of ways. In the sixties, visitors to Marnes-la-Coquette noted the occasional presence of a young female "nurse," and if Félix Paquet was on close enough terms with the show-business visitor, he would wink or otherwise hint that the "nurse" was there twice a week, to deal with Chevalier's sexual needs.

From November 1967 to September 1968, Chevalier stepped up the pace of his one-man shows in Europe, Latin America, the United States, and Canada, without, at first, announcing that he was ending his stage career. A photograph of him, taken on the boardwalk in Venice, California, shows a resplendent tanned Chevalier in a white suit and crew-neck black sweater after his concert at the University of Berkeley, heartened by the note slipped into his pocket by a girl student, reading: "On behalf of all the kids, thank you so much for everything. You are a beautiful person and will never get old—only more beautiful. From all of us." A sold-out concert at Lincoln Center was followed by tiring shows in Washington, Westbury, Chicago, and Detroit. Though he had announced his decision to retire at the time of his eightieth birthday while on a tour of South Africa, only François and Madeleine Vals took him seriously, for he had made several such threats to the press in years gone by. In March and April 1968, he was in Britain, crisscrossing from one major city to the next for sold-out one-night stands. Cameron Mackintosh, producer of the international hit musicals *Les Misérables* and *Miss Saigon*, then nineteen, watched Chevalier, in Glasgow, give a "magic performance." "The voice wavered a bit, but the overall effect was staggering. I had never seen anyone with his stage presence—I hadn't yet seen Judy Garland, or even Barbra Streisand—and the strange thing was that he didn't *do* that much onstage. He didn't have to." Afterward, Mackintosh recalled, Chevalier was mobbed by thousands of people, cheering him in the street.

He gave an emotional farewell performance at the London Palladium, recalling his appearance there in 1925 in the memorable flop, *White Birds,*

stopping off for his final English concert—in Coventry—before returning to Marnes-la-Coquette for a brief rest. Then came his final farewell
tour of the United States, beginning in Orlando on April 21, culminating in New York with an emotional farewell appearance—and a Tony
Award, presented to him by Audrey Hepburn.

Madeleine and François Vals alone fully understood the problems
retirement would bring in its wake, but after only halfheartedly sounding
him out on a change of mind, planned his farewell American tour with
their customary efficiency—to Washington, Westbury, Flint (Michi-
gan), Chicago, one of his favorite cities, with one final performance in
Newark's Symphony Hall, the old Mosque Theater. Alan G. Brannigan,
then theater reviewer for the *Newark* (New Jersey) *News*, went backstage
during the intermission. "He was sitting alone and looking rather depressed," Brannigan recalled. "Tomorrow morning," he said, "I am going
to fly back to Paris and I think I shall never be here again."*

The French student uprising of May 1968 had plunged France into
turmoil while Chevalier was still touring the United States. Temperamentally, he was ill-equipped to understand or sympathize with any of
its participants or their goals. Aragon, the celebrated French poet, only
a few years younger than Chevalier, whose intervention had been crucial
to him during the Liberation months, went out into the Latin Quarter
to fraternize with the students (and was copiously booed). But Chevalier,
in private, railed against these spoiled, overprivileged upstarts. His attitude was, "What is it they want that they haven't already got? *I* don't
have any complaints." He was used to meticulously prepared travel
plans, and incensed when he was compelled to fly to Brussels, not Paris
(for strikes had closed down the airports) and submit to a tiring drive
to Marnes-la-Coquette.

De Gaulle, after faltering briefly, recouped his authority, though he
would never entirely recover from the affront. Chevalier's morale, too,
improved, after a well-deserved short rest. May '68, with its iconoclastic
assault on traditional values, had shaken him considerably, inflicting, as
he wrote in his diary, "congestion of the heart and of the brain"—but

*He did return, but not to sing, in 1970.

he resumed his punishing schedule; going to Brazil, Argentina, Uruguay, Peru, Panama, Mexico, and Montreal, touching down in Paris only for his birthday party—a gala evening at the Lido, the proceeds earmarked for the Ris-Orangis retired actors' home. Chevalier no longer presided over this institution, having transferred his title to Charles Aznavour, but he remained a patron. Its reception hall, by now a Maurice Chevalier museum, displayed some of his memorabilia, including some of the autographed pictures he had collected over the years.

Organized with his usual flair by Georges Cravenne, his old friend, the birthday party was a memorable, emotional night for le tout Paris. At Chevalier's own table, the principal guests were Claudette Colbert and Noël Coward; a retrospective Sound and Light pageant, commented by Jean Yanne, the well-known film star, retraced his career from Ménilmontant to his current pinnacle of fame. Only the war years remained unmentioned. Twenty scantily clad Bluebell Girls pranced by the table of honor in single file, each brandishing a birthday cake in the shape of a straw hat topped by four candles. Chevalier was in fine form, dry-eyed, alert. Asked about the evening's impact on him, he said, "Me? I feel a bit like the Eiffel Tower—always there.* But I tell you, to be a Parisian monument is rather fun. One sees lots of people pass by. . . . To be eighty is grand, and in twenty years' time we will perhaps gather again at the Lido to celebrate the centenary of a happy kid called Maurice Chevalier."

Outside, on the Champs-Élysées, pandemonium reigned, as police attempted with little success to keep thousands of fans from mobbing him and other famous guests. It was all highly reminiscent of the hysterical scenes at Victoria Station that had marked his arrival in London in December 1930, with an additional touch of *The Day of the Locust*. The event deserved a *Guinness Book of World Records* mention, for no other star had maintained his popularity over such a long time span, or was likely to again.

---

*The Eiffel Tower was almost exactly the same age as Chevalier, completed six months before he was born.

Then he was off once more, for a farewell concert in Madrid and Palma de Mallorca, only three days before the start of his final, twenty-one-day recital at the Théâtre des Champs-Élysées—his last, emotional stage contact with Parisians, in the town where he had made his first appearance at the Café des Trois Lions in Ménilmontant, at the age of twelve.

It is difficult, still, for anyone who attended Chevalier's last show to talk about it dispassionately. Some, like Patachou, felt that on opening night (October 1, 1968), Chevalier appeared exceptionally old and frail, only a shadow of his former self. In his own diaries, Chevalier admitted that he had never experienced such stage fright. ("I started talking to myself: steady boy, you mustn't cry, think of your modest dignity, there, there now. . . ."). But these were no ordinary concerts, and the audiences attending the twenty-eight sold-out performances (there were seven matinees) were not ordinary either: Part of the theater was packed, night after night, with show-business celebrities, eager to pay a final tribute to the most famous French vaudevillian of all time, and some returned, again and again, to savor the historic moment. On the first night, Chevalier turned it all into a joke. "Thanks for coming along in such large numbers," he began, with his inimitable grin. "I really need your support because I'm scared out of my wits." ("*J'ai une trouille noire*"). As he got into his stride, Chevalier regained his composure, mastering his own, considerable emotion.

As always, he planned his singing "menu" carefully, as a retrospective of his entire career. Several numbers were new, specially written for the occasion—among them Charles Aznavour's lilting, melancholy ballad: "*Quand J'étais Gosse, Paris M'a Pris dans Ses Bras*," ("When I Was a Kid, Paris Took Me in Her Arms") and Jean Dréjac's effective song, with music by his veteran accompanist Fred Freed: "*Merci pour la ballade/Merci pour les grand soirs/Je vous dédie ma serenade/Au revoir*" ("Thanks for the journey/ Thanks for all those nights/This tune is for you all/I'm saying good-bye"), with which he closed the show. Sadly, his English-language songs, among his best, bored his audience. ("As for the English couplets," wrote Olivier Merlin in *Le Monde*, they can only irritate a Parisian audience, which cannot relate to them.")* On his final appearance, a 5:00 P.M. matinee on October 21, Chevalier's emotional farewell, at the close of an interminable standing ovation, "came," as he put it, "from my subconscious. I heard myself say, I started my career in a *café-conc* in Ménilmontant. I finish it here in this splendid Champs-Élysées Theater, after sixty-eight years of good and loyal services, and this is as it should be. *Adieu* is too sad a word, so I won't use it. I'll just say that this is my last appearance on the stage. In Ménilmontant, when I was just a kid, I dreamed of going on the stage. Now I can't believe, standing in front of you, that my great big dream has come true. But now it's time to say *au revoir*. With a smile of hope then, yes, *au revoir*." Most of the audience, even those aware of his consummate showmanship, were, like Chevalier himself, in tears.

In the immediate aftermath of that final stage appearance, Chevalier basked in the glow of this, his most memorable one-man show of all. There were valedictory programs on radio and TV, a Chevalier exhibition in Paris's Musée de la Chanson, thousands of congratulatory letters and phone calls. Olivier Merlin, the *Le Monde* critic, came across him at a lunch given by U.S. ambassador Sargent Shriver on November 26, 1968. He seemed at a loose end, Merlin recalled, but had an attractive young woman in tow, and epitomized the relaxed "Parigot" still.

Chevalier himself, as his letter to *Variety* showed, did not believe his career had come to a definitive end. "Dear Variety," his handwritten note (run as a full-page ad on January 8, 1969) read:

I am in my 81st year and have decided to quit doing "One man shows" while everybody is still asking from everywhere. That's that. But I still feel I could do a fine job in international television, also on the big screen. So—wish me luck with the same kind of heart that I wish the very best of luck—in 1969—to the great U.S.A."

Maurice Chevalier.

*Quant aux couplets Anglais, ils ne peuvent qu'agacer le public Parisien, qui n'a rien à en faire.

As this elegant but unmistakable "situation wanted" ad showed, the world's most durable, best-known vaudeville star was prepared to consider all suitable offers.

A similar, if slightly more oblique, message was delivered on the floor of the U.S. Senate by one of his oldest American friends, Senator Charles Percy, then chairman of the Foreign Relations Committee. After praising Chevalier as "the best ambassador of good will France has sent to the United States in this century," Percy said:

> To retire is the beginning of death.
>   He exclaims: "I am an old man who refuses to be an old man."
>   Thus he will continue to make records, to supervise television shows, to project the spirit of youth to his admirers. And he will, I am certain, assume with increasing effectiveness his role of public service, the humanizing influence which is his hallmark, the badge of his identity. Perhaps an American film producer will see the potential in the story of his remarkable life and his outlook on life.
>   He is a man who believes that the crime of loving is to forget: and, he explains, "I never forget." Nor is he likely to be forgotten. He has been the spirit of France, the essence of life well-lived, far too long for his warmth and vitality quickly to diminish in the eyes of the world. Nor does his Gallic spirit give evidence of diminishing. For, as he has said, "an artist carries on throughout his life a mysterious, uninterrupted conversation with his public."

At first, after his exhausting series of farewell appearances, he welcomed his new leisure, settling down to complete the latest volume of his autobiography, "*Môme aux Cheveux Blancs*" (*The White-haired Kid*). A Japanese promoter begged him to embark on one last tour—to Japan, where he had never been. Vals urged him to go, but Chevalier refused.

His sunny mood did not last long. He confidently expected film and TV producers to beat a path to his door. With one exception, they did not. Chevalier eagerly responded to Disney Productions' request that he sing the title song of the feature-film cartoon *The Aristocats* (1970), recorded in Paris. In his lifetime, the late Walt Disney had instructed his staff that if ever a Disney film was to be made in France, he wanted Chevalier, whom he greatly admired (a large autographed portrait of him hung on the wall behind Disney's desk), to be part of it.

With his old friend Robert Manuel, the Comédie Française veteran actor, Chevalier discussed strategy that might lead to a seat on the forty-member Académie Française, until it became clear to Manuel and others in Chevalier's entourage that the stuffy, hidebound academicians would never vote for the admission of a vaudeville entertainer with a writing sideline—not, at least, in sufficient numbers. His writing did not occupy enough of his time, and, as he may have realized, he had little to say that was either profound, new, or interesting about his later years.

He was still a highly sought-after guest. André Malraux invited him to lunch at Lasserre, the fashionable three-star restaurant, and, later, to share his box at the Opéra. ("Just Louise de Vilmorin*, Malraux and me. I can't believe it!") He still worried about real and imaginary slights, including the possibility that Brigitte Bardot had deliberately snubbed him at a dinner party given by the veteran French financier Paul-Louis Weiller and attended by Elsa Martinelli, Warren Beatty, Arthur Rubinstein, Salvador Dali, and the Pompidous.† He went to the movies, and to the theater, with increasing frequency—and was recognized in the street wherever he went; Paquet organized weekly luncheon parties, and Chevalier was still the perfect, somewhat formal host, invariably making a little speech at the end of the meal, eulogizing the guest of honor, but his depression, apparent only to his immediate entourage, was beginning to worry them.

It was difficult for Chevalier to adjust to the fact that he no longer needed to gear up to a public performance in the evening. His unaccustomed idleness bred melancholia, magnifying his already marked tendency to worry about insignificant problems. Three months after his last

*Malraux's constant companion

†"Madame Pompidou," he wrote in *I Remember It Well*, "seated at my left at table, soothed my aching complexes. Had Brigitte given me the cold shoulder? Had she snubbed me or not? I didn't stay to find out. I felt out of place in this high society and crept out after coffee."

public appearance, he wrote, "I am panic-stricken at the notion that I no longer have to do anything to deserve my name."

And while Félix Paquet did his best to entertain him and ensure his good mood, the Man Friday also began displaying his darker side. In all sorts of ways, he played on Chevalier's suspicious nature, especially on his tendency to believe unfavorable gossip. The seeds of discord, subtly planted, had a clear purpose: to discredit both François and Madeleine Vals and Janie Michels and her sons. This, he believed, would leave him in an impregnable position when Chevalier came to make, or revise, his will.

Already, long before Chevalier's retirement, Paquet had tried, and failed, to prejudice Chevalier against François Vals, hinting, behind his back, that he was inexperienced, and not sufficiently devoted to Chevalier's real interests. This was patently absurd, and, directly challenged by Vals at the time, Paquet had backed down. But now that Chevalier was no longer active, Vals's services were required less and less frequently. He came to Marnes-la-Coquette once a week at first, then, later, once or twice a month, and it was far easier for Paquet to resume his malicious whispering campaign.

With Janie Michels, Paquet used a similar technique. He claimed that her children were too noisy, too demanding, they were upsetting Chevalier, and their ubiquitous presence was not good for his peace of mind. Their constant presence at mealtimes was an unnecessary expense. On another tack, he hinted that Janie Michels was something of a gold digger. Had she not asked Chevalier for money to hire a gallery to exhibit her works? Imperceptibly, Chevalier responded to Paquet's campaign. When he finally concluded his work on "*Môme aux Cheveux Blancs*" (*I Remember It Well* in its American version), he was in a very dark mood indeed.

Thérèse de Saint-Phalle, his Éditions Julliard editor, found him in a "suicidal" state. "He was desperately lonely, needed company, and even asked me if I knew of anyone suitable to share his life," she recalled. Chevalier attached himself to her with almost childlike devotion. He called her "*marraine*" ("godmother") also making a play on words ("*ma reine*," my queen). After a party she threw in his honor, when, to her surprise, he behaved like a much younger man, dancing the Charleston, and staying up till three in the morning, he wrote to her:

> The other evening you were the Princess of today's worldly women. So kind, so gay, so full of life . . . and such a memory, a formidable performance. I'd like a list of your other guests' names, for I want to put down on paper my timid entry into this "new world" of all the most solid talents. What an evening! Many of them came up to talk to me and I'm sure I had the sympathy of people I admire. Please forgive me for taking French leave without saying good-bye to your husband. Very soon, I'll be coming to see you for a possible book-signing session in Deauville. Affectionately, your admirer, Maurice.*

In a further letter to her dated October 16, 1969, he wrote:

> I owe my euphoric mood to you, where nothing else matters—to you, marvelous Thérèse, and to your adorable employer. *The White-haired Kid* has enabled me to plant my feet firmly on the ground once more. Because you must have talked yourself hoarse at the Frankfurt Book Fair on my behalf, I enclose some excellent Swedish throat pastilles, and while I try and calm down a bit, be assured of my deepest gratitude, from the happiest of Maurices.

There may have been an additional explanation for his sunny mood. Four months previously, on June 20, 1969, he had autographed his book at the Galeries Lafayette. In anticipation of this, he had written to Saint-Phalle: "The weather's not at all good. Will anyone come?" As Thérèse de Saint-Phalle recalled, the book sale that day was a huge success: Five hundred people lined up after purchasing the book to get him to sign it. Among them was an attractive woman in her early forties, who said, as she presented her copy for Chevalier to autograph, "You don't remember me, do you?"

Chevalier shook his head.

*dated July 11, 1969

"I'm Odette Meslier. I was your 'Valentine' in your show, in 1952."[1]

Chevalier brightened. He wanted to know more, to hear how she had fared since those long-forgotten days. He may have felt a slight sentimental twinge at the idea they had once had a brief affair. There was a long line of people waiting behind her. "Write me," he said, and she did.

Her letter moved him. She had married, had a child, and divorced. Her daughter, Pascale, aged seven, was severely handicapped, and Odette spent most of her time looking after her. She lived alone, had been separated from her husband for some time—and he had recently committed suicide. She rarely went out and had been overjoyed to see Chevalier again. She did not mention a still ongoing if intermittent liaison with a French actor.

Soon afterward, she called on Chevalier in Marnes-la-Coquette, with her daughter. Lonely, disenchanted with Janie Michels—Paquet had done his work well—Chevalier saw Odette Meslier as a heaven-sent companion. As he wrote in his diaries for publication: "I am certain I have found a feminine hand to consolidate my new way of life, and someone in whom I can truly believe. A hand to hold my own, until the very end if need be." He rented a small apartment for her in Marnes-la-Coquette, and soon she was visiting Chevalier daily. He talked about old times. She, too, was a good listener. Unassuming, modest, eager not to disturb him, she did not appear to be any kind of a threat. Paquet hinted as much to Vals one day, with a knowing look. "We needn't bother about her, need we?" he said.

Paquet was wrong. Chevalier was in the process of transferring his dependency and need for affection onto Odette Meslier and her seven-year-old daughter, Pascale, whose striking good looks could not entirely conceal her condition. Encephalitis at the age of three had left her permanently disabled, unable to speak coherently. Chevalier insisted she go through round after round of tests, paying all the specialists' bills.

He prepared for his book-autographing appearances with the same meticulous attention to detail he formerly devoted to his one-man shows. "Môme aux Cheveux Blancs" was a slight book—little more than a series of diary entries, a trite, self-congratulatory chronicle of his most recent concert tours and of his meetings with celebrities after his retirement. Critics honored the veteran show-business phenomenon more than its actual contents: General de Gaulle, acknowledging its gift and addressing Chevalier as *"Cher Maître,"* said he had read it "with great pleasure. . . . Here is an opportunity for me to restate not only the enjoyment your magnificent talent has afforded me all these years, but my appreciation of it, and of your person, because your exceptional artistic influence has served France well and because you were, and remain, a man who has always taken risks and fought the good fight."

In the fall of 1970, accompanied by Thérèsè de Saint-Phalle, he went one last time to America, not to sing, but to promote *I Remember It Well.* "There was applause among the crowd at Kennedy Airport when they caught sight of him," she said. Clearly, he had lost none of his star aura. But the book reviews were at best lukewarm. The ingenuous optimism ("I am a simple sunshine salesman"), the name-dropping, the occasional dripping sentimentality, were more palatable in the original French. A typical entry read, "I did it. A simple music-hall public at the London Palladium has just given me an evening so charged with emotion and satisfaction that it can only be called colossal," and a caption under a recent photograph showing him in scholarly mood in Marnes-la-Coquette described him as "reader, thinker, philosopher, new young writer with hopes."

Especially harsh was *The New York Times.* Actors always tended to be larger than life, wrote Maurice Zolotow,

> but once in a while there appears a person of such outrageous narcissism he's on another plane. He just doesn't experience his environment and other people. Other people are vaguely felt shadows who enhance his own being. Such a character is Maurice Chevalier. . . . He journeys to Expo 67 in Montreal to begin his long farewell tour. He sees himself as more than a legendary performer. "I was the French flag personified." Going along with him—in spirit—are Sarah Bernhardt and general de Gaulle, two other widely travelled French luminaries. But he's still a little worried—until he recalls something Prince Charles of Belgium once said to him about "divine intervention." So now "a third figure joined me. No longer would I have to face that monumental crowd alone. Three other

THE GOOD FRENCHMAN · 393

people would be on the platform with me to whisper, "take heart, Momo," every time I faltered. *Incroyable, non?"*

Mocking his description of his "monastic existence" as the "missionary of the entertainment world," Zolotow savaged him for writing only about banalities in his reports of conversations with Jackie Kennedy, Malraux, ex-president Truman, and others. "He cannot convey an experience interestingly, he cannot evoke an exciting moment out of the past, he cannot recreate a simple incident in the form of an amusing or touching anecdote. And the reason he cannot is that he apparently does not experience other people, he doesn't live through events as the rest of us do. Other people impinge on him hardly at all."

Chevalier had misguidedly written that "you will probably laugh," but he was so little afraid of death that "I would not mind at all if they broadcast the crucial moment on color television. That way I could say my last goodbye to my international public and then turn over, pink-cheeked and cheerful, for the eternal sleep." "I did not laugh, Maurice," Zolotow concluded.

The Village Voice described the autographing scene at a book-launching party at Brentano's on Fifth Avenue (in the presence of his old friends and admirers Hermione Gingold and Alan Jay Lerner) as "the purest of parties—a non-event created by the press, for the press, to get *more* press to promote the entertainer's ode to himself. . . . Impeccable in a dark blue suit, crisp white shirt, matching tie and handkerchief, wearing the *Légion d'Honneur*, Maurice Chevalier sits on a dais at the far end of the bookstore, surrounded by cameras. . . . He clings to the sunny side of the street with a tenacity that deprives the landscape of dimension. Light without shade defines nothing. Real objects and people, Maurice, cast shadows." Occasionally, he displayed a more melancholic streak. "I don't sing anymore but I occasionally hum," he told McCandell Phillips of *The New York Times.* "I'm over 80 in a world where the young reject the old with more intensity than ever before. So what should an old man do? Fight to stay in the limelight? Try to impress the world when he doesn't understand what it wants anymore? Now I'd like my old age to be my best performance. Death is the best exit."

Back in Marnes-la-Coquette, he was still visited by journalists, still gave elaborate luncheon parties, was still much in demand as a celebrity—but by now it was clear to him that his television talk-show hopes were leading nowhere. Nor was he in the running, after *Aristocats*, for any more film work. He embarked on another book, also in diary form. Its title "*On Est Comme On Naît*," was a pun on words meaning both "One is as one was born" and "One is what one is.") Its tone reflected his somber mood. One entry read, "My nervous state is undoubtedly the result of my change in life. When I used to perform in the evenings, all my thoughts during the day focused on my osmosis with the public, that was the only thought in my mind. But since I gave up the stage, so many new, different things come to mind and lead to confusion." The next sentence, subsequently crossed out, read, "Under my skull I'm so much on the boil, the heat inside my brain is such that I'm beginning to fear that the lid may blow."

He returned, again and again, to thoughts of death and his beloved La Louque: "When the lady in black comes I can always make it acceptable by imagining that she comes in the form of La Louque, stretching out her arms to me, saying, "You've worked hard enough, come, my little one, let me look after you." A cryptic entry read, "I am going to attempt a new experience. I would rather not say what will happen if I fail." The manuscript was duly delivered to Éditions Julliard, but not to Thérèse de Saint-Phalle who was no longer working there.

His old friend Robert Manuel, one of the few visitors Paquet never turned away in the last year of Chevalier's life, remains convinced that the "new experience" was a reference to his sex life, involving Odette Meslier, and that it was the discovery that he had lost his sexual powers completely and irrevocably that led to what happened next. For one night in March 1971, Chevalier tried to kill himself.

He almost succeeded. "It was no starlet's token attempt," Vals recalled. He absorbed a huge quantity of sleeping pills, also slashing his wrists, was discovered only at dawn by Maryse Paquet, and was instantly rushed to the American Hospital in Neuilly, where he remained unconscious for forty-eight hours.

Vals believes there may have been an additional reason, for the circumstances were as follows: Like so many ordinary, middle-class French families, Chevalier used to watch television during dinner. That prior evening, as Félix Paquet later told Vals, the guest star on the program was Henri Charrière, the former Devil's Island convict whose somewhat romanticized autobiography, *Papillon*, had just become a runaway best-seller, turning him overnight into a media star. The sight of *Papillon* on TV infuriated Chevalier. "So one has to murder people and become a convict these days to appear on television!" he ranted, leaving the dinner table abruptly.

The French press either never knew, or chose to ignore, the real reason for his hospitalization, with the exception of *Minute*, an extreme rightwing French weekly, which very briefly, and ambiguously, hinted at a suicide attempt. (The news had been leaked to a reporter on the paper by his girlfriend, who worked at the American Hospital). Only a few of Chevalier's closest friends were aware of the attempt, for François and Madeleine Vals did their best to make light of the inevitable rumors. They of course were well aware of his intentions, for he had left the Valses, the Paquets, and his cook the identically worded pathetic note:

> I have had the finest career a kid from Ménilmontant could hope for. But the end of my life is pitiable. You all figure in my will. I ask your forgiveness. One day we will see each other Up There.*

To François Vals, a few days later, in his hospital bed, he once more assumed the language of the earthy, streetwise Paris *gavroche*. *"J'ai fait une vraie connerie,"* he told him. ("I did a real asshole thing.")

The Vals couple behaved admirably, if, in retrospect, perhaps unwisely so: Aware that Paquet's whispering campaign against them and Janie Michels had been resumed, with considerable effect, they toyed at first with the possibility of warning Chevalier against his majordomo. They wanted to say that Chevalier's rejection of Janie Michels and her sons to the status of unwanted, unseen houseguests was unfair, that it

---

*"J'ai eu la plus belle carrière que pouvait souhaiter un enfant de Ménilmontant. Mais j'ai une fin de vie pitoyable. Je vous demande pardon. Un jour on se verra là-haut."

would be good for his morale to see her occasionally, that Paquet's behavior, filling him with malicious gossip, monitoring his phone calls, determining who should visit, was not good for his physical or mental health.

But they also feared that if they spoke out, this might fuel Chevalier's growing paranoia. He had always been susceptible to tattletales, even as a young man, and their advice might well be counterproductive, confirming in Chevalier's ever-suspicious mind the notion that *they* were trying to discredit the Paquets—the unspoken stake, of course, being Chevalier's vast inheritance. So, instead, they simply urged him to put the attempted suicide behind him and overcome his temporary breakdown, as he had done in 1924. Chevalier rallied, and from then on, François and Madeleine Vals had freer access to him.

Shortly after his return to Marnes-la-Coquette, Chevalier summoned François Vals and ordered him to reclaim the manuscript of "*On Est Comme On Naît*" from Éditions Julliard. Vals pointed out that an advance had already been received, and the book was about to be published. "I don't care," Chevalier said. "Indemnify them. Pay them whatever you have to." Vals duly reimbursed the publisher and retrieved the manuscript.

Chevalier also requested that the three suicide notes he had written be returned to him. He now spent hours every day answering the many get-well letters he had received. His handwriting was so shaky that Vals did not post them all. Chevalier's thank-you notes had style. He quoted from a letter he had once received from the marquis de Cuevas, the famous socialite and patron of the arts who subsidized the Monte-Carlo-based ballet company of the same name for many years: "I apologize for giving you no sign of life," Cuevas had written Chevalier in 1954, "The reason is I have been too busy trying not to die."

The aftereffects of the suicide attempt were serious—more serious than Chevalier realized. He began suffering from memory lapses, and progressive kidney failure brought about renewed depression, provoking bouts of irrational, senile irritability. He unfairly upbraided a great-niece, Mimi (René's daughter), for leaving her parents' apartment to move into her own studio; he could no longer stand the presence of

Pascale, Odette Meslier's daughter, he once told Paquet. He wanted her kept out of sight. But this mood did not last. A few weeks later, a photographer took candid shots of an adoring Chevalier, nursing the small child on his lap, during a visit to the circus. Increasingly, he spent most of the day in bed, read less, watched television hardly at all. His weariness, compounded by insomnia, resulted in bouts of loathing for all around him. While Vals was on a visit, Odette Meslier phoned. "Do you wish to speak to her?" Vals asked. Chevalier made an unmistakable gesture of rejection, as if to say, "Can't you get her out of my life?"

He rewrote his will. Until his suicide attempt, its beneficiaries had been roughly aware of its contents. The chief beneficiaries had been Madeleine and François Vals, with Janie Michels, the Paquets, the housekeeper-cook couple, and various charities (including the home for destitute actors at Ris-Orangis) receiving substantial sums. The new will, notarized by Maître Serge Marchand, was substantially different—though this, of course, remained unknown to all but Odette Meslier.

On his good days, Chevalier still went to see movies, or to the circus, even received visitors. But on bad days, he often broke down in uncontrollable fits of weeping. On one of his last visits, Vals recalled, Chevalier whispered, "I'd rather die than go on living like this."

On his eighty-third birthday (September 12, 1971), a small family party took place. Janie Michels, and her two sons, though living on his doorstep, were not invited. One of his last foreign visitors, also on his birthday, was Jerry Lewis, a lifelong admirer, who went through his zany comic act at Chevalier's request and managed to make him laugh.

His kidney condition deteriorated alarmingly, and on December 12, 1971, while at a movie on the Champs-Élysées with his housekeeper's small son, he collapsed, was rushed to the Hôpital Necker, and put on a dialysis support machine. Before the ambulance came, he instructed Vals to keep the Christmas notes and presents he had already prepared for his household staff, and be ready to distribute them on Christmas Day, "in case anything happens to me."

There were contradictory reports of his state of health. Félix Paquet, the only person to visit Chevalier in the hospital, kept issuing reassuring health bulletins to the press, while doctors reported that his "deterioration is continuing slowly and persistently." Paquet kept all visitors away, on various pretexts: Doctors' orders, he told the Valses, his nephew René Chevalier, and Marlene Dietrich, who wished to see him. In his present condition, Chevalier did not want to see anyone, Paquet told others. The Necker Hospital director, Georges Cours, told René Chevalier that the patient was not responding to dialysis. The hospital was in a quandary: The machine was badly needed elsewhere, to help patients with a real chance of survival. Chevalier had none. On December 26, Cours told the press that "no further treatment with a dialysis machine was planned." This, he added, indicated that the patient could no longer tolerate the treatment, which had become useless. But almost to the very last, Paquet insisted Chevalier was getting better. "He was seated in an armchair," he told reporters that same day. He is better. . . . He is lucid. His treatment is continuing."

On January 1, 1972, *le Révérend Père* Alain Carré administered the last rites and the Eucharist. Chevalier slipped into a coma and died shortly afterward. His last words, Father Carré revealed during his funeral oration, were, *"Y'A d'La Joie"* ("There's Fun in the Air")—the title of the famous Charles Trenet song that had caused so much bad blood between them.

The funeral, and the church ceremony in Marnes-la-Coquette, in bitter January weather, was attended by a crowd of about a thousand people, including Grace Kelly, Jacques Duhamel, the French minister of culture, Tino Rossi, Georges Carpentier, and a group of film and vaudeville stars. This was far less than the estimated hundred thousand people who had attended Edith Piaf's funeral, but the relatively small numbers were understandable: His death had occurred in the middle of the New Year holidays, and Marnes-la-Coquette was not as easily accessible as Paris's Père Lachaise Cemetery. Chevalier was buried in his stage outfit—his midnight-blue tuxedo, with the straw boater on his chest. The Légion d'Honneur and World War I medals were displayed on his coffin. Among the wreaths was a large one from Yvonne Vallée, who was also present. Félix Paquet, who monitored the proceedings, made his presence felt, keeping most of the mourners out of the cemetery, including a number of erstwhile friends and acquaintances. The undertakers had been instructed to allow in only those to whom he gave the nod. Janie Michels watched the funeral proceedings from the street outside the church. "What are you doing here? Why aren't you in the procession, behind Maurice?" Fred Freed, Chevalier's pianist, asked her.

There were undignified scuffles among photographers at the cemetery, one of them falling into the open grave on top of Chevalier's coffin. From there he continued, phlegmatically, to shoot pictures, refusing the helping hand of the contrite paparazzo who had pushed him in.

The terms of Chevalier's will focused media attention on Odette Meslier for the first time in her life. Dressed in black, she told newsmen, "Maurice Chevalier was a marvelous grandfather for my little girl. He was a marvelous friend to me. I am in mourning." Chevalier's last, hitherto unknown girlfriend, they reported, had inherited his entire fortune.

This was not strictly accurate: In his final, handwritten testament, dated November 26, 1971, Chevalier divided his assets into twenty-eight equal parts, making "Odette Meslier, widow of Monsieur Junet, residing I rue Xavier Schlumberg at Marnes-la-Coquette, my residual legatee," and instructing her to dispose of them as follows: two of the twenty-eight shares were to go to the Ris-Orangis home for retired actors; three shares to Madeleine and François Vals; one share to "Mama" Delpierre, his former housekeeper; one share to his nephew Maurice; one share to Nita Raya; three shares to his favorite nephew, René; two shares to the SACEM* for the upkeep of the Chevalier Village (his former La Bocca house); three shares to Félix and Maryse Paquet; two shares to the Welfare Bureau of the Paris XXᵉ arondisse-ment (for underprivileged children and old-age pensioners); two shares to Pierre and Maria Le Mounier, his cook and housekeeper. In addition, Chevalier left the Vals couple a knit-goods workshop he had bought for them twenty years previously and made over to the Paquets a country house he had owned for years but hardly ever visited.

Odette Meslier became, overnight, extremely wealthy, for Chevalier

*Société des Auteurs et Compositeurs de Musique

willed her not only all eight of the remaining shares but also his Marnes-la-Coquette property, and his valuable real estate in Lausanne "and the assets thereof," i.e., the accumulated moneys from his Swiss tenants that were held in a Swiss bank. Another proof of her importance to him in the last months of his life was the specific mention in his will that "should she die before I do," all the assets willed to her were to go "to her father and mother, or to the latters' survivors"—a neat way of providing for Odette's handicapped daughter, Pascale, for life. The will made it clear that the beneficiaries were to be free of subsequent tax claims. "Since Maître Serge Marchand is aware of all my holdings," he wrote, "I ask him to make a complete list of all my worldly goods and give him the task of disposing of all my assets, including all my real estate, except for the forementioned ones, to dispose of them, to pay all inheritance and sales taxes (before calculating the amount available) for my beneficiaries." Among the buildings sold in Paris was the one at 72, Boulevard de Courcelles, where he had lived during the Second World War. There was no mention of Janie Michels anywhere in the will.[2]

Chevalier asked that Odette Meslier and Maître Marchand "dispose of all my personal belongings [wardrobe, trophies, Oscars, paintings, jewelry, etc.] to individuals of their choice." He also specified, "I want to be buried in the funeral concession I have acquired in Marnes-la-Coquette cemetery alongside my mother, and that no one else, with the exception of my mother and I, be buried there," he wrote.

François Vals remains convinced that, in part, at least, Chevalier's new will, as well as his decision to prevent publication of his last book, reflected his compulsive need to present a perfect picture to the world at large, to show that he had indeed found true love at last. Had the manuscript not been withdrawn, fans, readers, and critics alike might well have concluded that his attempted suicide was the consequence of the failure of the "new experience" hinted at in his last book draft: Loneliness, old-age impotence, and melancholy had no place in the "Chevalier myth" he was determined to preserve.

It was all part of his quest for perfection, in life as in his art, from the moment he first went on the stage of the Café des Trois Lions at the age of twelve. Behind the veteran, irrepressibly cheerful performer hypnotically charming his beloved public, there lurked an altogether more fragile, endearingly human personality: One's heart goes out to this "real," lonesome, insecure Chevalier, who all his life put up such a consistently optimistic front, weathered so many storms, overcame so many crises, and made so many astonishing comebacks during his incredibly long career, begun in the days of the Belle Epoque and lasting until shortly after May 1968.

This quintessentially "good Frenchman," the most durable stage star in history, in his later years astounding his audiences with his youthful persona and his mastery of his craft, remains an extraordinary landmark, an almost inexplicable phenomenon. No one in entertainment history was ever like him, for, good looks apart, he began his career with few of the assets most of his competitors took for granted. To achieve, and maintain himself at, the pinnacle of fame, as he did for so long, required incessant, grueling practice, a lifetime of endless rehearsals. He deserves more than token adulation, or the perpetuation of a stereotyped image of his own devising. Surely, it is not belittling him to show him as he really was?

Behind the walls of number 4, rue du Réservoir, Marnes-la-Coquette, renamed rue Maurice Chevalier after his death, his mansion has become a shrine, a private, seldom-visited Maurice Chevalier museum. His bedroom, splendid marble bathroom, leather-bound books, framed autographed photographs, rosewood furniture, and the formal layout of the house remain exactly as they were in the last few years of his life. Odette Meslier lives there part of the time with her daughter, but his personal quarters remain unoccupied. Even the pink champagne she serves occasional visitors and Chevalier pilgrims remains his favorite brand.

Madame Meslier is the reclusive guardian of this private museum—as well as of his memory. She does not want to talk about what happened in the last months of his life, beyond reiterating her veneration of "one of the greatest men who ever lived."

Others are less discreet. Odette Meslier, one member of the Chevalier "family" recalled, assumed her new role as *châtelaine* of the Chevalier estate with cold, hard-eyed practicality. Immediately after his death, she gave the Paquets, Janie Michels and her family, and François Vals two weeks' notice to clear out. François Vals was told to remove his personal effects from his office and leave all Chevalier's papers behind. Moving vans arrived at the appointed time. In the immediate aftermath of his death, one "family" member recalled, several pairs of Chevalier's glasses were collected—he had the habit of leaving them strewn all around the house. "What's to be done with them?" Odette Meslier was asked. "Get rid of them," she replied.

As a tiny footnote to the immediate post-Chevalier days in Marnes-la-Coquette, a local gas-station employee told how, before Chevalier's death, Odette Meslier used to be a frequent visitor, using her considerable charm to get him to repair, free of charge, her small, unreliable car, which was constantly breaking down. "After Maurice's death, there she was at the wheel of his Mercedes," he said, "haughty, not saying a word, behaving as if I were a complete stranger. She clearly wished to put the past behind her."

Though some pictures remain on the walls of the Chevalier estate, the more valuable Matisse, Picasso, and Utrillo paintings were auctioned in 1971.

Chevalier's erstwhile house at La Bocca, near Cannes, did not remain a SACEM-run "Chevalier Village" for long. It had functioned as a leisure center for artists and writers only until the midsixties: Henri Betti himself spent a few weeks there. Then, after the death of Albert Willemetz, the new SACEM executives determined the house was unsuitable, and too expensive to run, as an artists' home. It remained empty and was put up for sale in 1988, the year of the centenary of his birth. In 1992, it remained derelict and boarded up, about to be torn down and replaced by a high-rise apartment block.

François Vals invested in a chain of restaurants, becoming a highly successful entrepreneur. Ever since Chevalier's death, he and Madeleine Vals have spent the bulk of their time raising funds—in Chevalier's name—both for the Ris-Orangis retired actors' home and for "Soleil d'Enfance," the French branch of the worldwide Variety Club (to help handicapped children), which Chevalier also endowed in his lifetime.

René Chevalier, and his wife, Louise, after selling the butcher's shop they inherited from René's father, Paul, live modestly in Paris in a high-rise apartment near Belleville. They remain devoted to Chevalier's memory and treasure his last note to them, dated December 12, 1971 — the day before his final collapse.

Yvonne Vallée, ninety-two when this book was completed, was interviewed several times on the telephone but was reluctant to receive visitors. "I am too old and too frail," she said. She recalled the past without bitterness. "Maybe what happened to us was my fault," she said. "He worked too hard, I was alone too much." She was at pains to deny that Chevalier had ever taken drugs during their years together. "His war wound hurt him more than he would ever admit," she added.

Two years after Chevalier's death, Félix Paquet threw himself out of the window of a hotel while undergoing treatment for depression, dying instantly. He had never recovered from the aftermath of Chevalier's death—and the ensuing change in his life-style. Nita Raya and Maryse Paquet, both in excellent health still, remain great friends, and often meet and talk about their bygone years with Chevalier.

A centenary celebration for Chevalier was staged at the Lido in 1988. All male guests were asked to wear straw hats. Among them was one of the ten French prisoners of war released by the Germans after his controversial concert in Alten Grabow.

On February 23, 1990, President George Bush celebrated Chevalier's memory on the occasion of a special tribute to him organized in New York by the Alliance Française. "As one of the most popular French entertainers of the 20th century, Maurice Chevalier radiated an elegance of style and a carefree love of life that touched the hearts of all who were fortunate enough to see or hear him perform," Bush wrote. "Maurice Chevalier taught us that, as long as we believe in ourselves, all things are possible. If I may paraphrase a song title made famous by this wonderful artist, 'Thank Heaven for Maurice Chevalier.'"

Notes

CHAPTER ONE

1. Cudlipp, Percy, *Maurice Chevalier's Own Story, As Told to Percy Cudlipp* (London: Nash and Grayson Ltd., 1930).
2. Mistinguett, *Mistinguett by Mistinguett* (London: Elek Books, 1957).

CHAPTER TWO

1. Douglas Gilbert, *American Vaudeville, Its Life and Times* (New York: Dover Books [originally Whittlesey House], 1940).
2. Chance Newton, *Idols of the Halls* (London: Heath and Cranton, 1928).
3. Gilbert, op. cit.
4. Ibid.
5. Ibid.
6. Bernard Sobel, *A Pictorial History of Vaudeville* (Secaucus, N.J.: Citadel Press, 1961).
7. *Music-Hall Memories* (a quarterly magazine), London 1935–36.
8. Ibid.
9. Mistinguett, *Toute Ma Vie* (Paris: Presses de la Cité, 1953).
10. Sobel, op. cit.
11. Jacques-Charles, *La Révue De Ma Vie* (Paris: Éditions Fayard, 1958).
12. Ibid.

CHAPTER THREE

1. Émile Zola, *Paris* (1897).
2. Colette, *La Vagabonde* (Paris: Le Livre de Poche, originally published 1910).
3. Ibid.

CHAPTER FOUR

1. I am indebted to Nicole and Alain Lacombe, authors of *Fréhel* (Paris: Éditions Pierre Belfond, 1990) for details of her early life.

CHAPTER FIVE

1. I am indebted to Jean-Paul Neu, deputy mayor of Enghien and expert on local history, for a copy of Mistinguett's birth certificate and other family background details.
2. Jacques Damase, *Les Folies du Music-Hall*, (Paris: Éditions du Spectacle, 1960).
3. Mistinguett, *Toute Ma Vie*.
4. Michel Georges-Michel, *Nuits d'Actrices*, reproduced in Herbert Griffiths's *Mistinguett and her Confessions* (London: Hurst and Blackwell, 1938).
5. Ibid.
6. Interview with Jean Sablon, May 9, 1992.
7. Mistinguett, *Toute Ma Vie*.
8. Ibid.
9. Ibid.

CHAPTER SIX

1. Maurice Chevalier, *Ma Route et Mes Chansons*, Vol. I (Paris: Éditions Julliard, 1947).
2. Mistinguett, *Mistinguett by Mistinguett*.
3. Ibid.
4. Ibid.
5. Jacques-Charles, *La Révue de Ma Vie*, op. cit.
6. Ibid.
7. Maurice Chevalier, *Ma Route et Mes Chansons*, Vol. I.
8. Interview with Jean Sablon, May 9, 1992, who recalled past conversation with Jack Buchanan at Clifton Webb's Hollywood house in 1935.
9. Mistinguett, *Toute Ma Vie*.
10. Maurice Chevalier, *Ma Route et Mes Chansons*, Vol. I.

CHAPTER SEVEN

1. Mistinguett, *Mistinguett by Mistinguett*.
2. Ibid.
3. Maurice Chevalier, *Ma Route et Mes Chansons*, Vol. 2, 1956.
4. Interview in *The American Weekly*, August 24, 1958.
5. Mistinguett, *Mistinguett by Mistinguett*.
6. Elsie Janis, *So Far, So Good* (New York: E. P. Dutton, 1932).
7. Ibid.
8. Ibid.

9. Ibid.

10. Interview with Jean Sablon, recalling conversations in Hollywood in 1935–36 with Richman, at dinners in Clifton Webb's house.

11. Mistinguett, *Mistinguett by Mistinguett.*

12. Interview with Arletty in Paris, October 10, 1991.

13. Denis Brogan, *The French Nation 1814–1940* (New York: Harper Brothers, 1957).

14. Lucien Rioux, *Vingt Ans de Chansons* (Paris: Éditions Arthaud, 1966).

CHAPTER EIGHT

1. Interview with Jean Sablon, May 9, 1992.

2. Telephone conversation with Yvonne Vallée, May 1992.

3. Telephone conversation with Billy Wilder, October 1991.

4. Jesse Lasky, *I Blow My Horn,* (New York: Doubleday, 1957), pp. 224 ff.

CHAPTER NINE

1. Axel Madsen, *Gloria And Joe* (New York: Arbor House, 1988).

2. Alan Jay Lerner, *The Street Where I Live* (New York: W. W. Norton, 1980).

3. Adolph Zukor, *The Public Is Never Wrong* (London: Cassell's, 1954).

4. Ethan Mordden, *The Hollywood Studio* (New York: Alfred A. Knopf, 1988).

5. Jesse Lasky, op. cit.

6. Ibid.

7. Ibid.

8. I am indebted to Axel Madsen's excellent book *Gloria And Joe* for this and other details concerning Paramount just before the Great Crash of 1929.

9. Patrick McGilligan, *George Cukor: A Double Life* (New York: St. Martin's Press, 1991).

10. John Kobal, interview in *People Will Talk* (New York: Alfred A. Knopf, 1985).

11. Mordden, op. cit.

12. Ibid.

13. Lasky, op. cit.

14. James Robert Parish, *The Jeanette MacDonald Story* (New York: Mason/Charter, 1976).

15. Gavin Lambert, *On Cukor* (New York: G. P. Putnam's Sons, 1972).

16. Robert Spencer interview in Los Angeles, January 28, 1992.

17. Leslie Halliwell, *Halliwell's Filmgoer's Companion* (New York: Charles Scribner's Sons, 1985).

18. Robert Spencer interview.

CHAPTER TEN

1. Jean Sablon interview.

2. Robert Spencer interview.

3. Ibid.

4. Gene Ringgold and De Witt Bodeen: *The Films and Career of Maurice Chevalier* (Secaucus, N.J.: Citadel Press, 1973).

5. Maurice Chevalier, *Ma Route et Mes Chansons*, Vol. 2.

6. Kobal, op. cit.

7. Lambert, op. cit.

CHAPTER ELEVEN

1. Ringgold and Bodeen, op. cit.

2. Ibid.

3. Robert Spencer interview, January 29, 1992.

4. *Los Angeles Times*, December 29, 1931.

5. Robert Spencer interview.

6. Robert Spencer interview.

7. Bob Thomas, *Thalberg, Life and Legend* (New York: Doubleday, 1967).

8. The letter, signed by Thalberg, is part of a private collection owned by the late Sam Marx, formerly a Thalberg aide. With characteristic generosity, he provided many valuable insights concerning this Hollywood "golden age," of which he was one of the last survivors. It is a matter of deep regret that he died while the book was still being written.

9. Thomas, op. cit.

10. Grace Moore, *You're Only Human Once* (Los Angeles: G. Moore Parera, 1944).

11. Robert Spencer interview.

12. Ibid.

13. Interview with Jean Sablon, a frequent traveler aboard the *Île de France*, who recalled that Chevalier's generous distribution of photographs and contrasting parsimony with tips was the talk of the ship's staff.

14. William Paul, *Lubitsch's American Comedies* (New York: Columbia University Press, 1983).

15. Moore, op. cit.

CHAPTER TWELVE

1. Mistinguett, *Mistinguett by Mistinguett*.

2. Nita Raya's recollections of her years with Chevalier in this chapter are based on several interviews with her in Paris from June to September 1992.

3. Interview with Jo Siritsky, July 1992.

4. Maurice Chevalier, with Eileen and Robert Mason Pollock, *With Love* (New York: Little, Brown, 1960).

CHAPTER THIRTEEN

1. Otto Abetz, *Memoirs d'un Ambassadeur* (Paris: Éditions Fayard, 1954).

2. Robert Paxton, *Vichy France* (New York: Alfred A. Knopf, 1972).

3. Paxton, op. cit.

4. Ibid.

5. Robert Paxton, *Parades and Politics at Vichy* (Princeton, N.J.: Princeton University Press, 1966).

6. Interview with Pierre Galante.

7. Simone de Beauvoir, *La Force de l'Age* (Paris: Éditions Gallimard, 1961).

8. René Rocher, contribution to *France Under the German Occupation* (Stanford, California: Hoover Institution on War, Revolution and Peace, 1953).

9. In the winter of 1941, Jouvet took a repertory company on a tour of Latin America after which he sought asylum in America, spending the war years in Los Angeles and only returning to France after the war.

10. Rocher, op. cit.

11. Robert Aron, *Histoire de Vichy* (Paris: Éditions Fayard, 1954).

12. Abetz, op. cit.

13. Chevalier, *With Love*.

14. Henri Betti wrote extensively about his life and was kind enough to show me the unpublished manuscript containing details of his war years with Chevalier. Chapters 13 and 14 are based on extensive interviews with him in 1991 and 1992.

CHAPTER FOURTEEN

1. Henri Betti interview, August 1991.

2. Hoover Institution Archives, op. cit.

3. Jacques de Launay, *La Force de Pétain* (Paris).

4. André Halimi's little-known *Chantons Sous l'Occupation* (Paris: Éditions Orban, 1976) is an invaluable reference book, chronicling the movie, theater, music-hall, and nightclub boom in France during the Occupation years.

5. *Le Petit Parisien*, November 1, 1941.

6. Pierre Drieu la Rochelle, *Journal 1939–1945* (Paris: Éditions Gallimard, 1992). ("*La comédie de la collaboration aura été parfaitement humaine: des Allemands qui ne croyaient pas assez à Hitler chargés d'endoctriner des Français qui y croyaient trop.*")

7. Hervé Hamon and Patrick Rotman, *Tu Vois, Je N'ai Pas Oublié* (Paris: Éditions du Seuil/Fayard, 1990).

8. Chevalier, *Ma Route et Mes Chansons*, Vol 2.

9. *Le Petit Parisien*, September 12, 1941.

10. Interview with Henri Betti, September 1991.

11. Interview with Étienne Léandri, October 1991.

12. *Les Parfums Tocalon* was the American-owned company Léandri worked for, enabling him to obtain special gasoline coupons.

13. Abetz, op. cit.

14. Fabienne Jamet, *One-Two-Two* (Paris: Éditions Orban, 1975).

15. Chevalier, *Ma Route et Mes Chansons*, Vol. 2.

CHAPTER FIFTEEN

1. Henry Jadoux, *Sacha Guitry* (Paris: Librairie Perrin, 1982).
2. Maurice Chevalier, *Ma Route et Mes Chansons*, Vol. 3.
3. *Newsweek*, September 11, 1944.
4. Pierre Dac, *Un Français Libre à Londres* (Paris: Éditions France-Empire, 1971).
5. Lottman, op. cit.
6. Jacques Debû-Bridel, *La Résistance Intellectuelle* (Paris: Éditions Julliard, 1970).
7. Interview with Georges Cravenne.

CHAPTER SIXTEEN

1. *Chevalier, Photos de Madame d'Ora* (Geneva: Éditions René Kister, 1955).
2. Interview with Robert Manuel, October 1991.

CHAPTER EIGHTEEN

1. Lerner, op. cit.
2. Interview with Leslie Caron, July 1992.
3. The Hedda Hopper Archives, by kind permission of the Library of the Motion Picture Association.

CHAPTER NINETEEN

1. Interview with Thérèse de Saint-Phalle.
2. Chevalier's net worth, after taxes, was variously estimated in the press at between $5 million and $50 million. It was certainly in excess of $10 million, for when Chevalier and his former American "gofer," Robert Spencer, met briefly in the United States in 1947, Chevalier told Spencer then that he was already worth "at least ten million dollars."

Bibliography

Abetz, Otto. *Memoirs d'un Ambassadeur,* Paris: Éditions Stock, 1963.

Aron, Robert. *Histoire de Vichy.* Paris: Éditions Fayard, 1954.

Bach, Steven. *Marlene Dietrich, Life and Legend.* New York: William Morrow, 1992.

Beauvoir, Simone de. *La Force de l'Age.* Paris: Édition Gallimard, 1961.

Brogan, Denis. *The French Nation 1814–1940.* New York: Harper Brothers, 1957.

Cudlipp, Percy. *Maurice Chevalier's Own Story, As Told to Percy Cudlipp.* London: Mash and Grayson, 1930.

Chevalier, Maurice. *Ma Route et Mes Chansons,* 8 volumes. Paris: Éditions Julliard, 1947–1968.

Chevalier, Maurice, with Eileen and Robert Mason Pollock. *With Love.* New York: Little, Brown, 1960.

Chevalier, Maurice. *Môme aux Chevaux Blancs (I Remember It Well),* Paris: Éditions Julliard, 1970.

Colette. *La Vagabonde.* Paris: Livre de Poche, 1961.

Dac, Pierre. *Un Français Libre à Londres.* Paris: Éditions France-Empire, 1971.

Damase, Jacques. *Les Folies du Music-Hall.* Paris: Éditions du Spectacle, 1960.

Debû-Bridel, Jacques. *La Résistance Intellectuelle.* Éditions Julliard.

D'ora, Madame. *Chevalier, Photos.* Geneva: Éditions René Kister, 1955.

Drieu la Rochelle, Pierre. *Journal 1939–45.* Paris: Éditions Gallimard, 1992.

Flanner, Janet. *Paris Was Yesterday.* New York: Viking, 1972.

Flanner, Janet. *France Under the German Occupation,* Archives of the Hoover Institution on War, Revolution and Peace. Stanford, Calif.: Stanford University Press, 1959.

Gilbert, Douglas. *American Vaudeville, Its Life and Times.* New York: Dover Books, 1940.

Griffiths, Herbert. *Mistinguett and Her Confessions.* London: Hurst and Blackwell, 1938.

Greene, Abel, and Joe Laurie. *Show Biz—from Vaudeville to Video.* New York: Henry Holt, 1951.

Halimi, André. *Chantons Sous l'Occupation.* Paris: Éditions Orban, 1976.

Halliwell, Leslie. *Halliwell's Filmgoer's Companion.* New York: Charles Scribner's Sons, 1985.

Hamon, Hervé, and Patrick Rotman. *Tu Vois, Je N'ai Rien Oublié.* Paris: Éditions du Seuil/Fayard, 1990.

Harding, James. *Sacha Guitry: The Last Boulevardier.* London: Methuen, 1968.

Jacques-Charles. *La Révue de Ma Vie.* Paris: Éditions Fayard, 1958.

Jadoux, Henry. *Sacha Guitry.* Paris: Librairie Perrin, 1982.

Jamet, Fabienne. *One-Two-Two.* Paris: Éditions Orban, 1975.

Janis, Elsie. *So Far, So Good.* New York: E. P. Dutton, 1932.

Lacombe, Nicole, and Alain Lacombe: *Fréhel.* Paris: Éditions Pierre Belfond, 1990.

Lambert, Gavin. *On Cukor.* New York: G. P. Putnam's Sons, 1972.

Lasky, Jesse. *I Blow My Own Horn.* New York: Doubleday, 1958.

Lerner, Alan Jay. *The Street Where I Live.* New York: W. W. Norton, 1980.

Lottman, Herbert. *L'Épuration.* Paris: Éditions Fayard, 1968.

Marx, Samuel. *Mayer and Thalberg: The Make-Believe Saints.* New York: Random House, 1975.

Madsen, Axel. *Gloria and Joe.* New York: Arbor House, 1988.

McGilligan, Patrick. *George Cukor: A Double Life.* New York: St. Martin's Press, 1991.

Mistinguett. *Mistinguett par Mistinguett.* Paris, Presses de la Cité, 1957.

Mistinguett. *Mistinguett by Mistinguett,* trans. Herbert Griffiths. London: Elek Books, 1957.

Moore, Grace. *You're Only Human Once.* Los Angeles: G. Moore Parera, 1944.

Mordden, Ethan. *The Hollywood Studio.* New York: Alfred A. Knopf, 1988.

Newton, H. Chance. *Idols of the Halls.* London: Heath Cranton, 1928.

Parish, James Robert. *The Jeanette MacDonald Story.* New York: Mason/Charter, 1976.

Paul, William. *Lubitsch's American Comedies.* New York: Columbia University Press, 1983.

Paxton, Robert. *Parades and Politics at Vichy.* Princeton, N.J.: Princeton University Press, 1966.

Paxton, Robert. *Vichy France.* New York: Alfred A. Knopf, 1972.

Ringgold, Gene, and De Witt Bodeen. *Chevalier: The Films and Career of Maurice Chevalier.* Secaucus, N.J.: Citadel Press, 1973.

Rioux, Lucien. *Vingt Ans de Chansons.* Paris: Éditions Arthaud, 1966.

Sobel, Bernard. *A Pictorial History of Vaudeville.* Secaucus, N.J.: Citadel Press, 1961.

Spoto, Donald. *Dietrich.* New York: Bantam Books, 1992.

Stein, Charles W. *American Vaudeville.* New York: Alfred A. Knopf, 1984.

Thomas, Bob. *Thalberg, Life and Legend.* New York: Doubleday, 1967.

Weygand, Maxime. *Memoirs.*

Wilmot, Roger. *Kindly Leave the Stage.* London: Methuen, 1985.

Zola, Émile. *Paris.* Paris: Éditions Laffont (oeuvres complètes), 1970.

Zukor, Adolph. *The Public Is Never Wrong.* London: Cassell's, 1954.

The Songs of Maurice Chevalier

During a stage career spanning sixty-eight years, Chevalier's song repertoire was in the thousands. Less than a score are well known today. His early records are collectors' items, but in America he remains best known for those musical numbers that were devised for him either in prewar Hollywood and for the postwar classics—especially *Love in the Afternoon* and *Gigi*—films that are still shown regularly on late-night television.

His friend and admirer Marcel Pagnol, the playwright, wrote that "this is not a singer, this is not a *'diseur,'* this is not a conjurer of the fantastic, this is not a comedian, this is a creator of personages. That which he creates alone every evening on the stage is not a 'number,' is not even a recital. It is a work which belongs to the realm of dramatic art." Pagnol did Chevalier an injustice: Onstage, he was both a consummate *diseur*, comedian, and clown. Above all, he projected the image of the professional seducer/optimist—in such marked contrast to the events marking his private life.

When evaluating his performances, it is essential to remember that he was above all a product of the turn-of-the-century *café-conc*, the French popular music-hall theater. Without the benefit of any special effects, or indeed, until 1931, microphones, the *café-conc* performer had to strive for immediate attention, and Chevalier used his considerable stage skills to supplement what he himself knew was an extremely limited voice range. His typical music-hall "number"—in the style of Dranem, Mayol, and Polin—part song, part comic monologue or sketch, owed as much to the performer's presence and personality as it did to his vocal talent or the quality of his song. Chevalier's numbers invariably told a story, to the accompaniment of dance steps, mime, or gesture. Toward the end of his life, the story became, quite simply, Chevalier himself.

Though he was more mellifluous in his old age, he never quite lost his raucous tone. Some of his records (his version of "Swanee," for example) are at odd moments quite excruciatingly off-key. His composers quickly got into the habit of tailoring the tunes to his voice range.

Though hundreds of his songs have been recorded, it is the force of personality behind them that makes them memorable, for though Chevalier prided himself on singing "from the heart" he used every possible trick to overcome not only his singing limitations but the often-mediocre material at his disposal. Jean-Christophe Averty, the French film director, music-hall buff, and rare-record collector, who owns a huge collection of recorded Chevalier songs, devoted no less than twenty-four hourly programs on Chevalier on France-Inter, the French radio station, in 1988, the centennial year of Chevalier's birth. Listening to his tapes today, one's overall impression is of an art from another planet: His performances, in the twenties, were rooted in the tradition of the nineteenth-century music hall—the music almost invariably of the oom-pa-pa, brass-band variety, the subject matter rooted in sexual innuendo.

It would of course be absurd to judge his songs by current standards. What is remarkable to us today—the sheer crudity both of language and music in Chevalier's songs of the twenties, and its repetitiveness—delighted his audiences in the twenties and thirties; what is surprising, in his pre-Hollywood period, is that even the Maurice Yvain/Henri Christiné/Albert Willemetz numbers contain little that is truly memorable in terms of rhythm and original, felicitous lyrics. The occasional gems stand out, as with his later Hollywood career, when Rodgers and Hart provided him with adequate vehicles for his talent. One can only regret that in the twenties, his only Cole Porter song was "On the Level, you're a Little Devil." The existing Cole Porter tape may crackle with age, but the mildly syncopated rhythm, flawless delivery, and the quality of the lyrics ("There'll be no headache on the morning after") are in startling contrast to the rest of his 1920–21 repertoire.

If performed today, some of Chevalier's early songs would probably have angry feminist shock troops picketing theaters and disrupting his act: In song after song, Chevalier glorifies in his self-acknowledged status as male-chauvinist pig, as a predator intent on lightheartedly bedding every attractive woman in sight; women, in his twenties songs, are reduced to the status of stereotyped, passive sex objects, and we are in no doubt as to his cold-bloodedly catalogued sexual preferences. As he put it in one of his songs: "I like flowers and girls in the bud."* He liked them insignificant and compliant (as in "Les Petites Femmes de Rien du Tout" (1920). "Tall gals are an easy pickup/But small gals are quicker to jump into bed. They are between the sheets before there's time to close the door."** He liked curvaceous, plump girls best, he told his

---

*"Moi, j'aime les fleurs quand elles sont en boutons.
Et j'aime les femmes pour la meme raison.
Toutes les deux je les admi-i-i-re,
Et pour moi le vrai bonheur
C'est de frôler, du bout de mon nez,
Leurs calices parfumés."

**"On n'a pas le temps de refermer la garçonniere
qu'elle est déjà dans le dodo.
Une grande femme se lève facilement
La petite se couche plus rapidement." (From "Les Petites
Femmes de Rien du Tout," 1920)

audience, making the point with a truly hideous, untranslatable pun: "*Les tanagras je les aime bien/Les tanas maigres ça ne me dit rien.*"

This kind of innocent, if crude, sexual "political incorrectness" lasted until Chevalier was lured away to Hollywood, where his seducer image was brought into line with the more puritanical American standards, especially after the new (1933) MPA censorship rules. It would be unfair, of course, to reduce him to a mere seducer cliché—and the reluctance of Hollywood studios to allow him more varied roles was one of the reasons for his return to France in 1935.

Because of his limited voice range, Chevalier was never in the same musical class as his near contemporary Charles Trénet (still going strong in his eighties in 1992), but what he lacked in delicacy he made up in panache. R. A. Israel, who witnessed a marathon Chevalier recording session in New York in 1959, especially admired his skill in switching from one character to the next. In "Nobody Throw Those Bull," Chevalier "is a guttural French-Canadian Indian who proudly sings about his son who is performing in a rodeo in New York."

> Suddenly a transformation took place. The beguiling Chevalier charm was replaced by a new character—rough-hewn, tough, loud, boastful and thoroughly winning. Chevalier grimaced at the microphone, bent down low, shouted at the ceiling. . . . We had witnessed an artistic creation. The characterization, full of bravado and gusto, provided a magnificent curtain."*

Chevalier enjoyed these forays into non-Chevalier types, but heard today, they often disappoint: "*La P'tite Dame des Expos,*" sung at the time of the 1937 International Exhibition in Paris, a sketch about a man who follows a pretty girl from one pavilion to the next at this world fair, courting her in simulated Italian, Spanish, Mandarin, and German, only to discover she speaks with the pure accent of Ménilmontant, delighted thirties audiences—but Chevalier is no Peter Sellers or John Cleese. His foreign-language imitations are crude stereotypes. So was his Spanish spoof, "*À Barcelone,*" performed at the time with castanets, a bullfighter hat, and a surfeit of "Olés."

His early *café-conc* training came in handy during his first Hollywood career. As Israel pointed out, "he came from a different tradition. Every sentence is punctuated and accentuated by physical gestures; the movement of an arm, the jutting of the lip, the angle of the torso, all come into constant play to create a rhythmic personality that renders its [Hollywood] associates bland by comparison." What audiences saw, in the films of 1928–1935, was a "filmed stage performance in the grandest French music-hall tradition. The songs are American, but the interpretation is not."

What they could not know was the sheer effort involved: Unlike Gene Kelly or Fred Astaire, Chevalier was not an instinctive, naturally graceful stage performer; everything

---

*R. A. Israel, "The Seven Sunny Decades of Maurice Chevalier," *High Fidelity,* May 1959.

was rehearsed, down to the most detailed stage movements and voice inflections. Even at the height of his Hollywood stardom, in 1933, he insisted on grueling training sessions with the supremely gifted choreographer Hermes Pan, Astaire's adviser, amanuensis, and virtual alter ego, paying for them out of his own pocket.

Chevalier's earliest records were "acoustic," made by Pathé,* and they are of abysmal quality. Most were duplicated, between 1925 and 1928, by French Columbia, and these provide the best example of what he must have sounded like at the time. The orchestral accompaniments, *High Fidelity* magazine noted, were "lusty," the sound authentic—for the accompanying orchestra was that of the Casino de Paris, his almost daily partner. Some of the songs are sung to a two-piano accompaniment (Jean Wiener and Clement Doucet). These two were his favorite stage accompanists—and it shows.

Later (1929–1935) Chevalier recorded for Victor, in the United States, usually with a single pianist accompaniment, and these records are blander. They do, however, provide a fairly accurate rendition of his American one-man shows during this period. Later LP records—some available, some not—are listed as follows:

THE AMERICAN REPERTOIRE

Yesterday. Glen Osser, cond. and arranger. M-G-M E 3702P (LP).

Mimi; My Ideal; Livin' in the Sunlight; I Was Lucky; Walkin' My Baby Back Home; Louise; You Brought A New Kind of Love to Me; Valentine; One Hour with You; Hello Beautiful; Isn't It Romantic; The Yankee Doodle Boy.

Today! Glen Osser, cond. and arranger. M-G-M E 3703P (LP).

Something's Gotta Give; He Loves and She Loves; The Best Things in Life Are Free; Fascination; There's a Rainbow 'Round My Shoulder; Some of These Days; You Made Me Love You; Lucky Day; You Were Meant for Me; You Will Find Your Love in Paris; If I Could Be with You; I'm Looking Over a Four-Leaf Clover.

Maurice Chevalier Sings Broadway. Glen Osser, cond. and arranger. M-G-M E 3738 (LP).

Give My Regards to Broadway; I've Grown Accustomed to Her Face; C'est Magnifique; Just in Time; Some Enchanted Evening; It's All Right with Me; Get Me to the Church on Time; I Love Paris; All of You; Do It Again; A Newfangled Tango; Almost Like Being in Love.

*In the "Pathé 4000" series

Maurice Chevalier. Orchestra, Ray Ellis, cond. M-G-M K 12759 (45 rpm).

Nobody Throw Those Bull; Quel Temps.

Gigi. Recording from the sound track of the film. Original Cast. M-G-M E 3641 (LP).

THE FRENCH REPERTOIRE

Paris Je T'Aime. Columbia CL 568 (LP).

Paris Je T'Aime; Paris a Ses 2000 Ans; La Chasse; J'ai Fixé Mon Coeur; Trinque . . . Trinque; À la Française; Mais Qui Est-ce?; Moi J'ai Gardé; Ah Si Vous Saviez; Peut-être; Peintre en Batiment; Un Canne et une Casquette.

The Art of Maurice Chevalier. Orchestras; Paul Durand, Raymond Legrand, Fred Freed, conds. London TWB 91183 (LP).

Alhambra; Mimile; Quand un Vicomte; Môme de Môme; La Marche de Ménilmontant; Dans La Vie Faut Pas S'en Faire; A Las Vegas; Marie de la Madeleine; Monsieur Hibou; Mudam' Madame; Deux Amoureux sur un Banc; Mon P'tit Moustique; Loin du Pays.

Chevalier's Paris. Michel Legrand and His Orchestra. Columbia CL 1049 (LP).

Introduction, Medley. Rock and Roll; On the Sunny Side of the Street; Ah! Si Vous Connaissiez Ma Poule; Mon Plus Vieux Copain; Ma Pomme; Prosper; Valentine.

Index

About the Author

EDWARD BEHR is a veteran foreign correspondent and prize-winning author, film maker, and broadcaster who was brought up in both French and British cultures, experiencing firsthand some of the events that marked the later life of Maurice Chevalier.

Behr spent four years at Reuters, after which he became a foreign correspondent for Time-Life and roving editor for *The Saturday Evening Post*. He then joined *Newsweek*, for which he covered the Vietnam war before becoming Paris bureau chief, then European editor, and finally cultural editor of *Newsweek International*.

His books include *The Algerian Problem, Bearings, The Last Emperor*, a novel, *Getting Even*, and biographies of Emperor Hirohito and the Ceauşescus. His documentary on the Ceauşescus received an Emmy nomination in 1992 and he received the Gutenberg prize (the French equivalent of the Pulitzer) for *The Last Emperor*.

Behr, who divides his time between London, Paris, and the United States, is a frequent contributor to *GEO* magazine and remains a *Newsweek International* contributing editor.